D1552231

SAP PRESS e-books

Print or e-book, Kindle or iPad, workplace or airplane: Choose where and how to read your SAP PRESS books! You can now get all our titles as e-books, too:

- ▸ By download and online access
- ▸ For all popular devices
- ▸ And, of course, DRM-free

Convinced? Then go to **www.sap-press.com** and get your e-book today.

SAPUI5

 **PRESS**

SAP PRESS is a joint initiative of SAP and Rheinwerk Publishing. The know-how offered by SAP specialists combined with the expertise of Rheinwerk Publishing offers the reader expert books in the field. SAP PRESS features first-hand information and expert advice, and provides useful skills for professional decision-making.

SAP PRESS offers a variety of books on technical and business-related topics for the SAP user. For further information, please visit our website: *www.sap-press.com*.

Bönnen, Drees, Fischer, Heinz, Strothmann
SAP Gateway and OData (2nd edition)
2016, 785 pages, hardcover and e-book
www.sap-press.com/3904

Anil Bavaraju
SAP Fiori Implementation and Development
2016, 569 pages, hardcover and e-book
www.sap-press.com/3883

Dave Haseman, Ross Hightower
Mobile Development for SAP
2013, 617 pages, hardcover and e-book
www.sap-press.com/3248

James Wood, Shaan Parvaze
Web Dynpro ABAP: The Comprehensive Guide
2013, 784 pages, hardcover and e-book
www.sap-press.com/3021

Christiane Goebels, Denise Nepraunig, Thilo Seidel

SAPUI5

The Comprehensive Guide

Rheinwerk® Publishing

Bonn • Boston

Editor Sarah Frazier
Acquisitions Editor Kelly Grace Weaver
Copyeditor Melinda Rankin
Cover Design Graham Geary
Photo Credit Shutterstock.com/60010105/© tratong
Layout Design Vera Brauner
Production Marissa Fritz
Typesetting SatzPro, Krefeld (Germany)
Printed and bound in the United States of America, on paper from sustainable sources

ISBN 978-1-4932-1320-7
© 2016 by Rheinwerk Publishing, Inc., Boston (MA)
1st edition 2016

Library of Congress Cataloging-in-Publication Data
Names: Goebels, Christiane, author. | Nepraunig, Denise, author. | Seidel, Thilo, author.
Title: SAPUI5 : the comprehensive guide / Christiane Goebels, Denise Nepraunig, Thilo Seidel.
Description: 1st edition. | Boston : Rheinwerk Publishing, 2016. | Includes index.
Identifiers: LCCN 2016001818| ISBN 9781493213207 (print : alk. paper) | ISBN 9781493213214 (ebook) | ISBN 9781493213221 (print and ebook)
Subjects: LCSH: Application software--Development. | User interfaces (Computer systems) | HTML (Document markup language) | Software architecture.
Classification: LCC QA76.76.A65 G52 2016 | DDC 005.1/2--dc23 LC record available at http://lccn.loc.gov/2016001818

Contents at a Glance

Dear Reader,

Back in the days when I was still a young, naive user, I, like many users, lived under the fantasy that apps magically appeared out of thin air. Okay, sure, I wasn't chanting "Rain down your gifts upon me, oh Great App Giver from the Cloud," as I thumbed my way through the App Store, but I didn't give much thought to where these programs at my fingertips were coming from.

That all changed when I took my first web development class. Surviving the semester with an (admirable) B+, it was during this time that the curtain was pulled, so to speak, on my grandiose illusion to reveal that behind every app is the blood, sweat, and tears of developers. And while an omnipresent entity bestowing apps upon us seems pretty remarkable, what's even more impressive is the realization that behind every great app, is someone like you and me.

Working on this book with authors Christiane, Denise, and Thilo has reminded me again why developers truly are an amazing bunch. These modern technical wizards, besides being the coolest group of authors I've gotten to work with, have packed this book with the wisdom to take your SAPUI5 apps to the next level. Needless to say, you're in great hands. Now, roll up your sleeves, take a deep breath, man your keyboard, and get ready to work!

What did you think about *SAPUI5: The Comprehensive Guide*? Your comments and suggestions are the most useful tools to help us make our books the best they can be. Please feel free to contact me and share any praise or criticism you may have.

Thank you for purchasing a book from SAP PRESS!

Sarah Frazier
Editor, SAP PRESS

Rheinwerk Publishing
Boston, MA

sarahf@rheinwerk-publishing.com
www.sap-press.com

Contents

PART II   SAPUI5 In Action—Building Apps

PART III   Finishing Touches

12 Don'ts 551

Appendices 561

Acknowledgments

Our special thanks to all the colleagues in the central SAPUI5 teams in Walldorf, Germany and Sofia, Bulgaria who are constantly working on improving this framework, and without whose input this book would have been impossible to write.

Warm thanks also goes out to Chris Whealy for his help and guidance, on writing books in general, and for proofreading and his valuable feedback!

The authors would also like to extend their individual thanks…

Thank you to my partner, family, and friends for bearing with me, and not complaining when I declined an invitation for a night out for the 100th time because "I just need to finish chapter XY."

– Christiane Goebels

I would like to thank my friends, family, and colleagues who motivated and encouraged me through this whole book writing journey. A big thank you to my awesome co-authors Christiane and Thilo, it was a pleasure to work with you! Another big thank you to my manager, Christian Paulus, who supported this whole book project from the first second and was very understanding when I needed a last minute holiday when another book deadline was approaching.

A special thank you to our editor, Sarah Frazier, who did an amazing job, and whose encouraging words helped me to push through this whole project.

– Denise Nepraunig

I want to thank all the beautiful people building, supporting, using, and promoting SAPUI5. Especially the internal SAPUI5 development teams and colleagues who have never been too tired to answer all my lousy questions in the past years and especially while writing this book.

Additionally, I want to thank the OpenUI5 people that open-sourced crucial parts of SAPUI5. You rock!

Personally, I want to thank Sonia for being proud, Mattis for being there, and finally Denise and Christiane for making me a co-author for this book!

– Thilo Seidel

Preface

SAPUI5 is the latest user interface (UI) programming toolkit from SAP, and it is a major player in SAP's current technology strategy. Most notably, it is the technology used to design SAP Fiori applications, which have become the new standard for how modern SAP applications should look.

SAPUI5-created apps are responsive across browsers and devices, and provide built-in extensibility, feature-rich UI controls for complex patterns and layouts, language translation support, and accessibility features. Navigating all these features can seem daunting. That's where this book comes in! With this comprehensive guide, you'll hone your coding skills and become fluent in SAPUI5 lingo. Whether you're starting with the basic building blocks, or looking to implement some advanced features into your code, this book will carry you through all facets of your SAPUI5 journey.

Target Audience

This book is designed and written for all developers who have some prior basic knowledge of web development and JavaScript, and who would like to gain a deeper knowledge on how to build applications with SAPUI5. Developers with different backgrounds, don't let this statement deter you! When working with this book, we recommend you have either a good JavaScript book beside you, or look at one of the numerous online resources for the JavaScript basics before you start. And, for all you ABAP developers out there, because we feel your pain: remember, JavaScript is case-sensitive.

Objective

The purpose of this book is to provide you with everything you need to know to build full-fledged SAPUI5 applications. You will walk away with a thorough understanding of the concepts required to do this, as well as a practical understanding of how to apply these concepts to create real-world applications.

How to Read This Book

The book is designed to build upon itself, chapter by chapter, starting with the basics of building SAPUI5 applications and then gradually introducing more complicated concepts as you move forward through the book.

Part I introduces SAPUI5 and its architecture. The following chapters are covered in Part I of the book:

▶ **Chapter 1**, SAPUI5 at a Glance, provides an introduction to SAPUI5 in general, with information on its product history, evolution, features, use cases, competition, and its open source companion, OpenUI5.

▶ **Chapter 2**, Architecture, takes a deeper look at the architecture of SAPUI5, including its libraries, elements, and structural hierarchy.

Part II devotes itself to the steps in building apps with SAPUI5, starting with "Hello, World," and ending with advanced concepts like writing custom controls. The following chapters are covered in Part II:

▶ **Chapter 3**, Hello, SAPUI5 World, gets you started with a simple Hello, World application example, leading you through the first and most important steps in developing applications with SAPUI5. In this chapter, we'll look at the structure of a single-page application, as well as the core building blocks of SAPUI5: its controls, their functionality, and API.

▶ **Chapter 4**, Building MVC Applications, builds off of the concepts introduced in Chapter 3, and expands on concepts such as application models, views, and controllers.

▶ **Chapter 5**, Models and Bindings, discusses the general usage and types of models in SAPUI5. Here, we also explain the different types of data binding that can be performed in SAPUI5, including property, element, aggregation, and expression binding.

▶ **Chapter 6**, CRUD Operations, we begin to connect our applications to the real world—real services that is—and how to create typical requests to the backend.

You'll also learn important functions like filtering, sorting, grouping, and expanding.

▸ **Chapter 7**, Using OData, introduces one of the most important REST-based protocols out there: OData. In this chapter, we look at how to connect an application to an OData model and explain the additional features OData lends us.

▸ **Chapter 8**, Application Patterns and Examples, explores the most widely used application patterns in SAPUI5. We also look at deploying our apps in SAP Fiori Launchpad, which is the portal used for SAP Fiori and SAPUI5 applications.

▸ **Chapter 9**, Advanced Concepts, shows what it takes to take your applications to the next level! Learn how to use OData annotations to feed smart controls, or extend SAPUI5 functionality by writing your own controls.

Part III puts the finishing touches on our application development with information about how to tune, debug, and deploy SAPUI5 apps. The following chapters are covered in Part III:

▸ **Chapter 10**, Making Applications Enterprise-Grade, presents all the important enterprise features that can be used to enhance your applications further. From employing company themes to implementing security measures and performance enhancements. In addition, you'll find guidelines for making your applications accessible to users with disabilities.

▸ **Chapter 11**, Debugging and Testing Code, provides the steps for ensuring your applications are road tested and ready, from manually debugging to writing automated tests that guarantee robustness and error-free application code.

▸ **Chapter 12**, Don'ts, tells you everything you can do to make a mess of your applications. In this chapter, you'll discover worst practices and ways you can break your applications.

The book concludes with a number of helpful appendices that round out the SAPUI5 discussion:

▸ **Appendix A**, IDE Setup, provides basic setup guidelines for using common IDEs within SAP, including the SAP Web IDE and WebStorm.

▸ **Appendix B**, Accessing the Backend, presents tips and tricks for accessing the backend including SAP HANA Cloud Platform (HCP) destinations and Google Chrome security plugins.

- **Appendix C**, App Deployment, offers steps for deploying your apps on different platforms, including SAP HCP, SAP Web IDE, and the ABAP server.

- **Appendix D**, Cheat Sheets, as its name suggests, offers quick references to important coding concepts, such as starting an application, performing data bindings, and more.

- **Appendix E**, Additional Resources, contains a comprehensive list of resources to continue your learning, from links to openSAP courses and documentation to websites and Github repositories.

Book Supplements

Throughout the book, we will rely on examples, step-by-step instructions, and sample code to teach the concepts covered in a practical way. You can access the sample code and other extra content for this book on the book's website at *https://www.sap-press.com/3980/*.

We hope you have as much fun using this book as we had writing it. Now, turn the page and let's get started!

In this chapter, you will learn the basics of SAPUI5: What it is, where to consume it from, how it evolved, and which competitors it can best be compared with. You will also learn about OpenUI5, SAPUI5's open source sibling.

1   SAPUI5 at a Glance

By purchasing this book, you've taken the first step towards mastering the UI development toolkit for HTML5 (hereafter referred to as SAPUI5). Congratulations! At this point, we assume you have some knowledge of SAPUI5 but want to learn more so that you can build full-fledged SAPUI5 applications. During the course of this book, we will strive to teach you what you need to know to code your way through SAPUI5; we will introduce the basics before diving into more advanced concepts.

This chapter begins our journey. In this chapter, you will learn what SAPUI5 is, what it is not, its primary features and use cases, and how it differs from OpenUI5. Ready, set, let's begin!

1.1   What It Is and Where to Get It

SAPUI5 is a toolkit that enables you to easily build SAP- and non-SAP-related web applications. As a client-side tool, SAPUI5 is composed of CSS, HTML5, and JavaScript, and it allows you to completely decouple the frontend development of your applications from any backend development.

Although SAPUI5 was originally designed to create a new generation of SAP's own applications, it has now become a tool to develop any kind of web application.

SAPUI5 is available as an SAP NetWeaver add-on for SAP customers. It is also available for download from the SAP Service Marketplace and on SAP HANA Cloud Platform (HCP). You can find information on where to find the version valid for your license and details on how to install it at *https://help.sap.com/saphelp_uiaddon10/helpdata/en/7b/b04e05f9484e1b95b38a2e48ecef4f/content.htm?original_fqdn=help.sap.com*.

You can also consume SAPUI5 from a content delivery network (CDN). The CDN address for SAPUI5 is *https://sapui5.hana.ondemand.com/resources/sap-ui-core.js*. This URL will be used in the configuration part of the *bootstrap*, which is the script every SAPUI5 application will load at the very beginning. See more on bootstrapping SAPUI5 in Chapter 3, Section 3.2.2.

From the CDN, you will want to use the latest released version of SAPUI5. If you want to tie your application to a particular version, you can also use the version number in the URL—for example, if you go to *https://sapui5.hana.ondemand.com/1.32.9/resources/sap-ui-core.js*, your SAPUI5 application uses version 1.32.9 of SAPUI5 until you change the URL yourself.

By using this URL, you can easily switch between versions in your app or when experimenting on-the-fly, allowing you to explore new features, quickly see how everything works after an upgrade, or explore how a feature introduced in a newer release would look in your application. Note that SAPUI5 will stay backwards compatible, so you should not run into any regression problems on upgrade.

Now that you know what SAPUI5 is and how to get it, let's dive a bit deeper into the history and evolution of SAPUI5 technology.

1.2 History and Evolution

SAPUI5 is not the first UI framework developed by SAP, but it is certainly the most widely used for new SAP applications and is considered the state-of-the-art for a new generation of cross-platform-compatible SAP solutions. Originally developed under the project name *Phoenix*, SAPUI5 still includes a bird in its logo today.

The first project team began work on SAPUI5 in 2010 and consisted of only a few people. Now, there are several teams across several SAP subsidies in locations all over the world working on the code you can consume in the different libraries, and even more people are involved when you count the user experience designer teams that are responsible mainly for the beautiful and lightweight UIs you can build with SAPUI5. In 2014, the project teams behind the SAPUI5 framework convinced SAP that the toolkit would not be able to thrive behind closed doors, and so OpenUI5, SAPUI5's open source sibling, came to life. We'll discuss the differences between SAPUI5 and OpenUI5 in Section 1.6.

1.3   Features

Among its many features, SAPUI5 allows you to connect your apps to any service easily and consume data from that service. This allows for shorter update cycles and state-of-the-art frontend development while leaving backend functionality untouched. SAPUI5 consists of multiple libraries into which the tool's core and controls are organized.

> **Controls**
>
> The term *control* may sound unfamiliar. In other frameworks, controls may be called widgets, components, or just elements.

SAPUI5 is a toolkit based on modern web standards. It comes with a large number of controls you can use to build your UI quickly and to connect it easily to any backend service.

> **Number of Controls**
>
> At the time of writing, SAPUI5 has around 200 controls that range from typical form inputs to complex layouts to analytical tables with sophisticated sorting, grouping, and filtering.

In this section, we'll look at some of the prominent features of SAPUI5. We'll begin by looking at where you can go to find information on the newest and current features of SAPUI5: the SAPUI5 Demo Kit. We'll then dive into the Model-View Controller (MVC) concept, cross-browser compatibility, theming, localization, accessibility, and open source capabilities.

1.3.1   SAPUI5 Demo Kit

Before we look at an overview of SAPUI5 features, it's important to know where to look for current and emerging features. The easiest starting point for your own explorations is to use the SAPUI5 Demo Kit, available online at the following URLs, depending on the platform:

▸ SAP NetWeaver on demand: *https://sapui5.netweaver.ondemand.com/*

▸ SAP HANA on demand: *https://sapui5.hana.ondemand.com/*

The SAPUI5 Demo Kit provides an overview of the changes from release to release in the WHAT'S NEW IN SAPUI5 section (see Figure 1.1).

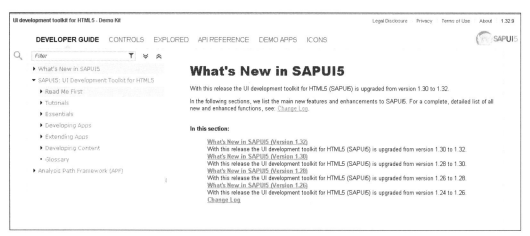

Figure 1.1 SAPUI5 Demo Kit

Release Cycles

A typical SAPUI5 release version number looks like this: SAPUI5 version **1.32**.*9*.

The **bold** characters indicate the major release number, whereas the *italic* character indicates the current patch version of the release. Every even-numbered release is an external release, available for SAP customers and partners. The odd numbers are internal releases, which are not made available to the public.

The SAPUI5 Demo Kit also includes the following sections:

▸ DEVELOPER GUIDE
   The developer's guide to SAPUI5 is written by developers, for developers. Most content has been created by the product teams directly working on the framework, including the authors of this book.

The developer guide includes additional documentation and a growing number of tutorials, which can help you get started with SAPUI5 development easily. The tutorials include a walkthrough for beginners, a tutorial on routing and navigation, and a tutorial on data binding, to name just a few (see Figure 1.2).

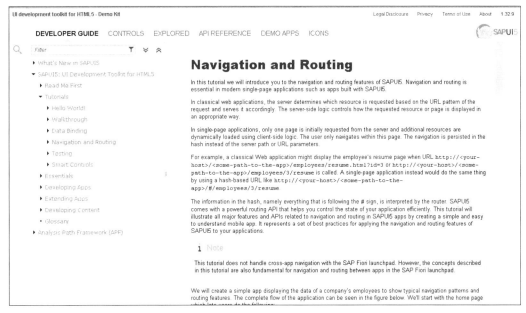

Figure 1.2 Tutorials in the SAPUI5 Demo Kit

► CONTROLS
  A gallery/glossary of the different kinds of controls in SAPUI5.

► EXPLORED
  The Explored app provides a detailed view of almost every control available. It includes samples that show how to use the different controls and what their particular purposes are, which SAPUI5 library they are contained in, and which application component a resource belongs to, in case you find an issue and want to alert the responsible SAP developers. As you can see in Figure 1.3, a searchable list resides on the left side in the Explored app, and when you select a particular control, you will see its details on the right side of the app. And several tabs in the upper part of the details area allows you to switch among a list of SAMPLES, PROPERTIES, ASSOCIATIONS, and EVENTS on this control.

Figure 1.3 Explored App, Showing the sap.m.Button Control

Click on a sample in the list to see the typical use cases in different configurations of the control; the button in the top-right corner (highlighted in Figure 1.4) will allow you to also view the corresponding sample code. The code itself can be downloaded and copied, so you can also try it out and use it in your own projects.

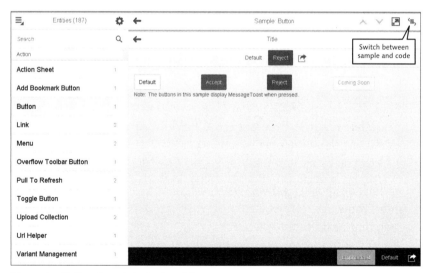

Figure 1.4 Button Sample in Explored App

▸ API Reference
  Complete API documentation for every resource available in SAPUI5.

▸ Demo Apps
  Showcases different example apps, such as Hello World.

▸ Icons
  Overview of the available icons in SAPUI5.

1.3.2 Model-View-Controller in SAPUI5

SAPUI5 follows the Model-View-Controller (MVC) paradigm for building applications. There are several model types available that make connecting to backend services and maintaining data within your app easy. All controls have corresponding functionality to bind to a model and to display and/or edit data.

There also are different view types available, so as a developer you can choose whether you want to write your views in JavaScript, XML, JSON, or HTML. The recommended option, however, is to use XML views, which have been preferred by our application developers due to their easy readability and maintainability. Most of the advanced chapters in this book therefore will focus on implementation with XML views.

1.3.3 Cross-Browser Compatibility

SAPUI5 is a device-agnostic framework, which means that it has mechanisms to detect which device, operating system, browser, and browser version you're using. It also detects screen sizes and has functionality that allows its controls and apps built with SAPUI5 to respond to changes in the display mode—switching from portrait to landscape, for example.

Most controls either adapt to different screen widths out of the box or, if the behavior desired by the developer is not so foreseeable, have configuration options that allow you to set this behavior according to your requirements.

These options include appropriate flexibility in, for example, widths, margins and paddings, and layouts and complex controls that can display or hide menus or columns depending on the available screen size. There is also an API that app developers can access for device information, so that they can flexibly react to this data in their own code.

Figure 1.5, Figure 1.6, and Figure 1.7 show the different screen sizes for desktop, tablet, and mobile phone from the Explored app.

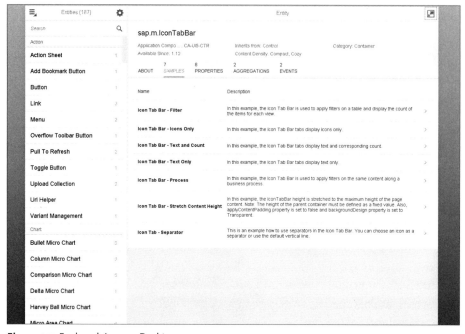

Figure 1.5 Explored App on Desktop

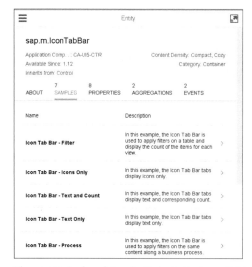

Figure 1.6 Explored App in Portrait Mode on Tablet

Figure 1.7 Explored App on Phone-Sized Screen

Screen behavior is specific for a particular control you can use as an overall layout in your application: the `sap.m.SplitApp` control. The pattern used in the Explored app is a typical master-detail pattern: On a large screen, a master-detail pattern will always show the master, which in this case is the list of controls you can inspect. The detail on the right side of the app will then show information about the control.

When you view this app on a tablet in portrait mode, it will not display the master by default. Instead, you can either swipe it in and out or reach it by tapping on the "hamburger" button ≡ in the top-left corner. On a phone, the master and the detail views will act as different pages, with navigation in between them.

This is just an example of the responsiveness of SAPUI5 controls, and there is no additional code you need to write in order to get this behavior in your application. Instantiate and configure the control, and you're done.

1.3.4 Theming

When you're building web applications for enterprises, it's not enough to build them in such a way that they both implement all the required functionality in terms of the workflow and look pretty. Depending on your customer's brand, you will want to use a toolkit to adopt colors and appearance of different flavors.

SAPUI5 can be easily set up with different themes of your own design via a tool called the UI Theme Designer. This tool allows you to create themes either based on existing SAP themes bundled into SAPUI5, or created from scratch on your own (see Figure 1.8).

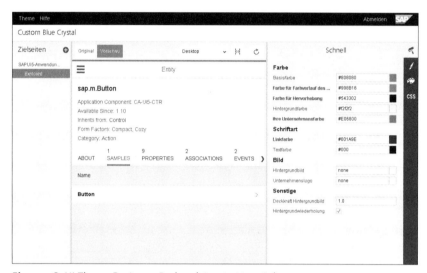

Figure 1.8 UI Theme Designer: Explored App in New Colors

You'll learn more about the UI Theme Designer and theming for SAPUI5 in general, in Chapter 10.

1.3.5 Localization

Another important feature in an enterprise environment is localization and translation. SAPUI5 has a built-in mechanism to detect which locale it should use at a given time. Most controls that require localization automatically adapt to the detected language settings, displaying data (e.g., dates, large numbers, and currency values) in the corresponding format.

Language constants can be localized automatically if there is a translation present. Texts can be kept in a so-called properties file, and there can be multiple properties files in an application, one for each language the application should be available in.

1.3.6 Accessibility

Because application developers should not and do not want to exclude anyone from using applications due to a visual impairment or any other disability, we need to make our applications accessible. This means that we need functionality in place to allow screen readers to gather and produce meaningful information from what's on the screen. It also means that navigation through UI elements should be possible by means other than using a mouse. Therefore, we need to build our UI so that the contrast of elements and text is high enough, and there should be a way to increase this contrast to a maximum by applying a high-contrast black theme.

We can do all of this in SAPUI5. All elements of SAPUI5 undergo thorough accessibility tests internally before they're released, including tests with the JAWS screen reader on Internet Explorer. Some features are built in automatically, and require you to configure them or keep them in mind while you code. In Chapter 10, you'll learn all about how to make your application fully accessible.

1.3.7 Open Source in SAPUI5

SAPUI5 has many famous and well-known open source components incorporated into its core, the most important of which is *jQuery*. jQuery is one of the most widespread and mature frameworks on the web today. It's easy to learn and has powerful document object model (DOM) manipulation. In addition, it evens out the behavior and different implementations of functionality across different browsers. SAPUI5 uses jQuery a lot internally, so it was only natural not only to bundle it into the SAPUI5 core, but also to do so in a way that allows application developers to use it in their SAPUI5 apps.

If you are not familiar with jQuery yet, be at ease: It's easy to learn, it's well documented, and there are many good jQuery tutorials on the web. It makes sense to have a look at this framework when you start programming your own SAPUI5 applications in order to get a better understanding of what's going on behind the scenes, but it's not a prerequisite.

Another open source library integrated into SAPUI5 is *datajs*, the JavaScript library for data-centric web applications. The `model` class in SAPUI5 that allows you to connect your application easily to any OData service is built on top of this library.

Handlebars are used in SAPUI5 for templating syntax in HTML views, and there are several more open source components.

1.4   Use Cases

In an SAP environment, many new applications based on SAPUI5 have been built in recent years—most famously, the *SAP Fiori applications*. SAP Fiori is a user experience concept central to a large set of new SAP applications. The design principles of SAP Fiori have been incorporated into the controls used in SAPUI5, particularly into the Blue Crystal theme, so SAP Fiori and SAPUI5 are closely related. They do not technically depend on each other; for example, you can build SAPUI5 applications that look and feel completely different than SAP Fiori apps.

SAP Smart Business cockpits are some examples of SAP Fiori apps, like SAP Smart Business cockpit for Cash Management, SAP Smart Business cockpit for Material Requirements Planning, SAP Smart Business cockpit for Project Execution, and SAP Smart Business cockpit for Sales Order Fulfillment.

There are three typical types of SAP Fiori apps:

▶ **Transactional apps**
Transactional apps let you perform transactional tasks, such as placing or approving an order.

▶ **Fact sheet apps**
Fact sheet apps display information and key facts about central objects used in business operations.

▶ **Analytical apps**
Analytical apps will let you collect and analyze data from real-time operations of your business.

Visit *https://fioriappslibrary.hana.ondemand.com/sap/fix/externalViewer/* to discover all the SAP Fiori applications currently available.

In essence, you can build any kind of single-page application with SAPUI5; the functionality is not restricted to building typical business apps. SAP developers have even created a browser-based game with the toolkit in their spare time, just for the fun of proving it works.

Typical SAPUI5 demo applications include Shopping Carts, Leave Request Management, Purchase Order Approvals, and more, allowing you to see how easy it is to handle larger amounts of data and display it for a user in a pleasant and intuitive manner. Let's look at a few example apps built with SAPUI5. Figure 1.9 shows a chart displaying an analysis path in an Analysis Path Framework (APF) app.

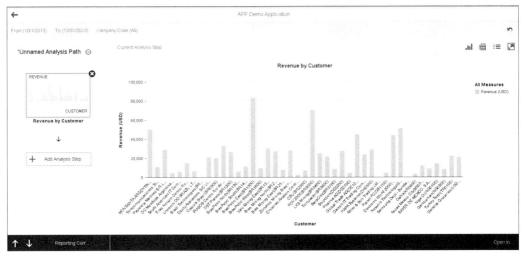

Figure 1.9 Analysis Path Framework (APF) Library Demo Application

Figure 1.10 shows the Manage Products demo app, which provides information such as which items are out of stock, are experiencing a shortage, or are fully stocked.

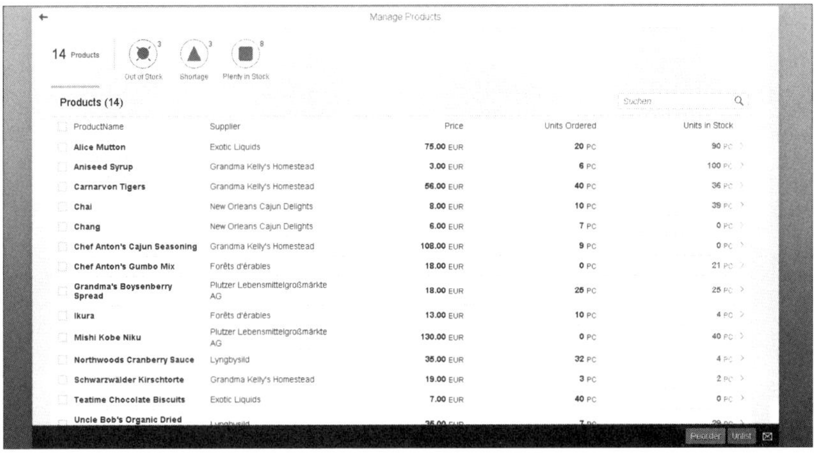

Figure 1.10 Manage Products Demo Application

Figure 1.11 shows a simple Shopping Cart app in which one side displays the items selected and the other provides details of the selected item.

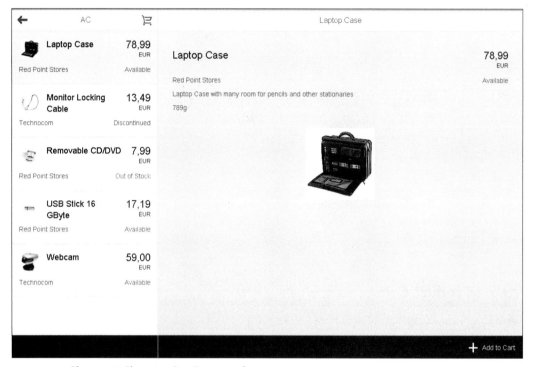

Figure 1.11 Shopping Cart Demo Application

To illustrate how different SAPUI5 applications can be from one another, let's look at one more example: The SAP Wall embedded into SAP Innovation Management (see Figure 1.12). This is a virtual collaboration board. Users can create items resembling sticky notes, or they can pin images or upload documents. They can share their walls—their personal boards—with other users and can help organize ideas and projects.

We have used the SAP Wall to organize our writing and divide the book into chapters. You currently have the complete book in hand (or on your device, if you're reading the e-book), so we can take this as proof of the app's usefulness.

Figure 1.12 SAP Wall, Part of SAP Innovation Management, Used Here as Scrum Board

1.5 Product Comparison

The most important competitor for SAPUI5 is not Angular, not React, and not any of the other open source frameworks currently out in the world and highly successful. Although these frameworks are not undeservedly famous and are well-liked, they do not have the same feature set as SAPUI5. Angular, for instance, does not include controls out of the box; there is a good reason that Angular is so often combined with Twitter Bootstrap. React, the framework built by Facebook, makes creating the view part of applications easy. However, as its own site states, it only cares about views, and React doesn't provide any functionality for backend connections, for example.

Most other current frameworks make it necessary for you as an application developer to decide which frameworks to combine and meld into your app. This decision can be hard at times, and there is certainly always a risk of incompatibilities or that your code may become bloated with lines trying to connect one framework to the other. With SAPUI5, you have all of the components you need in one framework. The developers of SAPUI5 integrated other open source libraries they've used carefully into their own code, so neither are they bloating the global namespace with their variables and functions, nor are there any namespace collisions between them.

To our knowledge, there is only one other competitor on the market with an equally rich feature set: Sencha. We are not Sencha experts, so we can only judge from the outside, but it seems that Sencha's Ext.js is SAPUI5's only peer in business application frameworks, covering areas such as accessibility, translation, theming, and so on. It comes with a useful number of UI widgets (the equivalent of controls in SAPUI5), which allow you to connect your app to a backend service through their functionality.

Originally, Sencha had not one but two frameworks with which to build HTML5-based web applications: Ext.js, the main library, and Sencha Touch, designed to build cross-platform mobile applications. Only in the latest version, Sencha has recently combined the two frameworks into one, leaving the UI widgets for different devices in two different toolkits.

Although some of the early SAPUI5 libraries and controls were designed to work on desktop and tablet only, SAPUI5 developers have been relying on one source for controls across all platforms in dozens of applications. With SAPUI5, applications you write do not require you to exchange one control set for another in order to have your application run on a desktop or phone.

Another key advantage SAPUI5 has over Ext.js is that it has an open source sibling.

1.6   SAPUI5 and OpenUI5

If you are not an SAP customer, you can still build applications using SAPUI5. In such a case, you will use OpenUI5 instead of SAPUI5. Most content explained in this book can be applied to both versions; the major difference between the two is that the latter is available under an Apache 2.0 license. It's fully open source, and the Apache license is flexible enough to let you use OpenUI5 for literally anything.

In December 2013, the decision was made to open source all the key parts of SAPUI5, and the code has been available on GitHub for a while. You can fork the project, you can file issues in the GitHub issue tracker for OpenUI5, and you can even contribute code yourself if you like. The open source version of SAPUI5 is no slower in getting updates then the SAPUI5 version itself, because the two share one code base. If you want to try out what SAPUI5 has in store for you, you can start with OpenUI5, and easily switch later to using SAPUI5 in your project.

Be careful about switching versions, because new features may be available in the latest version only. OpenUI5 versions follow the same version number pattern as SAPUI5 versions, so this is not a hard task.

OpenUI5 is available on the CDN and can be consumed from there, so again you do not have to download anything to get started. The CDN address for OpenUI5 is *https://openui5.hana.ondemand.com/resources/sap-ui-core.js*. The pattern we noted earlier about using the version number while consuming SAPUI5 from the CDN also applies to OpenUI5, so *https://openui5.hana.ondemand.com/1.32.9/resources/ sap-ui-core.js* will again indicate version 1.32.9 here.

1.7   Summary

In this chapter, we discussed what SAPUI5 is and what functionality it has in store for you. Based on this information you should now have an idea about what the later chapters in this book are going to cover. You have seen an overview of the features of SAPUI5, and you know something about SAPUI5's competitors. You also know where to get SAPUI5 if you do not have it already, and you know that there is an open source version called OpenUI5.

Maybe you already have particular questions in mind. If so, you can always skip to a particular chapter. Each stage of the application we're building throughout the chapters can be downloaded or viewed from our GitHub repository (see Appendix E). This means that if you want to start at one of the later chapters, you can get the code in the state the last chapter left it at and start the exercises in the following chapter from there.

In the next chapter, we will look at the architecture of the toolkit in detail, and in the subsequent chapters, we will start to build an application with SAPUI5. This application will be enhanced chapter after chapter, until by the end of the book you have worked through the entire application implementation process in SAPUI5.

This chapter provides an overview of the general architecture of SAPUI5. It explains the structure and hierarchy of the basic elements that comprise SAPUI5.

2   Architecture

The last chapter provided a brief overview over SAPUI5, its features, and its purpose. In this chapter, we'll walk through the architecture of the framework. Later, when you start programming your applications, you will have a better understanding of what's going on behind the scenes. This in turn will allow you to predict what your code will do and how your apps will behave. It will also help you track down errors more easily.

We'll start by looking at the different libraries the toolkit offers and see what each is best at.

2.1   The Libraries

As mentioned in Chapter 1, Section 1.3, SAPUI5 as a toolkit is organized into several libraries. The most important library is the `sap.ui.core` library, hereafter called the *core*. Without the core, SAPUI5 can't run at all. Within the core, you'll find all the basic functionality, from model, view, and controller base classes to render management for controls to the basic control classes to routing and navigation functionality, and so on.

The process of loading and initializing SAPUI5 is called *bootstrapping*. The path to the core library needs to point to the bootstrap of an SAPUI5 application (see Chapter 3 for how to bootstrap), and it's crucial to the application.

The core itself does not have any controls included. The controls reside in the other libraries. You need to pick the libraries you want to load, depending on the use case of your application.

If, for example, you want to build an SAP Fiori-like application running across different devices and browsers, you will most likely choose to load the `sap.m` library, in which the most important cross-browser-compatible controls are located. You may also want to load the `sap.ui.layout` library, as it contains controls that help you structure and display the content of your views.

Table 2.1 lists the key libraries that are part of SAPUI5 and what they are designed for.

Library/Namespace	Purpose
`sap.ui.core`	Core functionality of the toolkit: loads and manages all additional resources and contains models and render manager, a singleton which takes care of (re-) rendering views and controls, writing to the DOM.
`sap.m`	Contains the most important set of controls, from the very basic (like inputs) up to controls that can act as containers for your application views.
`sap.ui.layout`	Special controls designed to help you structure the display of elements in your views.
`sap.ui.unified`	Contains additional controls for both mobile and desktop applications.
`sap.ui.table`	Contains controls like the `AnalyticalTable`, the `Tree Table`, and so on. These controls are not designed to work on phone-sized screens; they have been built for applications handling large volumes of data.
`sap.viz`	Contains `sap.viz.ui5.controls.VizFrame`, which allows you to use different types of charts in your application. Most other parts of the `sap.viz` namespace are deprecated. Please see the API documentation in the demo kit for details.
`sap.ui.comp`	Contains smart controls like the `SmartField`, `SmartFilterBar`, `SmartTable`, `SmartForm`, `ValueHelpDialog`, and so on.
`sap.suite`	There are three libraries under the `sap.suite` namespace: the `sap.suite.ui.commons`, which contains even more controls, and two others that contain additional resources, like types and templates.
`sap.ushell`	Under the `sap.ushell` namespace, there are several libraries that contain all unified shell service-related functionality.

Table 2.1 SAPUI5 Libraries

Library/Namespace	Purpose
sap.uxap	Contains more controls, including breadcrumbs and ObjectPage-Header.
sap.ui.commons	This is a library in maintenance mode; no new controls or control features are developed here. This library was designed for desktop and tablet screen sizes only. The controls inside this library have pendants in the sap.m library that are completely cross-platform compatible and adapt to any screen size, large or small. This library is not deprecated, but must be used with care when combined with other libraries; see Figure 2.1 for more details.
sap.ui.richtexteditor	Contains all functionality required for the RichTextEditor control in SAPUI5. The control is built by wrapping TinyMCE.
sap.ui.suite	A library of controls designed for the new SAP Business Suite applications.
sap.ui.ux3	Controls designed mainly for desktop and tablet applications. Originally designed to run in the SAP Gold Reflection theme, which was the predecessor of Blue Crystal.
sap.ui.vk	Contains functionality and controls to display 3-D models.

Table 2.1 SAPUI5 Libraries (Cont.)

There are some limitations for which libraries are compatible with each other. For example, it's not recommended to mix controls from sap.ui.commons and sap.ui.ux3, or to mix sap.ui.richtexteditor with controls from sap.m.

Figure 2.1 illustrates the key libraries and their compatibilities with each other.

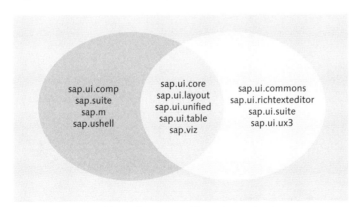

Figure 2.1 Compatible and Incompatible SAPUI5 Libraries

The libraries in the intersection of the two circles can be used together with libraries from the left circle and with libraries from the right one.

However, libraries from the left and the right sides should not be combined together in one project; these combinations are not tested and therefore also are not supported.

2.2   MVC Overview

It's important to get a full view of your application's structure, models, view, and controllers. Chapter 4 will provide an in-depth look at the Model-View-Control (MVC) concept, but here we'll prove a brief overview of the basic elements of MVC. We'll quickly look at how the model, view, and controller work together, then discuss the lifecycle hooks available in SAPUI5.

2.2.1   MVC Interaction

To understand how the MVC paradigm is implemented and used in SAPUI5, see Figure 2.2.

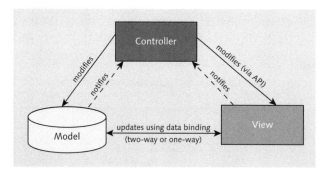

Figure 2.2 MVC in SAPUI5

As you can see, the typical interaction between the model, view, and controller is such that a view, after its controller has been instantiated, can react to user interaction with methods defined in its controller. The controller gets access to the model instance through the view.

Depending on the functionality executed in the controller, the controller can trigger an update of the data in the model and an update of the view. For example, say a user edits some data. When a `press` event on a particular button occurs, this user input is processed. Simultaneously, the currently displayed view switches from editing mode to read-only mode.

The view has access to the data in the model through data-binding mechanisms within SAPUI5. When data in the view is changed, the model itself can also react on these changes, depending on the model type and binding mode (for more details, see Chapter 5). The model can then notify the controller of the changes.

Models set to a parent element like a component or a view inside of an application are propagated down to their children. This means that when you set a model to an app component, all views and controls nested inside will have access to the data in the model and can be bound accordingly.

2.2.2 View Instantiation and the Controller Lifecycle

Note that in SAPUI5 views are instantiated before their controllers. This is important to know, because it helps you understand which information can be accessed in the different lifecycle phases of the controller.

SAPUI5 provides predefined lifecycle hooks for implementation. You can add event handlers or other functions to the controller, and the controller can fire events, for which other controllers or entities can register. Figure 2.3 shows the view and controller lifecycle in SAPUI5.

Let's go over SAPUI5's lifecycle hooks shown in Figure 2.3:

▶ `onInit`
Called when a view is instantiated and its controls (if available) have already been created. This is used to modify the view before it is displayed, to bind event handlers, and perform other one-time initialization tasks.

▶ `onExit`
Called when the view is destroyed. This is used to free resources and finalize activities.

▶ `onAfterRendering`
Called when the view has been rendered; therefore, its HTML is part of the document. This is used to perform post-rendering manipulations of the HTML. SAPUI5 controls access this hook after being rendered.

▶ onBeforeRendering

Invoked before the controller view is re-rendered but not before the first rendering. Uses onInit for invoking the hook before the first rendering.

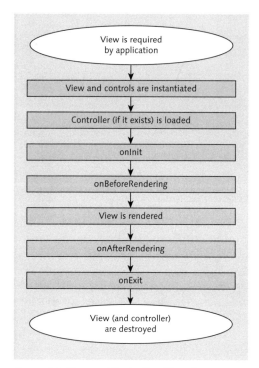

Figure 2.3 View and Controller Lifecycle

2.3 Architecture of a Typical SAPUI5 Application

Applications in SAPUI5 usually apply the following pattern: sap.ui.core.Component acts as the encapsulating element for the application. This component has a configuration that determines which root view to instantiate on startup, which routing paths and targets can be used within the app, which libraries need to be loaded, and which models should be instantiated. This way, the application is independent from any particular starting page and can also run in application containers like the SAP Fiori Launchpad.

In the following chapters, you will learn how to set up such a configuration from within the component, and later you'll learn how to do this in the App Descriptor.

The App Descriptor is the central configuration file for each full-blown SAPUI5 application.

When an application starts, SAPUI5 is first loaded and initialized. The graph in Figure 2.4 shows what happens internally and in what order.

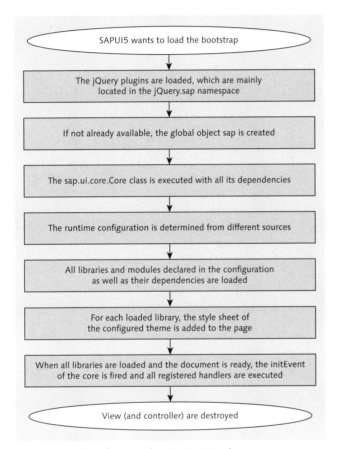

Figure 2.4 Order of Steps When SAPUI5 Loads

Next, the actual app is started, usually by instantiating a `ComponentContainer`, which will in turn create an instance of the component.

Once the component has been instantiated, a `sap.ui.core.routing.Router` instance and the root view are successively instantiated as well. The root view itself then creates an instance of its controller, if it has a controller, and normally takes care of creating instances for the correct child controls and views. As you learned in

Section 2.2, views in SAPUI5 can be nested into each other, and most apps will contain more than one view.

Figure 2.5 shows in what order each code is invoked.

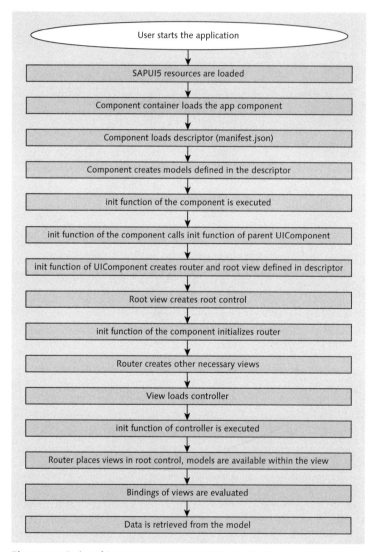

Figure 2.5 Order of Events on Starting SAPUI5 Application

Other resources within an SAPUI5 application typically include the files containing the language constants, local data required for the application, assets such as images the app wants to use, and controls or other extensions to the SAPUI5 libraries that may have been developed for a particular application. There should also be some testing resources (which are not necessarily shipped, but this is a different topic).

You can have more than one component within your application; this makes sense particularly when you are reusing and sharing code across several applications.

Dependencies like libraries that need to be loaded can be bundled with your application, but do not necessarily need to be. Dependencies can also be served from a CDN, but it depends on where your application is running.

Figure 2.6 shows a typical directory structure for an SAPUI5 app. This structure recommended by SAPUI5 for making files easier to find. Note that this is only a recommendation or best practice guideline; it is not mandatory.

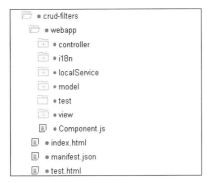

Figure 2.6 Typical Directory Structure

You can see that the above structure contains all the file types of SAPUI5 mentioned so far, and for each file you need to edit, it will be easy to guess which directory it is in. Many SAPUI5 applications have been built using this pattern, so sticking to it will also help other SAPUI5 application developers and the SAPUI5 teams within SAP to find and maintain your coding.

2.4   Class Hierarchy

It would not make sense to describe the complete inheritance tree for every single class in SAPUI5 in this book (otherwise, this book would be on nothing else). However, it is important to know the key classes you as app developer will encounter every day and to understand where these classes have inherited their particular behavior from. This will give you a better feeling for how SAPUI5 is structured. We will therefore have a look at two examples: one will be the proto-type chain of a regular SAPUI5 control from the `sap.m` library, and the other an important model type, the OData model.

The base class for all objects inside of SAPUI5 is the `sap.ui.base.Object`. In the `sap.ui.base` namespace, there are other classes that are equally deep at the root of SAPUI5. Even `sap.ui.core.Core` inherits from `sap.ui.base.Object`.

The `sap.ui.core` namespace itself contains all SAPUI5 jQuery plugins (`jQuery.sap.*`), the core itself and all components belonging to it, and base classes for controls, components, and MVC classes.

In this section, we will discuss the inheritance for both controls and models to paint a picture of class hierarchy in SAPUI5. Let's have a look at the prototype chain for an SAPUI5 control.

2.4.1 Inheritance for Controls

Figure 2.7 illustrates the inheritance tree for an example control, `sap.m.CheckBox`, along with a description of the most important functionality for each class in the tree.

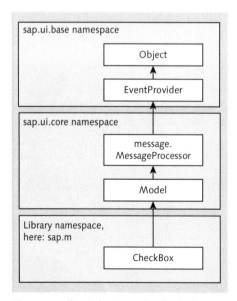

Figure 2.7 Class Inheritance for Control

Table 2.2 explains the important functionality each parent lends to the control.

Class	Important Functions
sap.ui.base.Object	This is the base class for all objects in SAPUI5. In this class, functions like extend or getMetadata are implemented. The extend function is invoked every time a new class is created that inherits from (=extends) a parent class. Even the core inherits from this class.
sap.ui.base.EventProvider	This class provides the functionality required to fire events and attach or detach handlers from events.
sap.ui.base.ManagedObject	In this class, all functionality for managed properties of an object, managed aggregations and associations, and their state is provided. *Managed* in this case means that the properties, aggregations, and associations are not just member properties of a class, but can also be accessed and modified through getters and setters (e.g., the methods getProperty and setProperty). ManagedObject also provides binding capabilities and keeps bound values in sync.
sap.ui.core.Element	This class extends ManagedObject, adding functionality to add and remove custom data and dependents (important for some controls when added to views; see Chapter 9). It also provides methods to get and set an element binding (see Chapter 3), lay out data, access the DOM reference of an element, and set tooltips. As you can see, we're getting closer to the layer in which the actual rendering of controls is involved, even if we're not there yet.
sap.ui.core.Control	This class provides functionality that all SAPUI5 controls build upon (e.g., adding style classes, setting the visibility of a control, or setting the busy state). It also provides basic functionality concerning the control lifecycle (onBeforeRendering, onAfterRendering).
sap.m.CheckBox	As a manifestation of an actual control, this class provides functionality like the actual rendering and behavior of CheckBox. It contains all information required to create the corresponding DOM element and methods that react on user input.

Table 2.2 Class Inheritance for a Sample Control

Accessing Methods

Note that you should always access methods from the last object in this chain, so if methods have been overwritten at the checkbox (e.g., a property setter or getter), you should use these methods instead of falling back to the more generic functions higher up the inheritance chain.

2.4.2 Inheritance for Models

A second example may be important for you as an application developer, so we'll show the inheritance for a particular model class. We're using the OData model here to show which functionality is derived from which parent class (see Figure 2.8).

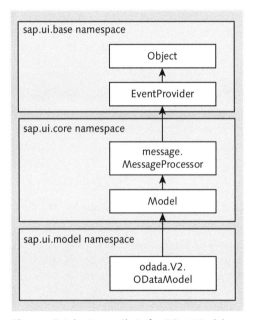

Figure 2.8 Inheritance Chain for ODataModel

Table 2.3 shows the class inheritance for the OData model and provides details of the most important functions of each class.

Class	Important Functions
sap.ui.base.Object	The same base class the controls inherit from (see Table 2.2).
sap.ui.base.EventProvider	This class provides the functionality required to fire events and attach or detach handlers from events.
sap.ui.core.message.MessageProcessor	This is an abstract base class which mainly introduces methods for message handling (checkMessage, attachMessageChange, etc.), which are usually implemented in the child classes.
sap.ui.core.Model	The Model class is the base class for all models in SAPUI5. It provides important common methods for data-binding mechanisms, like getObject to retrieve a particular object from the model data, or bindProperty, bindList, and bindContext, which are propagated to the child model classes and have specific implementations there. In the base model class, there are also events for requests (requestSent, requestCompleted, and requestFailed) and the corresponding methods to attach to and detach from these events again. This functionality is important for your applications, because it makes it possible to react on the outcome of requests from a model to a service.
sap.ui.model.odata.V2.ODataModel	The ODataModel class implements all functionality needed to connect an application to an OData service. It has functionality for loading the specific metadata for such a service, methods to retrieve and write back data in single mode or batch mode, and some functions that are required to handle ODataAnnotations. It adds events to those coming from the base model class, such as metadataLoaded or annotationsLoaded, and events for batch requests (batchRequestSent, batchRequestCompleted, batchRequestFailed).

Table 2.3 Class Inheritance for OData Model

If we tried to draw inheritance diagrams for all the major classes in SAPUI5, this book would become a different version of our API documentation. More important than seeing the particulars of each class in the hierarchy is knowing how to get to the information these diagrams are based upon. The API documentation is

53

available with your local installation of SAPUI5 when you're on an ABAP back-end, but it's also available at several points on the web—for instance:

https://sapui5.netweaver.ondemand.com/#docs/api/symbols/sap.ui.html

Under the API REFERENCE tab, you'll see a tree menu organized into the name-spaces of the different classes and libraries. For each class in the API, you will always see

▸ What properties it has

▸ What methods and events it provides

▸ Where methods and events are inherited from

You will also find a description of the parameters and functionality behind the methods in this documentation. For ODataModel, for example, you'll see the screen shown in Figure 2.9.

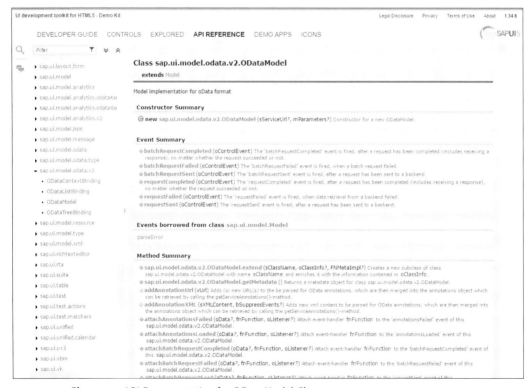

Figure 2.9 API Documentation for ODataModel Class

You should already be familiar with the demo kit and where the API documentation shown in Figure 2.9 resides. As you can see, there is a clear separation between methods implemented by the class itself and those inherited from a parent. In the API documentation, it's easy to get an overview of the relations between the different classes and their hierarchy.

2.5   Summary

This chapter provided an overview of the general architecture of SAPUI5; you should now have an idea of how the toolkit works and how it's constructed.

Don't worry if you feel like you don't completely understand every detail covered. All concepts described here will be covered in more detail in other chapters to come. In the next chapter, you'll have the chance to get your hands dirty and code your first SAPUI5 application.

PART II

SAPUI5 In Action—Building Apps

Starting with a simple application, this chapter guides you through the first and most important steps when developing applications with SAPUI5. It explains the structure of an SAPUI5-based single-page application as well as the core building blocks of SAPUI5, the controls, their functionality, and the API.

3   Hello, SAPUI5 World

In the last two chapters, we looked at general concepts and ideas behind SAPUI5. Now, it's time to start writing your own apps. In this chapter, we'll look at the basics of SAPUI5 development, how to create a simple application, how controls work, and how event handlers can be used. We'll build a simple application as a warm-up exercise for the following chapters.

You can start coding in the IDE of your choice. See Appendix A for how to get started in the SAP Web IDE or Web Storm, for instance. To get started quickly, however, we recommend registering for a trial account on the SAP HANA Cloud Platform (HCP), where you can obtain access to the SAP Web IDE, a browser-based development tool that makes creating SAPUI5 applications easy without requiring a lot of effort of configuration upfront. You'll find the link to register for a trial in Appendix A, Section A.2.

3.1   Coding Guidelines

There are guidelines you should be aware of before beginning your coding adventure. Understanding the dos and don'ts of coding in SAPUI5 will help you to better understand the framework code, give your code a more consistent look, and make your code easier to read and maintain.

Some of these guidelines are for JavaScript in general, whereas others are specific to SAPUI5 and concern themselves only with characteristic features of the framework. We only mention rules for JavaScript in general in cases in which there are several flavors of JavaScript available in the web development world, and we explain why we prefer one flavor over another.

> **Don'ts of SAPUI5**
>
> This section briefly covers some of the no-no's of SAPUI5 coding. For a more in depth analysis, see Chapter 12.

In this section, we'll look at guidelines for using global variables and private object members, the finer points of formatting code, and recommendations for variable naming conventions.

3.1.1 Global Variables

Do not use global JavaScript variables. Global variables in JavaScript are variables declared outside of a function scope. Global objects should be organized in a global namespace (e.g., `yourApp.*`). SAP follows the OpenAjax concept for namespaces and reserves the `sap` namespace officially for SAP. Therefore, all objects, functions, classes, and so on developed by SAP and visible globally, must be members either of that namespace or of one of its subnamespaces.

> **OpenAjax Concept**
>
> The OpenAjax alliance has specified rules for JavaScript libraries used in Ajax-powered applications; libraries such as SAPUI5. Respecting these rules should guarantee the best possible compatibility when you have multiple different libraries working in one page. Web application developers often want to use different libraries from different vendors together in their applications, be it because they care for different concerns in an app, or because one library is lacking functionality that another offers. Rules like proper namespacing ensure that the use of multiple libraries is possible without causing any issues.

Applications and controls developed by customers and partners must not use the `sap` namespace prefix in order to avoid namespace clashes that break applications. This is also why using other global namespaces, like `window.xyz`, is not desirable.

We noted in Chapter 2 which methods SAPUI5 provides to help handle namespaces:

- `jQuery.sap.declare(sModuleName)`
- `sap.ui.namespace(sNamespace)`

On that note, also *do not* use undeclared variables. Undeclared variables immediately become a member of the global object and can cause equally as much damage as global JavaScript variables. When you need to use global variables because they have been introduced by other libraries that your application is using and you don't have under your control, declare their use in a special global comment: `/*global JSZip, OpenAjax */`.

This makes it possible to track which global variables may be present within an application easily.

3.1.2 Private Object Members

Do not access internal (private) members of other objects. Stability of internal members of SAPUI5 objects is not part of any contract, so there's a potential danger in relying on certain member variables within your code; on the next SAPUI5 update, these object members may be gone or renamed, which could break your application.

Do not use `console.log()`. The console object is not available within certain browsers while the developer tools are not available.

You can instead use `jQuery.sap.log.xyz`, where *xyz* stands for the specific log level you want to use. Possible values for log levels include the following:

- `jQuery.sap.log.Level.DEBUG` (debug level)
- `jQuery.sap.log.Level.ERROR` (error level)
- `jQuery.sap.log.Level.FATAL` (fatal level)
- `jQuery.sap.log.Level.INFO` (info level)
- `jQuery.sap.log.Level.NONE` (do not log anything)
- `jQuery.sap.log.Level.TRACE` (trace level)
- `jQuery.sap.log.Level.WARNING` (warning level)

3.1.3 Code Formatting

SAPUI5 uses a set of formatting rules generally agreed upon on in the JavaScript developer community. In order to ensure that these rules are always applied, all SAPUI5 code undergoes an *ESLint* check during build. ESLint is a pluggable JavaScript linter tool for reporting on patterns in JavaScript in order to catch suspicious bugs or code that doesn't follow the SAPUI5 formatting rules. Some of these rules are applied strictly; others will only lead to warnings. For your own code, we recommend using ESLint. If you decide not to use such a tool, we still recommend sticking to the most important rules for code formatting:

▶ Add a semicolon (;) after each statement, even if it's optional.

▶ No spaces before and after round parentheses (function calls, function parameters), but...

▶ ...use spaces after `if/else/for/while/do/switch/try/catch/finally`, around curly braces {}, around operators, and after commas.

▶ Ensure that opening curly brace (functions, `for`, `if-else`, `switch`) appear on the same line as the conditional statement they belong to. For example, `if (a === true) {`.

▶ Use "`===`" and "`!==`" instead of "`==`" and "`!=`";

The last rule makes a comparison between two JavaScript variables becoming type-sensitive in such a way that the compared variables need to not only have the same value but also be of the same type.

You can read more about particular rules and their reasons in the ESLint documentation at *http://eslint.org/*.

3.1.4 Variable Naming Conventions

Throughout SAPUI5, the Hungarian notation is used for variable names. In this notation, names for variables and object properties are prefixed with an indicator for the type of the variable. For API method parameters, however, such prefixes are not necessary, because the method documentation itself specifies the types in detail. (All methods in SAPUI5 are documented in the code and in the API documentation.)

In the Hungarian notation, variable names start with a lowercase character as a prefix for the type and then continue with a longer form, normal name for the variable, using an uppercase letter for the beginning of each separate word within the variable name.

In Table 3.1, you can find examples for proper variable names according to their type.

Name Sample	Data Type
sId	String
oObject	Object
$DomRef	jQuery object
iCount	Int
mParameters	map/assoc. array
aEntries	Array
dToday	Date
fDecimal	Float
bEnabled	Boolean
rPattern	RegExp
fnFunction	Function
vVariant	Variant types

Table 3.1 Variable Naming Conventions

DOM attribute names starting with `data-sap-ui-` and URL parameter names starting with `sap-` and `sap-ui-` are reserved for SAPUI5. There are other coding conventions within SAPUI5 besides the ones listed in Table 3.1, which we'll cover in other chapters when we take a closer look at each corresponding topic.

3.2 Setup

From here on, we will work with code, code, and more code. You now have an idea of what SAPUI5 is about, its use cases, and what to pay attention to while coding. The only thing left to do is work with real and proper code.

3.2.1 Setting Up Your HTML Start Page

The page content for a start page of an SAPUI5 application is similar to most other HTML pages on the web. The skeleton for such a start page will look like in Listing 3.1.

```
<!DOCTYPE HTML>
<html>
  <head>
```

```
    <meta http-equiv="X-UA-Compatible" content="IE=edge" />
    <meta charset="UTF-8">
    <title>Your App Title Goes Here</title>
  </head>
  <body class="sapUiBody" id="content">
  </body>
</html>
```

Listing 3.1 HTML Start Page for an App

We start by declaring the DOCTYPE as being HTML. Next, we add the opening <html> tag, and within it open the <head> section with the corresponding tag.

In the head section, we declare some metatags: The first metatag will tell Internet Explorer to always use the highest supported document mode for its version. More on Internet Explorer document modes can be found at *https://msdn.micro-soft.com/en-us/library/ff406036(v=vs.85).aspx*. Furthermore, we declare our character set to be UTF-8. More on the different character sets can be found at *https://www.w3.org/TR/html4/charset.html*.

Next, we specify the app title within the <title> tag. We then close the head section and start the body section. The <body> tag has a class sapUiBody, and an ID content. Why these two are important will become visible later when we add our first controls.

Last, we need to add the closing </html> tag. As you can see, this is indeed a structure of a very normal HTML page.

Now that you know the basic layout of your HTML start page, in the next section we'll dive into bootstrapping in SAPUI5.

3.2.2 Bootstrapping SAPUI5

In order to load SAPUI5 into your application, you must first tell your application where to retrieve the SAPUI5 resources from and of the many resources that belong to SAPUI5, which you need and want to load.

As previously discussed, SAPUI5 is organized into several libraries. We have never heard of a case in which an application has tried to use all the libraries. As you'll recall, not all libraries play nicely together; for example, sap.m does not like to be in one page with sap.ui.commons. So how do you tell SAPUI5 which resources to load?

There are only a few lines of code you need to add to your HTML start page (Listing 3.2). In this book, we'll refer to the HTML starter page as *index.html*.

```
<script
  id="sap-ui-bootstrap"
  src="http://<<server>>:<<port>>/resources/sap-ui-core.js"
  data-sap-ui-libs="sap.ui.m"
  data-sap-ui-theme="sap_bluecrystal" >
</script>
```

Listing 3.2 Bootstrap Script

The bootstrap code goes into the head section of our html page. The complete code will look like Listing 3.3.

```
<!DOCTYPE html>
<html><head>
  <meta http-equiv="X-UA-Compatible" content="IE=edge">
  <meta charset="UTF-8">
  <title>Hello World</title>

  <script id='sap-ui-bootstrap'
      src='resources/sap-ui-core.js'
      data-sap-ui-theme='sap_bluecrystal'
      data-sap-ui-libs='sap.m'>
    </script>
</head>
<body class="sapUiBody" id="content">
  </body>
</html>
```

Listing 3.3 Bootstrap Added to Heading of index.html

Let's go over the lines of code inserted in the bootstrap of SAPUI5:

▶ `src`

The `src` attribute points the application to where the SAPUI5 library is located. You need to adapt the path where the resources are located (<<server>>: <<port>>) according to your installation.

To access SAPUI5 on SAP HCP, for example, use `src="https://sapui5.hana. ondemand.com/resources/sap-ui-core.js"`.

▶ `data-sap-ui-theme`

The `data-sap-ui-theme` parameter tells SAPUI5 which theme to load. The applications currently developed and offered by SAP use the Blue Crystal theme (sap_bluecrystal). However, other themes are available, and you can also create your own theme, which will be discussed in Chapter 10.

▶ **data-sap-ui-libs**
  The data-sap-ui-libs attribute tells SAPUI5 which libraries it's supposed to load. In this example, we'll be using the sap.m library. This library contains most of the controls, and controls within it will run on any device and screen size.

When you run this application, you will only see a blank page for now. However, you can check whether there were any errors in the developer tools console to make sure the app could successfully load the SAPUI5 resources specified. If you are not familiar with the developer tools in the browser, you can refer to *https://developer.chrome.com/devtools*. This website will point you to the documentation for Google Chrome, as this is the browser with the most advanced developer tools available.

Now, let's start to add some content to our application.

3.3   Adding a Simple Control

In this section, we'll pick a simple control from the sap.m library we loaded and add it to our page.

For the first step, we'll use an image control. In order to add the control to the page, perform the following steps:

1. Create an instance from the sap.m.Image control class.

2. Place it somewhere on the page.

The code to achieve this looks like Listing 3.4.

```
<script>
  sap.ui.getCore().attachInit(function () {
    var oImage = new sap.m.Image();
    oImage.setSrc("img/UI5_logo.png");
    oImage.setDecorative(false);
    oImage.setAlt("SAPUI5 Logo");
    oImage.placeAt("content");
  });
</script>
```

Listing 3.4 Creating a Control Instance and Placing It in the Page

In the second line of Listing 3.4, the code attaches to the `Init` event of the core before trying to access any SAPUI5 API in order to make sure that all necessary resources have successfully loaded beforehand.

Within the event handler, which is defined as an anonymous function, the first line creates a new instance of the `sap.m.Image` control type. An *anonymous function* is a function that is declared without assigning it to any named identifier. You cannot call an anonymous function later by its name, because it has none. In the case of our event handler, the function is specified inline, as a parameter to the `attachInit` function. It acts as a callback function, which is invoked as soon as the `Init` event at the core is fired.

Next, some properties on the control are set, such as the source, the `decorative` property (which is relevant for accessibility settings), and the `alt` text (which is specified for the image). Finally, the control is placed within a DOM element, which needs to be present in the application. In this case, simply make SAPUI5 place the control within the body of the document, passing the ID of the body tag into the `placeAt` function SAPUI5 offers for this case.

For this first control, we're using the SAPUI5 logo as an image source. This logo needs to be put into the file structure of the application.

Create a folder on the same level as index.html and name it *img*; it will contain all the images for the new application. The structure of the app now looks like this:

```
|--- webapp
| |--- index.html
| |--- img
| | |--- UI5_logo.png
```

Now, pass the path to the image into the image's own `setSrc` method, using the path as stated in Listing 3.4: `oImage.setSrc = "img/UI5_logo.png"`.

The app should now look like Figure 3.1.

Even if this app is still rather empty, you've now added your first control to your very first SAPUI5 application! This is an important milestone, because this is what creating a UI with SAPUI5 is all about. In the next step, you'll learn how to add functionality to the application that will react to your users' actions.

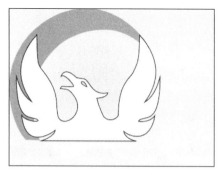

Figure 3.1 SAPUI5 "App" with Single Control

3.4   Defining an Event Handler

An *event handler* is a function dedicated to reacting on a particular user action, such as clicking on a button, hovering over an image, or pressing a key. You can define event handlers for every control, depending on the events the control offers. The image control, for instance, will fire a `press` event, which performs an event when a user clicks or taps (in the case of a touch device) on the image.

You can find out which events are supported in the API documentation, and we'll look at this in more detail in Section 3.6. For now, we'll just use the `press` event on the image, as we just noted that it's available.

We'll now explain how to implement the behavior you would like to see when a user clicks on the image control added to the application. To implement this behavior, you need to do two things:

1. Write the corresponding event handler function.

2. Attach the event handler to the event coming from the control.

Let's first examine what such an event handler should look like.

3.4.1   Simple Event Handler

Event handlers are functions that are invoked when a certain event is fired. The code lines ahead show a basic example that does nothing more than say "Hello UI5!" to the user who clicks it. Because it's a named function, we can easily access it in our code later on.

```
var onPressImage = function(){
  alert("Hello UI5!");
}
```

You can now attach the event handler to the `press` event on the control and make the app invoke this event handler when a `press` event is triggered.

One way to do this is to add the function right in the constructor call of the control, as in Listing 3.5.

```
var oImage = new sap.m.Image({
  src: "img/UI5_logo.png",
  decorative: false,
  alt: "SAPUI5 Logo",
  press: onPressImage
});
```

Listing 3.5 Adding the Function in the Constructor Call on the Control

In Listing 3.5, we're simply passing the name of the event handler function into the control by defining the `press` event like we would do for a property.

We could also have added the event handler as an anonymous function when we instantiated the control. The corresponding code would then look like Listing 3.6.

```
var oImage2 = new sap.m.Image({
  src: "img/UI5_logo.png",
  decorative: false,
  alt: "SAPUI5 Logo",
  press: function(oEvent) {
 alert("Hello UI5!");
  }
});
```

Listing 3.6 Adding an Event Handler as an Anonymous Function

If we only need the event handler we are defining in this case for a single control, it's valid to define it as an anonymous function within the control's constructor call.

Let's try the different versions and add an event handler to the first image, then instantiate a second image with an anonymous press handler.

The code for the application should now look like Listing 3.7.

```
<!DOCTYPE html>
<html><head>
```

```
<meta http-equiv='X-UA-Compatible' content='IE=edge'>
<title>Hello World</title>

<script id='sap-ui-bootstrap'
  src='../resources/sap-ui-core.js'
  data-sap-ui-theme='sap_bluecrystal'
  data-sap-ui-libs='sap.m'>
</script>
<script>
  sap.ui.getCore().attachInit(function () {
    var onPressImage = function(){
      alert("Hello UI5 World!");
    };
  var oImage = new sap.m.Image({
      src: "img/UI5_logo.png",
      decorative: false,
      alt: "SAPUI5 Logo",
      press: onPressImage
    }).placeAt("content");
  var oImage2 = new sap.m.Image({
      src: "img/UI5_logo.png",
      decorative: false,
      alt: "SAPUI5 Logo",
      press: function(){
        alert("Hello UI5!");
      }
    }).placeAt("content");
});
  </script>
</head>
<body class='sapUiBody'>
  <div id='content'></div>
</body>
</html>
```

Listing 3.7 Different Ways to Attach Event Handlers in SAPUI5

Your application should now display in the browser as shown in Figure 3.2.

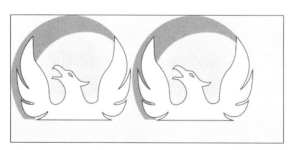

Figure 3.2 App with Two Images

Clicking on the first image should produce an alert saying "Hello UI5 world!", whereas clicking on the second image should produce the alert "Hello UI5!"

Now that you have a general idea of what an event handler does, let's look at the parameters an event handler can receive and modify our app again so that we can reuse one event handler function for the two images and still display two different texts. As a prerequisite, we'll give our two controls fixed IDs, as shown in Listing 3.8, to be able to identify them better in the next step.

```
var oImage = new sap.m.Image("Image1", {
    src: "img/UI5_logo.png",
    decorative: false,
    alt: "SAPUI5 Logo",
    press: onPressImage
}).placeAt("content");

var oImage2 = new sap.m.Image("Image2", {
    src: "img/UI5_logo.png",
    decorative: false,
    alt: "SAPUI5 Logo",
    press: function(){
      alert("Hello UI5!");
    }
}).placeAt("content");
```
Listing 3.8 Provide IDs for Controls

Note that the ID is passed as a first parameter to the controller and is not part of the object of the parameters we have previously used.

3.4.2 Using Event Information within an Event Handler

Modify the onPressImage function to get access to the parameter it receives with the following code:

```
var onPressImage = function(oEvent){
  alert("Hello UI5 World!");
};
```

The parameter oEvent passed to this function is an event object the function receives, and this object carries a lot of information about the event itself (e.g., which control it's been fired on). We can access the source property to find out which image was clicked on.

Within the event handler, ask for the event source using the following line of code:

```
var oSrc = oEvent.getSource();
```

The object returned is a control, which in turn we can ask for its ID like so:

```
var sId = oSrc.getId();
```

Now we can decide which text to produce, depending on the ID of the control.

We can also chain the two methods:

```
var sId = oEvent.getSource().getId();
```

The new event handler will thus look like Listing 3.9.

```
var onPressImage = function(oEvent){
  var sId = oEvent.getSource().getId();
  if (sId === "Image1") {
    alert("Hello UI5 World!");
  } else {
    alert("Hello UI5 World!");
  }
};
```

Listing 3.9 Modified Event Handler Checking the Event Source

Check whether everything works as expected by reloading your application. Do you still see two different alerts? Also, inspect the code in the developer tools of your favorite browser. Put a breakpoint into your new event handler and see if your app gets to the breakpoint when you click an image.

We now have two important components of every SAPUI5 applications: controls and events. Next, we'll look at how to find out more about the controls, their properties, and their events from the API reference.

Whenever you encounter a control and need to find out about its specifics, the API reference is the place to look. It's part of the SAPUI5 Developer's Guide, which you can find either on your own local SAPUI5 installation or at *https://sapui5.netweaver.ondemand.com/#docs/api/symbols/sap.ui.html*.

3.5   Complex Controls

So far, we've used a control with some properties and an event—but there are also more complex controls that we can use, which can have references to other controls inside your application.

There are two different types of such references: *aggregations* and *associations*. In this section, we'll look at the differences between the two and how to use each.

As an example, we'll use a `RadioButtonGroup` containing several instances of `RadioButton`, both controls served from the `sap.m` library again.

3.5.1   Aggregations

Aggregations are references from *parent* controls to *child* controls. They can have a cardinality of 0:1 or of 0:n, meaning that there can be aggregations taking only one child control as well as aggregations taking several. A child control can never have more than one parent, however.

In our example, `RadioButtonGroup` is a control that can have an aggregation of multiple `RadioButton`. These `RadioButton` will share the lifecycle of the parent control, so when the parent control is destroyed, for instance, the aggregated controls will also share this fate.

To add children to a control's aggregation, perform the following steps:

1. Instantiate the controls.
2. Add the controls with the corresponding method offered by the parent.

The children don't need to be placed on the page somewhere on their own, so we won't need the `placeAt` method for any of the child controls. Instead, they will be rendered when their parents are rendered.

You can add controls to an aggregation in several ways. All controls inherit the method `addAggregation` from `ManagedObject`. This method takes two parameters: the aggregation name specified in the control API and the control that should be added to the aggregation. Most controls, however, offer typed methods for their aggregations. `RadioButtonGroup`, for instance, has an aggregation called `buttons` and also offers a method called `addButton`. Adding a new `RadioButton` to the `RadioButtonGroup` would look like this: `oRadioButtonGroup.addButton(oRadio-Button)`.

Listing 3.10 shows you how the complete code looks like when we are adding several of the `RadioButton` to a `RadioButtonGroup`. Plus, another simple control of type `sap.m.Label` will explain what the `RadioButtonGroup` is for.

```
//instantiating a label with an ID and a text property
var oLabel = new sap.m.Label("rbgLabel",{
  text: "Which logo do you like better?"
}).placeAt("content");

//instantiate the RadioButton
var oRadioButton = new sap.m.RadioButton({
  text: "Left Logo"
});
var oRadioButton2 = new sap.m.RadioButton({
  text: "Right Logo"
});
// instantiate RadioButtonGroup with one attribute specifying the
// number of columns
var oRadioButtonGroup = new sap.m.RadioButtonGroup({
  columns: 2
});
// add the RadioButtons to the Button aggregation of the group
oRadioButtonGroup.addButton(oRadioButton);
oRadioButtonGroup.addButton(oRadioButton2);

//display the group onscreen
oRadioButtonGroup.placeAt("content");
```
Listing 3.10 Adding RadioButtons to the Button Aggregation of a RadioButtonGroup

When you reload your application, it should look like Figure 3.3.

Figure 3.3 App with RadioButtonGroups and Aggregated RadioButtons

> **Note**
>
> Whenever the cardinality of an aggregation allows for multiple aggregated controls, the method for adding a control to the aggregation will be called `addAggregationName`. If, however, the cardinality was only 0:1, the method would instead be named `setAggregationName`.

We're not finished yet! We have a label for `RadioButtonGroup` here, but in terms of ARIA-compliance, the label and `RadioButtonGroup` are not connected yet. ARIA stands for Accessible Rich Internet Applications, and there are rules defined on how to make web apps accessible for everyone. This includes, for example, features like zooming-capability, or information required for non-graphical browsers. Currently, any screen reader might miss the information that the label is there for a particular element on the screen. More on accessibility will be covered in Chapter 10, Section 10.4.

We'll now add this relationship and we'll look at associations while we do so in the next section.

3.5.2 Associations

Associations, just like aggregations, are references from one control to another. The main difference between aggregations and associations is that associated controls do not share the lifecycle of their parent. The label can exist separately from the `RadioButtonGroup` in our example, and you'll see in a minute why this makes perfect sense.

Let's now enhance the example app again by adding the label to the `ariaLabelledBy` association of `RadioButtonGroup`. Let's assume that the example app is a poll to determine which logo is more beautiful. After the user has chosen his or her favorite, we want to hide the `RadioButtonGroup` and then show the overall result of the poll. We'll display this information with a different control, but the label will remain the same. Hence, it will have to be associated with the next control it labels as well. The process of adding a control to an association of another control is similar to adding a child control to an aggregation.

You will need to instantiate the associated control—which is the label in our case—and then invoke a corresponding method on the parent. These methods are again implemented into the `ManagedObject`, which makes it possible to call `oControl.addAssociation("associationName", oAssociatedControl)`. As you saw in the case for aggregations, many controls also offer typed methods for adding associations. In the case of `RadioButtonGroup`, you can also call `oRadioButtonGroup.add ariaLabelledBy(oLabel)`.

The same mechanism for method naming is applied here as we discussed for aggregations. For associations with cardinalities of 0:n, the method will be prefixed with the word *add*; for 0:1 references, the method will be prefixed with *set*. Listing 3.11 shows highlighted how the labels are added to the `ariaLabelledBy` association of the `RadioButtonGroup`.

```
sap.ui.getCore().attachInit(function() {
    var oImage = new sap.m.Image({
      src: "img/UI5_logo.png",
      decorative: false,
      alt: "SAPUI5 Logo"
    }).placeAt("content");

    oImage.ontap = function(oEvent) {
      alert("Hello UI5 World!");
    };

    // defining the event handler on instantiation:
    var onPressImage = function(oEvent) {
      alert("Hello UI5!");
    }
    var oImage2 = new sap.m.Image({
      src: "img/UI5_logo.png",
      decorative: false,
      alt: "SAPUI5 Logo",
      press: onPressImage
    }).placeAt("content");

    var oLabel = new sap.m.Label("rbgLabel", {
      text: "Which logo do you like better?"
    }).placeAt("content");

    var oRadioButton = new sap.m.RadioButton({
      text: "Left Logo"
    });
    var oRadioButton2 = new sap.m.RadioButton({
      text: "Right Logo"
    });
    var oRadioButtonGroup = new sap.m.RadioButtonGroup({
      columns: 2,
      ariaLabelledBy: oLabel
    });
    oRadioButtonGroup.addButton(oRadioButton);
    oRadioButtonGroup.addButton(oRadioButton2);

    oRadioButtonGroup.placeAt("content");

    new sap.m.Label("rbg2Label", {
      text: "Do you speak JavaScript?"
    }).placeAt("content");
```

```
new sap.m.RadioButtonGroup({
  columns: 2,
  buttons: [
    new sap.m.RadioButton({
      text: "Yes"
    }),
    new sap.m.RadioButton({
      text: "No"
    }),
  ],
  ariaLabelledBy: "rbg2Label"
}).placeAt("content");
  });
```

Listing 3.11 Setting the ariaLabelledBy Association of the RadioButtonGroups

3.6 Controls API

In the previous chapter, we mentioned that all controls inherit from a base control class in SAPUI5. This class in turn inherits from `ManagedObject`; this means that for every control property, a getter and setter method comes from this parent. Most controls also come with typed getter and setter methods for their properties.

For example, the image `src` property provides two options for setting it:

```
oImage.setProperty("src", "path-to-image");
```

and

```
oImage.setSrc("path-to-image");
```

If the typed method is not overwritten at the control, you could use either method to the same effect. If the typed methods on the control are overwriting or extending the original getters and setter, however, using `setProperty` or `getProperty` would bypass the additionally specified control behavior. It is therefore better to use the methods implemented at the control itself wherever possible.

The same principle can also be applied to aggregations and associations at the control. There are always methods to add and remove items and to destroy an aggregation or association, which can be implemented into the `ManagedObject`. Again, it is better to use the typed methods where possible.

Note

Some controls can have aggregations of any type of control (e.g., layouts), whereas others specify exactly which child controls are allowed into their aggregations. In the case of `RadioButtonGroup`, only children of type `sap.m.RadioButton` are allowed.

To determine which getters, setters, and so on are available for the control, look at the control API documentation. All controls within SAPUI5 have their documentation written into their code, using comments that automatically end up in the API reference. The comments follow the rules of JSDoc, which eventually also generates the API reference. JSDoc is a framework which allows you to generate your API documentation automatically from code comments following the specified rules. More on the framework can be found at *http://usejsdoc.org/*.

Important

Never use parts of the control functionality starting with an underscore (_) in your application. Properties, aggregations, and so on prefixed with this character are considered private by the framework, and while it may be tempting sometimes to use them, you should really respect their private status, because there is no contract at all saying that the inner DOM or inner CSS classes of a control will not change. When you rely on such functionality, chances are high that your application will break at some point during an update.

3.7 Layouts

A particular type of control we have not talked about yet is crucial for every application: layouts. You've probably already noticed that positioning controls within our app is not exactly elegant. However, SAPUI5's layout controls will come to the rescue. *Layout controls* are controls that—as the name implies—are concerned with tasks such as positioning other controls correctly on screen. They are usually able to take in all elements of type `Control` into the aggregation(s) holding their content, so layout controls can also be nested. They are organized in a different library, the `sap.ui.layout` library. Let's now add this library to our application.

In order to make our UI look a little better, we'll use the `sap.ui.layout.Grid` layout control for the overall structure of the app.

Simply instantiate the grid as any other control and place it on the screen. The other controls that were previously placed on the page individually are now added to the content aggregation of the grid, which will take care of rendering them in the right position.

We can also get rid of the `div` element within the HTML body, because the layout will be rendered into the body itself.

We'll also add one more CSS class to the page in order to prevent the controls in the page from being glued to the upper left of the window with no margin at all. The CSS class we've used is available at the framework level itself and adds some margins to the page: `sapUiResponsiveMargin`. Information on these CSS classes and how to use them correctly can be found at *https://sapui5.hana. ondemand.com/ #docs/guide/91f0a22d6f4d1014b6dd926db0e91070.html*.

Listing 3.12 shows what the code will now look like. Highlighted you can see the code for the layout and the CSS class we have added.

```
<!DOCTYPE html>
<html>
<head>
  <meta http-equiv="X-UA-Compatible" content="IE=edge">
  <title>Hello World</title>
  <script id="sap-ui-bootstrap"
    src="../resources/sap-ui-core.js"
    data-sap-ui-theme="sap_bluecrystal"
    data-sap-ui-libs="sap.m,sap.ui.layout">
  </script>
  <script>
    sap.ui.getCore().attachInit(function() {
      var oImage = new sap.m.Image({
        src: "img/UI5_logo.png",
        decorative: false,
        alt: "SAPUI5 Logo"
      });

      oImage.ontap = function(oEvent) {
        alert("Hello UI5 World!");
      };

      // defining the event handler on instantiation:
      var onPressImage = function(oEvent) {
        alert("Hello UI5!");
      }

      var oImage2 = new sap.m.Image({
```

```
      src: "img/UI5_logo.png",
      decorative: false,
      alt: "SAPUI5 Logo",
      press: onPressImage
  });

  var oLabel = new sap.m.Label("rbgLabel", {
    text: "Which logo do you like better?"
  });

  var oRadioButton = new sap.m.RadioButton({
    text: "Left Logo"
  });

  var oRadioButton2 = new sap.m.RadioButton({
    text: "Right Logo"
  });

  var oRadioButtonGroup = new sap.m.RadioButtonGroup({
    columns: 2,
    ariaLabelledBy: oLabel
  });
  oRadioButtonGroup.addButton(oRadioButton);
  oRadioButtonGroup.addButton(oRadioButton2);

  var oLabel2 = new sap.m.Label("rbg2Label", {
    text: "Do you speak JavaScript?"
  });

  var oRadioButtonGroup2 = new sap.m.RadioButtonGroup({
    columns: 2,
    buttons: [
      new sap.m.RadioButton({
        text: "Yes"
      }),
      new sap.m.RadioButton({
        text: "No"
      }),
    ],
    ariaLabelledBy: "rbg2Label"
  });

new sap.ui.layout.Grid({
  content: [
    oImage,
    oImage2,
    oLabel,
    oRadioButtonGroup,
    oLabel2,
    oRadioButtonGroup2
```

```
      ]
    }).placeAt("content");
  });
 </script>
</head>
<body id="content" class="sapUiBody sapUiResponsiveMargin">
</body>
</html>
```

Listing 3.12 SAPUI5 App with Layout Control and CSS

When you shrink your browser window, your app will be running at a width smaller than 1,024 px, and now you can see what the grid is doing. Resize your window once so that it covers the size of a mobile phone (< 800 px) and you'll see it even better: Depending on the screen size a user is on, the grid will reposition elements.

The grid itself is a 12-column layout in which all columns cover an equal part of the screen width. The controls inside the grid allow you to define how many of the columns a single control is allowed to cover.

By default, the configuration of the grid will allow controls inside to cover three columns on large and extra-large screen sizes, six columns (half of the screen width) on medium-sized screens (such as on tablets), and 12 columns (the complete screen width) on phone-sized screens.

We can influence this default behavior by overriding the configuration and setting the `defaultSpan` property to a different value. `defaultSpan` is a string property that expects a value that follows a particular pattern:

`"XL[a] L[b] M[c] S[d]"`

where `[a]`, `[b]`, `[c]`, and `[d]` will be replaced by the number of columns you want the controls nested into the grid to cover.

We can also influence the behavior of single controls within the grid when they need to deviate from the default. For the grid (and most other layout controls), you can define different `LayoutData` for each nested control. The layout data for the grid inherits from the basic `sap.ui.core.LayoutData` class in SAPUI5 and includes some additional settings. The class we need to use is the `sap.ui.layout.GridData`. Let's now use this class for `RadioButtonGroups` and `Labels` in order to display them below each other on large screens. The complete application code should now match Listing 3.13. Highlighted, again, you can see which code we added for the layout data.

81

```
<!DOCTYPE html>
<html>
<head>
  <meta http-equiv="X-UA-Compatible" content="IE=edge">
  <title>Hello World</title>
  <script
id="sap-ui-bootstrap"
src="../resources/sap-ui-core.js"
data-sap-ui-theme="sap_bluecrystal"
data-sap-ui-libs="sap.m,sap.ui.layout">
  </script>
  <script>
    sap.ui.getCore().attachInit(function() {
      var oImage = new sap.m.Image({
        src: "img/UI5_logo.png",
        decorative: false,
        alt: "SAPUI5 Logo"
      });

      oImage.ontap = function(oEvent) {
        alert("Hello UI5 World!");
      };

      // defining the event handler on instantiation:
      var onPressImage = function(oEvent) {
        alert("Hello UI5!");
      }

      var oImage2 = new sap.m.Image({
        src: "img/UI5_logo.png",
        decorative: false,
        alt: "SAPUI5 Logo",
        press: onPressImage
      });

      var oLabel = new sap.m.Label("rbgLabel", {
        text: "Which logo do you like better?",
        layoutData: new sap.ui.layout.GridData({
          span: 'XL12 L12 M12 S12'
        })
      });

      var oRadioButton = new sap.m.RadioButton({
        text: "Left Logo"
      });

      var oRadioButton2 = new sap.m.RadioButton({
        text: "Right Logo"
      });
```

```
    var oRadioButtonGroup = new sap.m.RadioButtonGroup({
      columns: 2,
      layoutData: new sap.ui.layout.GridData({
        span: 'XL12 L12 M12 S12'
      }),
      ariaLabelledBy: oLabel
    });
    oRadioButtonGroup.addButton(oRadioButton);
    oRadioButtonGroup.addButton(oRadioButton2);

    var oLabel2 = new sap.m.Label("rbg2Label", {
      text: "Do you speak JavaScript?",
      layoutData: new sap.ui.layout.GridData({
        span: 'XL12 L12 M12 S12'
      })
    });

    var oRadioButtonGroup2 = new sap.m.RadioButtonGroup({
      columns: 2,
      buttons: [
        new sap.m.RadioButton({
          text: "Yes"
        }),
        new sap.m.RadioButton({
          text: "No"
        }),
      ],
      layoutData: new sap.ui.layout.GridData({
        span: 'XL12 L12 M12 S12'
      }),
      ariaLabelledBy: "rbg2Label"
    });

    new sap.ui.layout.Grid({
      content: [
        oImage,
        oImage2,
        oLabel,
        oRadioButtonGroup,
        oLabel2,
        oRadioButtonGroup2
      ]
    }).placeAt("content");
  });
  </script>
</head>
<body class="sapUiBody sapUiResponsiveMargin" id="content">
```

```
</body>
</html>
```
Listing 3.13 Grid LayoutData

When you run the application, it will appear as shown in Figure 3.4 on a larger screen.

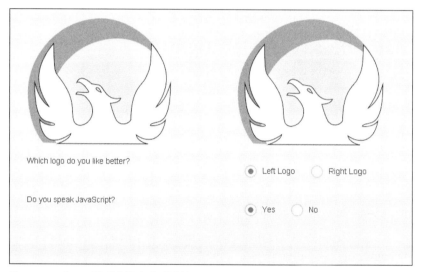

Figure 3.4 App with GridData in Grid Layout

As you can see, the labels and `RadioButtonGroup` now cover the complete column width, making each next element appear on the next line.

3.8 Summary

In this chapter, you learned about and used several of the most important concepts, controls, and patterns you'll need to develop apps with SAPUI5. You've learned how to bootstrap SAPUI5, what rules we apply to the way we code, how to pick controls and layouts for your applications, and how to set them to action. However, the code we've written in this chapter is not well structured, at least not when you think of writing a larger application like this. So far, all our code is in one file, and we have not made use of the MVC capabilities built into the toolkit. In the next chapter, this will change, and you'll see how easy it is to write well-ordered applications with SAPUI5.

84

In this chapter, you'll learn all about the Model-View-Controller (MVC) concept and how it's used in SAPUI5. This knowledge will help you structure your application.

4   Building MVC Applications

In the last chapter, we built code examples to help you familiarize yourself with SAPUI5. We wrote all the coding into the index.html file; this worked for our small example, but would end in a total mess as our examples get bigger.

A well-thought-out structure enhances the maintainability and extensibility of your SAPUI5 application. In this chapter, we'll focus on the MVC concept, which is an integral part of SAPUI5 application development. With MVC, you'll be able to structure your application files into an appropriate file and folder structure. Throughout this chapter, you'll also learn how to encapsulate your application further via components, and you'll see some basic routing features in action.

4.1   Models, Views, and Controllers

MVC is a software architectural pattern that divides applications into three connected parts: the model, the view, and the controller. This pattern was originally developed for desktop applications but has also been widely adopted by web application frameworks. Each part has its own responsibilities:

- **Model**
  Holds all the application data.
- **View**
  Represents the application data and UI.
- **Controller**
  Handles the application data and user interaction.

The best way to understand this pattern is to look at a concrete example. Throughout this chapter, we'll build an application in which we can display suppliers. The *model* will hold the application data, like the name and the ID for each supplier. Application data is normally loaded from a web service, but it's also possible to load the data directly from a file or by using hard-coded values. Within an application, you can use several different models. One model could hold resources like translated texts, for example, and another model could hold the application data.

After we have loaded the required data into the model, we need to display the data; therefore, we need some UI elements, like labels or tables. All the UI elements will be put into a *view*. An application can consist of one or more views. We could have a view that displays general information about a supplier and another view with more detailed information about the supplier and its products. There could also be views to create a new supplier or modify an existing one. A view can also contain other views. For example, a view could contain UI elements to display the address data for suppliers, and we can then reuse that view in our application in several different places.

A view can include several different UI elements with which a user could interact, like buttons, lists, or tables. For those interactions, you will need a *controller*. The controller of the corresponding view will take care of all those events. It is also possible for a view to lack a controller, such as when a view just acts as a container for other views or when the view doesn't need to react to user interaction. One controller could also be used by several views. In our example, the app will react when the user clicks on a table row that contains supplier information, and then it will navigate to a detail view.

Now that you understand the general concepts behind models, views, and controllers, in the next section we'll dive into the MVC application structure.

4.2   Structure

To begin our discussion of the MVC application structure, let's put all of our code into a single HTML file to see the basic building blocks of our application. As you continue coding throughout this chapter, you'll split several parts into corresponding files and folders. This will help you get a deeper understanding of the

MVC concept within SAPUI5. Let's begin by looking at the file and folder structure before we begin coding:

```
mvc-app-simple
| index.html
```

This doesn't look like much of a structure at the moment, but by the end of this chapter, your file structure should resemble Listing 4.1.

```
mvc-app-simple
|    index.html
+---webapp
|   |    Component.js
|   |    manifest.json
|   |
|   +---controller
|   |        Detail.controller.js
|   |        Master.controller.js
|   |
|   +---i18n
|   |        i18n.properties
|   |
|   +---service
|   |        data.json
|   |
|   \---view
|            App.view.xml
|            Detail.view.xml
|            Master.view.xml
```

Listing 4.1 Full Application File and Folder Structure

As you can see, we start with a simple index.html file and end with a well-structured and maintainable source code structure. The final structure provides a glimpse into the MVC concepts involved. In Listing 4.1, you can see separate folders for certain views and controllers. The data for the application models are stored in *src/service/data.json* and for the translation model in *src/i18n/i18.properties*. Throughout this chapter, you'll see different options to instantiate the corresponding models and load their data.

The detailed concepts behind the Component.js and manifest.json files will be explained at the end of this chapter. The *Component.js* file sets up the whole application, including configuring the routing, creating the models, and instantiating views. Information about the routing and the involved models can be stored in a separate file—manifest.json, which is also called the *Application Descriptor*. The

Application Descriptor contains information about the application, like its name, version, and description, the SAPUI5 libraries used, the different models used and the location of its data, the routing information, and more. We'll discuss the Application Descriptor further in Section 4.7.

4.2.1 Application Overview

To begin, let's create the example application without the MVC concept. In Chapter 3, you used some of the basic building blocks, like sap.m.App and sap.m.Page, that we need for this application.

The first page in the app will contain an overview of suppliers. For that, we'll use sap.m.Table. Clicking on a table row will navigate to a second page, where the app will display more detailed information. To display detailed information, we'll use sap.m.ObjectHeader. Through this example, you'll learn the basics of data binding and how to send information from one page to another. Data binding will be discussed in depth in Chapter 5.

Figure 4.1 shows the final application we're going to build throughout this chapter.

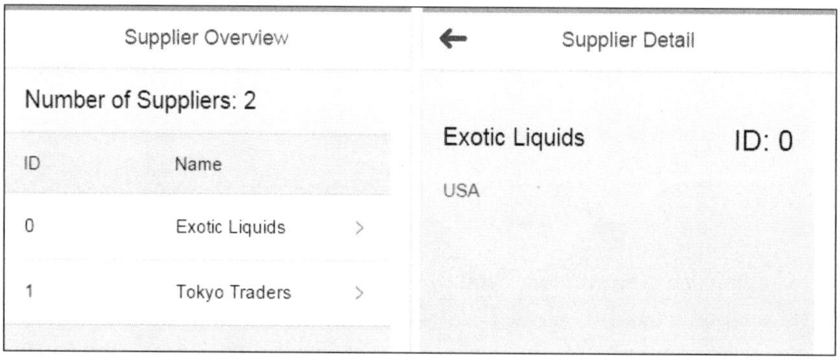

Figure 4.1 Final Example Application

Table 4.1 shows the building blocks of the application and its hierarchical structure. Figure 4.1 and Table 4.1 help illustrate how to put the application together. You'll see such a hierarchical structure again when you start to create views not via code, but via declarative syntax, like XML, JSON, or HTML.

Master Page	Detail Page
Page	Page
Suppliers Table	Name ID ObjectHeader
# Suppliers Toolbar	Address/Country ObjectAttr.
ID | Name Colmun Header	
ID | Name ColumList Item	

Table 4.1 Hierachical Overview of Application

We'll use a hands-on approach throughout this chapter, so that you can see results quickly and get an idea of how concepts fit together. We're going to use rather complex controls right away so that you get a feeling for how to develop a realistic application. Don't be discouraged when things don't work right away or you don't understand every little piece; your knowledge will expand throughout this book, and the concepts will become clearer.

First, create the *index.html* page with the code shown in Listing 4.2. This should look similar to the HTML start page we showed you back in Chapter 3, Section 3.2.1.

```
<!DOCTYPE HTML>
<html>

<head>
  <meta http-equiv="X-UA-Compatible" content="IE=edge" />
  <meta charset="UTF-8">
  <title>MVC App</title>
  <script id="sap-ui-bootstrap"
    src="resources/sap-ui-core.js"
    data-sap-ui-libs="sap.m"
    data-sap-ui-theme="sap_bluecrystal"
    data-sap-ui-compatVersion="edge">
  </script>
  <script>
  // your coding will go here
</script>
</head>
<body class="sapUiBody" role="application">
  <div id="content"></div>
</body>
</html>
```

Listing 4.2 Basic Structure for MVC Example

With the index.html page created, we can now start building the first page.

4.2.2 Building the First Page

We're going to create an application in which we display information about suppliers. We have two suppliers with their respective data, like ID, name, and address. The data is in JSON format. SAPUI5 provides the `sap.ui.model.json.JSONModel` model type for handling data in JSON format. Other model types handle XML, resources, or OData formats. In this chapter, you'll become familiar with the resource model as well, which is used for translation. Later in this book, you will use OData models heavily. In SAPUI5, we need models for data binding. When we load data into the application, we'll want to display it somewhere within the UI.

The example data includes two suppliers, and we want to display the number *2* in the header of the table to indicate the number of suppliers. Therefore, we need to bind this number information to the header of the table. There are one-way and two-way data bindings. For the JSON model, the two-way binding is the default. Whenever the model data updates, the changes must be reflected in the UI. If the changes in the UI directly manipulate the data, then that's a two-way binding; otherwise, it's a one-way binding. The model data can be bound to the whole SAPUI5 core, a view, or a specific control.

Listing 4.3 shows the application data, the model creation, the assignment of the data to the model, and, last but not least, setting the model for the whole SAPUI5 core.

The application model data has the following structure:

- CountSuppliers
- Suppliers
    - ID
    - Name
    - Address
        - Street
        - City
        - State
        - ZipCode
        - Country

Write this structure as shown in Listing 4.3.

```
// application data
var oData = {
  "CountSuppliers" : "2",
  "Suppliers":[
    {
      "ID":0,
      "Name":"Exotic Liquids",
      "Address":{
        "Street":"NE 228th",
        "City":"Sammamish",
        "State":"WA",
        "ZipCode":"98074",
        "Country":"USA"
      }
    },
    {
      "ID":1,
      "Name":"Tokyo Traders",
      "Address":{
        "Street":"NE 40th",
        "City":"Redmond",
        "State":"WA",
        "ZipCode":"98052",
        "Country":"USA"
      }
    }
  ]
};

// model creation and setting data
var oModel = sap.ui.model.json.JSONModel();
oModel.setData(oData);

// setting the model to the core
// so that it's available in the whole application
sap.ui.getCore().setModel(oModel);
```

Listing 4.3 Creation of Data and Model

Now that we've created the structure, let's create the table. The table consists of columns, a table header, and the repeating entries for the supplier data. The column data is used as column headings, and the table header displays the number of suppliers. Listing 4.4 shows how to create the table; add this coding after the application data and model creation.

```
// the columns will act as column headers
var aColumns = [
  new sap.m.Column({
    header : new sap.m.Text({
      text : "ID"
    })
  }),
  new sap.m.Column({
    header : new sap.m.Text({
      text : "Name"
    })
  })
];

// in the template we'll display the supplier information
var oTemplate = new sap.m.ColumnListItem({
  type: "Navigation",
  cells : [
    new sap.m.ObjectIdentifier({
      text : "{ID}"
    }),
    new sap.m.ObjectIdentifier({
      text : "{Name}"
    })
  ]
});

// in the header we're displaying the number of suppliers
var oTableHeader = new sap.m.Toolbar({
  content : [
    new sap.m.Title({
      text : "Number of Suppliers: {/CountSuppliers}"
    })
  ]
});

// we create the table with the columns and header
var oTable = new sap.m.Table({
  columns : aColumns,
  headerToolbar : oTableHeader
});

// we bind the table items to the /Suppliers entries
// and to our template
oTable.bindItems("/Suppliers", oTemplate);
```
Listing 4.4 Creating the Table

In Listing 4.4, you'll see different options to bind data. When we're binding values from the model directly to a property (like a text property), we can use curly braces ({ }). The value in the curly braces will be replaced by the data from the model. You see different examples on how to bind data in the following list:

▶ `text: "{ID}"`

This is a simple binding in which the value of `{ID}` will be set by the ID values of the suppliers—in this case, 0 and 1.

▶ `text: "Number of Suppliers: {/CountSuppliers}"`

This is a complex binding in which we can combine the text "`Number of Suppliers`" and the value of `CountSuppliers`. As in the prior example, the value between the curly braces will be replaced by the model data—in this case, 2.

Pay special attention to the slash at the beginning of `/CountSuppliers`. We need this slash because we're referencing a root node of the model. The model has the root nodes `CountSupplier` and `Suppliers`.

▶ `bindItems("/Suppliers", oTemplate)`

Here, the data binding happens via coding and not while creating the controls. We don't need curly braces, just the name of the data property. We also need the slash here, because we're again referencing a root node.

To display the table in the application, we'll add the table to a page. After that, we'll add the page to an app and add the page to our UI area. For these steps, add the coding from Listing 4.5 after the table creation coding.

```
var oPageMaster = new sap.m.Page("masterPage", {
  title : "Supplier Overview",
  content : [oTable]
});

var oApp = new sap.m.App("myApp");

oApp.addPage(oPageMaster);
oApp.placeAt("content");
```

Listing 4.5 Creation of Master Page and App

You now can run the application. You should see the supplier information displayed in the table and see the number of suppliers in the table header (see Figure 4.2).

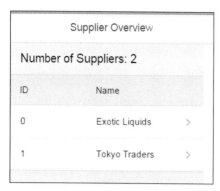

Figure 4.2 Supplier Overview Table

4.2.3 Table Coding

Next, we'll describe how the table works in combination with data binding. For that, let's revise Listing 4.4 and look at the different parts. When you look at the table we created, you'll see the assigned columns and `headerToolbar`, as shown:

```
var oTable = new sap.m.Table({
columns : aColumns,
headerToolbar : oTableHeader
});
```

One `sap.m.Column` instance includes `sap.m.Text` with the text "ID" or "Name" in its header aggregation, as you can see in Listing 4.6.

```
var aColumns = [
  new sap.m.Column({
    header : new sap.m.Text({
    text : "ID"
  })
}), ...
```

Listing 4.6 Column Creation

The table header contains `sap.m.Toolbar` with `sap.m.Title` as its content (see Listing 4.7).

```
var oTableHeader = new sap.m.Toolbar({
  content : [
    new sap.m.Title({
      text : "Number of Suppliers: {/CountSuppliers}"
    })
```

```
    ]
});
```
Listing 4.7 Table Header Creation

The most important part of this process is creating `oTemplate`, in which we create `sap.m.ColumnListItem` and put two `sap.m.ObjectIdentifier` instances into the cell's aggregation. The text of the `sap.m.ObjectIdentifier` instances are bound to the `ID` and `Name` of our data model. The table itself has an items aggregation. We then bind the items with `bindItems` to the root node with `/Suppliers` to our `oTemplate`. The template will be repeated twice because there are two suppliers (don't forget the slash in the binding!). The first row will be bound to the first supplier and the second row to the second supplier. Listing 4.8 shows the necessary coding.

```
var oTemplate = new sap.m.ColumnListItem({
 type: "Navigation",
 cells : [
  new sap.m.ObjectIdentifier({
   text : "{ID}"
  }),
  new sap.m.ObjectIdentifier({
   text : "{Name}"
  })
 ]
});
...
oTable.bindItems("/Suppliers", oTemplate);
```
Listing 4.8 Template Creation for Table Rows

We've finished the first part of the application and put everything into one HTML file. Now it's time to split up the app into parts and create a suitable file and folder structure.

4.3   Building a Simple View

In SAPUI5, we can create different view types. We can create them via JavaScript coding or declaratively with XML, JSON, or HTML. The most common view type used by SAP is the *XML view*, which is used mainly in SAP Fiori and upcoming SAP S/4HANA SAPUI5 applications.

The second most frequently used view type is the *JavaScript view*. These views are used in some SAPUI5-based products and are also convenient when writing unit tests or creating views inside a single HTML file. We will discuss view types further in Section 4.4.

Let's start by refactoring our folder structure. Create a new *webapp* folder with a *view* and a *controller* subfolder. Now, create two empty files: *Master.controller.js* (in the *controller* folder) and *Master.view.js* (in the *view* folder). You can see the folder structure in Listing 4.9.

```
mvc-app-simple
|    index.html
|    |
+---webapp
|    |
|    +---controller
|    |        Master.controller.js
|    |
|    \---view
|             Master.view.js
|
```
Listing 4.9 Folder Structure for MVC Example

In terms of naming conventions, it's important that the view files are named according to this naming scheme: *ViewName.view.viewtype*. Table 4.2 lists the file naming conventions for different view types.

View Type	File Ending
JavaScript view	.view.js
XML view	.view.xml
HTML view	.view.html
JSON view	.view.json

Table 4.2 File Extensions for Different View Types

In this section, we'll begin by looking at the SAPUI5 namespaces and resource paths, before creating our master JavaScript view, master controller, and detail view.

4.3.1   Namespaces and Resource Path

Before we continue refactoring, let's discuss the importance namespaces in SAPUI5 and where your application loads its corresponding source files (like views and controllers).

SAPUI5 has built-in support for *modularization*. This means that instead of loading one large SAPUI5 JavaScript file, SAPUI5 can be split into smaller parts and loaded on demand—for example, loading `sap.m.Dialog` or loading views and controllers. These are examples of modules. It's also possible to preload the whole `sap.m` library, which you'll see in Section 4.7 when we talk about components and the Application Descriptor.

When you start your current SAPUI5 application and look at the console output, you'll see the initial registration of the module paths:

```
registerResourcePath ('', 'resources/') - sap.ui.ModuleSystem
URL prefixes set to: - sap.ui.ModuleSystem
(default) : resources/ - sap.ui.ModuleSystem
```

This happens automatically because we referenced the location of the SAPUI5 library with `src="resources/sap-ui-core.js"` within the script part of our HTML file. As you can see in the console output, the default location was set to `resources/`. When you look back at Listing 4.9, in which we defined the folder structure, we didn't include have a *resource* folder, so this folder refers to resources from SAPUI5. When we want to use our application folder structure, we need to tell SAPUI5 where to find it.

We also need to define a *namespace* for our application, a unique identifier for the application. A namespace is also important when an app runs inside the SAP Fiori Launchpad. For this example application, we'll use the namespace `sapui5.demo.mvcapp`. You can use whatever namespace you like for your application. You can also use the common reverse domain name notation—for example, "myproduct.example.com"—which is used in Java programming.

To define the location of our files for our namespace, we can add the parameter `data-sap-ui-resourceroots` to the script tag in our HTML file, as shown in Listing 4.10. The parameter expects a JSON notation; pay attention to the single and double quotes.

```
<script id="sap-ui-bootstrap"
  src="resources/sap-ui-core.js"
  data-sap-ui-libs="sap.m"
```

```
data-sap-ui-theme="sap_bluecrystal"
data-sap-ui-preload="async"
data-sap-ui-compatVersion="edge"
data-sap-ui-xx-bindingSyntax="complex"
data-sap-ui-resourceroots='{"
    sapui5.demo.mvcapp": "./webapp/"}'>
```

Listing 4.10 Defining Namespace and resourceroots

When you now restart the application and look at the console, you'll see that the new path has been registered (see Listing 4.11). You'll also see that the dots in sapui5.demo.mvcapp have been replaced with slashes: sapui5/demo/mvcapp.

In the last line of the code, you'll see the important part: Whenever SAPUI5 comes across the path sapui5/demo/mvcapp (also in its dot notation, sapui5.demo.mvcapp), it looks for resources in the folder *./webapp* (*./* means *current directory*). This is exactly what we wanted, because all our files (except the HTML file) will be stored in that *webapp* folder.

```
registerResourcePath ('', 'resources/') - sap.ui.ModuleSystem
registerResourcePath ('sapui5/demo/mvcapp', './webapp/') -
sap.ui.ModuleSystem
URL prefixes set to: - sap.ui.ModuleSystem
(default) : resources/ - sap.ui.ModuleSystem
'sapui5/demo/mvcapp' : ./webapp/ - sap.ui.ModuleSystem
```

Listing 4.11 Console Output: resourcePath Registration

We've now finished mapping source code folders with the namespace. You also could have written this information into the JavaScript coding of the app—for example, before the definition of oData. The following code snippet shows an example what the JavaScript coding would look like:

```
jQuery.sap.registerModulePath('sapui5.demo.mvcapp', './webapp/');
var oData = {
"CountSuppliers" : "2",
...
```

4.3.2   Creating the Master JavaScript View

After all of this preparation, you can create your first JavaScript view. Open the empty *webapp/view/Master.view.js* file, or create it now if you haven't done it before. Here, you'll see the namespace again. Add the coding from Listing 4.12 into your Master.view.js file.

```
sap.ui.jsview("sapui5.demo.mvcapp.view.Master", {
  getControllerName: function() {
    return "sapui5.demo.mvcapp.controller.Master";
  },
  createContent: function(oController) {
    // here we will create our UI via JS coding
  }
});
```

Listing 4.12 JavaScript View

The two most important functions every JavaScript view must have are `getCon-trollerName` and `createContent`. The controller coding doesn't exist yet, but we'll create it in one of the next steps. Now, look at the first line of Listing 4.12, where you'll see the name of the view:

```
sap.ui.jsview("sapui5.demo.mvcapp.view.Master", {
```

The `sapui5.demo.mvcapp` resource will be mapped to the folder *./webapp*, so the resource `sapui5.demo.mvcapp.view.Master` will be mapped to *./webapp/view/Master.view.js*. `view.js` will be added automatically because you defined a Java-Script view. You'll see the location later in the network trace when you instantiate the view.

Let's create the content for our view. Cut the coding from where we created the table and its content and the master page from the HTML file and paste it into the `createContent` function. You just need to make one small change: At the end of the `createContent` function, you must return the page (see Listing 4.13).

One change we made in the coding is that we no longer return the name of the page in the view—so instead of writing

```
var oPageMaster = new sap.m.Page("masterPage", { …
```

we only write

```
var oPageMaster = new sap.m.Page({…
```

We do this because SAPUI5 would otherwise create IDs automatically in the view, and these IDs would not match the desired name, `masterPage`. We'll assign the name of the master page later in the coding of the index.html file.

```
createContent: function(oController) {

  var aColumns = [
```

```
    new sap.m.Column({
      ...

  var oTable = new sap.m.Table({
    columns: aColumns,
    headerToolbar : oTableHeader
  });

  oTable.bindItems("/Suppliers", oTemplate);

  var oPageMaster = new sap.m.Page({
    title: "Supplier Overview",
    content: [oTable]
  });
  return oPageMaster;
}
```

Listing 4.13 Content of Master.view.js

4.3.3 Creating the Master Controller

According to the MVC concept, we also need a controller. In the `getController-Name` function in `Master.view.js`, we've returned the `sapui5.demo.mvcapp.controller.Master` controller, which we'll create now.

Open the empty *webapp/controller/Master.controller.js* file, or create it now if you haven't done so yet. Insert the coding from Listing 4.14.

```
sap.ui.define([
  "sap/ui/core/mvc/Controller"
], function(Controller) {
  "use strict";
  return Controller.extend("sapui5.demo.mvcapp.controller.Master", {
  });
});
```
Listing 4.14 Initial Coding of Master.controller.js

In Listing 4.14, we're using the new module-loading syntax of SAPUI5. The old module-loading syntax was `jQuery.sap.declare` and `jQuery.sap.require`, which are synchronous.

The aims of `sap.ui.define` and `sap.ui.require` are the same as in RequireJS: to provide the option to organize your code in modules, to load those modules asynchronously, and to resolve their dependencies (asynchronous loading is good for performance reasons). This is referred to as an *asynchronous module definition* (AMD). When you organize your code in modules, you can easily assemble your application with those modules. As a result, you'll see that your code is loosely coupled and easier to maintain.

Let's take a closer look at those module concepts. In JavaScript version 5, there was no built-in option to organize your code in modules and define their dependencies. Therefore, two concepts were invented:

▸ **CommonJS modules**
This is the dominant implementation in node.js. It has the following traits:

▹ Main use: server

▹ Compact syntax

▹ Designed for synchronous loading

▸ **Asynchronous module definition**
The most popular implementation in RequireJS. It has the following traits:

▹ Main use: browser

▹ Slightly more complicated syntax

▹ Designed for asynchronous loading

Let's look at why and when to implement these module concepts and what their main functions are.

When you have a JavaScript project in which one file depends on two other files, you need to write the script files in the correct order into the script tag of the HTML page. This isn't a big deal if you only have a few files, but as your coding grows ever bigger, it becomes ever more complicated. In the next version of JavaScript (ECMAScript 2015), there will be built-in support for defining and loading modules. You can read about the final syntax at *http://www.2ality.com/2014/09/ es6-modules-final.html*.

Because SAPUI5 runs in the browser, we'll focus on the AMD approach. If you want an introduction into the most popular implementation of RequireJS, we recommend the easy tutorial found at *http://www.sitepoint.com/understanding-requirejs-for-effective-javascript-module-loading/*.

However, don't get lost in the different implementation details of RequireJS; focus on the `define`/`require` syntax of SAPUI5. You can read about specific implementation details and differences from RequireJS at *https://sapui5.hana.ondemand.com/ sdk/#docs/api/symbols/sap.ui.html#.define*.

The basic syntax of `sap.ui.define` is as follows:

```
sap.ui.define(sModuleName?, aDependencies?, vFactory, bExport?)
```

In Listing 4.14, we used the following syntax:

```
sap.ui.define([
"sap/ui/core/mvc/Controller"
], function(Controller) {
```

We have omitted the first parameter, `sModuleName`. We provided an array of dependencies—in this example, just the value `sap/ui/core/mvc/Controller`—and put it into an anonymous function with the parameter `Controller`. We also omitted the last parameter, `bExport`.

After all the dependencies have been loaded—in this case, only the SAPUI5 controller class—the anonymous function will be executed. As you can see in the previous code, the dots have been replaced with slashes. If we wanted to load `sap.m.Dialog`, we'd just need to require `sap/m/Dialog`.

After we've required the `sap.ui.core.mvc.Controller`, we now have it in the `Controller` variable. The code continues `with return Controller.extend...`. It's important that we return our newly created module in our coding so that another file also could load our module. We'll examine this further at the end of the chapter when we provide `BaseClass` for a controller and require it in the controller coding.

Because we omitted the first parameter, `sModuleName`, the name of the module will be generated automatically, which is considered a best practice. The global namespace for our master controller is `sapui5.demo.mvcapp.controller.Master`. When you use `sap.ui.require`, no namespace is generated.

Keep the following module-loading conventions in mind:

▶ Use `sap.ui.define` to define a global namespace for your modules and to load dependent modules.

▶ Use `sap.ui.require` to load dependent modules without declaring a global namespace.

▶ You don't need to provide the file ending .js; this happens automatically.

▶ Name the function parameter as the artifact (in this case, `Controller`) and not like the namespace (`sap.ui.core.mvc.Controller`).

- You can use ./ when you're referring to your current directory.
- The order of the loaded modules in the dependencies array is not guaranteed.
- When your application needs to ensure synchronous module definition or synchronous loading of dependencies, you must use `jQuery.sap.declare` or `jQuery.sap.require`.

We've now done all the preparation work and can load the view, which will load its controller automatically in the index.html file. To load the view, we need to adapt the coding where we loaded the master page of our application; the changes are marked in bold in Listing 4.15. Pay close attention to the fact that we've given the view the name of the master page. We're also setting the property `initialPage` of our application, because we're going to add another page soon. This parameter helps us to set the initial page of the application (as its name suggests) so that we do not have to depend on the order of adding our pages with `oApp.addPage()`. The initial page is always shown first.

```
...
sap.ui.getCore().setModel(oModel);

var oPageMasterView = sap.ui.view("masterPage", {
  type: sap.ui.core.mvc.ViewType.JS,
  viewName: "sapui5.demo.mvcapp.view.Master",
});

var oApp = new sap.m.App({
  initialPage: "masterPage"
});
oApp.addPage(oPageMasterView);
oApp.placeAt("content");
```

Listing 4.15 Instantiation of Master View in index.html

In this example, we used the `sap.ui.view` function syntax. This is a factory function that will create the view for us. You see that we did not need to use the keyword `new` in front of `sap.ui.view`. We provided the view type via the `type` parameter and set it to `sap.u.core.mvc.ViewType.JS`. We also could have used the factory function `sap.ui.jsview`, in which case we would have not needed to provide the view type.

We've achieved the first step in organizing our file structure from a single HTML file into a more convenient MVC structure. When you run the application now, you won't see any differences. However, as promised earlier, you can look into your network traffic (here, we used Google Chrome). You'll see that the module definition with its resource path has worked, and the files have been loaded from the correct folder locations (see Figure 4.3).

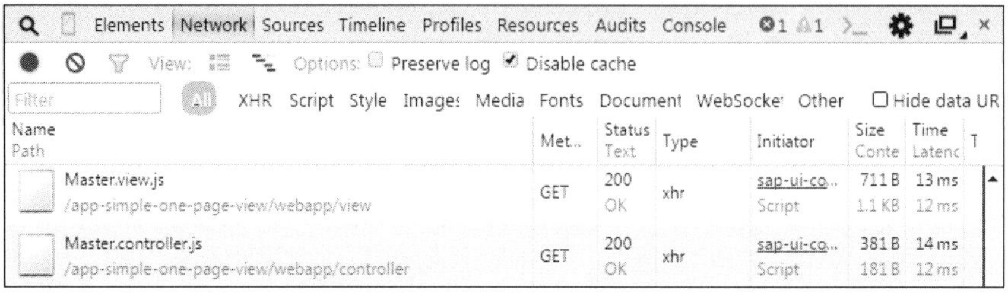

Figure 4.3 Network Traffic of Master View and Controller

The registration of the resource root `'sapui5/demo/mvcapp' : ./webapp/` has ensured that the master view with the `sapui5.demo.mvcapp.view.Master` namespace was loaded from the *./webapp/view/Master.view.js* folder. You can see that *.view.js* has been added automatically to the request, because we requested a view from the JavaScript type.

4.3.4 Creating a Detail View and Controller

Now that we have a convenient file structure in place and you've learned about some important aspects of creating views and controllers, let's enhance our application by adding a second page. When a user clicks on one of the table rows from the master page, we want the app to navigate to the detail page. There, we'll use an object header to display the information. Create the new files Detail.controller.js and Detail.view.js in their corresponding folders (see the folder structure in Listing 4.16).

```
mvc-app-simple
|   index.html
|   |
+---webapp
|   |
|   +---controller
|   |       Detail.controller.js
|   |       Master.controller.js
|   |
|   \---view
```

```
|              Detail.view.js
|              Master.view.js
```
Listing 4.16 Folder Structure for Detail Controller and View

Let's start with the detail view. Here, we're creating `sap.m.ObjectHeader` and placing it into `sap.m.Page`. Put the coding from Listing 4.17 into your */webapp/view/Detail.view.js* file.

```
sap.ui.jsview("sapui5.demo.mvcapp.view.Detail", {

  getControllerName: function() {

    return "sapui5.demo.mvcapp.controller.Detail";
  },

  createContent: function(oController) {

    var oObjectHeader = new sap.m.ObjectHeader({
      title: "{Name}",
      number: "ID: {ID}",
      attributes: [
        new sap.m.ObjectAttribute({
          text: "{Address/Country}"
        })
      ]
    });

    var oPageDetail = new sap.m.Page({
      title: "Supplier Detail",
      showNavButton: true,
      navButtonPress: [oController.onNavPress, oController],
      content: [oObjectHeader]
    });

    return oPageDetail;
  }
});
```
Listing 4.17 Detail View

The detail page also has a navigation button, as you can see in the coding for `showNavButton: true`. Next, we define the event handler for that button once it is clicked with `navButtonPress`. As you can see in the signature of the `createContent` function, we're also passing in a reference to the controller with `oController`.

We're assigning an array to the `navButtonPress` function: `[oController.onNav-Press, oController]`. We could also just assign `oController.onNavPress`. We're passing in an array here because the second value in the array (`oController`) is used as the `this` reference inside the controller. In the event handlers of the controls (in this case, the navigation button), `this` would reference the control itself and not the controller. This could lead to unexpected behaviors in your code; most times you would get "undefined is not a function" error, because SAPUI5 tried to invoke a controller function on your control.

Therefore, it's a good practice to always use the array syntax in your event handlers so that `this` is always what you're expecting it to be: the controller. This practice is not needed when we use declarative view types.

In the object header, you'll see the data binding syntax with the curly braces for the name, ID, and the country of the address of our supplier. We are referencing the path of the country via "Address/Country". Recall that our dataset has the following structure:

- ▶ CountSuppliers
- ▶ Suppliers
  - ▹ ID
  - ▹ Name
  - ▹ Address
    - – Street
    - – City
    - – State
    - – ZipCode
    - – Country

We're using the slash to access a nested property (Country) inside the Address. You may be wondering which supplier this page is bound to: the first or the second? Currently, there is no binding to a particular supplier. We'll set this up this later via the coding in our master view. Now, let's continue with *Detail.controller.js*. Review the code shown in Listing 4.18.

```
sap.ui.define([
  "sap/ui/core/mvc/Controller"
], function(Controller) {
```

```
  "use strict";

  return Controller.extend("sapui5.demo.mvcapp.controller.Detail", {

    onNavPress: function() {
      oApp.back();
    }
  });
});
```
Listing 4.18 Detail Controller

In the coding of the detail controller, you'll see the event handler for the navigation button `onNavPress`. We're referencing `oApp` here. This is the global variable from our index.html file. Using global variables is not a good practice and should be avoided when possible. For our current example, however, this is OK, and it works out of the box. We'll modify the coding throughout this chapter.

Now, we're going to modify the master view. The table row needs an event handler for when a user clicks on it. Let's add a press handler, `onListPress`, for the column list item template (which represents our row). Listing 4.19 shows the changes needed in bold.

```
… // listening shortend
var oTemplate = new sap.m.ColumnListItem({
  type: "Navigation",
  press: [oController.onListPress, oController],
  cells: [
    new sap.m.ObjectIdentifier({
      text: "{ID}"
    }),
    new sap.m.ObjectIdentifier({
      text: "{Name}"
    })
  ]
});
```
Listing 4.19 Master View Press Handler

Now, we can create the event handler in the master controller. Add the bold code from Listing 4.20 to your *Master.controller.js* file.

```
sap.ui.define([
  "sap/ui/core/mvc/Controller"
], function(Controller) {
  "use strict";
```

```
    return Controller.extend("sapui5.demo.mvcapp.controller.Master", {

  onListPress: function(oEvent) {
    var sPageId = "detailPage";
    oApp.to(sPageId);

    var oPage = oApp.getPage(sPageId);
    var oContenxt = oEvent.getSource().getBindingContext();
    oPage.setBindingContext(oContenxt);
  }
 });
});
```
Listing 4.20 Master Controller Press Handler

We'll go into detail about how setting the binding context works after we've set up the whole application. Now, let's add the second page to our app. Open the index.html file and adapt the coding as shown in Listing 4.21.

```
...
var oPageDetail = sap.ui.view("detailPage", {
  type: sap.ui.core.mvc.ViewType.JS,
  viewName: "sapui5.demo.mvcapp.view.Detail",
});

var oApp = new sap.m.App({
  initialPage: "masterPage"
});
oApp.addPage(oPageMaster).addPage(oPageDetail);
oApp.placeAt("content");
```
Listing 4.21 Second Page in index.html File

When you run the application, you'll see that you can navigate to the second page. On the second page, which is the DETAIL page, you'll see the corresponding supplier information, as shown in Figure 4.4.

Figure 4.4 Supplier Details

When you set a breakpoint after `oContext` in the *Master.controller.js* and click on the first table row, you'll see that the clicked row was bound to "`Supplier/0`" (`sPath` property in `oContext`), which is the first supplier. Figure 4.5 shows the debugging.

Figure 4.5 Debugging of Binding Context

This means that the second page is bound to the first supplier, and the corresponding data is shown correctly for this supplier. You'll learn more about data binding in Chapter 5; for now, just think of the binding context as information about which corresponding entries in the data set the control is bound to. In Section 4.6, you'll learn another way to set the binding of the second page.

The following are some important controller conventions to keep in mind:

▸ Controller names are capitalized.

▸ Controller filenames end with *.controller.js.

▸ Controllers should have the same name as their corresponding views.

▸ Event handlers are prefixed with `on`.

Later, we'll look at the standard methods a controller provides. Now that you have a basic idea of how to write controllers and views and the MVC structure, let's dive into the different view types. It's important that you are able to switch mentally between a JavaScript and an XML view, because those are the most used view types.

4.4 View Types

SAPUI5 supports four different view types: JavaScript, XML, HTML, and JSON. XML and JavaScript views are the most common options, and these two view types have the most features. You can see a features overview in Table 4.3.

Features	JavaScript View	XML View	JSON View	HTML View
Controls from standard and custom libraries	Yes	Yes	Yes	Yes
Self-contained registration of custom library locations	Yes	No	No	No
Properties of types string, integer, boolean, float	Yes	Yes	Yes	Yes
Properties of other types (object)	Yes	No	No	No
Aggregation 1:1, 1:n; Association 1:1, 1:n	Yes	Yes	Yes	Yes
Single event listener registration (maybe limited to scope, for example, controller/window)	Yes	Yes	Yes	Yes
Multiple event listeners and/or without scope	Yes	No	No	No
Simple data binding (e.g., path, default, or named model, template approach)	Yes	Yes	Yes	Yes
Customized data binding (e.g., formatter, data type, factory approach)	Yes	Yes	No	No
Embedded HTML (without use of HTML control)	No	Yes	No	No
Dynamic control creation (e.g., based on model data, but outside of data binding features)	Yes	No	No	No
Code completion	Yes	Yes	No	No
Templating	Yes	Yes	No	No
Validation	No	Yes	No	No

Table 4.3 View Type Comparison

JavaScript view types provide the most flexibility because they involve pure Java-Script coding, which allows you to put code together in any way you want. The big advantage of XML views is that they can be validated automatically. It's also easy to get an impression of the final view layout with XML views because of their hierarchical structure. When working with JavaScript views, you can put the different UI elements together in any order you want. In XML views, you must write them down in the correct final position.

It's unusual to use XML in modern JavaScript UI frameworks, and you may wonder why someone would choose XML over an HTML implementation—but when we look at some short code snippets, you'll see that the syntax of XML views is much more compact than that of the corresponding HTML ones.

When thinking about XML and JSON, you may wonder why someone would prefer XML; JSON is much more modern and has a smaller file size. XML views are much more verbose in their syntax than JSON views, but the verbose XML syntax is not always a bad thing. If you are manually putting together a big, nested JSON view and you're trying to match all those "},]" - characters and get an idea about the correct indenting, then you'll find that this can be a difficult venture—and JSON is especially picky about extra or missing commas. A closing } doesn't mean much; a closing `</Button>` is much more meaningful.

When you create an SAPUI5 application, you won't create hundreds of view files, and a view will not be that big—so we can disregard the file size aspect. One downside of XML views is that it isn't easy to write them inline in another file; you'll see this later in a separate code listing. XML views also cannot be uglified and will always show up in clear text. They can be packaged inside a *Component-preload.js* file, which we will see in Chapter 10.

As developers, we tend to want to write everything with code. If you're used to creating your views with code, you may find writing XML medieval, but it's still worth a try. Note that all examples in the SAPUI5 Explored app are written with XML views, and SAP wrote all its SAPUI5 SAP Fiori applications with XML views. XML is currently the preferred way to create views, and the tools provided by SAP—namely, the Layout Editor provided in the SAP Web IDE—only work with XML views at the time of writing (July 2016). Therefore, we'll also focus on XML views in this book.

XML Views

As a rule of thumb, you should use XML views whenever possible. When you're writing unit tests with inline view coding, however, use JavaScript views.

Now that you've learned about the different view types, let's look at their different implementations. We'll first work through a simple example so that the different implementations can be understood more easily.

We've provided a small example with the four different view types; in the example, every view displays the same `sap.m.Button` object with a press handler. The button is inside `sap.m.Panel`, and the panel is inside `sap.m.Page`. The example is called `app-very-simple-view-types`. Listing 4.22 shows the file and folder structure, and Listing 4.23 shows the view structure.

```
app-very-simple-view-types
|    index_html_view.html
|    index_js_view.html
|    index_json_view.html
|    index_xml_view.html
|    |
+---webapp
|    |
|    +---controller
|    |       View.controller.js
|    |
|    \---view
|            View.view.html
|            View.view.js
|            View.view.json
|            View.view.xml
|
```

Listing 4.22 File Folder Structure View Types Example

```
View
  controller: sapui5.demo.viewtypes.controller.View
  Page
    title: Hello World!
    Panel
    Button
      text: Hello World!
      icon: sap-icon://action
      type: Accept
      width: 200 px
      press: onPress
```

Listing 4.23 Structure of View

All four views have the same controller, and every view is instantiated in its corresponding HTML file.

Let's look at coding from the index_js_view.html file in Listing 4.24. `data-sap-ui-resourceroots` has been set to `'{"sapui5.demo.viewtypes": "./webapp/"}'`. The only part that differs among the four index_*_view.html files is the bold part of Listing 4.24, in which we define the view type.

```
var oPage = sap.ui.view("page", {
  type: sap.ui.core.mvc.ViewType.JS,
  viewName: "sapui5.demo.viewtypes.view.View",
});

var oApp = new sap.m.App();
oApp.addPage(oPage);
oApp.placeAt("content");
```
Listing 4.24 index_js_view.html coding

When you look at the coding from index_xml_view.html, you can see that the page instantiation happens with this coding—only the type of the view was changed:

```
var oPage = sap.ui.view("page", {
type: sap.ui.core.mvc.ViewType.XML,
viewName: "sapui5.demo.viewtypes.view.View",
});
```

The controller code is the same for all four different view types and is shown in Listing 4.25. The controller is saved in *webapp/controller/View.controller.js*.

```
sap.ui.define([
  "sap/ui/core/mvc/Controller"
], function(Controller) {
  "use strict";

  return Controller.extend("sapui5.demo.viewtypes.controller.View", {
    onPress: function() {
      alert("Hello World!");
    }
  });
});
```
Listing 4.25 Controller for Different View Types

You can see that we have just one function in the controller: the `onPress` event handler, which will be executed upon button press in the view. Now, let's look at the different view types. You'll see that it's possible to suppress the default aggregation content from `sap.m.Page` in the XML and HTML views.

When looking at the different view types, pay attention to how the different controls are defined and how their properties are set. We'll then take a detailed look at the XML views. You'll see the different view types in Listing 4.26 through Listing 4.29.

```
sap.ui.jsview("sapui5.demo.viewtypes.view.View", {

  getControllerName: function() {

    return "sapui5.demo.viewtypes.controller.View";
  },

  createContent: function(oController) {

    var oButton = new sap.m.Button({
      text: "Hello World!",
      icon: "sap-icon://accept",
      width: "200px",
      type: "Accept",
      press: [oController.onPress, oController]
    });

    var oPanel = new sap.m.Panel({
      content: [oButton]
    });

    var oPage = new sap.m.Page({
      title: "Hello World!",
      content: [oPanel]
    });
    return oPage;
  }
});
```

Listing 4.26 JavaScript View Type Example

```
<mvc:View
  xmlns="sap.m"
  xmlns:mvc="sap.ui.core.mvc"
  controllerName="sapui5.demo.viewtypes.controller.View">
  <Page title="Hello World!">
    <Panel>
      <Button
        text="Hello World!"
        icon="sap-icon://action"
        type="Accept"
        width="200px"
```

```
        press="onPress">
      </Button>
    </Panel>
  </Page>
</mvc:View>
```

Listing 4.27 XML View Type Example

```
<template data-controller-name="sapui5.demo.viewtypes.controller.View">
  <div data-sap-ui-type="sap.m.Page"
    data-title="Hello World!">
    <div data-sap-ui-type="sap.m.Panel">
      <div data-sap-ui-type="sap.m.Button"
        data-text="Hello World!"
        data-icon="sap-icon://accept"
        data-type="Accept" data-width="200px"
        data-press="onPress"></div></div></div>
</template>
```

Listing 4.28 HTML View Type Example

```
{
  "Type": "sap.ui.core.mvc.JSONView",
  "controllerName": "sapui5.demo.viewtypes.controller.View",
  "content": [{
    "Type": "sap.m.Page",
    "title": "Hello World!",
    "content": [{
      "Type": "sap.m.Panel",
      "content": [{
        "Type": "sap.m.Button",
        "text": "Hello World!",
        "icon": "sap-icon://accept",
        "width": "200px",
        "type": "Accept",
        "press": "onPress"
      }]
    }]
  }]
}
```

Listing 4.29 JSON View Type Example

Now that you've seen all the different view type examples, you can choose your favorite one. However, keep in mind that the XML view is the preferred option by SAP, followed by the JavaScript view. Now, let's move on and discuss the specialties for XML views.

4.4.1 XML Views

When you are using XML views, it's important that you define the namespaces for the view. You can choose whatever namespaces you want. It's a best practice to choose the standard, empty namespace for `sap.m`.

If you are new to this XML namespace concept and its use within SAPUI5 XML views, you can think of namespaces as short alias references to the corresponding SAPUI5 libraries. Let's look at the namespace definition from the XML view example:

```
<mvc:View
xmlns="sap.m"
xmlns:mvc="sap.ui.core.mvc"
controllerName="sapui5.demo.viewtypes.controller.View">
```

Namespaces are marked in bold. You see that the first namespace—which is defined with `xmlns="sap.m"`—has no colon after `xmlns`. Therefore, you can use any `sap.m` control without needing it to prefix it; we just wrote `<Button>` to use a `sap.m.Button`. The second namespace is defined for `sap.ui.core.mvc`, and its prefix is `mvc` (note the characters "mvc" after the colon in `xmlns:mvc`).

Pay special attention when you are copying and pasting examples from the Explored app to ensure that you are using the correct namespaces! If you forgot to define the namespace for `sap.ui.layout` and tried to reference a horizontal layout in your view, you would see an error in your browser console:

```
Uncaught Error: resource sapui5/demo/viewtypes/view/Layout.view.xml
could not be loaded from ./webapp/view/View.view.xml. Check for 'file
not found' or parse errors. Reason: Error: Invalid XML
```

The layout example is shown in Listing 4.30. As you can see, it's preferable to use short namespaces; here, just l is used for `sap.ui.layout`.

```
<mvc:View
  controllerName="sap.ui.layout.sample.HorizontalLayout.C"
  xmlns:l="sap.ui.layout"
  xmlns:mvc="sap.ui.core.mvc"
  xmlns="sap.m">
  <l:HorizontalLayout>
    <Image
      src="pic1.png"
      width="250px">
    </Image>
    <Image
      src="pic2.png"
```

```
        width="250px">
      </Image>
    </l:HorizontalLayout>
</mvc:View>
```

Listing 4.30 Layout Example with XML Namespace

Now that you've seen the different view types and examples, let's sum up some view conventions to keep in mind:

▶ View names are capitalized.

▶ All views are stored in the *view* folder.

▶ Views always end with *.view.viewtype* (where *viewtype* is js, xml, html, or json).

▶ Use XML views whenever possible, and JavaScript views as a second choice.

▶ The default namespace for XML views is `sap.m`.

▶ Other XML namespaces are referenced by an alias.

▶ Use short names for those aliases—for example, `l` for `sap.ui.layout`.

4.4.2 Transforming JavaScript Views into XML Views

In the previous section, we discussed the differences between the different view types. We looked at a simple example that was implemented in all four view types. Let's apply this knowledge and transform our master and detail JavaScript views into XML views. Throughout Listing 4.32 to Listing 4.36 you'll see the view codes side by side. Try to implement the XML view by yourself while looking at the JavaScript view; this is an important exercise!

This exercise helps when you're looking at the API documents of SAPUI5 and trying to implement an JavaScript view into an XML view. It will also help when you're working the other way around: looking at the SAPUI5 Explored XML view examples and trying to understand the API documents.

Let's start with the listings for the master view (Listing 4.32 and Listing 4.33). The various controls are marked in bold. In JavaScript coding, you would first create all the different parts of the table and then assign them to the table. In XML, you write the table first, because that's the way it's structured naturally; the same is true for the page.

```
mvc-app-simple
|   index.html
```

```
|    |
+---webapp
|    |
|    +---controller
|    |        Detail.controller.js
|    |        Master.controller.js
|    |
|    \---view
|             App.view.xml
|             Detail.view.xml
|             Master.view.xml
```

Listing 4.31 File and Folder Structure for XML Views

```
createContent: function(oController) {
  var aColumns = [
    new sap.m.Column({
      header: new sap.m.Text({ text: "ID" }) }),
    new sap.m.Column({
      header: new sap.m.Text({ text: "Name" }) })
  ];

  var oTemplate = new sap.m.ColumnListItem({
    type: "Navigation",
    press: [oController.onListPress, oController],
    cells: [ new sap.m.ObjectIdentifier({ text: "{ID}" }),
             new sap.m.ObjectIdentifier({ text: "{Name}" }) ]
  });

  var oTableHeader = new sap.m.Toolbar({
    content: [ new sap.m.Title({
        text: "Number of Suppliers: {/CountSuppliers}" }) ]
  });

  var oTable = new sap.m.Table({
    columns: aColumns, headerToolbar: oTableHeader });

oTable.bindItems("/Suppliers", oTemplate);

  var oPageMaster = new sap.m.Page({
  title: "Supplier Overview", content: [oTable] });
  return oPageMaster;
}
```

Listing 4.32 Master View JavaScript createContent

```
<mvc:View
  controllerName="sapui5.demo.mvcapp.controller.Master"
  xmlns:mvc="sap.ui.core.mvc" xmlns="sap.m">
```

```
  <Page title="Supplier Overview">
    <content>
      <Table items="{/Suppliers}">
        <headerToolbar>
          <Toolbar>
            <Label id="tableHeader"
               text="Number of Suppliers: {/CountSuppliers}" />
          </Toolbar>
        </headerToolbar>
        <columns>
          <Column><header><Text text="ID" /></header></Column>
          <Column><header><Text text="Name" /><header></Column>
        </columns>
        <items>
          <ColumnListItem type="Navigation" press="onListPress">
            <cells>
              <ObjectIdentifier text="{ID}" />
              <ObjectIdentifier text="{Name}" />
            </cells>
          </ColumnListItem>
        </items>
      </Table>
    </content>
  </Page>
</mvc:View>
```

Listing 4.33 Master View XML Implementation

```
var oObjectHeader = new sap.m.ObjectHeader({
  title: "{Name}",
  number: "ID: {ID}",
  attributes: [
    new sap.m.ObjectAttribute({
      text: "{Address/Country}"
    })
  ]
});

var oPageDetail = new sap.m.Page({
  title: "Supplier Detail",
  showNavButton: true,
  navButtonPress: [oController.onNavPress, oController],
  content: [oObjectHeader]
});

return oPageDetail;
```

Listing 4.34 Detail View JavaScript createContent

Pay attention to how the event handlers are used. You don't need to put the `oCon-troller` as the second parameter into the `navButtonPress` function to get the right `this` context. In XML views this happens automatically, you just write `navButtonPress="onNavPress"`.

Note that aggregations in the XML views are also used with lowercases, like `content`, `columns`, `attributes` and `items`. The names of the controls begin with an uppercase letter, like `Text` or `Page`.

Instead of the : (colon) you use to set the properties in JavaScript, you use the = (equal sign) in XML views. So, `title: "Supplier Detail"` is written as: `title="Supplier Detail"`. The curly braces for data binding work exactly the same in JavaScript and XML views, as in `"{Address/Country}"` (see Listing 4.35).

```
<mvc:View
  controllerName="sapui5.demo.mvcapp.controller.Detail"
  xmlns:mvc="sap.ui.core.mvc"
  xmlns="sap.m">
  <Page
    navButtonPress="onNavPress"
    showNavButton="true"
    title="Supplier Detail">
    <content>
      <ObjectHeader
        title="{Name}"
        number="ID: {ID}">
        <attributes>
          <ObjectAttribute
            text="{Address/Country}" />
        </attributes>
      </ObjectHeader>
    </content>
  </Page>
</mvc:View>
```

Listing 4.35 Detail View XML

Note how the aggregation binding of the items is performed. In JavaScript, you had to define a template and bind the items with the template to the "`Suppliers`":

```
oTable.bindItems("/Suppliers", oTemplate);
```

In the XML views, you bind the table items to the supplier and write your template inside the items aggregation (without any special template syntax):

```
<Table items="{/Suppliers}"> …
… <items> <ColumnListItem type="Navigation" press="onListPress"> …
</items> …
</Table>
```

Now that we've refactored the two views from JavaScript into XML, you may wonder if there's also a way to turn the coding of the sap.m.App into a view: The answer is *yes*. The coding for the app looks quite simple, so this won't be a big deal. While we're doing this, we'll see an interesting feature of the XML views, one that will break our current navigation code when we create App.view.xml!

SAPUI5 creates automatic IDs for our elements in our views. What's surprising about this is that when we create views within another view, they're prefixed with the name of the outer view. This creates a new ID for the view even though we gave the view a fixed ID.

Let's investigate this behavior as we implement the app view. Create the file *App.view.xml* in the folder in *webapp/view*. Here's a recap of the main functionality from the app view:

```
var oApp = new sap.m.App({
initialPage: "masterPage"
});
oApp.addPage(oPageMaster).addPage(oPageDetail);
```

Create an app, set its initial page, and add the two pages. The pages have two IDs, masterPage and detailPage:

```
var oPageMaster = sap.ui.view("masterPage", { …
var oPageDetail = sap.ui.view("detailPage", { …
```

"Translating" this into XML would result in the code shown in Listing 4.36. We also added a new property called displayBlock and set it to true to get rid of the scroll bars in the application.

```
<mvc:View
  xmlns:mvc="sap.ui.core.mvc"
  displayBlock="true"
  xmlns="sap.m">
  <App id="app">
    <pages>
      <mvc:XMLView
        id="masterPage"
        viewName="sapui5.demo.mvcapp.view.Master" />
      <mvc:XMLView
        id="detailPage"
        viewName="sapui5.demo.mvcapp.view.Detail" />
```

```
    </pages>
  </App>
</mvc:View>
```
Listing 4.36 App View XML

You can see that we've now embedded `sap.m.App` inside an XML view. The two other views were also embedded into the `pages` aggregation of the app, as we did in our coding before with `oApp.addPages(…)`. To embed views, put the view name inside the `viewName` property in the `mvc:XMLView` tag. We've also put the views' IDs inside this view tag. We don't need the `initialView` property anymore, because the first page in the aggregation will be displayed first. Also note that `sap.m.App` now has an ID, "app": `<App id="app">`. This is necessary to access the app in our coding.

Now, we can adapt the index.html file to instantiate the newly created app view. First, remove the coding to create the other two pages; we don't need it anymore, because it happens automatically in the app view. Note that we're now instantiating a view with the new `oAppView` variable—and don't create `sap.m.App`! To access the app inside the app XML view, use the `byId` function of the view (because we need this for navigation). The modified coding of index.html is shown in Listing 4.37.

```
…
sap.ui.getCore().setModel(oModel);
var oAppView = sap.ui.view("appview", {
  type: sap.ui.core.mvc.ViewType.XML,
  viewName: "sapui5.demo.mvcapp.view.App",
});
var oApp = oAppView.byId("app");
oAppView.placeAt("content");
```
Listing 4.37 Modified index.html to Instantiate App.view.xml

You can run the app now, but won't be able to navigate to the second page. To investigate this issue, let's check the IDs that SAPUI5 created for us. After that, we'll look at the part of our code that's now failing in the debugger.

We inspected the HTML from SAPUI5 with Google Chrome and have highlighted the term `masterPage` (see Figure 4.6). We also highlighted the IDs for `appview` and `app` so that you can see how SAPUI5 created the IDs. You won't find the `detailPage`, because it's not currently rendered in the DOM, but the view is already loaded.

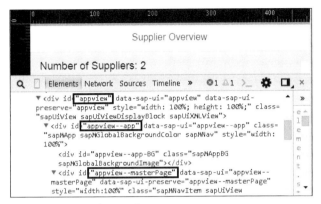

Figure 4.6 Created View IDs

You can see that the ID of our app ("app") was prefixed with the ID `appview`, which resulted in `appview--app`, but in the previous coding we were still able to access it via "app":

```
// the app was prefixed with "appview-app"
// but we are able to access it via "app"
var oApp = oAppView.byId("app");
```

This is possible because when you are calling `byId` on a view, the view is able to return it to you via its original ID. If you wanted to access the app via the SAPUI5 core you would have needed the whole ID — `"appview--app"`—which we typed into the console in Figure 4.7.

As previously mentioned, when we click on an item in our table currently, we'll see the following error in the console:

```
Uncaught TypeError: Cannot read property 'setBindingContext' of null
```

To see what's happening, set a breakpoint at `oPage.setBindingContext(oContext);` in the Master.controller.js file. The Google Chrome debugger displays the values of our variables inline as we're debugging (see Figure 4.8). You'll see that our variable `oPage` is `null` and therefore we can't call `setBindingContext` on it.

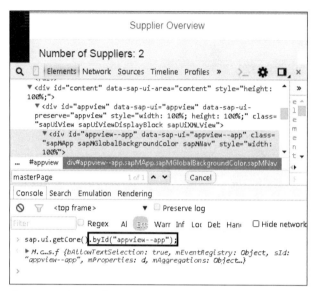

Figure 4.7 Getting the App via sap.ui.getCore()

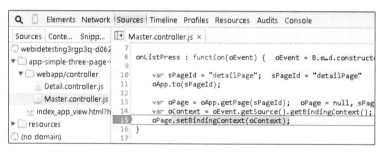

Figure 4.8 Breakpoint at oPage.setBindingContext(oContext)

Let's examine what's happening and how to solve our problem in the console while we're still at this breakpoint. In Listing 4.38, the > in our input and the < is the output of the console.

```
>  oPage
<  null
>  oApp.getPages();
<  [M.createClass.f, M.createClass.f]
>  oApp.getPages()[1];
<  M.c... s.f {
     bAllowTextSelection: true,
     mEventRegistry: Object,
```

```
      sId: "appview--detailPage",
      mProperties: d,
      mAggregations: Object...
   }
>   oApp.getPages()[1].getId();
<   "appview--detailPage"
```

Listing 4.38 Console Commands for Debugging oPage Is Null

Now, retrieve all the pages of the app. Then, check the second page—the detail page—which translates to index 1 in the `getPages()` array. Our coding doesn't work, because the original ID `detailPage` was set to `appview--detailPage`. We can fix our coding now with two possible options:

▶ Change the value of `sPageId` to the new ID hard coded:

```
var sPageId = "appview--detailPage"
```

▶ Change the value of `sPageId` to the new ID dynamically:

```
var sPageId = oApp.getPages()[1].getId();
```

In our example coding, we used option 2 and commented out option 1. When you restart the application with this change made, everything should work again. You can see that navigation with IDs—depending on how you've created them—can be a cause of errors. We'll address this error-prone approach when we dive into Section 4.6.

Feel free to try to set IDs at different points in views and look at the HTML generated by SAPUI5. Sometimes, you'll find that some IDs have been ignored by SAPUI5—for example, if you set an ID inside the app view, as demonstrated in Listing 4.39 and in the corresponding screenshot in Figure 4.9. If you want to keep this coding, take care to use the correct IDs in the master controller for navigation, as in the previous example.

```
// App.view.xml – added a fixed ID
<mvc:View
id="appview"
xmlns:mvc="sap.ui.core.mvc"
displayBlock="true"
xmlns="sap.m">
<App id="app">
...
// index.html - removed the fixed ID
...
var oAppView = sap.ui.view({
type: sap.ui.core.mvc.ViewType.XML,
```

```
viewName: "sapui5.demo.mvcapp.view.App",
});
...
```

Listing 4.39 Experiment with Setting IDs for Views

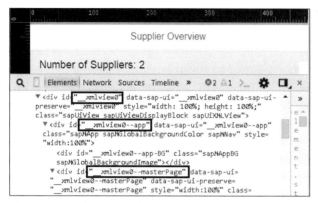

Figure 4.9 Resulting IDs When Setting the View ID in the App View Itself

Now that we've set up all the necessary views for our application, we can take the next step for optimizing our application. As you know, we still have a lot of coding happening in the index.html file, and this file, which is responsible for starting the application, should contain as little code as possible. Let's split our application into reuseable components that can be instantiated easily—which is also important if we want to use our application inside the SAP Fiori Launchpad.

4.5   Components

We introduced the MVC concept in the last sections, and now we'll introduce another important aspect of SAPUI5 applications: components. A component doesn't really fit into one of the MVC categories. It's not a view, not a controller, and definitely not a model. A component is a more abstract concept that involves encapsulation and reuse. As mentioned previously, the component file is important when running an application from SAP Fiori Launchpad, because the launchpad starts your application via the component file and not via your HTML file.

There are two different types of components: *faceless* (without a UI) and *UI components*. Throughout the rest of this chapter, we'll focus on UI components, because our application has a UI. Faceless components can be useful for applications such as a service that delivers data from the backend.

The component we're using is the "startup" script for your application, which defines the locations of our services, instantiates the different models, creates the initial view, describes your application (e.g., the title and description), and sets up the routing.

4.5.1 Creating the Component File

Throughout this chapter, we'll also apply some small visual enhancements to our application once we have the component up and running. Now, let's create a component for our project. As a best practice, the component file should be inside the *webapp* folder, and it must be named Component.js. From now on, all our application files are relative to that component file. Create *webapp/Component.js*; you'll see the file structure in Listing 4.40.

```
mvc-app-simple
|    index.html
|    |
+---webapp
|    |    Component.js
|    |
|    +---controller
|    |        Detail.controller.js
|    |        Master.controller.js
|    |    |
|    \---view
|             App.view.xml
|             Detail.view.xml
|             Master.view.xml
```

Listing 4.40 Folder Structure for Component.js

The content of the component file is shown in Listing 4.41.

```
sap.ui.define([
  "sap/ui/core/UIComponent",
  "sap/ui/model/json/JSONModel"
], function(UIComponent, JSONModel) {
  "use strict";

  return UIComponent.extend("sapui5.demo.mvcapp.Component", {

    createContent: function() {
      UIComponent.prototype.createContent.apply(this, arguments);
```

```
    var oData = {
        ...
    };
    var oModel = new JSONModel();
    oModel.setData(oData);

    // important to set the model on the component
    this.setModel(oModel);

    var oRootView = sap.ui.view("appview", {
      type: sap.ui.core.mvc.ViewType.XML,
      viewName: "sapui5.demo.mvcapp.view.App"
    });

    oApp = oRootView.byId("app");
    return oRootView;
  }
 });
});
```

Listing 4.41 Component.js Initial Coding

In the component listing, you'll see that we're using the `sap.ui.define` syntax and requiring the `sap.ui.core.UIComponent` as `UIComponent` and the `sap.ui.model.json.JSONModel` as `JSONModel`. The component also has a `createContent` function, which we're using to create our content. We extend the `UIComponent` and give it the name `sapui5.demo.mvcapp.Component`. It is necessary that the name ends with `.Component`; otherwise, SAPUI5 won't be able to find it when searching for it.

Because we're overwriting the `createContent` function, it's also important to call the function from the super class—which we can do via `UIComponent.prototype.createContent.apply(this, arguments)`. This lets you call a function with the first parameter as the `this` value and the second parameter as the parameters for the function in an array or array-like object.

Every function in JavaScript contains the array-like variable `arguments`, which contains all current arguments of the called function. If you're unfamiliar with the `prototype` syntax and the corresponding inheritance in JavaScript, refer to the article "Introduction to Object-Oriented JavaScript" from the Mozilla Developer Network (MDN), found at *https://developer.mozilla.org/en-US/docs/Web/JavaScript/ Introduction_to_Object-Oriented_JavaScript*.

If you want to dig deeper into this topic, we can suggest another great resource. The free book *You Don't Know JS: this & Object Prototypes* is hosted on the Github repository by Kyle Simpson, along with his other titles; visit *https://github.com/getify/You-Dont-Know-JS/*.

Returning to coding the component, you'll see that we're setting the model directly onto the component with `this.setModel(oModel)` and not onto the SAPUI5 core. This is important, because otherwise your application would run inside the SAP Fiori Launchpad and every app would set the model to the SAPUI5 core, which would lead to a mess, and your app wouldn't work anymore.

We're creating the root view of the application (the app view) in the same way we did in the index.html file. As previously discussed, we name the variable for the root view `oRootView`. After doing so, we can still access the `oApp` variable, which is a global variable; we'll improve the `oApp` later in Section 4.6. At the end of the `createContent` function, we return the root view.

To startup the component, we need to modify the *index.html* file. While we're doing this, we're also introducing another important event in the application: the `attachInit` event from the SAPUI5 core. This event will be fired when SAPUI5 has finished its startup. To avoid blocking the UI, the `attachInit` event and modifying the index.html must happen asynchronously; therefore, we need a new line in the index.html file bootstrap:

```
...
data-sap-ui-compatVersion="edge"
data-sap-ui-preload="async"
data-sap-ui-resourceroots='{"sapui5.demo.mvcapp": "./webapp/"}'>
```

The modified script part of the index file is shown in Listing 4.42 in bold. When we instantiate the component, we have to put it into a container that can display it. For that, we'll use `sap.ui.core.ComponentContainer`. Note that we're still using the global variable `oApp` for navigation purposes.

```
var oApp;
sap.ui.getCore().attachInit(function() {
  sap.ui.require([
    "sap/ui/core/ComponentContainer",
    "sapui5/demo/mvcapp/Component"
  ], function(ComponentContainer, Component) {
    new ComponentContainer({
      height: "100%",
      component: new Component({
        id: "mvcAppComponent"
```

```
        })
    }).placeAt("content");
  });
});
```

Listing 4.42 Index.html File Creating a Component

You can see that we've acquired the component file via the path *sapui5/demo/mvcapp/Component* and referenced it as `Component` in the code. The component itself is inside `ComponentContainer`. The container is a `sap.ui.core.Component-Container` element, which has a `component` association. It's important to set the `height` of the `ComponentContainer` to `100%`; otherwise, a user would only see the title of the application. Last but not least, we also gave the component an ID: `"mvcAppComponent"`.

When you start the application now, you'll see that nothing has changed visually, but we've taken a big step forward in terms of modularization. In the network trace, you'll see that everything is as expected: The component was loaded first, then the app view, and then the master and detail views with their corresponding controllers. Figure 4.10 shows the network trace, as captured in Google Chrome.

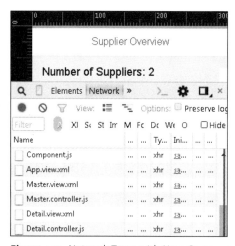

Figure 4.10 Network Trace with New Component.js

4.5.2 Adding a Shell Around the Component

After setting up the component file, we can start to enhance the look of the application. Currently, if you open the application to a full screen, you'll see that the page is pretty big and covers the whole area from left to right. When you look at SAP Fiori applications, you may notice that they're centered in the middle with equal space on the left and right sides. In web design, it's a common practice to restrict the page content to a certain width, a technique called *letterboxing*. Figure 4.11 shows a demo SAP Fiori application from the SAP Fiori, demo cloud edition, which has letterboxing enabled.

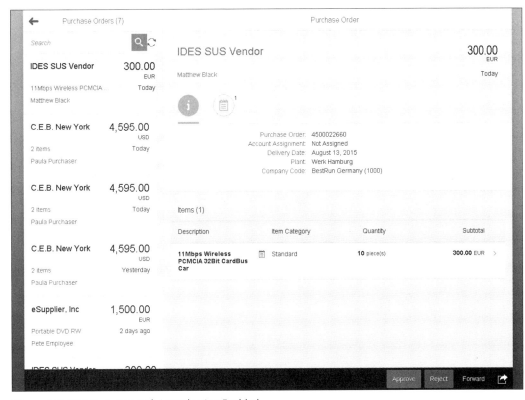

Figure 4.11 SAP Fiori App with Letterboxing Enabled

We can achieve the same effect in our application with the `sap.m.Shell` control. Don't use `sap.ui.unified.Shell` if you want to run your application inside the SAP Fiori Launchpad; the unified shell adds a title bar that the launchpad already provides. Only use the unified shell if you're running your application as a stand-alone app. Creating `sap.m.Shell` is pretty easy; we'll adapt the coding in our current index.html file. The changes are marked in Listing 4.43 in bold.

```
var oApp;
sap.ui.getCore().attachInit(function() {
   sap.ui.require([
      "sap/m/Shell",
      "sap/ui/core/ComponentContainer",
      "sapui5/demo/mvcapp/Component"
   ], function(Shell, ComponentContainer, Component) {
      new Shell({
        app: new ComponentContainer({
           height: "100%",
           component: new Component({
              id: "mvcAppComponent"
           })
        })
      }).placeAt("content");
   });
});
```

Listing 4.43 Component Inside sap.m.Shell

We acquired the sap.m.Shell, referenced it as Shell, and put the ComponentContainer inside default aggregation app. When you run the application now in full screen, you'll see that letterboxing is enabled and the application is centered nicely (Figure 4.12 shows before and after screenshots).

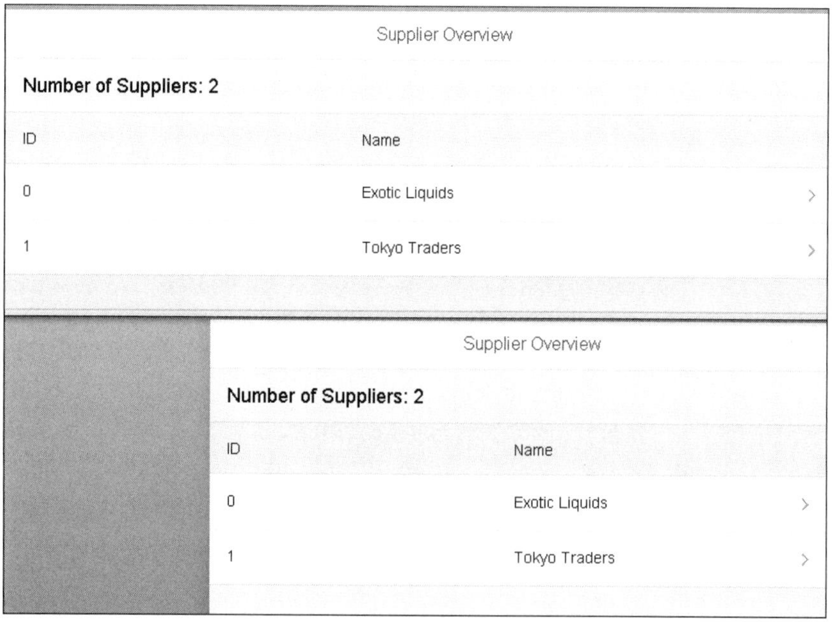

Figure 4.12 Letterboxing Enabled with sap.m.Shell

4.5.3 Enhancing the Look of a Table

There is one final visual enhancement we can make to the table. You'll see that at the moment the table touches the page on the left and right in full-screen mode; this would be OK on mobile phones. We can change this by adding a predefined style class to the table. It's important to set the width of the table to "auto" so that SAPUI5 can calculate the correct values. You'll find examples of different padding and margin classes in the SAPUI5 Developer Guide in the "Using Predefined CSS Margin Classes" and "Using Container Content Padding CSS Classes" sections.

We'll use a responsive margin to add some space around the table control. For that, we need to add the two bold lines to our Master.view.xml (see Listing 4.44).

```
...
<Table
  class="sapUiResponsiveMargin"
  width="auto"
  items="{/Suppliers}">
    ...
```

Listing 4.44 Table Margins

When you run the application now on different screen sizes, you'll see that the margin was adapted accordingly (see Figure 4.13).

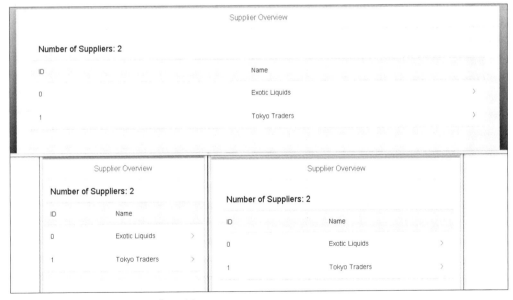

Figure 4.13 Responsive Margin for Table

4.5.4 Component Metadata

In the component file, the `metadata` section allows for configuration. Here, you can configure the routing or the locations of your models, for example. Let's start with a simple configuration that handles the root view, which is App.view.xml. Open the Component.js file and apply the changes set in bold in Listing 4.45.

```
return UIComponent.extend("sapui5.demo.mvcapp.Component", {
  metadata: {
    "rootView": "sapui5.demo.mvcapp.view.App"
  },
  createContent: function() {
    // call the base component's createContent function
    var oRootView =
      UIComponent.prototype.createContent.apply(this, arguments);
```

Listing 4.45 Metadata Configuration of Component

We can now directly assign the result of the function call `UIComponent.proto-type.createContent.apply(this, arguments)` to the `oRootView` variable. The result is `App.view.xml`, because it's configured as the `rootView` in the `metadata` section.

If we didn't have a `createContent` function (which we currently need for creating our model), then the creation of the view would happen automatically; that is, the prototype's `createContent` function would be called automatically and would create the view. Throughout this chapter, we'll add additional properties to this `metadata` section. When you run the application now, you'll notice that nothing's changed.

4.5.5 Storing the Hard-Coded Model Data in a Separate data.json File

Let's go one step further and save the hard-coded model data into a separate file. Copy and paste the data from the model (see Listing 4.3), beginning with the opening curly brace and ending with the last curly brace without the semicolon, and save it into *webapp/service/data.json*. After that, delete the `oData` variable. You can see the folder structure in Listing 4.46 and an excerpt of the data.json file in Listing 4.47. Pay special attention to all the property names inside the JSON file, all of which must be inside quotation marks.

```
mvc-app-simple
|    index.html
|    |
+---webapp
|    |    Component.js
|    |
|    +---controller
|    |         Detail.controller.js
|    |         Master.controller.js
|    |
|    +---service
|    |         data.json
|    |
|    \---view
|              App.view.xml
|              Detail.view.xml
|              Master.view.xml
```

Listing 4.46 Folder Structure for data.json File

```
{
  "CountSuppliers": "2",
  "Suppliers": [{
    "ID": 0,
    "Name": "Exotic Liquids",
    "Address": {
      "Street": "NE 228th",
      ...
    }
  }]
}
```

Listing 4.47 Excerpt of webapp/service/data.json

Now, we need to modify the coding in the component. We'll create a new section in which we can configure the URL for the data file. The new section is called `"config"`, and the property is the `"serviceUrl"`. For now, this points to the JSON file, but in later chapters, when we connect to backend services, it will point to a server URL. Listing 4.48 shows the modified coding in the component file.

```
return UIComponent.extend("sapui5.demo.mvcapp.Component", {
  metadata: {
    "rootView": "sapui5.demo.mvcapp.view.App",
    "config": {
      "serviceUrl": "webapp/service/data.json"
    }
  },
```

```
createContent: function() {
  var oRootView =
    UIComponent.prototype.createContent.apply(this, arguments);
  var oModel =
    new JSONModel(this.getMetadata().getConfig().serviceUrl);
  this.setModel(oModel);
...
```
Listing 4.48 Instantiating the Model via Configuration Service URL

You now have access to the metadata of the component via `this.getMetadata()`, and you can access the configuration via `getConfig()`. Earlier, we said that the resources will be loaded relative to the component file, but we had to write the folder name `webapp` in front and could not use `./` to point to the current folder. The URL resolution for such resources work differently, because they're still relative to the root folder of the application. If your file was not get loaded correctly, open the network trace in your browser, determine from which location your other files have been loaded, and adapt your path accordingly.

Because we're using a local resource, we also could have referenced it via dot notation and retrieved the correct path via the `jQuery.sap.getModulePath` helper function. To try out this coding, set a breakpoint inside the `createContent` function of the component (see Listing 4.49).

```
// serviceUrl: "sapui5.demo.mvcapp.service.data"
var sServiceModule = this.getMetadata().getConfig().serviceUrl;
var sModulePath =
  jQuery.sap.getModulePath(sServiceModule, ".json");
var oModel = new JSONModel(sModulePath);.
```
Listing 4.49 Instantiating the JSON Model with Data from a JSON file

This dynamic determination of the path is important if your application will run from SAP Fiori Launchpad, but it's unlikely that you would use static data from a local JSON file for your application; therefore, we'll stick with the simple path solution for learning purposes.

The following are some important component conventions to keep in mind:

▸ The component file must be named Component.js.

▸ The index.html file should contain as little coding as possible.

▸ Put the component file inside the *webapp* folder.

4.6   Routing

Now, it's time to get rid of the clumsy global variable oApp that we've been using to navigate inside the app. In this section, you'll learn a better approach to navigation via SAPUI5 routing.

Routing isn't just about navigating from one page to another. Via routing, we can make our applications bookmark enabled and send the bookmarked link to another person. We can directly access different application states of the application—for example, the application may be currently showing the master view or perhaps the detail view of a certain supplier.

The different states—or locations—are represented in the URL after the hash sign (#). Examples of such URLs patterns are listed in Table 4.4.

URL Pattern	Location
index.html#	Start page
index.html#/detail/0	Displays details of entry number 0
index.html#/detail/0/moredetail	Displays further details for entry number 0
index.html#/detail/0?query=param	Displays details of entry number 0 and appends a custom query

Table 4.4 URL Pattern Examples

In our application, we'll use the first two patterns shown in Table 4.4. The idea in routing is that you want define those URL patterns and configure which view should be shown. We have to make several changes throughout all of our files to set up the routing. The steps are as follows:

1. Get rid of the oApp variable in the index.html file.

2. Delete the oApp variable inside the createContent function of Component.js also.

3. Delete the rootView.

4. Configure the routing in the metadata section of Component.js.

5. Initialize the routing within the init function of Component.js.

6. Delete the master and detail view in the pages aggregation of App.view.xml.

7. Adapt the coding of Master.controller.js to make use of the routing.

8. Adapt the coding of Detail.controller.js to use the routing and adapt the data binding.

It's important that you complete all the preceding steps; otherwise, the app will break if you run it. Steps 1 and 2 are easy enough to do on your own, and we'll guide you through steps 3 to 7 in the following section. While performing the steps, you can look ahead to the final solution in `simple-routing-simple` in the source code from this chapter.

4.6.1 Routing Configuration

After you've deleted the `oApp` variable in index.html and the component file, we'll continue with the configuration in the component file. Insert the bold sections from Listing 4.50 into the `metadata` section, as shown.

```
metadata: {
  "rootView": "sapui5.demo.mvcapp.view.App",
  "config": {
    "serviceUrl": "webapp/service/data.json"
  },
  "routing": {
    "config": {
      "routerClass": "sap.m.routing.Router",
      "viewType": "XML",
      "viewPath": "sapui5.demo.mvcapp.view",
      "controlId": "app",
      "controlAggregation": "pages",
      "transition": "slide"
    },

    "routes": [{
      "pattern": "",
      "name": "master",
      "target": "master"
    }, {
      "pattern": "detail/{ID}",
      "name": "detail",
      "target": "detail"
    }],

    "targets": {
      "master": {
        "viewName": "Master",
        "viewLevel": 1
```

```
      },
      "detail": {
        "viewName": "Detail",
        "viewLevel": 2
      }
    }
  }
},
...
```

Listing 4.50 Routing Configuration

Let's work through this coding step by step. The following sections will identify the different parameters and the configuration that needs to occur.

config

First, apply the routing configuration via the `config` parameter. This section contains the global configuration for the router and provides default values. To begin, use the router class provided by SAPUI5, which is `sap.m.routing.Router`. Set the view types to XML, and set the default view path to `sapui5.demo.mvcapp.view`, because all of the views are contained in the *view* folder. The control ID `"app"` is again the ID inside App.view.xml, which we used previously in the `oApp` variable. This means that the placement of the views should happen inside this control (which is an `sap.m.App` control).

Next, specify the aggregation in which the views should be placed. We did this manually in the app view when we put the views inside the `pages` aggregation. Now, you can let the router handle this and just reference `pages` as `controlAggregation`. At the end, provide a transition; the default is `"slide"`. We also could have used `"flip"` or `"show"`.

routes

Next, let's look at the routes in which you'll define the URL patterns for the application. It's important that the routes have a name; we'll use this name later when we're navigating. In this example, we've provided two patterns.

The first pattern is an empty string, which means that after the hash, there is no text. This pattern would match the following:

```
index.html#
```

139

The second pattern means that there will be the text `detail` after the hash, followed by a slash and the mandatory parameter ID. The curly braces in this case indicate that the parameter is mandatory. This patterns would match the following:

```
index.html#/detail/0
index.html#/detail/1
```

We've added a slash before the hash; this happens automatically via the routing. When you define the routes, it's important to be careful about the order in which you define them, because only the first route would match. In the routes, you also define a target, which refers to a target in the `targets` section.

targets

The targets define which view should be displayed; we'll refer to the master and detail views. The view level is important when you're using the slide or flip transition to ensure that the view slides or flips in the right direction. Here, define a slide transition so that when a user clicks on a table entry the master view slides to the left and shows the detail view. When you navigate back from the detail view, it slides to the right and shows the master view.

We didn't need to specify the full qualified name of our views, like `sapui5.demo.mvcapp.view.Master`, because we defined the view path in the config section with `sapui5.demo.mvcapp.view`; therefore, we can just use `Master`.

4.6.2   Router Initialization

Inside Component.js, create a new `init` function right after the `metadata` section and before the `createContent` function. We'll also call the base component's `init` function via `UIComponent.prototype.init.apply(…)` like we did before in the `createContent` function. Then, we'll initialize the router.

As you can see in Listing 4.51, the router is globally available via the `this.getRouter()` function inside the component. We'll make use of this later when we adapt our master and detail controllers.

```
// metadata
},
init: function() {
```

```
  // call the base component's init function
  UIComponent.prototype.init.apply(this, arguments);

  // create the views based on the url/hash
  this.getRouter().initialize();
},
  createContent: function() { ...
```
Listing 4.51 Router Initialization

It is important that you don't forget to initialize the router manually. Otherwise, you'll just see a blank screen (blue if you're using the Blue Crystal theme) without any errors in the console. The only point that you would notice is that in the NET-WORK tab, neither App.view.xml nor Master.view.xml is loaded.

4.6.3 Adjusting the App View

This is a simple step; just delete the two XML views and the pages aggregation. We don't need to specify the pages aggregation, because it's the default aggregation of the sap.m.App control, and we defined the controlAggregation pages inside the routing configuration. The resulting app view is rather small and is shown in Listing 4.52.

```
<mvc:View
  xmlns:mvc="sap.ui.core.mvc"
  displayBlock="true"
  xmlns="sap.m">
  <App id="app">
    <!-- pages will be filled automatically via routing -->
  </App>
</mvc:View>
```
Listing 4.52 App View without Nested XML Views

4.6.4 Using Routing inside the Master Controller

Next, we'll use the routing inside the master controller. Therefore, completely replace Listing 4.52 with the contents of Listing 4.53.

```
onListPress: function(oEvent) {
// also possible:
// var oRouter = this.getOwnerComponent().getRouterFor(this);
  var oRouter = sap.ui.core.UIComponent.getRouterFor(this);
  var oItem = oEvent.getSource();
```

```
  oRouter.navTo("detail", {
    ID: oItem.getBindingContext().getProperty("ID")
  });
}
```
Listing 4.53 Master Controller with Routing

Here, we access the router via a function provided by the component: Access the component via the static function `sap.ui.core.UIComponent` and then call `getRouterFor(this)`. The value of `this` is the controller in this case.

Save the reference to the router in the `oRouter` variable. We still need to figure out the binding context of the clicked-on table row, which we'll store in an `oItem` variable. Then, call the `navTo` function from our router. The first parameter is the name of the route—in this case, `"detail"`. The second parameter is an object. Let's look at this object in detail:

```
oRouter.navTo("detail", {
ID: oItem.getBindingContext().getProperty("ID")
});
```

Note that we're passing the mandatory parameter `ID`, which we defined in the `detail` pattern earlier; Listing 4.54 shows an extract of the route.

```
"routing": {
  ...
  "routes": [{
      "pattern": "",
      ...
    }, {
      "pattern": "detail/{ID}", ...
```
Listing 4.54 Routing Pattern of Detail Route

Now, we're only passing the value of the ID—`getProperty("ID")`—when we call `navTo` instead of the whole binding context. Sending the whole binding context would not work now, because the context doesn't match the pattern we defined. We're expecting a string, but the binding context itself is an object. If you would send the binding context, like so:

```
oRouter.navTo("detail", {
// CAUTION!!! Just for showing the error message!!!
ID: oItem.getBindingContext()
}
```

then you'll see an error message in the console thrown by *crossroads.js*, a third-party library used by SAPUI5 for the routing. The error message looks quite cryptic and is shown in Listing 4.55.

```
Uncaught Error: Invalid value "?oModel=
EventProvider%20sap.ui.model.json.JSONModel&sPath=/Suppliers/0&
constructor=
function%20(m,p)%7Bsap.ui.base.Object.apply(this);this.oModel=
m;this.sPath=p;%7D&getMetadata=function%20()%7Breturn%20v;%7D&getModel=
function%20()%7Breturn%20this.oModel;%7D&getPath=
function%20(p)%7Breturn%20this.sPath+(p?%22/%22+p:%2222);%7D&
getProperty=
function%20(p)%7Breturn%20this.oModel.getProperty(p,this);%7D&
getObject=function%20(p)%7Breturn%20this.oModel.getObject(p,this);%7D&
toString=function%20()%7Breturn%20this.sPath;%7D&destroy=
function%20()%7B%7D&getInterface=function%20()%7Bvar%20i=
new%20I(this,this.getMetadata().getAllPublicMethods());this.getInterfac
e=q.sap.getter(i);return%20i;%7D" for segment "{ID}".
```

Listing 4.55 Error Message Thrown by crossroads.js

The significant clues are at the beginning and the end: `"Invalid value for seg-ment "{ID}"`, which indicates that we provided the wrong value for the ID. Make sure you're using the correct coding when you continue through this exercise:

```
oRouter.navTo("detail", {
ID: oItem.getBindingContext().getProperty("ID")
});
```

4.6.5 Using Routing inside the Detail Controller

The biggest changes for the example application happen inside the detail controller; you can see the whole coding in Listing 4.56. The detail controller itself also has an `onInit` function which will access the router and save it inside a private variable, because we are going to reuse the router in our controller.

Inside the `onInit` function, we'll attach the `_onDetailMatched` function when the pattern of the `detail` root has been matched.

Controller Lifecycle Methods

The `onInit` method is one of the four lifecycle methods of a controller. The others are `onExit` (when the controller is destroyed), `onBeforeRendering`, and `onAfterRendering`. *Rendering* refers to the rendering of the connected view.

The _onDetailMatched function recreates the binding path with the provided ID from the routing and saves it in the sObjectPath variable. Then, we can access the view via this.getView() and bind the whole view via bindElement to this object path. This means that we're binding the view to the corresponding supplier. You'll learn more about bindElement in Chapter 5.

When we want to navigate back, we'll use the router and access the browser history. To do so, we have to require sap.ui.core.routing.History and reference it as History. We're asking the history if there was a previous hash, and if so, we navigate back to this hash via the native browser history. We'll call window.hisotry.go(-1) to navigate one page back. Otherwise, we'll navigate to the master route.

You can test this this behavior in the application when you're on the *index.html/#/detail/0* page; manually enter *index.html/#/detail/1*. When you click on the BACK button from the detail page, you'll first navigate back to the previous supplier and then be returned to the master page.

```
sap.ui.define([
  "sap/ui/core/mvc/Controller",
  "sap/ui/core/routing/History"
], function(Controller, History) {
  "use strict";
  return
Controller.extend("sapui5.demo.mvcapp.controller.Detail", {
    onInit: function() {
      this._oRouter = sap.ui.core.UIComponent.getRouterFor(this);
      this._oRouter.getRoute("detail").attachPatternMatched(this._
onDetailMatched, this);
    },
    _onDetailMatched: function(oEvent) {
      var sObjectPath =
        "/Suppliers/" + oEvent.getParameter("arguments").ID;
      var oView = this.getView();
      oView.bindElement(sObjectPath);
    },
    onNavPress: function() {
      var oHistory = History.getInstance();
      var sPreviousHash = oHistory.getPreviousHash();

      if (sPreviousHash !== undefined) {
        // history contains a previous entry
        window.history.go(-1);
      } else {
        this._oRouter.navTo("master");
      }
```

```
    }
  });
});
```

Listing 4.56 Detail Controller with Routing

Now we've modified all the parts of the application to set up the routing. When you run the application, you can see in the URL that the corresponding hashes are applied, as highlighted in Figure 4.14.

Figure 4.14 Routing with Detail Hash

Now we've finished the routing example, but we've just scratched the surface of it. With routing, you can restore the sorting for a table, this means, for example, if the table has been sorted by a product name in descending order, this specific table sorting could be restored. You can also preserve search parameters when searching inside a table, or preserve the status of an opened dialog with routing.

> **Additional Information**
>
> Learn more about routing and its possibilities in the official SAPUI5 documentation. Navigate to *https://sapui5.hana.ondemand.com/* and choose DEVELOPER GUIDE • TUTORIALS • NAVIGATION AND ROUTING.

4.7   Application Descriptor

Until now, we've put all the application-specific settings inside the Component.js file, in the `metadata` section. Now, let's put those settings inside a separate file called *manifest.json* to further decouple the application coding from the application settings. The Application Descriptor also includes some nice features, like automatic model instantiation, which is supported as of SAPUI5 version 1.30. Putting your application settings in the Component.js file is still supported, but not recommended; use the Application Descriptor instead. The Application Descriptor file is also interpreted by SAP Fiori Launchpad.

You can migrate your existing application settings from the Component.js file inside manifest.json via copying and pasting the settings to the right group and including some small adaptations. We'll use the example app `app-mvc-simple` from this chapter's source code and migrate it. You'll find the end result in `app-mvc-simple-app-descriptor`. Open the `app-mvc-simple` files and compare them with the source code in Listing 4.57 and Listing 4.58 to see how the migration works.

Let's start by copying the `app-mvc-simple` example. Adapt i18n.properties to include the following lines:

```
#Application descriptor
appTitle=Simple Application descriptor Demo App
appDescription=Demo application showcasing the application descriptor
```

Create a new manifest.json file inside the *webapp* folder; Listing 4.57 shows what manifest.json should look like. You'll notice that the application settings are now grouped inside specific settings, like `sap.app`, `sap.ui`, or `sap.ui5`. The settings in `sap.app` and `sap.ui` are new; we didn't maintain them before.

```
{
  "_version": "1.1.0",
  "sap.app": {
    "_version": "1.1.0",
    "id": "sapui5.demo.mvcapp",
    "type": "application",
    "i18n": "i18n/i18n.properties",
    "applicationVersion": {
      "version": "1.0.0"
    },
    "title": "{{appTitle}}",
    "description": "{{appDescription}}",
    "dataSources": {
      "mainService": {
        "uri": "./service/data.json",
        "type": "JSON"
      }
    }
  },
  "sap.ui": {
    "_version": "1.1.0",
    "technology": "UI5",
    "deviceTypes": {
```

```
        "desktop": true,
        "tablet": true,
        "phone": true
      },
      "supportedThemes": [
        "sap_bluecrystal"
      ]
    },
    "sap.ui5": {
      "_version": "1.1.0",
      "rootView": {
        "viewName": "sapui5.demo.mvcapp.view.App",
        "type": "XML"
      },
      "dependencies": {
        "minUI5Version": "1.30.0",
        "libs": {
          "sap.m": {}
        }
      },
      "contentDensities": {
        "compact": true,
        "cozy": true
      },
      "models": {
        "": {
          "dataSource": "mainService"
        },
        "i18n": {
          "type": "sap.ui.model.resource.ResourceModel",
          "settings": {
            "bundleName": "sapui5.demo.mvcapp.i18n.i18n"
          }
        }
      },
      "routing": {
        "config": {
          "routerClass": "sap.m.routing.Router",
          "viewType": "XML",
          "viewPath": "sapui5.demo.mvcapp.view",
          "controlId": "app",
          "controlAggregation": "pages",
          "bypassed": {
            "target": "notFound"
          }
        },
        "routes": [{
          "pattern": "",
          "name": "master",
          "target": "master"
```

```
    }],
    "targets": {
      "master": {
        "viewName": "Master",
        "viewLevel": 1
      },
      "detail": {
        "viewName": "Detail",
        "viewLevel": 2
      },
      "notFound": {
        "viewName": "NotFound",
        "viewId": "notFound"
      }
    }
  }
 }
}
```

Listing 4.57 Migrate Application Settings to manifest.json File

The settings inside sap.ui5 are basically the same as those that were in the meta-data section from the Component.js file. Adapt the Component.js file as shown in Listing 4.58.

```
sap.ui.define([
  "sap/ui/core/UIComponent"
], function(UIComponent) {
  "use strict";

  return UIComponent.extend("sapui5.demo.mvcapp.Component", {

    metadata: {
      manifest: "json"
    },

    init: function() {
      UIComponent.prototype.init.apply(this, arguments);
      this.getRouter().initialize();
    }
  });
});
```

Listing 4.58 Adapted Component.js file with Reference to Application Descriptor

Notice the translations {{appTitle}} and {{appDescription}}, which we maintained in the i18n.properties file before. The {{ }} characters are a specific syntax that replaces the values they contain with the real values (appTitle, appDescription) when the application runs. Another cool feature of the Application Descriptor is the automatic model instantiation mentioned before. In sap.app, we define a data source mainService with the type JSON, and in the sap.ui5 group in the models section this data source is referenced and automatically creates and instantiates a SAPUI5 JSONModel. The "" characters indicate that this is an unnamed model. On the next line, a model with the name "i18n" is defined and is also automatically instantiated. You'll learn more about this automatic model instantiation in Chapter 5.

When you look at the new Component.js file and compare it with the previous one, you'll notice that the coding is now much simpler. We just reference manifest: "json" inside metadata, and in the init function we initialize the prototype of UIComponent and initialize the router. All the manual model instantiation coding—which had to happen at during right lifecycle method (init or createContent)—is now gone. When you run the application now, you should notice no difference. When you create a new application with the SAP Web IDE templates, then the Application Descriptor file is automatically created for you. Your application is now much more structured, and the coding has been simplified, so use the Application Descriptor instead of maintaining your application settings inside Component.js.

> **Note**
>
> For another example of how to migrate from Component.js metadata application settings to manifest.json, visit the SAPUI5 walkthrough tutorial: Navigate to *https://sapui5.hana.ondemand.com/* and select Developer Guide • Tutorials • Walkthrough • Descriptor for Applications.
>
> To learn more about the different settings inside the Application Descriptor, navigate to *https://sapui5.hana.ondemand.com/* and select Developer Guide • Essentials • Structuring: Components and Descriptor • Descriptor for Applications, Components and Libraries.

We have listed the most important Application Descriptor settings in Table 4.5.

sap.app	
The `sap.app` namespace contains application-specific attributes.	
`id`	Namespace of your application; must be unique and not exceed 70 characters.
`type`	Defines what is described—an application in the example.
`i18n`	Path to the resource bundle file.
`title`	Description of the application.
`description`	Short description of the application.
`applicationVersion`	The version of the application.
sap.ui	
The `sap.ui` namespace contains UI-specific attributes.	
`technology`	Specify the UI technology—SAPUI5 in the example.
`deviceTypes`	Specify which device types are supported (desktop, tablet or phone; all true by default).
`supportedThemes`	An array of supported themes, such as Blue Crystal (`sap_bluecrystal`).
sap.ui5	
The `sap.ui5` settings will be interpreted by SAPUI5 itself.	
`rootView`	The root view will automatically instantiated by the Component.
`dependencies`	The depended libraries which you use in your application like `sap.m` or `sap.ui.layout`.
`models`	Models defined in this section will be automatically instantiated.
`routing`	Here the application routing can be defined.

Table 4.5 Most Important Application Descriptor Settings

4.8   Summary

We started with a simple approach in which we wrote all of our application coding into one HTML file. Throughout this chapter, you learned how to structure your application into a useful file and folder structure. While we were showing you this, we explained what the MVC concept means in SAPUI5 and how to apply it in your applications. We also touched on the basic concepts of data binding; you'll learn more about this in the next chapter. You also learned about the role components play and how to implement them in an application. With a component in place, you were able to learn about and apply the basics of routing. What's missing in our application is the ability to make it multilingual, which we'll discuss in the next chapter.

This chapter covers the general usage and types of models in SAPUI5 and includes a discussion on data binding.

5   Models and Bindings

In the previous chapter, we discussed how models work as data containers that hold all the business data your application will work with. SAPUI5 comes with several predefined model classes ready for use. In the example application, you've seen both a JSON model and a resource model in action. In this chapter, we'll explain these model types in more depth and learn more about the binding functionality you'll use throughout your applications.

Data binding involves connecting data residing in a specific model in an application to a particular part of the UI on the screen. This connection can be either a *one-way* or a *two-way connection*. The former will only serve the data from the model and will leave the model data untouched when data is changed in the UI. The latter will keep the data from the UI and the model in sync, as you've seen in the running example with the input fields in the last chapter.

For most models, you can decide yourself whether you would like to use one-way or two-way binding. A one-way binding mode, however, does not mean that data in such a model can't be updated at all. Instead, there are simply special actions that need to be taken in order to update the model. This concept makes more sense when we take a closer look at the amount of data our application can access and where this data comes from.

To begin, let's look at a JSON example.

5.1   Using Models: A JSON Sample

JSON models are client-side models, which means that once the model object is instantiated and the data has been loaded, the application has access to all data the model contains.

Other models—like the OData model, for example—are server-side models. On instantiation of a particular model object, there is no data loaded automatically at all; data has to be requested and will then be loaded on demand only. This can either happen through deliberate actions taken in the application code (e.g., calling the corresponding functions on the model) or happen automatically when data from such a model is bound to some element on screen using certain binding types. The model object itself will then take care of requesting the data from the service. More details about this will be given in the next chapter, where we'll dive into the depths of the OData model itself.

As in the previous chapter, let's use a JSON model and see how it can be used in the application and how to apply the different binding types that exist in SAPUI5.

5.1.1 Instantiation and Loading of Data

First, let's recap the model structure of the example application and revisit what we've achieved as of the previous chapter. We have all the business data we need for our application in a JSON structure. As you've seen, instantiating a JSON model is fairly easy, using the constructor function of the corresponding model class as shown:

```
// model creation and loading the data
var oAppModel = sap.ui.model.json.JSONModel(this.getMetadata().
  getConfig().serviceUrl);
```

You already know what's happening here: SAPUI5 creates a new object, the prototype of which is `sap.ui.model.json.JSONModel`.

Next, we need some data for this model, which we want available to the controls in our application. As before, we don't simply use a JSON object, but will load the data from a separate file to simulate the answer we would get from a service.

In the background, the JSON model distinguishes between two options: whether it has received 1) a URL or 2) an object as a parameter to its constructor. We've passed a URL this time, so the constructor function of the model realizes this and automatically tries to load the file from the URL, using the `setData` function of the model, as you can see when you take a look at the constructor function itself (see Listing 5.1).

```
var JSONMoel = ClientModel.extend("sap.ui.model.json.JSONModel", {
  constructor : function(oData) {
    ClientModel.apply(this, arguments);
```

```
    if (oData && typeof oData == "object") {
      this.setData(oData);
    }
  },

  metadata : {
    publicMethods : ["setJSON", "getJSON"]
  }
});
```
Listing 5.1 sap.ui.model.JSONModel Constructor

When the data has successfully been retrieved, it's stored in the model object, particularly in a property of the model called oData. Note that this property is not meant for direct access and is mentioned here only to clarify for you where the data ends up.

Apart from this automatic loading on instantiation, there is another option to trigger the request for the data. The JSON model also has a method called loadData, which we can use to trigger the loading of data manually, as shown in Listing 5.2.

```
// model creation and loading the data
var oAppModel = sap.ui.model.json.JSONModel();

// loading the JSON data from the URL and storing it in the model
oAppModel.loadData("service/data.json");
```
Listing 5.2 Instantiating the Model and Loading the Data Manually

This convenience method is actually a wrapper for an XHR request, which we otherwise have to create ourselves if we wanted to decide on our own when the request to load data should be fired. It also gives us a means to directly influence some of the default behavior inherited from the parent sap.ui.model.Model class.

We'll leave the default behavior as is for the moment, however, and look closer at what exactly happens when the loadData function is invoked (see Listing 5.3; we've omitted code lines that you currently don't need to focus on).

```
JSONModel.prototype.loadData =
 function(sURL, oParameters, bAsync, sType, bMerge, bCache, mHeaders){
[…]
  this.fireRequestSent({url : sURL, type : sType, async : bAsync,
  headers: mHeaders, info : "cache=" + bCache + ";bMerge=" +
  bMerge, infoObject: {cache : bCache, merge : bMerge}});
  this._ajax({
  [….]
success: function(oData) {
```

```
[…]
that.setData(oData, bMerge);
 that.fireRequestCompleted({url : sURL, type : sType, async : bAsync,
 headers: mHeaders, info : "cache=" + bCache + ";bMerge=" + bMerge,
 infoObject: {cache : bCache, merge : bMerge}, success: true});
  },
  error: function(XMLHttpRequest, textStatus, errorThrown){
[…]
  });
 };
```

Listing 5.3 Excerpt from loadData Function of JSON Model

You can see that apart from the actual request, there is code that fires particular events that inform listeners about the status of the request. These events help you determine in your application when you can start working with the data from the model securely or when the request has failed; you may want to react upon such a failure. These events are fired on the model, so you can easily attach event handlers to them.

Whenever such a request is sent, the requestSent event is fired on the model. More important for our next experiments with the model, however, is the event that fires on success (or failure): the requestCompleted event.

5.1.2 Accessing Model Values

You'll now learn how to access and manipulate values in a JSON model via the getProperty and setProperty methods. However, to be sure about when the data should be available in the model and when we can start working on it, we need to attach to the requestCompleted event.

Let's switch to a smaller and more isolated app example for the remainder of this introduction to data binding, which we'll call *Databinding First Steps*; this example will help keep our first tentative steps in the model more transparent. We'll return to the larger application example from time to time also in order to implement what we've learned.

The index.html file for this new, tiny sample application looks like Listing 5.4.

```
<!DOCTYPE HTML>
<html>
  <head>
    <meta http-equiv="X-UA-Compatible" content="IE=edge" />
    <meta charset="UTF-8">
```

```
      <title>JSON First Steps</title>
<script id="sap-ui-bootstrap"
 src="../resources/sap-ui-core.js"
 data-sap-ui-libs="sap.m"
 data-sap-ui-theme="sap_bluecrystal"
 data-sap-ui-compatVersion="edge"
 data-sap-ui-xx-bindingSyntax="complex">
    </script>
    <script>
      // instantiate the model
      var oModel = sap.ui.model.json.JSONModel();

      //load the data asynchronously
      oModel.loadData("service/data.json");
 //
 attach to the requestCompleted event in order to know when manipulatio
n of the data is safe:
      oModel.attachRequestCompleted(function(oEvent){
        //get and manipulate particular value:
        var sSupplierName = oModel.getProperty("/Suppliers/0/Name");
        sSupplierName = sSupplierName + " Sammamish";
        oModel.setProperty("/Suppliers/0/Name", sSupplierName);
      });

      sap.ui.getCore().setModel(oModel);
      var oText = new sap.m.Text({text: "{/Suppliers/0/Name}"});
      oText.placeAt("content");
  </script>
</head>
 <body class="sapUiBody" role="application">
  <div id="content"></div>
 </body>
</html>
```

Listing 5.4 First JSON Sample Application

This sample app also includes JSON data in a file called *data.json* within a folder
called *service*, just as in earlier examples; the file currently resembles Listing 5.5.

```
{
    "Suppliers": [
        {
            "ID": 0,
            "Name": "Exotic Liquids",
            "Address": {
                "Street": "NE 228th",
                "City": "Sammamish",
                "State": "WA",
                "ZipCode": "98074",
```

```
                        "Country": "USA"
                    }
                },
                {
                    "ID": 1,
                    "Name": "Tokyo Traders",
                    "Address": {
                        "Street": "NE 40th",
                        "City": "Redmond",
                        "State": "WA",
                        "ZipCode": "98052",
                        "Country": "USA"
                    }
                }
            ]
        }
```

Listing 5.5 JSON Model

Running this application will leave you with a not overly populated screen (see Figure 5.1).

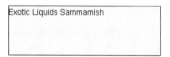

Figure 5.1 First Display of Sample Application

In this application, we'll first retrieve the data from our model file manually by invoking the `loadData` function. Next, we want to access and manipulate one of the values in the model. We can use the methods `getProperty` and `setProperty` for this, which are implemented for the JSON model itself. With these methods, you can operate on particular nodes in your model, accessing the values with the path syntax you saw briefly in Chapter 4. You'll learn how to determine the path you need soon, but first let's address what seems to be a timing problem we've encountered here. This problem becomes the most visible when you run this application in the browser and inspect the model object during runtime.

If you want to see the effect for yourself, put a breakpoint right after the line of code in which the model is instantiated and look at the model object in the debugger of your favorite browser. You can see that there's no data in the model to work on yet (see Figure 5.2).

```
> oModel
  ▼ Factory {mEventRegistry: Object, mMessages: Object, id: "id-1433892459672-0", oData: Object, bDestroyed: false…}
    ▶ aBindings: Array[0]
    ▶ aPendingRequestHandles: Array[1]
      bCache: true
      bDestroyed: false
      bLegacySyntax: false
      iSizeLimit: 100
      id: "id-1433892459672-0"
    ▶ mContexts: Object
    ▶ mEventRegistry: Object
    ▶ mMessages: Object
    ▶ mSupportedBindingModes: Object
    ▼ oData: Object
      ▶ __proto__: Object
      sDefaultBindingMode: "TwoWay"
      sUpdateTimer: null
    ▶ __proto__: ClientModel.extend.constructor
```

Figure 5.2 oModelnspected in the Google Chrome Developer Tools Console before Data Has Been Loaded

When we put the next breakpoint into the function, we call on requestCompleted. If the request has been successful, you'll immediately see a result like this when you reach that breakpoint (see Figure 5.3).

```
> oModel
  ▼ Factory {mEventRegistry: Object, mMessages: Object, id: "id-1433892459672-0", oData: Object, bDestroyed: false…}
    ▶ aBindings: Array[5]
    ▶ aPendingRequestHandles: Array[0]
      bCache: true
      bDestroyed: false
      bLegacySyntax: false
      iSizeLimit: 100
      id: "id-1433892459672-0"
    ▶ mContexts: Object
    ▶ mEventRegistry: Object
    ▶ mMessages: Object
    ▶ mSupportedBindingModes: Object
    ▼ oData: Object
      ▼ Suppliers: Array[2]
        ▶ 0: Object
        ▶ 1: Object
          length: 2
        ▶ __proto__: Array[0]
      ▶ __proto__: Object
      sDefaultBindingMode: "TwoWay"
      sUpdateTimer: null
    ▶ __proto__: ClientModel.extend.constructor
```

Figure 5.3 oModelnspected in the Google Chrome Developer Tools Console after Data Has Been Loaded

You can see that now the oData property of the model has been populated with the corresponding data from the data.json file.

Now, let's start working on the data using the methods mentioned previously; the callback function is only invoked when the requestCompleted event has been fired:

```
oModel.attachRequestCompleted(function(oEvent){
// callback function here
});
```

Let's populate this callback function now. In order to access any value within the model, there is only one piece of information you need: the path to the node you want to work with.

Most models in SAPUI5 have a hierarchical structure that allows you to access nodes and values by specifying their respective paths. The corresponding syntax simply separates the model node levels leading to the desired value with slashes:

```
/Suppliers/0/Name
```

This path will access the value of the `Name` property assigned to the first supplier in the model of the sample application. The first part of the path points to the collection of suppliers in the model, the next part allows us to pick the order of the supplier in the model, and the last part leads to the particular property we want to bind our control property to; therefore, this path accesses the highlighted values in the model code below:

```
{
  "Suppliers":[
    {
      "ID":0,
      "Name":"Exotic Liquids",
      "Address":{
        "Street":"NE 228th",
        "City":"Sammamish",
        "State":"WA",
        "ZipCode":"98074",
        "Country":"USA"
      },
[…]
    },
    {
      "ID":1,
      "Name":"Tokyo Traders",
      "Address":{
        "Street":"NE 40th",
        "City":"Redmond",
        "State":"WA",
        "ZipCode":"98052",
        "Country":"USA"
      },
  […]
    }
```

```
    ]
}
```
Listing 5.6 Path to Particular Node in the Model

Note that the leading slash indicates that this path starts at the model root. When a leading slash is present, it's means we're looking at an absolute path. We can also use relative paths, which will become more useful when we talk about binding contexts starting in Section 5.2.

Now that we know the path, we can use it as parameter in the getProperty and setProperty methods in the application within the callback function. We just pass the path to the value we want to access as a parameter into the getProperty method on the model.

Next, we'll manipulate the value to our liking, and then pass the manipulated value back into the model again, using the setProperty method. This method again takes the path as the parameter, along with the value that you want to assign, so that the code finally looks like Listing 5.7.

```
oModel.attachRequestCompleted(function(oEvent){
  //get and manipulate particular value:
  var sSupplierName = oModel.getProperty("/Suppliers/0/Name");
  sSupplierName = sSupplierName + " Sammamish";
  oModel.setProperty("/Suppliers/0/Name", sSupplierName);
});
```
Listing 5.7 Final Callback Function to the requestCompleted Event

When you save the code and display this page, you'll see that the value for the first supplier indeed has been changed on the model as well as on the UI. The latter happens because the model itself detects that data has been changed and notifies the UI that there is a value to be updated.

> **getProperty**
>
> The getProperty method does not necessarily return a simple value, but will return an object or array of objects depending on the nature of the data found at the corresponding path. Pointing the getProperty function to the path /Suppliers/0 will return a JavaScript object with properties populated from the JSON model.

Next, let's look at how this particular connection is established, because the controls within our application are already making use of it.

5.2   Property Binding

Now that we have the model in place, we have the information we need about its structure, its content, and which values from the model we want to display in the application. As discussed in Chapter 4, one way to get values from a model displayed on screen is *property binding*. Property bindings allow us to connect the properties of controls with particular values in a model. Once such a connection has been established, any change to the value in a model will also be reflected on the control property and, because we're currently using a two-way binding mode, vice versa.

To establish a binding from a control property to a value in the model, you need two parameters:

▸ The path to the value in the model

▸ The name of the property that you want to bind

Next, we'll look at the methods for binding a control's property before diving into the use of data types and defining custom data types.

5.2.1   Methods for Binding a Control's Property

There are two basic methods you can use to bind a control's property:

▸ **Control settings**
You can use the `settings` object in the constructor of a control when you're using nondeclarative view types, or otherwise just use the `settings` object in the value specified for the attribute when you're in an XML view, for example.

▸ `bindProperty`
This method can be used at the control anytime in your code, to notify the system which value in the model a property should be bound to

In the next two subsections, we'll look at these two methods and provide examples of their use. We'll then look at using data types and defining custom data types.

Control Settings

In the control settings method of binding a control's property, curly braces enclosing a property value usually indicate that normal string parsing will be suspended and instead the data-binding mechanisms will take over.

In Figure 5.4, we instantiated a simple text control by using the constructor function in the JavaScript code:

```
var oText = new sap.m.Text({
text: "{/Suppliers/0/Name}"
});
```

As you can see, we're passing a value to the constructor that is assigned to the text property of the control. This value now contains the path to the value in the JSON model. Whenever the JSON model value updates, the value of the control property will update as well.

In a two-way binding scenario, this will also work the other way around. Replacing the text control with an input will immediately give the user an opportunity to adjust the model values. We can prove this by adding another control to our sample application: sap.m.Input.

In Listing 5.8, we instantiate a sap.m.Input control and place it in the content div.

```
var oInput = new sap.m.Input({
  value: "{/Suppliers/0/Name}"
});
oInput.placeAt("content");
```

Listing 5.8 sap.m.Input Instantiation

When you add this code to the sample, the application should look like Figure 5.4.

Figure 5.4 Sample Application with sap.m.Input

You can see that the input field has been assigned the same value as the text above it. With two-way binding, there's more to this than what you see right away. As mentioned previously, both of these controls are now connected to the same value from the model. When we manipulate either one, the model is updated as well. The model then in turn notifies all controls connected to it that the value has changed. This notification will cause a re-rendering of the respective controls and will hence be reflected in every one.

Try entering a different value into the text field, and see what happens once you press the ⌈Enter⌋ key or tab out of the field. The value from the input is immediately taken over for the text of the `text` control and displayed above the input field.

> **Live Value**
>
> The live value of the input field is only reflected in the value attribute of the control when a change event has been triggered. This change event is usually triggered if a user hits a key such as ⌈Enter⌋ or otherwise leaves the field by clicking or tabbing out of it.

In XML views, the particular properties of a control can be bound in the same way as in the settings of a control instantiation in JavaScript. Simply put the curly braces into the attribute at the corresponding tag for your control, like this:

```
<Input value="{/Suppliers/0/Name}" />
```

bindProperty

If you want to bind the property of a control to a model value not on instantiation but at a later point in your code, you can use the `bindProperty` method every control in SAPUI5 provides:

```
oInput.bindProperty("value", path: "{/Suppliers/0/Name}");
```

If you want to suppress the automatic data flow and deactivate the two-way binding mode for one particular control, you can specify this at the control as follows:

```
oInput.bindProperty("value", {
path: "{/Suppliers/0/Name}"
mode: sap.ui.model.BindingMode.OneWay
});
```

In the latter example, we make use of the object-literal syntax to define the binding, as we showed in the binding specified in the constructor call.

The API documentation tells us that the `bindProperty` method is available for every class inheriting from the `sap.ui.base.ManagedObject` parent class. For many control properties, aggregations, and associations, there are also typed methods available. Whether a control offers a typed method for a property is determined by the `bindable` flag in the control metadata.

In the case of our input, the control has inherited the value property from the `InputBase` class. When you open the InputBase.js file in the `sap.m` library, you can see these lines in the constructor, defining the property `value` as `bindable` (see Listing 5.9).

```
var InputBase = Control.extend("sap.m.InputBase", /
** @lends sap.m.InputBase.prototype */ { metadata: {
  library: "sap.m",
  properties: {
  value: { type: "string", group: "Data", defaultValue: null,
      bindable: "bindable" },
[…]
```

Listing 5.9 Excerpt from sap.m.InputBase

For each property defined with the `bindable` flag, the following methods will be automatically generated and added to the prototype of the class:

▶ `get[PropertyName]`

▶ `set[PropertyName]`

▶ `bind[PropertyName]`

▶ `unbind[PropertyName]`

For our input, this will result in the following methods being available:

▶ `getValue`

▶ `setValue`

▶ `bindValue`

▶ `unbindValue`

These methods will allow for the same parameters as the untyped variants. This means that in the previous examples, we also could have used the lines of code shown:

```
oInput.bindValue({
path: "{/Suppliers/0/Name}"
mode: sap.ui.model.BindingMode.OneWay
});
```

The typed functions are simply convenient methods that can make your code easier to write and read: nothing more, nothing less.

Note that complementary to the `bindProperty` method, there is also an `unbindProperty` method that will remove the connection of your control property to the model. When you use this method, the last value set on the property at the control is maintained; it is no longer updated when the value changes on the model.

The logic used for the property binding on a JSON model is implemented into the `sap.ui.model.json.JSONPropertyBinding` class. Most of its functionality is available for all property bindings throughout SAPUI5, because it's inherited from a common `sap.ui.model.ListBinding.js` class. All property bindings therefore share the getters and setters for value, type, formatter, external value, and binding mode (see Listing 5.10).

```
var PropertyBinding = Binding.extend("sap.ui.model.PropertyBinding",
/** @lends sap.ui.model.PropertyBinding.prototype */ {
  constructor : function (oModel, sPath, oContext, mParameters) {
    Binding.apply(this, arguments);
  },
  metadata : {
    "abstract" : true,
    publicMethods : [
      "getValue", "setValue", "setType", "getType", "setFormatter",
      "getFormatter", "getExternalValue", "setExternalValue",
      "getBindingMode"
    ]
  }
});
```

Listing 5.10 Inherited Getters and Setters for Property Bindings

5.2.2 Using Data Types

When you use property binding on certain model properties—for example, float values—you'll notice that sometimes it may be useful to make the data type known not only to the model, but also to the UI. This can be helpful if, for example, you want to ensure that only a number is inserted into a text field for a price, an amount, or the like, or only a date for a date of birth.

To achieve this and a certain amount of automatic data formatting, parsing, and validation, you can use data types on the bindings in SAPUI5.

A set of simple types are delivered with SAPUI5 and can be used out of the box:

- `sap.ui.model.type.Integer`
- `sap.ui.model.type.Float`
- `sap.ui.model.type.String`
- `sap.ui.model.type.Boolean`
- `sap.ui.model.type.Date`
- `sap.ui.model.type.Time`
- `sap.ui.model.type.DateTime`

Returning to the input example, we can directly pass a particular data type we want to use as a parameter to the constructor, as shown in Listing 5.11.

```
new sap.m.Input({
  value: {
    path:"/Suppliers/0/Address/ZipCode",
    type: new sap.ui.model.type.Integer({
      minimum: 5,
      maximum: 8
    })
  }
});
```

Listing 5.11 Specifying Type in Control Constructor Call

We can also stick to the `bindProperty` approach and simply pass the type into this method as a third parameter, as shown in Listing 5.12.

```
oInput.bindProperty("value", path: "{/Suppliers/0/Name}",
  new sap.ui.model.type.Integer({
    minimum: 5,
    maximum: 8
  })
});
```

Listing 5.12 Specifying Type in bindProperty Call at Control

Let's investigate in the details and functions involved when a data type is used along with the binding.

Each simple data type in SAPUI5 has three functions:

► `formatValue`

When a control property is bound to a value on the model, the `formatValue` function will be executed when a change in model data is supposed to be reflected on the control.

► `parseValue`

The `parseValue` function acts as a formatter in the other direction; it's executed whenever a property value is changed on UI side, and this change should be transported back into the model.

► `validateValue`

The `validateValue` function is executed to see if any value constraints were violated.

All functions throw corresponding exceptions when the requirements are not fulfilled—namely, `FormatException`, `ParseException`, and `ValidateException`.

To react on any such exceptions when they are thrown, it's not necessary to catch the exceptions yourself. Rather, you are supposed to attach to the events fired by SAPUI5 in such cases via the following controls:

► `attachFormatError`

► `attachParseError`

► `attachValidationError`

► `attachValidationSuccess`

You can easily react on a user's erroneous input by attaching to `validationError`, for example, which will be fired when a user's input violates constraints defined by the type.

Let's look at what happens when we use an integer type within our sample application. The constructor of the `sap.ui.model.type.Integer` takes two optional parameters of the type object—`oFormatOptions` and `oConstraints`—so a new instance can be instantiated like this:

```
var oType = new sap.ui.model.type.Integer(oFormatOptions, oConstraints);
```

When neither of the two parameters are specified, default values for the type are used.

Below the following input:

```
var oInput = new sap.m.Input({
value: "{/Suppliers/0/Name}"
});
oInput.placeAt("content");
```

we'll add another input that will take the zip code of the supplier's address as a value (see Listing 5.13). We expect an integer-type input.

```
var oZipInput = new sap.m.Input({
  value: {
    path:"/Suppliers/0/Address/ZipCode",
    type: new sap.ui.model.type.Integer({
      minimum: 1,
      maximum: 99999999
    })
  }
});
oZipInput.placeAt("content");
```

Listing 5.13 Using a Type with Constraints for an Input

Note that we've left the format options parameter for the `Integer` constructor as an empty object for the moment; we'll soon see what the parameter is best used for.

Let's now attach to the corresponding events in order to be able to give the user feedback when he tries to input something incorrectly (see Listing 5.14).

```
oZipInput.attachParseError(function(oControlEvent){
  alert("Parse Error occurred - this is no integer");
});
oZipInput.attachValidationError(function(oControlEvent){
  alert ("Validation error occurred -
 some constraints were violated: " + oControlEvent.getParameters().newV
alue + " is not between minimum and maximum");
});
```

Listing 5.14 Attaching to the Validation Events from the Type

When you reload the application and try to insert a number larger than specified in the constraints, you'll see an alert indicating that you've violated the minimum or maximum length.

When you insert some non-numerical characters, you'll see the alert from the `parseError` instead.

For each error that occurs, the attached event handler takes over. We can access the erroneous value by using a parameter from the `oControlEvent` object that the event handler receives and provide the user with some information has about what's gone wrong before we decide to remove the invalid value from the input.

The new value the user has tried to set is available as `newValue` parameter. You can likewise access the old value, the data type, and the element for which a property initiated the attempt to update the model.

Note that the additional constraints (for the `sap.ui.model.type.Integer`, there are only the two we have used available) will only be taken into account when validation takes place, which will only happen when the update on the model is attempted.

There are other parameters you can pass to the `Integer` type. These parameters, however, are part of the pattern used when the source value of a control is supposed to be transformed into a string, because a control property is of this type. This means that whenever you are outputting a source value of an `Integer` type with a certain number of digits—for example, to a `sap.m.Input` value property—there will be a pattern applied when the value is written to this control property, as the property itself is of type `string`.

For `sap.ui.model.type.Integer`, you can specify the following values, for example:

```
minIntegerDigits: 1, // minimal number of non-fraction digits
maxIntegerDigits: 99 // maximal number of non-fraction digits
```

These parameters are part of the `formatOptions` object we left empty in the first attempt to use this data type. When you add some of these format options to the sample, you can see immediately what happens when you try to insert a value that doesn't follow the pattern.

Let's specify a minimum number of digits, for example, and change the input field for the zip code as shown in Listing 5.15.

```
var oZipInput = new sap.m.Input({
  value: {
  path:"/Suppliers/0/Address/ZipCode",
  type: new sap.ui.model.type.Integer({
    minIntegerDigits: 5
   },{
    minimum: 1,
    maximum: 99999
```

```
    })
  }
});
```
Listing 5.15 Specifying Format Options for a Type

When you reload the application now and try to insert a one-digit number, for example, you'll see that as soon as the change event on the input is fired, the value you have inserted will be transformed according to the pattern we specified, turning the one-digit entry into 00001 (see Figure 5.5).

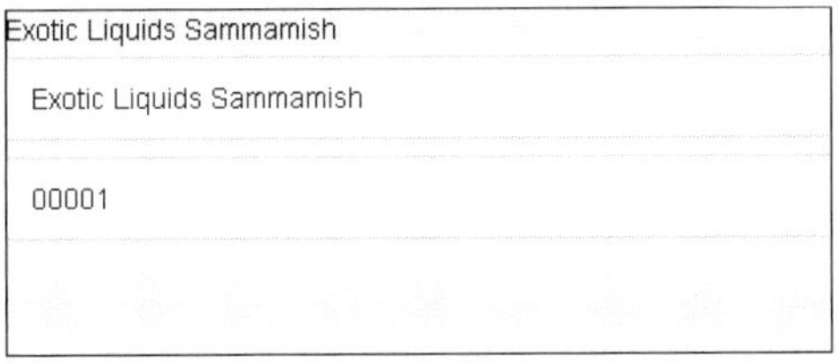

Figure 5.5 Application with Zip Code Input

There are several options for each of the other types as well, and for float values, you can define how many decimals a number should be allowed to have. For the complete list of options, see `sap.ui.model.type` in the API REFERENCE tab of the SAPUI5 Demo Kit.

5.2.3 Defining a Custom Data Type

You've seen which important methods the data types in SAPUI5 contains, and now we'll look at how to define our own custom data types.

Assuming you have a data type you want to apply in more than one place in your application, you can easily write your own custom type, extending the `sap.ui.model.SimpleType` class. You can then realize your particular requirements by implementing the three methods discussed in Section 5.2.2.

Say you need a special data type for phone numbers, following the pattern +01 1234 456789, which you want to reuse across the application. In this case, it makes sense to define your own type, because you're expecting a particular format for phone numbers. Because the sample application will also accept user input, it will be useful to have the `validateValue` function from the type ensure that the information entered fulfills the format requirements. Otherwise, it will throw an error and fire the `validationFailed` event you've seen before.

Let's first enhance the model with the phone number for the supplier, as shown in Listing 5.16.

```
{
  "Suppliers": [
    {
      "ID": 0,
      "Name": "Exotic Liquids",
      "Address": {
        "Street": "NE 228th",
        "City": "Sammamish",
        "State": "WA",
        "ZipCode": "98074",
        "Country": "USA",
        "PhoneNumber": "+1-123-123-1234"
      }
    },
    {
      "ID": 1,
      "Name": "Tokyo Traders",
      "Address": {
        "Street": "NE 40th",
        "City": "Redmond",
        "State": "WA",
        "ZipCode": "98052",
        "Country": "USA",
        "PhoneNumber": "+1-123-123-1235"
      }
    }
  ]
}
```

Listing 5.16 Enhanced JSON Model Data

In the next step, we'll create a new type by extending the `sap.ui.model.SimpleType` class and providing the three methods mentioned previously (see Listing 5.17).

```
sap.ui.model.SimpleType.extend("sap.test.phoneNumber", {
  formatValue: function(oValue) {
    return oValue;
  },
  parseValue: function(oValue) {
    return oValue;
  },
  validateValue: function(oValue) {
    if (! /\+*\D*[0-9]*\-([2-9]\d{2})(\D*)([2-9]\d{2})(\D*)(\d{4})\D/
.test(oValue)) {
```

```
      throw new sap.ui.model.ValidateException("phone number must
follow the pattern +1 234-567-890!");
          }
        }
    });
```
Listing 5.17 Defining New Type

For the first two methods, leave the value untouched and return it as is from the model. For the third method, use a regular expression to see if the user input matches the pattern we predefined for phone numbers.

We can now set the type of a new input for the phone number in the sample app to the custom type (see Listing 5.18).

```
var oPhoneInput = new sap.m.Input({
  value: {
    path: "/Suppliers/0/Address/PhoneNumber",
    type: new sap.test.phoneNumber()
  }
});
oPhoneInput.placeAt("content");
```
Listing 5.18 Using a Custom Type

Finally, we'll attach to the validationError event. This time, we'll use the message from the validation exception we defined ourselves to inform the user about what went wrong (see Listing 5.19).

```
oPhoneInput.attachValidationError(function(oControlEvent){
    alert ("Validation error occurred -
 constraints were violated: " + oControlEvent.getParameter("message"));
    });
```
Listing 5.19 Using the Validation Exception to Output an Error to the User

The sample application will now resemble Figure 5.6.

| Exotic Liquids Sammamish |
| Exotic Liquids Sammamish |
| 98074 |
| +1-123-123-1234 |

Figure 5.6 Phone Number Added to Sample Application

Now, when a user types in something that doesn't match the regular expression from the custom type, a new alert will indicate that the user has not followed the predefined pattern.

5.3   Using Formatters

In addition to formatting values by data types, you can also define your own formatters if you want to influence not the value in the model, but rather the output on the UI. A formatter generally makes sense wherever the formatting of a model value is one-way only, as opposed to a type, which is far more powerful, as you've learned.

We can pass a formatter function as a parameter into the constructor of the control, as shown:

```
oText.bindProperty("value", "/Suppliers/0/Name", function(sValue) {
return sValue && sValue.toUpperCase();
});
```

Or we can pass it when calling the `bindProperty` method for the corresponding property (see Listing 5.20).

```
oText = new sap.m.Text ({
    value: {
        path: "/Suppliers/0/Name",
        formatter: function(sValue) {
            return sValue && sValue.toUpperCase();
        }
    }
})
```

Listing 5.20 Using Formatter for sap.m.Text Control

Note that in both cases, the formatter function is an anonymous callback function that will be executed when the view is instantiated.

You can also define a formatter function nonanonymously in a view controller or, if it will be reused across your application, it may even make sense to have a separate formatter.js file in your application that can be referenced by multiple views.

In the first case, all you need to do is implement the function in the controller as shown in Listing 5.21.

```
onInit: function(){
[…]
},
onExit: function(){
  […]
}
toUpperCase: function(sName){
   return sName && sName.toUpperCase();
}
```

Listing 5.21 Formatter Code in Controller

You can then use this formatter instead of the anonymous function from the previous example, like so:

```
oText.bindProperty("value", "/Suppliers/0/Name", toUpperCase);
```

Returning to our MVC application, we can also make use of the formatter, by transferring the formatter from Listing 5.21 to the controller of the detail view. Insert the lines from Listing 5.21 into the Detail.controller.js file. The detail controller will now look like Listing 5.22.

```
sap.ui.define([
  "sapui5/demo/mvcapp/controller/BaseController"
], function(BaseController) {
  "use strict";

  return BaseController.extend("sapui5.demo.mvcapp.controller.Detail",
{

    /* ======================================================== */
    /* lifecycle methods                                        */
    /* ======================================================== */

    /**
     * Called when the worklist controller is instantiated.
     * @public
     */
    onInit: function() {
      this.getRouter().getRoute("detail").attachPatternMatched(this._
onObjectMatched, this);
    },

    /* ======================================================== */
    /* event handlers                                           */
```

```
/* =================================================== */

/**
 * Navigates back to the Master
 * @function
 */
onNavPress: function() {
  this.myNavBack("master");
},

/* =================================================== */
/* formatters                                          */
/* =================================================== */

/**
 * Formats a given string to uppercase.
 *
 * @function
 * @param {string} sName string to be formatted
 * @public
 */
toUpperCase: function(sName) {
  return sName && sName.toUpperCase();
},

/* =================================================== */
/* internal methods                                    */
/* =================================================== */

/**
 * Binds the view to the object path.
 *
 * @function
 * @param {sap.ui.base.Event} oEvent pattern match event in route '
object'
 * @private
 */
 _onObjectMatched: function(oEvent) {
 var sObjectPath = "/Suppliers/
" + oEvent.getParameter("arguments").ID;
 this._bindView(sObjectPath);
},

/**
 * Binds the view to the object path.
 *
 * @function
 * @param {string} sObjectPath path to the object to be bound
 * @private
 */
```

```
    _bindView: function(sObjectPath) {
      var oView = this.getView();
      oView.bindElement(sObjectPath);
    }
  });
});
```
Listing 5.22 Detail Controller in MVC App

In the detail view, we can now use the formatter as shown in Listing 5.23.

```
<mvc:View
  controllerName="sapui5.demo.mvcapp.controller.Detail"
  mlns:mvc="sap.ui.core.mvc"
  xmlns="sap.m">
  <Page
    id="page"
navButtonPress="onNavPress"
showNavButton="true"
title="Supplier Details">
    <content>
      <ObjectHeader
        id="objectHeader"
        title="{
          path: 'Name',
          formatter: '.toUpperCase'
        }"
        number="ID: {ID}">
        <ObjectAttribute
          text="{Address/Country}">
        </ObjectAttribute>
      </ObjectHeader>
    </content>
  </Page>
</mvc:View>
```
Listing 5.23 Detail View in MVC App

The "." in front of the formatter function name tells the framework that it should be looking for a formatter within the current controller.

Running the application and loading one of the supplier's details will now produce the screen shown in Figure 5.7.

As you can see, the supplier name is now displayed uppercase. The value on the model is not touched by this change.

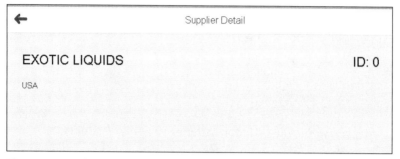

Figure 5.7 Detail View with Formatter in Action

However, the greatest reusability will be gained by transferring formatter functions to a separate file that will be available across the application. When writing larger applications, it's good practice to collect all formatters you would like to use in more than one view. Let's define our own formatter.js file for our apps. We'll put this file into a new *model* folder, because it belongs to functionality related to the model and its values. When you transfer the toUpperCase function to this file, the complete code will look like Listing 5.24.

```
sap.ui.define([], function() {
  "use strict";

  return {

    /**
     * Formats a given string to uppercase.
     *
     * @function
     * @param {string} sName string to be formatted
     * @public
     */
    toUpperCase: function(sName) {
      return sName && sName.toUpperCase();
    }
  };

});
```

Listing 5.24 formatter.js for MVC Application

When this formatter is loaded from a controller, it returns an object with the toUpperCase function available as member function.

We'll now make sure the controllers also know about this additional function by including it in the controller definition of the detail view. The controller will now look like Listing 5.25.

```
sap.ui.define([
  "sapui5/demo/mvcapp/controller/BaseController",
  "sapui5/demo/mvcapp/controller/formatter"
], function(BaseController, formatter) {
  "use strict";
  return BaseController.extend("sapui5.demo.mvcapp.controller.Detail",
{

    formatter: formatter,
    /* ================================================== */
    /* lifecycle methods                                  */
    /* ================================================== */

    /**
     * Called when the worklist controller is instantiated.
     * @public
     */
    onInit: function() {
this.getRouter().getRoute("detail").attachPatternMatched(this._
onObjectMatched, this);
    },

    /*================================================== */
    /* event handlers                                     */
    /* ================================================== */

    /**
     * Navigates back to the Master
     * @function
     */
    onNavPress: function() {
      this.myNavBack("master");
    },

    /* ================================================== */
    /* internal methods                                   */
    /* ================================================== */

    /**
     * Binds the view to the object path.
     *
     * @function
     * @param {sap.ui.base.Event} oEvent pattern match event in route '
object'
     * @private
```

```
  */
  _onObjectMatched: function(oEvent) {
    var sObjectPath = "/Suppliers/
" + oEvent.getParameter("arguments").ID;
    this._bindView(sObjectPath);
  },

  /**
   * Binds the view to the object path.
   *
   * @function
   * @param {string} sObjectPath path to the object to be bound
   * @private
   */
  _bindView: function(sObjectPath) {
    var oView = this.getView();
    oView.bindElement(sObjectPath);
  }
 });
});
```

Listing 5.25 Including the Formatter into the Controller

Note that within the controller, the corresponding formatter function has been deleted.

In the view, we now need to access the formatter slightly differently. As mentioned, we now load the formatter file and pass the object it returns to the controller as a parameter. It's then available as a property called formatter at the controller. We therefore need to change ObjectHeader in Detail.view.xml where we want to use the formatter as shown in Listing 5.26.

```
<ObjectHeader
  id="objectHeader"
  title="{
    path: 'Name',
    formatter: '.formatter.formatUpperCase'
  }"
  number="{ID}">
  <ObjectAttribute
    text="{Address/Country}">
  </ObjectAttribute>
</ObjectHeader>
```

Listing 5.26 Excerpt from Detail.view.xml

When we've done everything correctly, reloading the application will still show the same result in the browser. We haven't changed anything about the formatting results, but have just made the formatter's location more reusable. From here, we could include it in multiple controllers across our application.

We'll now display some more information to our supplier and will start by adding some additional fields to the object header in the detail view. We want to add the address of a supplier and his phone number now, using the data type from the previous example for the phone number.

Create a types.js file similar to the formatters.js file within the *model* directory of the MVC application, and copy and paste the data type for the phone number from Section 5.2.3. We'll make use of the define syntax again and will make the module return an object with particular types as properties.

The complete code within the types.js file looks like Listing 5.27.

```
sap.ui.define([
    "sap/ui/model/SimpleType"
    ], function (SimpleType) {
  "use strict";
  return {

    /**
     * Data Type for phone numbers.
     *
     * @public
     */
    PhoneNumber : SimpleType.extend("sap.test.phoneNumber", {
      formatValue: function(oValue) {
        return "Phone number:" + oValue;
      },
      parseValue: function(oValue) {
        return oValue;
      },
      validateValue: function(oValue) {
        if (!/\+*\D*[0-9]*\-([2-9]\d{2})(\D*)([2-9]\d{2})(\D*)(\d{4})\
D/.test(oValue)) {
          throw new sap.ui.model.ValidateException("phone number must f
ollow the pattern +1 234-567-890!");
        }
      }
    })
  };
});
```

Listing 5.27 Separate types.js File to Be Used in the Application

Next, we have to extend the model in this app a little, similar to what we've done before in the smaller sample application, in order to have the information ready for display. The model.json file will now look like Listing 5.28.

```
{
  "Suppliers":[
    {
      "ID":0,
      "Name":"Exotic Liquids",
      "Address":{
        "Street":"NE 228th",
        "City":"Sammamish",
        "State":"WA",
        "ZipCode":"98074",
        "Country":"USA",
        "PhoneNumber": "+1-123-123-1234"
      },
  [...]
  ,{
      "ID":1,
      "Name":"Tokyo Traders",
      "Address":{
        "Street":"NE 40th",
        "City":"Redmond",
        "State":"WA",
        "ZipCode":"98052",
        "Country":"USA"
        "PhoneNumber": "+1-123-123-1235"
      },
  [...]
}
```

Listing 5.28 Model Excerpt: Added Phone Number to Suppliers

Now we need to tell the controller again where to find the type we want to use in the view. As with the formatter, simply add the types to the modules loaded in the `define` section of the controller (see Listing 5.29).

```
sap.ui.define([
    "sapui5/demo/mvcapp/controller/BaseController",
    "sapui5/demo/mvcapp/model/formatter",
    "sapui5/demo/mvcapp/model/types"
  ], function (BaseController, formatter, types) {
    "use strict";
    return BaseController.extend("sapui5.demo.mvcapp.controller.Detail"
, {
```

```
    formatter: formatter,
    types: types,
[...]
```
Listing 5.29 Excerpt from Detail.controller.js

Finally, we can combine the new model values with the data type and formatter to enhance the detail view. Add the additional object attribute to the view as shown:

```
<ObjectAttribute text="{
path: 'Address/PhoneNumber',
type: '.types.PhoneNumber'
}" />
```

Run the application and pick a supplier from the list, and it should now look like Figure 5.8.

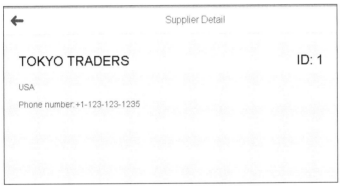

Figure 5.8 Detail View with Type for Phone Number

5.4   Aggregation Binding

So far, we've looked at the property bindings within the application, but there is also a different type of binding called *aggregation binding*, which will automatically generate items for a control aggregation from model data.

We can find an example of this in Master.view.xml, as shown in Listing 5.30.

```
<Table
  id="table"
  width="auto"
```

```
      class="sapUiResponsiveMargin"
      items="{/Suppliers}"
      noDataText="No data"
      growing="true"
      growingScrollToLoad="true">
[...]
<items>
  <ColumnListItem
      type="Navigation"
press="onListPress">
    <cells>
  <ObjectIdentifier
    text="{ID}"/>
  <ObjectIdentifier
    text="{Name}"/>
</cells>
</ColumnListItem>
</items>
```

Listing 5.30 Excerpt from Master View Showing Aggregation Binding

The items aggregation for the table is automatically filled with one item per model node that has been referenced by the path given in the items attribute in Listing 5.30. For each item, a template needs to be applied. This template is then cloned for each value from the model, setting the binding path of the aggregated element to the corresponding model node.

As noted in Chapter 4, when you want to instantiate the parent control within a JavaScript view and pass the aggregation binding parameters directly to the control constructor, use the code shown in Listing 5.31.

```
var aColumns = [
  new sap.m.Column({
    header: new sap.m.Text({
      text: "ID"
    })
  }),
  new sap.m.Column({
    header: new sap.m.Text({
      text: "Name"
    })
  })
];

var oTemplate = new sap.m.ColumnListItem({
  cells: [
    new sap.m.ObjectIdentifier({
```

```
      text: "{ID}"
    }),
    new sap.m.ObjectIdentifier({
      text: "{Name}"
    })
  ]
});

var oTable = new sap.m.Table({
  columns: aColumns,
  items: {
 path: "/Suppliers"
   template: oTemplate
 }
});
```
Listing 5.31 Aggregation Binding in JavaScript

Within the XML view, this template is declaratively specified within the `<items></items>` aggregation boundaries.

Some controls provide a default aggregation, which you can identify from the control metadata in the corresponding control class. If you look at `sap.m.Object-Header` in the sample application, you'll see the following bolded line in its metadata (see Listing 5.32):

```
[Property definitions here...]
  },
  defaultAggregation : "attributes",
  aggregations : {
[Aggregation definitions follow here…]
```
Listing 5.32 Default Aggregation Defined in the Metadata of a Control

These default aggregations are automatically used when you do not specify the aggregation within an XML view (see Listing 5.33).

```
<ObjectHeader id="objectHeader"
  title="{
    path: 'Name',
    formatter: '.formatter.formatUpperCase'
  }"
  number="ID: {ID}">
    <ObjectAttribute text="{Address/Country}">
    </ObjectAttribute>
    <ObjectAttribute text="{
      path: 'Address/PhoneNumber',
```

```
    type: '.types.PhoneNumber'
  }" />
</ObjectHeader>
```

Listing 5.33 Excerpt from Detail.view.xml without Explicit Usage of Default Aggregation

The code from Listing 5.33 and from the following Listing 5.34 will produce the very same DOM, even if only the latter contains extra tags for opening and closing the default aggregation:

```
<ObjectHeader id="objectHeader"
  title="{
    path: 'Name',
    formatter: '.formatter.formatUpperCase'
  }"
  number="ID: {ID}">
  <attributes>
    <ObjectAttribute  text="{Address/Country}">
      </ObjectAttribute>
        <ObjectAttribute text="{
          path: 'Address/PhoneNumber',
          type: '.types.PhoneNumber'
        }" />
  </attributes>
</ObjectHeader>
```

Listing 5.34 Excerpt from Detail.view.xml with Explicit Usage of Default Aggregation

It's a good practice to use the default aggregations without explicitly using the tags to indicate them. Only for nondefault aggregations do the corresponding boundaries need to be given.

Note that controls created within an aggregation binding take part in the lifecycle of their parents. They're instantiated when the parent controls are instantiated and are destroyed along with their parents.

We'll enhance our sample application with another aggregation binding on the detail view now by adding another `sap.m.Table` control that contains all products offered by a particular supplier.

Let's add this table to the Detail.view.xml file, right below the closing `</Object-Header>` tag, as shown in Listing 5.35.

```
<Table id="table"
  width="auto"
```

```
    class="sapUiResponsiveMargin"
    items="{Products}"
    noDataText="No Data"
    growing="true"
    growingScrollToLoad="true">
  <headerToolbar>
    <Toolbar>
      <Title id="tableHeader" text="Suppliers Products" />
    </Toolbar>
  </headerToolbar>
  <columns>
    <Column id="idColumn">
      <header>
        <Text text="ID:" id="IDColumnTitle" />
      </header>
    </Column>
    <Column id="nameColumn">
      <header>
        <Text text="Name:" id="nameColumnTitle" />
      </header>
    </Column>
    <Column id="priceColumn" hAlign="Right">
      <header>
        <Text text="Price:" id="priceColumnTitle" />
      </header>
    </Column>
  </columns>
  <items>
    <ColumnListItem>
      <cells>
        <ObjectIdentifier text="{ID}" />
        <ObjectIdentifier text="{Name}" />
        <ObjectNumber number="{Price}" unit="USD" />
      </cells>
    </ColumnListItem>
  </items>
</Table>
```

Listing 5.35 Products Table in Detail View

When you add this aggregation, there will be one item instantiated for every product associated with the supplier in the model. The application should now look like Figure 5.9.

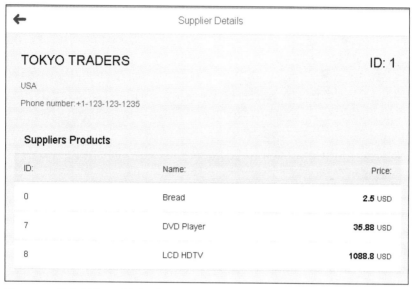

Figure 5.9 Detail View with Products

5.4.1 bindAggregation

Instead of declaring the aggregation template and binding within the XML view, we can use the corresponding method on the parent control—namely, the `bind-Aggregation` function. This method, just like the `bindProperty` method, can be used when you want to bind the desired aggregation on not instantiation of the parent control, but at a later point in your code.

The function takes two parameters: the name of the aggregation and an `oBindingInfo` object. This object can contain several parameters itself; we'll look at some of them in the following subsections.

As for the `bindProperty` method, some controls also offer typed methods for aggregation binding. In the control metadata, this is determined by the `bindable` flag at the aggregation definition. Note that these methods are generated automatically by the `sap.ui.base.ManagedObject` parent class but can be overridden at the particular control.

In the case of `sap.m.Table` in the previous example, we could also have called

```
oTable.bindItems("Products", oBindingInfo);
```

Complementary to the `bindAggregation` method, there is also an `unbindAggrega-tion` method, analogous to the `unbindProperty` method you already know.

5.4.2 Using a Factory

One major advantage of the programmatic approach is that you can use a factory along with the `bindAggregation` function. A common use case for a factory is the dynamic creation of your UI—for example, if you need to display additional or different child controls depending on whether some criteria are met or not.

Let's assume that in our application we do not want to show every product the same way; we want to adjust the display for products with certain ingredients. This part of the exercise will be slightly off the path the sample application will take during the remainder of the chapter, so please make sure you save a version of your work before you implement the next steps. We'll get back to the running example after this section.

Let's first enhance the JSON model to reflect this information, then remove the declarative aggregation binding within our view and instead programmatically implement the products aggregation we want to show in the controller (see Listing 5.36).

```
{
  "Suppliers": [{
    "ID": 0,
    "Name": "Exotic Liquids",
    "Address": {
      "Street": "NE 228th",
      "City": "Sammamish",
      "State": "WA",
      "ZipCode": "98074",
      "Country": "USA",
    "Phone Number":"001555789789789"

    },
    "Location": {
      "type": "Point",
      "coordinates": [-122.03547668457,
        47.6316604614258
      ]
    },
    "Products": [{
      "ID": 1,
      "Name": "Milk",
```

```
        "Description": "Low fat milk",
        "ReleaseDate": "1995-10-01T00:00:00",
        "DiscontinuedDate": null,
        "Rating": 3,
        "Price": 3.5
      }, {
        "ID": 2,
        "Name": "Vint soda",
        "Description": "Americana Variety - Mix of 6 flavors",
        "ReleaseDate": "2000-10-01T00:00:00",
        "DiscontinuedDate": null,
        "Rating": 3,
        "Price": 20.9
      }, {
        "ID": 3,
        "Name": "Havina Cola",
        "Description": "The Original Key Lime Cola",
        "ReleaseDate": "2005-10-01T00:00:00",
        "DiscontinuedDate": "2006-10-01T00:00:00",
        "Rating": 3,
        "Price": 19.9
      }, {
        "ID": 4,
        "Name": "Fruit Punch",
        "Description": "Mango flavor, 8.3 Ounce Cans (Pack of 24)",
        "ReleaseDate": "2003-01-05T00:00:00",
        "DiscontinuedDate": null,
        "Rating": 3,
        "Price": 22.99
      }, {
        "ID": 5,
        "Name": "Cranberry Juice",
        "Description": "16-Ounce Plastic Bottles (Pack of 12)",
        "ReleaseDate": "2006-08-04T00:00:00",
        "DiscontinuedDate": null,
        "Rating": 3,
        "Price": 22.8
      }, {
        "ID": 6,
        "Name": "Pink Lemonade",
        "Description": "36 Ounce Cans (Pack of 3)",
        "ReleaseDate": "2006-11-05T00:00:00",
        "DiscontinuedDate": null,
        "Allergenics": "Milk, Soy, Edible Nuts, Gluten",
        "Rating": 3,
        "Price": 18.8
      }]
    }, {
      "ID": 7,
      "Name": "Green Lemonade",
```

```
    "Description": "36 Ounce Cans (Pack of 3)",
    "ReleaseDate": "2006-11-05T00:00:00",
    "DiscontinuedDate": null,
    "Allergenics": "Milk, Soy, Edible Nuts, Gluten",
    "Rating": 3,
    "Price": 18.8
  }]
},

[…]
]
}
```

Listing 5.36 Altered JSON Model to Display Additional Product Information

You can see that some of products have now been enhanced with information about allergens they contain. In order to clearly show this information in the list of products, we'll add a control to the list item when this information is present in the model.

We'll first remove part of the table definition from the previous example again so that the detail view code now looks like Listing 5.37.

```
<mvc:View controllerName=
"sapui5.demo.mvcapp.controller.Detail" xmlns:mvc=
"sap.ui.core.mvc" xmlns="sap.m">
  <Page id="page" navButtonPress="onNavPress" showNavButton=
"true" title="Supplier Details">
    <content>
      <ObjectHeader id="objectHeader" title="{
        path: 'Name',
      formatter: '.formatter.formatUpperCase'
    }" number="ID: {ID}">
        <attributes>
          <ObjectAttribute text="{Address/Country}">
          </ObjectAttribute>
          <ObjectAttribute text="{
              path: 'Address/PhoneNumber',
              type: '.types.PhoneNumber'
            }" />
        </attributes>
      </ObjectHeader>
      <Table id="table" width="auto" class=
"sapUiResponsiveMargin" noDataText="No Data" growing=
"true" growingScrollToLoad="true">
        <headerToolbar>
          <Toolbar>
            <Title id="tableHeader" text="Suppliers Products" />
```

```
        </Toolbar>
      </headerToolbar>
      <columns>
        <Column id="idColumn">
          <header>
            <Text text="ID:" id="IDColumnTitle" />
          </header>
        </Column>
        <Column id="nameColumn">
          <header>
            <Text text="Name:" id="nameColumnTitle" />
          </header>
        </Column>
        <Column id="priceColumn" hAlign="Right">
          <header>
            <Text text="Price:" id="priceColumnTitle" />
          </header>
        </Column>
      </columns>
    </Table>
  </content>
</Page>
</mvc:View>
```

Listing 5.37 Detail View without Items Aggregation for Table

When you reload the application now in the browser, you'll still see the table itself, but it won't display any line items; it will only show the `noDataText`.

In the detail controller, in the `_onObjectMatched` function, we'll now make a call to another private function, like this:

```
createProductsAggregation(sObjectPath);
```

Next, we have to implement this function, which will create the items aggregation in the table. In this function, we want to use a particular control—namely, `VerticalLayout` from the `sap.ui.layout` library. We need to make sure that the controller knows this control, so we include it in the `define` part of the controller, as in Listing 5.38.

```
_createProductsAggregation: function() {
  var oTable = this.getView().byId("table");

  oTable.bindAggregation("items", "Products", function(sId, oContext) {
    var sAllergens = oContext.getProperty("Allergens");
    var oColumnListItem = new sap.m.ColumnListItem(sId);
    oColumnListItem.addCell(new sap.m.ObjectIdentifier({
      text: "{ID}"
```

```
    }));

    if (sAllergens) {
      //
  we have found allergens, so we provide a VerticalLayout instead
      //
  of just displaying the product name. The VerticalLayout then takes
      //
  the product name plus the allergens into its own content aggregation
      oColumnListItem.addCell(new VerticalLayout({
        content: [
          new sap.m.Text({
            text: "{Name}"
          }),
          new sap.m.Text({
            text: "{Allergens}"
          })
                      ]
      }));
    } else {
      // no allergens there, we display the name as usual
      oColumnListItem.addCell(new sap.m.ObjectIdentifier({
        text: "{Name}"
      }));
    }

    oColumnListItem.addCell(new sap.m.ObjectNumber({
      number: "{Price}",
      unit: "USD"
    }));
    return oColumnListItem;
  });
}
```

Listing 5.38 Binding Items Aggregation Using a Factory

You can see in the code that we're now instantiating the controls within the aggregation by passing a factory function into the `bindAggregation` method we call at the parent control. When the parent control is now instantiated and the aggregation is created, the factory is executed for every entry in the model. Depending on whether a product contains an allergen or not, we either display just the name of the product as usual or make a column containing the `sap.ui.layout.VerticalLayout` control type, which will allow us to specify more than one content control for the vertical layout.

We then simply use two text controls that will both go into the content aggregation of `VerticalLayout`. This shows some of the power of using factories with aggregation binding, because you as a developer can decide whether you want to display the same information a bit differently depending on your data, or even exchange a complete control for another.

When you reload the page, you can see that there are products carrying additional information within another control inside of the description cell, and other products without such additional information.

Note that the controls generated for the aggregation via the factory behave like any other aggregation element, too. That means they also take part in the lifecycle of their parent.

With the newly added items, the application's detail view should now look like Figure 5.10.

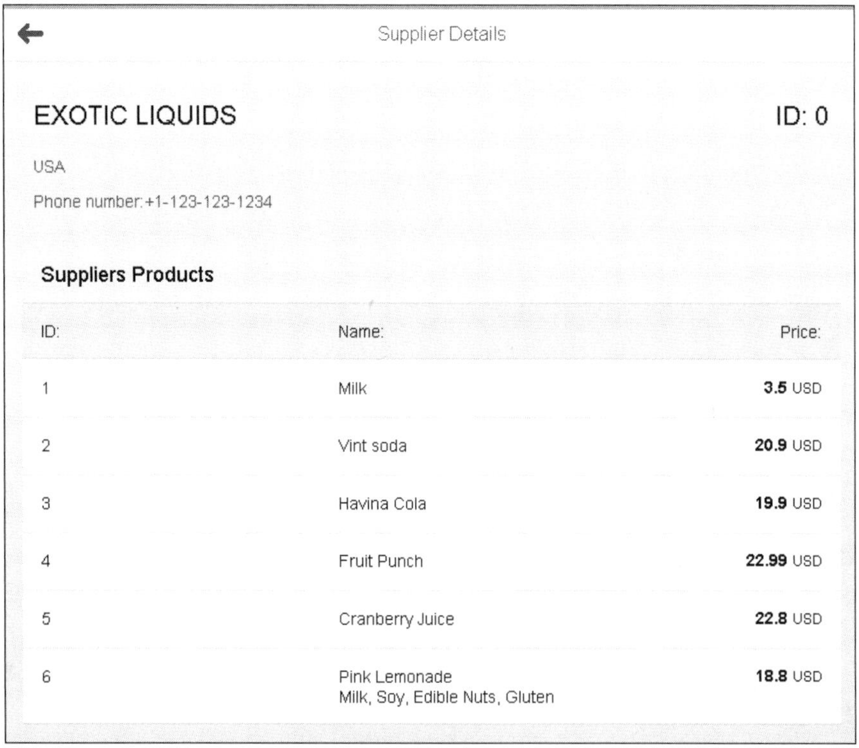

←   Supplier Details

EXOTIC LIQUIDS   ID: 0

USA

Phone number:+1-123-123-1234

Suppliers Products

ID:	Name:	Price:
1	Milk	**3.5** USD
2	Vint soda	**20.9** USD
3	Havina Cola	**19.9** USD
4	Fruit Punch	**22.99** USD
5	Cranberry Juice	**22.8** USD
6	Pink Lemonade Milk, Soy, Edible Nuts, Gluten	**18.8** USD

Figure 5.10 Supplier's Products with Information about Allergens

5.5   Element Binding

You've seen that when we switch from the master view to the detail view, the information displayed depends on which of the suppliers in the table we've picked. In the aggregation binding, we've now also made use of a relative binding path to the products. In order to make this relative binding path adapt to the chosen supplier, the parent of the List control that contains the aggregation needs to know how to resolve this path correctly. To achieve this, we'll use a third type of binding: *element binding*.

An element binding allows us to create a context for all relative bindings inside of an element. To understand what this means, let's look at an example.

Within the detail view are some property bindings that will always display the information about the chosen supplier. The same applies to sap.m.List, where we've defined our items aggregation so that it displays the products of a particular supplier. None of these paths begin with a slash, which indicates that you're looking at a relative binding path.

Let's look at where the information about how to resolve these paths is coming from.

When you inspect the code instantiating the detail controller a little more closely, you can see an element binding used in the method that handles the route-Matched event (see Listing 5.39).

```
_onObjectMatched : function (oEvent) {
  var sObjectPath = "/Suppliers/
" + oEvent.getParameter("arguments").ID;
  this._bindView(sObjectPath);
},

_bindView : function (sObjectPath) {
  var oView = this.getView();
  oView.bindElement(sObjectPath);
}
```

Listing 5.39 Binding the View to an Element

When someone clicks on a supplier in the master view, the information about the supplier's ID is passed to the detail view via routing. The parameter is then available at the event that is passed into the corresponding event handler.

We can hence determine which supplier the detail view is supposed to display by putting the path information together, combining the name of the collection in the model with the ID from the event parameter. This is done within the `onObjectMatched` event.

Next, we use this information within our private `_bindView` method, where we explicitly call `bindElement` on the view. The `bindElement` function then creates a binding context for a SAPUI5 control and receives the model name as well as the path to an item in a configuration object. This will trigger an update of the UI controls that we connected with the model fields.

When the element binding is set to a different binding context—for example, if we switch to a different supplier—all the controls inside of the view will be updated with the corresponding values again.

The `bindElement` function is inherited from the `sap.ui.base.Element` class and can be invoked on any child. Like for the other binding types, there is also an `unbindElement` function that can be used to remove the specific binding context created at an element.

5.6 Expression Binding and Calculated Fields

You've now seen how values from the models can be used for different binding types and how they can be formatted, either using formatter functions or by using a data type. However, so far we have only operated on one value at a time.

What if we want to combine several values from the model in one control property? That's where *expression bindings* or *calculated fields* come into play. Let's combine some of the supplier's information in the detail view in one place, using the city and the state as an example.

5.6.1 Calculated Fields

Calculated fields can be passed into the property you want to bind similarly to the usual binding. The only difference is that you now need to pass more than one part of the value, which is why the implementation lets you specify these as just that: parts.

In the detail view, let's change `ObjectHeader` with the supplier information as in Listing 5.40.

```
<ObjectHeader
  id="objectHeader"
  title="{
    path: 'Name',
    formatter: '.formatter.formatUpperCase'
  }"
  number="ID: {ID}">
  <attributes>
    <ObjectAttribute
      text="{Address/City}, {Address/Country}">
    </ObjectAttribute>
    <ObjectAttribute
      text="{
        path: 'Address/PhoneNumber',
        type: '.types.PhoneNumber'
      }" />
  </attributes>
</ObjectHeader>
```

Listing 5.40 Object Header in Detail View

As you can see, we're simply passing the two values into the detail view, which will make SAPUI5 perform an automatic concatenation of the two. The framework creates a composite binding automatically, and this composite binding will take care of combining the data and providing it to the UI.

When you reload the page now, you'll see that this behavior makes the calculated field appear as shown in Figure 5.11.

Figure 5.11 Object Header: Calculated Field

When you want to use this kind of binding within JavaScript code, you need to explicitly specify the parts of the binding, as in Listing 5.41.

```
var oObjectHeaderAttribute = new sap.m.ObjectAttribute({
    text: {
        parts: [
                {path: "Address/
City", type: new sap.ui.model.type.String()},
                {path: "Address/Country"}
            ]
        }
});
```

Listing 5.41 Creating an Object Header

You can specify a different type for each path, but it's not mandatory. In this case, however, you'll have to attend to the formatting yourself, which is why you can also pass in a custom formatter here. If you do not do so, the framework will use the default concatenation mechanism, which simply combines the two strings here.

Passing in a formatter is easy. You can either pass it within the object literal, as in Listing 5.42, or you can pass it as a parameter into the (typed or untyped) `bindProperty` method at the control.

```
oObjectHeaderAttribute.bindText({
    parts: [
      {path: "Address/City", type: new sap.ui.model.type.String()},
      {path: "Address/Country"}
    ]
  },
  formatter: function(sCity, sCountry){
    if (sCity && sCountry) {
      return sCity + ", " + sCountry;
    }
});
```

Listing 5.42 Passing the Formatter to the Binding Method

You can combine as many values into a calculated binding as you like, and only need to worry about the kind of concatenation you want to see within this function. When the layout becomes more complex, however, you'll want to fall back to using more than one control, most likely in combination with some kind of SAPUI5 layout control. Do not try to output HTML code here; it'll be hard to format and may even break the structure of your page.

Special Note

When using calculated fields binding, you need to be aware that it only works one way. There is currently no mechanism that will allow a two-way binding for such fields, because the algorithm that would be needed to cover all potential use cases for backwards calculation would become impossibly complex for the framework to foresee and implement.

When you want to give your users the opportunity to change the value of an input with a calculated field, you need to implement the logic that will reflect these changes into the model yourself.

5.6.2 Expression Binding

Expression binding is an additional data binding feature in SAPUI5 that can be used instead of a formatter if you need your binding to be based on certain conditions. Whenever you find yourself programming a rather trivial formatter that will only compare two values, you should think about whether expression binding might also do the job.

You could think about rewriting the code from the factory in Section 5.4.2 and simply use an expression to determine whether you want to have the text control showing the allergens for a product visible or not. In that case, you would have to simply alter the view a little instead of enhancing the controller much. The items part of your detail view would then look like Listing 5.43.

```
<items>
  <ColumnListItem>
    <cells>
     <ObjectIdentifier
       text="{ID}"/>
        <layout:VerticalLayout>
          <Text text="{Name}"/>
          <Text text="{Allergenics}" visible="{= ${Allergenics} !==
 '' }"/>
        </layout:VerticalLayout>
      <ObjectNumber
        number="{Price}"
        unit="USD" />
    </cells>
  </ColumnListItem>
</items>
```

Listing 5.43 Using Expression Binding instead of Formatting

Expression binding is only recommended when the expressions do not become overly complex. The downside of this approach is that the vertical layout would still be rendered as such, even if one of the controls inside it was invisible and would hence pollute the DOM with unnecessary elements. For more complex use cases, the other implementation options we covered—formatters or factories for aggregation bindings—may be more suitable.

There are several operators you can use within expressions—equality operators, multiplicative and additive operators, and several more. See the API REFERENCE tab in the SAPUI5 Demo Kit for details.

5.7 Resource Models and Internationalization

A *resource model* is a special type of client-side model used for internationalization purposes within SAPUI5. It acts as a wrapper for resource bundles. A *resource bundle* is a file used to store the translatable texts used within your application. These files have a simple internal structure, which contains a set of name/value pairs separated by an equals sign. For instance:

```
appTitle=Suppliers And Products
```

It is important to understand that within a *.properties* file, there is no concept of an object hierarchy. The structure is entirely flat.

In this section, we'll look at the file locations, file naming conventions, and code page for resource bundles. We'll then look at using a resource model in our example application.

5.7.1 File Location

Resource bundle files are typically placed into the *i18n* folder within your app's directory structure. All these files end with the suffix *.properties*, which is why they are also referred to as "dot properties" files.

When we inspect our sample application closely, you will see that there are some texts that are not part of the business data supplied in the JSON model. Instead, there are texts that act as labels or titles that should be translated should the user decide to run the application in a different language.

5.7.2   File Naming Convention

SAPUI5 resource bundle files follow the same naming convention as is used for Java resource bundles. Any file ending in *.properties* is assumed to contain simple name value pairs which language will be determined by locale identifiers present in the file name. Table 5.1 shows an example of a few resource bundle files.

File Name	Description
i18n.properties	No language defined; therefore, the default language is assumed. Exactly which language acts as the default is determined by the larger context within which your application is being run. For instance, if your default corporate language is English, then the texts contained within this file will be in English – but this is an assumed default and cannot be derived from the file name itself.
i18n_en.properties	A resource bundle containing English text.
i18n_en_GB.properties	A resource bundle containing text in British English.
i18n_de.properties	A resource bundle containing German text.
i18n_de_AT.properties	A resource bundle containing text in the Austrian dialect of German.

Table 5.1 Resource Bundle Naming Conventions

When determining which language resource file to open, the browser always requests the most specific file first. For instance, if your browser is set to a UK locale, the browser will request *i18_en_GB.properties*. If this file cannot be found, then the browser requests the next most specific file, which in this case would be *i18n_en.properties*. If this file cannot be found, then it removes any locale values from the file name and simply requests the resource bundle containing text in the default language—*i18n.properties*. This is known as the *language determination fallback process*.

5.7.3   Code Page

It is important to understand that the specification for resource bundle files states that all text will belong to the ISO-8859-1 (LATIN-1) code page. This has two important consequences:

- The use of the LATIN-1 code page immediately assumes the text belongs to a left-to-right language.

- Text belonging to languages that require the use of some other code page, for instance, far eastern languages must be entered into the resource bundle file using Unicode encoding and not using the language's native script.

For instance, if you wish to enter Hebrew text into a resource bundle file, then you must account for the fact that 1) Hebrew is a non-LATIN-1 language, and 2) it is a right-to-left language. Hebrew for "Hello World" translates into English as "Shalom Olam."

To remedy this, first, you must create a resource bundle file called i18n_he.properties; however, it is incorrect to enter the Hebrew script directly into this file. In spite of the fact that the Hebrew script is perfectly correct, the following example is incorrect:

```
helloWorld=‫עולם שלום!‬
```

Instead, you should enter:

```
helloWorld=\u05E9\u05DC\u05D5\u05DD \u05E2\u05D5\u05DC\u05DD!
```

Not only have the Hebrew characters been converted to their hexadecimal Unicode values, but the character order of the Hebrew phrase has had to be reversed. This is important, because all text in a .properties file are assumed to be specified in left-to-right format—even if such text belongs to a right-to-left language!

The browser will automatically reverse the order of characters within this string so that it is rendered correctly. See the `dir="RTL"` attribute for UI controls for more information.

5.7.4 Using a Resource Model

Let's go through with our example application now and replace all texts that you think should be translatable with values from a properties file.

First, you need to create the *i18n* directory within your application root folder. Next, you need to create the properties file within the i18n directory. Within this directory, you can have properties files for every language you want your app to be translatable into. A typical properties file for our application could look like Listing 5.44.

```
notFoundTitle=Not Found
notFoundText=The resource was not found
backToMaster=Back to Master List

masterViewTitle=Supplier Overview
tableNoDataText=No data
masterTableTitle=Supplier
tableIDColumnTitle=ID
tableNameColumnTitle=Name

detailTitle=Supplier Detail
ID=ID
```
Listing 5.44 Default Properties File for Example Application

In the next step, we need to instantiate the resource model. We'll do this in the component, because this model should be available across the application.

There are two areas in the component code that we'll change. The first is part of the component metadata—namely, the configuration. Define the path to the model as shown in Listing 5.45.

```
metadata : {
  "rootView": "sapui5.demo.mvcapp.view.App",
  "dependencies": {
    "minUI5Version": "1.28.0",
    "libs": [ "sap.ui.core", "sap.m" ]
  },
  "config": {
  "i18nBundle": "sapui5.demo.mvcapp.i18n.i18n",
  "serviceUrl": "webapp/service/data.json"
},
```
Listing 5.45 Excerpt from Component Metadata

The second area is the init method of the component. Here, access the configuration value, instantiate the resource model from the path you've retrieved, and then set it to the component, which will in turn propagate it to its children, the views (see Listing 5.46).

```
init : function () {
  var mConfig = this.getMetadata().getConfig();
  // call the base component's init function
  UIComponent.prototype.init.apply(this, arguments);

  // set the internationalization model
  this.setModel(new ResourceModel({
```

```
    bundleName : mConfig.i18nBundle
  }), "i18n");
},
```
Listing 5.46 Init Function in Component

We can now replace the hard-coded strings in the application with values from the model. Because this is a named model, we can access the values within the bindings with a prefix, such as i18n>detailTitle, as you can see in Listing 5.47.

```
<mvc:View controllerName="sapui5.demo.mvcapp.controller.Detail"
  xmlns:mvc="sap.ui.core.mvc"
  xmlns:layout="sap.ui.layout"
  xmlns="sap.m">
  <Page id="page"
    navButtonPress="onNavPress"
    showNavButton="true"
    title="{i18n>detailTitle}">
    <content>
      <ObjectHeader
        id="objectHeader"
        title="{
        path: 'Name',
      formatter: '.formatter.formatUpperCase'
  }"
        number="{i18n>ID}: {ID}">
```
Listing 5.47 Excerpt from Detail View with Resource Model

As you can see from the object header carrying the ID value from the supplier, it's also possible to combine values from two different models—say, from the resource model and business data model—into one binding.

You should go through the application now and replace the remainder of the hard-coded strings in order to make application fully translatable. If you wish, you can add another properties file to the *i18n* folder afterwards, using the suffix for your desired target language, and translate the properties from your source file.

When you switch the application language in the browser, you can see how certain strings are replaced with the corresponding language.

As an example, we've provided an additional German properties file, which will be called i18n_de.properties (see Listing 5.48).

```
notFoundTitle=Nicht gefunden
notFoundText=Die Resource wurde nicht gefunden
backToMaster=Zurück zur Master-Liste

masterViewTitle=Anbieter-Überblick
tableNoDataText=Keine Daten
masterTableTitle=Anbieter
tableIDColumnTitle=ID
tableNameColumnTitle=Name
tablePriceColumnTitle=Preis

detailTitle=Anbieter-Detail
detailTableHeader=Anbieter-Produkte
ID=ID
detailFilterLabel=Produkte Filtern
```

Listing 5.48 i18n.properties File with Translatable Texts for the Application

You can switch between different languages by specifying the language parameter for your application in the browser's address bar, like this:

http://yourpathtoyourapplication?sap-ui-language=fr

To identify a language, the framework generally uses a language code of type `string`. Typically, this includes strings like the BCP-47 standard, de, en-US, zh-Hans-CN, and so on, but the Java locale syntax and SAP proprietary language codes also are accepted. See the Developer Guide for more details.

The current language is determined from several sources. The following list shows all sources in the reversed order of their priority. That means the last in the list gets precedence over the others:

▶ Hard-coded SAPUI5 default locale 'en'

▶ Potentially configured browser language (`window.navigator.browserLanguage`); for Internet Explorer this is the language of the operating system

▶ Potentially configured user language
`window.navigator.userLanguage`; for Internet Explorer this is the language in the REGION settings

▶ General language information from the browser
`window.navigator.language`

▶ Android: Language contained in the user agent string
`window.navigator.userAgent`

▸ Locale configured in the application coding
`jsdoc:symbols/sap.ui.core.Configuration`

▸ Locale configured via URL parameters

If you want to use the API to access the current language, you can so via the corresponding method at the configuration object:

```
var sCurrentLocale = sap.ui.getCore().getConfiguration().getLanguage();
```

If you need to access a value from a resource model directly from the code—for example, if you need to make use of a value within a formatter—you can use the `jQuery.sap.resources` module. This module contains an API that allows you to retrieve a resource bundle, depending on the URL and locale you pass to the module.

Note, however, that you need to make sure the module is indeed present and loaded in your application. You can do so by explicitly requiring the module as follows:

```
jQuery.sap.require("jquery.sap.resources");
```

Then, you can use the module to retrieve the desired resource bundle:

```
var oBundle = jQuery.sap.resources({url : sUrl, locale: sLocale});
```

For more information, see `jQuery.sap.resources` in the API REFERENCE tab of the SAPUI5 Demo Kit. Once you have the resource bundle loaded within your application, you can use the `getText` method on the bundle to access any particular text by its key:

```
var sText = oBundle.getText(sKey);
```

5.8   View Models and the Device Model

The last two models covered in this chapter are not actually different model types. They can be any kind of model, but we'll again be making use of JSON models within the example application.

5.8.1 Using View Models

A *view model* can keep track of the states of different elements on your view. It can establish a connection between values calculated by application logic within your controller and the UI elements that need to be enabled/disabled, visible/invisible, or active/inactive, to name just a few examples.

Whenever you can't pass a value from your business data model to your view using the typical binding methods but have to calculate values based on several conditions, it's a good practice to use a view model. It helps keep the controller logic and view declaration separate, because it prevents the controller from needing to know something about the particular controls within the view and their respective states.

Let's look at an example to make this clearer. We'll implement a function that will allow us to flip through the suppliers within the application. When a user enters the detail view for one supplier, they'll see a forward and or backward button in the upper-right corner of the view, and when he clicks on one of the buttons, it will trigger a routing event and send him to the corresponding next or previous supplier.

The detail view in the application will now look like Listing 5.49.

```
<mvc:View controllerName="sapui5.demo.mvcapp.controller.Detail"
  xmlns:mvc="sap.ui.core.mvc"
  xmlns:layout="sap.ui.layout"
  xmlns="sap.m">
  <Page id="page"
    navButtonPress="onNavPress"
    showNavButton="true"
    title="{i18n>detailTitle}">
    <subHeader>
      <Toolbar>
        <ToolbarSpacer/>
        <Button icon="sap-icon://slim-arrow-up" press="onPageUp" />
        <Button icon="sap-icon://slim-arrow-down" press="onPageDown" />
      </Toolbar>
    </subHeader>
<content>
[…]
```

Listing 5.49 Altered Page Header in Detail View

Note that we're making use of special icons for the two buttons, which were designed for paging purposes. (ToolbarSpacer is there to make sure the buttons are right-aligned.) The challenge now is to enable and disable these buttons depending on whether there is a next or previous supplier at all. When the first supplier in the list is displayed, it doesn't make sense to have an active BACK button, after all.

We could go forward and use the methods that we've worked with previously to retrieve information about the position of the supplier in the list. However, in order to dynamically enable and disable the buttons from the controller, we'd then have to write code into the controller that would update the state of the button whenever the binding context in the view changes to a different supplier. In addition, the controller would have to know exactly which buttons are in the view, by accessing them by their IDs, for example. To decouple this in order to make our code as reusable and maintainable as possible, it's a better practice to keep the controller logic independent of knowing which buttons are in the view.

Fortunately, there's an easy way out of this dilemma: Create another model in the onInit event of the detail view.

This model is a normal JSON model, which we'll set to the view as a named model. It doesn't hold much data (in this particular case, only two values are necessary), which is why we can specify the model's values right where the model is instantiated.

The onInit handler in the detail view will now look like Listing 5.50.

```
onInit : function () {
    this.getRouter().getRoute("detail").attachPatternMatched(this._
onObjectMatched, this);
    var oModel = new sap.ui.model.json.JSONModel({
      buttonPrev: false,
      buttonNext: false
    });
    this.getView().setModel(oModel, "viewModel");
},
[…]
```

Listing 5.50 Instantiating a View Model

You can see that the two properties hold Boolean values, which we'll use to bind the enabled properties from the buttons to. We can do this by using the normal property-binding syntax in the view. Therefore, let's add another property to each of the two buttons—namely, the enabled property—and bind these to the view model, as shown in Listing 5.51.

```
<Toolbar>
  <ToolbarSpacer/>
    <Button icon="sap-icon://slim-arrow-up" press="onPageUp" enabled=
"{viewModel>/buttonPrev}" />
    <Button icon="sap-icon://slim-arrow-down" press=
"onPageDown" enabled="{viewModel>/buttonNext}" />
</Toolbar>
```
Listing 5.51 Binding to the View Model

When you reload the page, you'll see that the buttons are both disabled now, and no matter which supplier you go to, you will not be able to click on either one (see Figure 5.12).

What we're still missing is the logic that will update the view model whenever the `bindingContext` element for the view changes and the functionality for the navigation.

Figure 5.12 Supplier Detail with Object Header

We need to implement this logic in such a way that it will be triggered whenever the `bindElement` function on the view is invoked, which happens in the `onObjectMatched` method on the detail view.

For the sake of code clarity, we'll write our own function to determine the correct state and then call this function from within the `onObjectMatched` method.

The new function needs to retrieve the current position of a supplier in the model and calculate the state the buttons should be in based on this information. We will also store the information about the position in the view model, because it will be reused in the navigation event handler.

We can retrieve the information and update the view model by adding the lines of code in Listing 5.52 to the detail controller.

```
/**
 * Updates the view model according to whether there are previous
 * and/or next suppliers.
 *
 * @function
 * @param {string} sObjectID path to the current supplier object
 * @private
 */
  _updateViewModel : function() {
  //find out if there is a next object in the line:
    var oModel = this.getView().getModel();
    var oViewModel = this.getView().getModel("viewModel");
    var nextObjectId = parseInt(this.sObjectID) + 1;
    var prevObjectId = parseInt(this.sObjectID) - 1;
    // check if there is a next object by adding +1 to the supplier ID
    //we assume we get a field we can safely order from the server
    var bNext = !!oModel.getProperty("/Suppliers/" + nextObjectId);
    var bPrev = !!oModel.getProperty("/Suppliers/" + prevObjectId);
    oViewModel.setProperty("/buttonNext", bNext);
    oViewModel.setProperty("/buttonPrev", bPrev);
}
```

Listing 5.52 Binding the View to the Correct Context and Calculating Button Enablement

Here, we try to retrieve the next and previous suppliers by adding or subtracting 1 from the current ID, which assumes that the ID field is a field we can safely use to determine an order (which would probably not work most of the time). Usually, the service should be able to deliver information about the next or previous object in a collection.

Next, we need to add the line of code triggering this function (see Listing 5.53).

```
[...]
/**
 * Binds the view to the object path and maintains the paging
 * button state.
 *
 * @function
 * @param {sap.ui.base.Event} oEvent pattern match event in
 * route 'object'
 * @private
 */
_onObjectMatched : function (oEvent) {
      this.sObjectID = oEvent.getParameter("arguments").ID;
    this.sObjectPath = "/Suppliers/" + this.sObjectID;
```

```
    this._bindView();
    this._updateViewModel();
},
[...]
```

Listing 5.53 Updating the Bound Supplier and the View Model from the _onObjectMatched Function

Note how we also updated the documentation for this method. When you now reload the page, you can see that depending on whether we're on the first or the last supplier, the correct button state is maintained. However, we still can't navigate with these buttons, because the corresponding event handlers for the press events are still missing.

We'll add the onPagingButtonPress method to both the XML view as the event handler for the buttons, and to the controller, where the actual navigation is implemented. Because we're already using proper routing within the application, we can now simply make use of this routing by invoking the corresponding navTo function with the information about the next or previous supplier.

In our scenario, as mentioned, we can just assume we can increment or decrement the index of the supplier by one to get to the next or previous supplier. We therefore simply need to write the two functions in Listing 5.54.

```
onPageUp : function(oEvent) {
  var sID = oEvent.getSource().getBindingContext().sPath;
  sID = parseInt(sID.substr(sID.lastIndexOf("/")+1));
  sID = sID-1;
  this.getRouter().navTo("detail", {ID: sID});
},

onPageDown : function(oEvent) {
  var sID = oEvent.getSource().getBindingContext().sPath;
  sID = parseInt(sID.substr(sID.lastIndexOf("/")+1));
  sID += 1;
  this.getRouter().navTo("detail", {ID: sID});
},
```

Listing 5.54 Navigation Functions for Paging through Suppliers via Arrow Buttons

We are using the path from the event object passed into the event handler, and we are extracting the current supplier number out of that path. We convert it to an integer, as adding +1 would cause a string concatenation. Then, we either subtract one, in case a user clicks on the arrow up, or we add one, when the user navigates down. We pass the result to the navTo function as ID parameter, so the navigation to the next or previous supplier will be triggered and they will be displayed accordingly.

5.8.2 Using the Device Model

The *device model* is a normal JSON model, which we treat separately because it has a special meaning within the application. This model is not implemented for a particular view, however, but is more generally used throughout the application. It keeps track of control properties that need to be adapted depending on whether the application is displayed on a desktop or on a mobile (touchscreen) device.

This makes sense particularly for some properties that influence appearance, such as the active states of a control you've tapped or clicked on. Because this model can be used in more than one view, we implement it separately and instantiate it within the component.

The implementation for the model itself will go into a separate file, which we'll put into the existing *model* directory of the application, and we'll call it *models.js*.

The code for this model is shown in Listing 5.55.

```
sap.ui.define([
 "sap/ui/model/json/JSONModel",
 "sap/ui/Device"
], function (JSONModel, Device) {
  "use strict";
  return {
createDeviceModel: function () {
var oModel = new JSONModel(Device);
oModel.setDefaultBindingMode("OneWay");
    return oModel;
    }
  };
});
```

Listing 5.55 Implementing Device Model for the Application

The parameters passed into the `sap.ui.define` call are two classes that we'll need within this model in order to get all the information about our current client from the `sap.ui.Device` API and be able to store it within a JSON model.

When this module is invoked, it will return a new function named `createDevice-Model`. Within this function, we're creating a new JSON model from the data retrieved from the device API, and because this model delivers its information in key-value pairs, we can pass the object to the JSON model constructor.

We then set `bindingMode` to `OneWay` because it doesn't make any sense to manipulate the values within this model from the application code. Finally, we return the newly created model. When we now go back to the application component, we just need to include the new model in the component.

We need to add the corresponding resource to the `define` section of the component as in Listing 5.56.

```
sap.ui.define([
  "sap/ui/core/UIComponent",
  "sap/ui/model/resource/ResourceModel",
  "sap/ui/model/json/JSONModel",
  "sap/ui/Device"
], function (UIComponent, ResourceModel, JSONModel, Device) {
  "use strict";
```

Listing 5.56 Adding the Resources for the Device Model

Within the `init` function of the component, insert the code for the additional model instantiation as in Listing 5.57.

```
init : function () {
  var mConfig = this.getMetadata().getConfig();

  // call the base component's init function
  UIComponent.prototype.init.apply(this, arguments);

  // set the internationalization model
  this.setModel(new ResourceModel({
    bundleName : mConfig.i18nBundle
  }), "i18n");

  // create the device model here
  var oModel = new JSONModel(Device);
  oModel.setDefaultBindingMode("OneWay");
  this.setModel(oModel, "Device");

  // create the views based on the url/hash
  this.getRouter().initialize();
},
```

Listing 5.57 Device Model Instantiated in init Function of Application

Now, we can access the device model from our views. We can use the information about which device is accessing the app to determine if we want to show or hide controls, alter some of their behavior, or show information in a different control altogether. We could, for instance, choose to display the paging buttons we created for the suppliers only on phone screens.

In this case, all we had to do was change the lines in the detail view instantiating the corresponding text control as shown in Listing 5.58.

```
<Toolbar>
  <ToolbarSpacer/>
<Button
  icon="sap-icon://slim-arrow-up"
  press="onPageUp" enabled="{viewModel>/buttonPrev}"
  visible="{device>/system/phone}" />
<Button
  icon="sap-icon://slim-arrow-down"
  press="onPageDown"
  enabled="{viewModel>/buttonNext}"
  visible="{device>/system/phone}"/>
</Toolbar>
```
Listing 5.58 Using Properties from the Device Model for Binding

You'll see that the application now looks a bit different when in desktop mode, in which the arrow buttons in the detail view have disappeared.

We can bring them back by switching into emulation mode in Google Chrome, however, to see what the app now looks like on the phone.

5.9 Summary

In this chapter, you learned about client-side models and their usage in SAPUI5. You've seen how models are instantiated and have made use of the typical data-binding methods in the sample application.

Using this knowledge, we extended the application to a point at which the most common features in enterprise-grade applications have been touched upon. We've made the application multilingual by using a resource model and have made it more cross-platform compatible by implementing a device model for those features that need to be handled differently on a desktop than on typical mobile devices.

In the next chapter, we'll enhance the application even more by adding the means to manipulate data in a model from the application—and this time, we'll be operating on a real service instead of using local mockup data.

This chapter explains how to connect to a real service instead of only using local models and how to create typical backend requests.

6   CRUD Operations

In the previous chapter, you learned how to work with different model types and how data binding mechanisms work in SAPUI5. In this chapter, we'll add even more functionality to the running example application.

Most applications not only will display data to the user, but also will allow users to add, edit, and delete entries. We'll take a closer look at how to connect to a REST service, as opposed to relying on locally stored JSON files as we've done so far.

6.1   What Is REST? What Is CRUD?

Representational State Transfer (REST) describes a programming paradigm most often applied to web services: One URL of a REST service will always represent particular content, so multiple requests to this URL will each produce the same response. A REST service provides an API that follows a certain rule set. When we have a service dealing with suppliers and products, for example, suppliers will typically be requested with *yourservicedomain.com/suppliers*, and products analogously with *yourservicedomain.com/products*. A single product, for example, could be accessed via *yourservicedomain.com/products/17*.

The REST programming paradigm makes machine-to-machine communication on the web easy, because an application server can rely on data being present via a stable set of URLs. Each URL of a REST service has all the information coded into it that the service needs to answer the request. As a result, a RESTful service is *stateless*, meaning that there is no session information held at the server. For each request, all information has to be passed to the server again.

REST services provide an API with a set of standard verbs that can be used to access any resource. These are GET, PUT, POST, PATCH, and DELETE and are used for the typical CRUD (Create, Read, Update, and Delete) operations. These operations allow you to manipulate REST services, read data with the GET method, update existing data using the PUT method, create new datasets using the POST method, and delete data using the DELETE method. The actual method is sent as part of the HTTP request from a client to a service, which tells the service which action to carry out.

Another feature of REST services is that there is usually more than one format a resource can be delivered in—for example, XML or JSON.

We'll now implement a REST service in the sample application. We'll use the data from the data.json file, but we'll need a service that will now deliver the data to the application.

> **Note**
>
> The way services are implemented—for example, in terms of which URLs can be used to access certain entities—varies widely. We've chosen a particular flavor for the example featured in this chapter. If you're using a different service, you may have to adapt the code accordingly.

6.2   Connecting to REST Services

There are many ways to create a REST. What's more, the way services are implemented can also vary widely. Therefore, we've provided a *mock service* (e.g., suppliers and products) for you which you can use to run your application and so you don't have to create the REST service yourself. This mock service is essentially a piece of code that will intercept all the CRUD calls that would normally go out to a remote service and simulate the correct responses.

Our collection of suppliers is available under the path */Suppliers*, and for a particular supplier the location will be */Suppliers/1*, for example. We'll use these paths in the requests we send in order to retrieve and send data. We do not need a basic service URL, because the mock service will be configured to intercept requests matching the corresponding paths.

Sending a request of type GET to our service asking for a particular supplier—for example, */Suppliers/1*—will deliver a response with JSON data in its body. For this request, the response body from the REST service will look like Listing 6.1.

```
[
  {
    "id":0,
    "Name":"Exotic Liquid",
    "Address":{
      "Street":"NE 228th",
      "City":"Sammamish",
      "State":"WA",
      "ZipCode":"98074",
      "Country":"USA",
      "PhoneNumber":"+1-123-123-1234"
    },
    "Location":{
      "type":"Point",
      "coordinates":[
        -122.03547668457,
        47.6316604614258
      ]
    }
  },
  {
    "id":1,
    "Name":"Tokyo Traders",
    "Address":{
      "Street":"NE 40th",
      "City":"Redmond",
      "State":"WA",
      "ZipCode":"98052",
      "Country":"USA",
      "PhoneNumber":"+1-123-123-1235"
    },
    "Location":{
      "type":"Point",
      "coordinates":[
        -122.107711791992,
        47.6472206115723
      ]
    }

  }
]
```

Listing 6.1 Service Response Body for GET Request for /Suppliers/1

We'll now begin by configuring our mock data, so we have data from the service to work with. Second, we will extend our JSONModel class in order to establish the connection correctly.

6.2.1 Configuring the Mock Service

To get the mock service started, we need to include a library that's freely available on the web. For the purposes of this example, we'll use FakeRest. This is a JavaScript library made available on GitHub at *https://github.com/marmelab/FakeRest* thanks to the developer Francois Zaninotto. This JavaScript library is based on sinon.js, a useful testing framework that will be covered in greater detail in Chapter 11.

For now, you only need to download the corresponding files for FakeRest and include both FakeRest and sinon into your application. Once you go to *https://github.com/marmelab/FakeRest*, click the DOWNLOAD ZIP button, as shown in Figure 6.1.

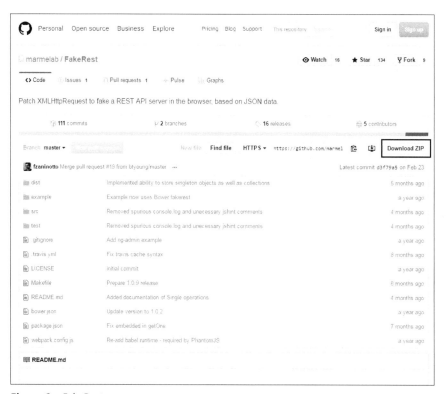

Figure 6.1 FakeRest

Downloading FakeRest will provide you with a ZIP file; you'll need to extract its contents. It doesn't matter where you extract the contents to, because we'll only need one file to put into our application directory.

When you have extracted FakeRest, make sure that you move the FakeRest.min.js file from the *dist* folder into the *service* folder of your web application. The path to FakeRest.min.js file will then be */webapp/service/FakeRest.min.js*.

Let's include this path in the example application's index.html page. Enter the following line of code either directly before or after the SAPUI5 bootstrap script in your index.html:

```
<script src="webapp/service/FakeRest.min.js"></script>
```

Now, we need to make sure that sinon.js is loaded as a dependency when we load the actual application. We'll therefore modify how the component loads, as in Listing 6.2.

```
sap.ui.require([
  "sap/m/Shell",
  "sap/ui/core/ComponentContainer",
  "sapui5/demo/mvcapp/Component",
  "sap/ui/thirdparty/sinon"
], function (Shell, ComponentContainer, Component) {
```

Listing 6.2 Defining sinon.js as Dependency

Next, we need to load the JSON data again, which will act as mock data for the service (see Listing 6.3).

```
jQuery.ajax({
  url : "service/suppliers.json",
  success : function(oData) {
    initAppWithFakeRest(oData);
  },
  error : function() {
    alert("Could not start server");
  }
});
```

Listing 6.3 Loading Mock Data for the Mock Service

In the `success` callback of the Ajax call in Listing 6.3, we're invoking a new function, `initAppWithFakeRest`. Within this function, we'll initialize the mock service itself, and we'll instantiate the shell and load the actual component. By doing so, we can make sure that the service has started before the app itself loads. The initAppWithFakeRest function is shown in Listing 6.4.

```
var initAppWithFakeRest = function(oData){
  // initialize fake REST server
  var restServer = new FakeRest.Server();
  restServer.init(oData);
  var server = sinon.fakeServer.create();
  server.xhr.useFilters = true;
  server.autoRespond = true;
  server.autoRespondAfter = 0;

  server.xhr.addFilter(function(method, url) {
    //whenever the this regular expression returns true the
    //request will not be intercepted by FakeRest
    return !url.match(/Suppliers/);
  });

  // use sinon.js to monkey-patch XmlHttpRequest
  server.respondWith(restServer.getHandler());
  // initialize the UI component
  new Shell({
    app: new ComponentContainer({
      height : "100%",
      component : new Component({
        id: "mvcAppComponent"
      })
    })
  }).placeAt("content");
}
```

Listing 6.4 Initializing Mock Service in index.html

To prevent FakeRest from intercepting all XmlHTTPRequests coming from the application and limit it to the requests targeting our service, we'll add a filter to the xhr object at the service (bolded in Listing 6.4). This filter will return true when nothing needs to be intercepted and false when the regular expression matches. In the latter case, the mock service will deliver the response that would normally come from a real service.

Note

To use a real service within this application later, make sure to remove the code for the mock service and the mock data loading. You then just need to pass the real service URL as a parameter to the AppModel constructor in your component.

6.2.2 Extending the JSON Model

We'll now refactor the existing code for the data binding a little so that the application can use the JSON data from the remote service just as it's used the data from the local JSON file in the past.

For our purposes, we'll still be using a JSON model—kind of. We'll extend `sap.ui.model.json.JSONModel` from SAPUI5, because it lacks some functionality we need for binding the data, and we'll do so again later on for updating, creating, and deleting entries.

To extend the JSON model, we'll create a new file in the *model* directory and will call the file AppModel.js. As you know, you can extend classes delivered with SAPUI5 by invoking the `extend` method on them. The skeleton code for the model extension will look like Listing 6.5.

```
sap.ui.define([
  "sap/ui/model/json/JSONModel"
], function(JSONModel) {
  "use strict";

  return JSONModel.extend("sapui5.demo.mvcapp.model.AppModel", {
  // our own methods go here
  });
});
```

Listing 6.5 Skeleton for Extended JSONModel

We'll define the dependencies again and extend `sap.ui.model.json.JSONModel`, giving the new child class the name `saui5.demo.mvcapp.model.AppModel` (combining the `app` namespace and the new class name).

In the component, instead of using the JSON model for business data as before, we'll now use the new model extension. We need to declare it as a dependency for the component before we can use it, so the component's array of dependencies will look like Listing 6.6.

```
sap.ui.define([
  "sap/ui/core/UIComponent",
  "sap/ui/model/resource/ResourceModel",
  "sap/ui/model/json/JSONModel",
  "sapui5/demo/mvcapp/model/AppModel",
  "sap/ui/Device"
], function (UIComponent, ResourceModel, JSONModel, AppModel, Device) {
```

Listing 6.6 Define Section of Component, Now Requiring AppModel

Next, we need to pass this new dependency as a parameter into the function instantiating the component. In the `onInit` method of the component, we'll now instantiate `AppModel` instead of the regular `JSONModel` from the previous chapter. The `onInit` function will now look like Listing 6.7.

```
init : function () {
  // call the base component's init function
  UIComponent.prototype.init.apply(this, arguments);

  // create the device model here
  var oModel = new JSONModel(Device);
  oModel.setDefaultBindingMode("OneWay");
  this.setModel(oModel, "device");
  var oAppModel = new AppModel();

  jQuery.ajax({
    contentType : "application/json",
    url : "/Suppliers",
    dataType : "json",
    success : function(oData) {
      oAppModel.setData(oData);
    },
    error : function() {
      console.log("an error occurred retrieving the Data");
    }
  });
  this.setModel(oAppModel);
  // create the views based on the url/hash
  this.getRouter().initialize();
},
```

Listing 6.7 Instantiating New Model in init Method on the Component

With this code, we load all suppliers from the service, along with the products they can deliver. We only need to change the binding paths in the master view, because suppliers will now be available in the model under the "/" path instead of /suppliers/.

When done correctly, your application should still run as it did before. The connection to the REST service has not been made yet; we've simply provided the means to do so.

CORS

When you're using a different service from some other host, make sure that the requests to this service are proxied correctly in order to avoid Cross-Origin Resource Sharing (CORS) issues if the service itself is not CORS enabled.

In the SAP Web IDE, this can be achieved by adding a destination to your configuration. More on how to do this can be found in Appendix B.

Now, we have to revise the application in order to use the new service. We'll still be using a JSON model, but now we have to connect it to the mock service in order to get results from there.

6.3 Using CRUD Operations

In the previous section, we took the first step to implement CRUD functionality into the application. We'll continue with our example and create a form for editing data that's already available in the service. Next, we'll add functionality that allows us to add new data, and then we'll implement the means for deleting such data from the service.

6.3.1 Editing an Existing Entry

In this section, we'll create a form for editing the data available in the service. The following is an overview of the steps we'll walk through:

1. Add a new button to the detail view; this button will bring the user to a new view from which he can edit a supplier.

2. Add a new route and a new target to the routing configuration in the component.

3. Implement the `onEdit` method in the controller of the detail view, which will trigger navigation.

4. Create the new edit view.

To begin, we'll first provide the means for our users to reach the new edit view we'll create later. Let's begin by adding a new button to the detail view that will allow users to switch to edit mode from an existing object's details.

Because the view uses `sap.m.Page`, we can simply add the EDIT button to the footer aggregation of the control from within the XML view (see Listing 6.8).

```
<footer>
  <Toolbar>
    <ToolbarSpacer/>
    <Button text="{i18n>Edit}" press="onEdit" />
  </Toolbar>
</footer>
```

Listing 6.8 Add to Footer of a Page Control within Detail View

Add the corresponding key-value pair for the button to the i18n.properties file:

```
btnEdit=Edit
```

Now, we'll make sure that the navigation from the detail view to the edit view happens when a user clicks on the EDIT button. To do so, we'll create a new target for our routing configuration so that the target's object will look like Listing 6.9.

```
"routing":{
  "config":{
    "routerClass":"sap.m.routing.Router",
    "viewType":"XML",
    "viewPath":"sapui5.demo.mvcapp.view",
    "controlId":"app",
    "controlAggregation":"pages",
    "bypassed":{
      "target":"notFound"
    }
  },
  "routes":[
    {
      "pattern":"",
      "name":"master",
      "target":"master"
    },
    {
      "pattern":"detail/{id}",
      "name":"detail",
      "target":"detail"
    },
    {
      "pattern":"edit/:id:",
      "name":"edit",
      "target":"edit"
    }
  ],
```

```
  "targets":{
    "master":{
      "viewName":"Master",
      "viewLevel":1
    },
    "detail":{
      "viewName":"Detail",
      "viewLevel":2
    },
    "notFound":{
      "viewName":"NotFound",
      "viewId":"notFound"
    },
    "edit":{
      "viewName":"Edit",
      "viewId":"edit",
      "viewLevel":3
    }
  }
}
```

Listing 6.9 Routing Configuration in Component

Next, we'll implement the `onEdit` function in the detail controller. We want to navigate to the new view when someone clicks on the EDIT button. To do so, we'll use the `navTo` function at our router. We'll pass two parameters to this function:

1. The name of the route we want to navigate to (defined in the component configuration)

2. The object ID of the object we want to edit

The second item needs to be passed within the parameters object that the `navTo` function takes as a second parameter. The object ID has to be added to the parameters as a property with the name we defined in the configuration, which means that a route configured with the pattern `edit/:id:` expects us to deliver a matching property `id` to the `navTo` function. Note that the surrounding colons mean that the `id` parameter is optional; this will become important later on when we implement the `Create` functionality.

We now need to read the current ID from the binding context of the detail view and wrap it in an object, as shown in Listing 6.10.

```
onEdit : function() {
//we need to strip the leading slash from the path to get the ID
  var sObjectPath =
 this.getView().getElementBinding().getPath().substr(1);
```

```
    this.getRouter().navTo("edit", {
      id: sObjectPath
    }, false);
  },
```

Listing 6.10 onEdit: Triggered When User Clicks on Edit Button from Detail View

Finally, we need a view to navigate to—that is, the edit view we'll implement now. Let's first create the skeleton code for this view (see Listing 6.11). This code goes into the *view* folder in the application, and the file will be called *Edit.view.xml*.

The application will have a BACK button in the page header, which is why we're assigning the onNavPress function to the navButtonPress property we'll later implement. We also need to set the showNavButton property at the page control to true.

We'll also have a SAVE button in the footer. This button will have its own event handler, a method we will call onSave, which we'll implement later in the edit controller.

```xml
<mvc:View
   controllerName="sapui5.demo.mvcapp.controller.Edit"
   xmlns:mvc="sap.ui.core.mvc"
   xmlns:layout="sap.ui.layout"
   xmlns:form="sap.ui.layout.form" xmlns="sap.m">
   <Page
id="page"
navButtonPress="onNavPress"
showNavButton="true"
title="{i18n>detailTitle}">
     <content>
     </content>
     <footer>
       <Toolbar>
         <ToolbarSpacer/>
         <Button text="{i18n>btnSave}" press="onSave" />
       </Toolbar>
     </footer>
   </Page>
</mvc:View>
```

Listing 6.11 Skeleton for Edit View

On the view, users will be able to edit some attributes of a supplier, including all of those that are displayed in the ObjectHeader control present in the detail view—except for the ID, which can't be updated, because it acts as the unique identifier for each supplier.

We'll use a new control in the edit view that was designed for the purpose of creating a form: `sap.ui.layout.form.SimpleForm`. This control can take input fields of all kinds into its content aggregation. It will display these fields aligned correctly, but differently on tablets and phones than on a desktop. On a phone or a tablet, it's better to have larger input fields to make it easier for users to select such fields with touch gestures. We've all seen web apps that make it hard to tap an input field with a finger because the fields are just too small. The `SimpleForm` control takes care of this problem.

Internally, `SimpleForm` makes use of the `Grid` layout control you used in Chapter 3. The code for `SimpleForm` goes into the content aggregation of the `Page` control within the edit view, and will look like Listing 6.12.

```
<form:SimpleForm
  id="form"
  layout="ResponsiveGridLayout"
  editable="true"
  class="sapUiResponsiveMargin"
  width="auto"
  labelSpanL="3" labelSpanM="3"
  emptySpanL="4" emptySpanM="4"
  columnsL="1" columnsM="1">
  <form:content>
    <Label id="nameLabel" text="Name" />
    <Input id="nameInput"
      value="{
      path : 'Name',
      type : 'sap.ui.model.odata.type.String'}" />
    <Label id="cityLabel" text="City" />
    <Input id="cityInput" value="{Address/City}" />
    <Label id="countryLabel" text="Country" />
    <Input id="countryInput" value="{Address/Country}" />
    <Label id="phoneLabel" text="Phone Number" />
    <Input id="phoneInput"
      value="{
      path: 'Address/PhoneNumber',
      type: '.types.PhoneNumber'
      }" />
  </form:content>
</form:SimpleForm>
```

Listing 6.12 SimpleForm Control in Edit View

You can see that the code for SimpleForm mostly contains the labels and inputs for the data we want to edit; the rest is the SimpleForm configuration. The property values configured for SimpleForm make the form display differently for the different screen sizes. width="auto" is self-explanatory. A property value set to "auto" indicates that the form will take as much space as its content will require.

The labelSpan properties determine the number of grid column labels that will cover certain screen sizes:

```
labelSpanL="3" labelSpanM="3"
emptySpanL="4" emptySpanM="4"
columnsL="1" columnsM="1">
```

The emptySpan property determines how much space in terms of grid columns there will be at the end of each row, and the columns properties determine how many form columns there will be on large and medium screens. Depending on the columns, there can be one or more form containers within one line.

More about the configuration options for SimpleForm in combination with ResponsiveGridLayout can be found in the Explored app or in the API documentation (see Appendix E).

We're still missing a proper controller for the new view; it will have to take care of enabling the correct binding for the form and its input fields, among other things. We'll reuse BaseController from the previous chapters for the edit view, and we'll also make use of the formatter and types previously defined in the sample application.

We therefore need to declare the corresponding files as dependencies in the array we're passing as the first parameter to the sap.ui.define function. Next, we can extend our BaseController class and create the new controller for the edit view. The file goes into the *controller* folder and will be called Edit.controller.js.

Within the onInit lifecycle method of the new controller, we'll make the new controller react when the edit routing pattern is matched and the view configured for the edit target—our edit view—is displayed. We'll use the attach-Display method on the router to register the corresponding event and create the correct binding.

The path for the binding will be retrieved in the onEditObjectMatched event handler, which in turn will call the private method _bindView. This method will create the element binding for the edit view.

In this controller, we'll also define what should happen when someone clicks the BACK button in this view; we want the app to navigate back to the master view. Therefore, we'll also implement the onNavPress event handler we assigned to the press event of the BACK button in the view. The new controller will now look like Listing 6.13.

```
sap.ui.define([
  "sapui5/demo/mvcapp/controller/BaseController",
  "sapui5/demo/mvcapp/model/formatter",
  "sapui5/demo/mvcapp/model/types"
], function(BaseController, formatter, types) {
  "use strict";
  return BaseController.extend("sapui5.demo.mvcapp.controller.Edit", {
    formatter: formatter,
    types: types,
/* ======================================================= */
/* lifecycle methods                                       */
/* ======================================================= */

    /**
     * Called when the edit controller is instantiated.
     * @public
     */
     onInit : function () {
       var oRouter, oViewModel;
       oRouter = this.getRouter();

       oRouter.attachRoutePatternMatched(this._onRouteMatched, this);
     },
    /* ======================================================= */
    /* event handlers                                          */
    /* ======================================================= */
    /**
     * Navigates back to the Master.
     * @function
     */
    onNavPress: function() {
      this.myNavBack("master");
},
/* ======================================================= */
/* internal methods                                        */
/* ======================================================= */

/**
 * Binds the view to the object path.
 *
 * @function
```

```
 * @param {sap.ui.base.Event} oEvent pattern match event in route 'object'
 * @private
 */
_onRouteMatched : function (oEvent) {
  var oEventData = oEvent.getParameter("arguments");
  this.sObjectPath = "/" + oEventData.id;
  this._bindView();
},
/**
 * Creates the actual element binding.
 *
 * @function
 * @param {string} sObjectPath path to the object to be bound
 * @private
 */
    _bindView: function() {
      var oView = this.getView();
      oView.bindElement(this.sObjectPath);
    }
  });
});
```

Listing 6.13 Controller for Edit View

The edit view will be displayed as shown in Figure 6.2.

Figure 6.2 Edit View

The last step to complete the editing scenario is to enable the SAVE button. For this button, we'll implement the onSave method in Edit.controller.js. When a user clicks on SAVE, the only thing we need to do is update the data on the remote server. To do so, we'll use a `PUT` request to write data to the service.

Because `sap.ui.model.json.JSONModel` doesn't have any convenient methods that can be called in order to update data on a remote service, we'll write a method ourselves that can be used for either of our update operations.

Because the JSON model we're using for our business data is a two-way-binding model by default, we can rely on our changes being applied from the input field values to the model when the focus leaves the corresponding field—for example, through tabbing out or clicking elsewhere.

The code for the `onSave` event handler will use the changes reflected in the model and update the service with this information. Implement a `saveEntry` method into `AppModel` via the code shown in Listing 6.14.

```
saveEntry : function(oObject, sUrl, sLocalPath){
  var sType,
      that = this,
      oData;
  // local path indicates whether we are updating an existing object
  // or creating a new one
  oData = JSON.stringify(oObject);
  jQuery.ajax({
    type : PUT,
    contentType : "application/json",
    data: oData,
    url : sUrl,
    dataType : "json",
    success : function() {
      //store the new/updated entry in the model
      that._updateModel(sLocalPath, oObject);
      //call createEntry to reset the dummy property to empty values
      that.createEntry("/");
      that.fireRequestCompleted();
    },
    error : function() {
      that.fireRequestFailed();
    }
  });
},
```

Listing 6.14 New saveEntry Method in AppModel

This method will send an Ajax request using the `jQuery.ajax` method, which is available in jQuery. The parameters for this method are `oObject`, containing the updated supplier data, `sUrl`, containing the URL on the service belonging to the supplier, and `sLocalPath`, for the path at which the supplier can be found in the local model.

As previously mentioned, we need to prepare the data we get as an input before passing it on to the service. We're passing the updated data to the request using `JSON.stringify`, a native JavaScript function, in order to convert the JSON object we get from the model into a string we can send.

The request will be sent asynchronously, and when it succeeds we store the updated data in the model and fire the `requestCompleted` event on the model. The corresponding method to fire this event is inherited from the JSON model we've extended. If the request fails, we fire the `requestFailed` event.

The `_updateModel` method is still missing in `AppModel`, so presently the only way to get the updated data to display in the list is to reload the app. We'll change this now by telling the app to save the data not only to the server, but also to the local model:

```
_updateModel : function(sLocalPath, data){
  this.setProperty(sLocalPath, data);
}
```

We could also write this code snippet into the `saveEntry` method itself, but we'll enhance this function later on to update the model with new entries or update it on delete.

In the edit controller, we need to call the `saveEntry` method on the model and provide the data in the `onSave` method. In addition, we'll attach `success` to the `requestCompleted` event fired on the model and on the `requestFailed` method.

If successful, we want to navigate back to the detail view and display the updated supplier. In case of an error, we'll have a message toast to tell the user something has gone wrong.

In order to display the message toast, we need to implement one more change to the `define` section of the controller, and then we'll have all the parts in place for the `onSave` handler. We need to require the message toast as a dependency in the edit controller, so the dependencies array will look like Listing 6.15.

```
sap.ui.define([
  "sapui5/demo/mvcapp/controller/BaseController",
  "sapui5/demo/mvcapp/model/formatter",
```

```
  "sapui5/demo/mvcapp/model/types",
  "sap/m/MessageToast"
], function (BaseController, formatter, types, MessageToast) {
```

Listing 6.15 Define Section of Edit Controller

For this message toast to show translatable text, we also need to retrieve the text from the resource bundle, as shown in Listing 6.16.

```
onSave: function(){
  var sLocalPath,
      sUrl = "",
      oRouter = this.getRouter(),
      sPath = this.getView().getElementBinding().getPath(),
      oModel = this.getModel(),
      oObject = oModel.getProperty(sPath),
      oBundle = this.getResourceBundle();

   sUrl = sUrl + "/Suppliers/" + oObject.id;
  sLocalPath = sPath;

  oModel.attachEventOnce("requestCompleted", function(){
    oRouter.navTo("master");
    this.getModel("viewModel").setProperty("/createMode", false);
  }, this);

  oModel.attachEventOnce("requestFailed", function(){
    MessageToast.show(oBundle.getText("updateFailed"));
  });
  oModel.saveEntry(oObject, sUrl, sLocalPath);
},
```

Listing 6.16 onSave Handler Triggered When User Clicks on Save Button in Edit View

Finally, we need to add the text for the updateFailed message toast to the i18n properties file(s):

```
updateFailed = Saving the supplier failed
```

6.3.2 Creating a New Entry

For the Create scenario, we'll reuse the edit view. We'll use another JSONModel instance to act as a view model in this view and thus will create two different modes for this view.

In this example, when a user wants to create a new entry, he clicks on an ADD button from the master view. The user will then be redirected to the edit view, but in a different mode: the *create mode*. In create mode, an additional field for the supplier's ID is visible (because we don't currently have any server-side means to automatically generate an ID). When the user clicks SAVE, he will trigger the `saveEntry` method in `AppModel` again, but we'll refactor this method in order to send either a PUT or a POST request depending on whether we're creating a new supplier or updating an existing one.

Let's first create the ADD button in the master view. The code in this view now looks like Listing 6.17.

```
<mvc:View
  controllerName="sapui5.demo.mvcapp.controller.Master"
  xmlns:mvc="sap.ui.core.mvc"
  xmlns="sap.m">
  <Page
id="page"
navButtonPress="onNavBack"
showNavButton="true"
title="{i18n>masterViewTitle}">
    <content>
      <Table id="table"
        width="auto"
        class="sapUiResponsiveMargin"
        items="{/}"
        noDataText="{i18n>tableNoDataText}">
      <headerToolbar>
        <Toolbar>
          <Title id="tableHeader" text="{i18n>SuppliersList}" />
          <ToolbarSpacer />
          <Button icon="sap-icon://add"
            tooltip="{i18n>btnAddSupplier}"
            press="onAddSupplier"/>
        </Toolbar>
      </headerToolbar>
      <columns>
        <Column id="nameColumn">
          <header>
            <Text id="IDColumnTitle"
              text="{i18n>tableIDColumnTitle}" />
          </header>
        </Column>
        <Column id=" nameColumn">
          <header>
            <Text id="nameColumnTitle"
              text="{i18n>tableNameColumnTitle}" />
          </header>
        </Column>
      </columns>
```

```
      <items>
        <ColumnListItem type="Navigation" press="onListPress">
          <cells>
            <ObjectIdentifier text="{id}" />
            <ObjectIdentifier text="{Name}" />
          </cells>
        </ColumnListItem>
      </items>
    </Table>
  </content>
</Page>
</mvc:View>
```

Listing 6.17 *Master View with Button to Add New Supplier*

The ADD button, highlighted in Listing 6.17, will trigger the onAddSupplier function, which we need to implement in the master controller now. We'll again make use of the router instantiated at the component, reusing the target we used before. The onAddSupplier method will thus look like this:

```
onAddSupplier : function(){
  this.getRouter().navTo("edit");
}
```

Note that we're not passing the optional id parameter to the navTo function now. When this parameter is not set, the app will react in edit view accordingly and display the view in a create mode instead of update mode. In create mode, form fields are not prepopulated with existing supplier data.

In the edit controller, we'll now implement this part of the functionality, creating the view model and setting the value according to the parameter we get through the router. The corresponding code needs to go into the onInit method for instantiating the view model. The onInit method in the edit controller will now look like Listing 6.18.

```
onInit : function () {
  var oRouter, oTarget, oViewModel;
  oRouter = this.getRouter();
  oTarget = oRouter.getTarget("edit");
  oViewModel = new JSONModel({
    "createMode": false
  });
  this.getView().setModel(oViewModel, "viewModel");

  oRouter.attachRoutePatternMatched(this._onRouteMatched, this);
},
```

Listing 6.18 *onInit Refactored in Edit View*

237

We have refactored the method formerly called _onObjectMatched, because the name doesn't fit anymore. After all, when we reach this part of the code in create mode, we don't have any objects to be matched; we're just generating a new one. From now on, the method will be called _onRouteMatched, a better name to describe what happens inside the code. Listing 6.19 displays the new method code.

```
/**
 * Binds the view to the object path.
 *
 * @function
 * @param {sap.ui.base.Event} oEvent pattern match event in route 'object'
 * @private
 */
_onRouteMatched : function (oEvent) {
  var oEventData = oEvent.getParameter("arguments");
  if (oEvent.getParameter("name")==="master"){
    return;
  }
  if(oEventData && oEventData.id){
    this.sObjectPath = "/" + oEventData.id;
  } else {
    this.getView().getModel("viewModel").setProperty("
    /createMode", true);
    this.getModel().createEntry("/");
    this.sObjectPath = "/createEntry";
  }
  this._bindView();
},
```

Listing 6.19 _onDisplay Method, Differentiating between Create and Edit Modes

You can see that we now can differentiate between the view when we edit an existing supplier and the view when we create a new supplier based on the optional id parameter we pass to the router—or not. In the onRouteMatched function, because it's an event handler, we again get the event object (here called oEvent) automatically passed in from SAPUI5. For this object, we can retrieve any other parameters and additional arguments the event object has. To check whether a supplier ID was sent along with the navigation event, we'll check the arguments parameter for a property called id. We do so by calling getParameter("arguments") at the event object. When we find id, we know we're editing an existing supplier. If id isn't found, we're creating a new supplier.

If the routePatternMatched event is only matched because we're navigating back to the master, however, we don't want to recreate the empty object. This is why we implement the check for the route name and return it in this case without doing anything in the event handler.

When we do not have a new supplier ID, we need to create an empty entry in the model so that we can bind the view as usual. We thus do not have to change anything about the property binding in the view, and we profit from the two-way-binding mode here. We'll invoke a new function, `createSupplier`, and implement it in `AppModel`, which will create this empty entry for us. This method in the `AppModel` will now look like Listing 6.20.

```
createSupplier : function(){
  this.setProperty("/createEntry",
    {
      "id" : "",
      "Name" : "",
      "Address" : {
        "Street" : "",
        "City" : "",
        "State" : "",
        "ZipCode" : "",
        "Country" : "",
        "PhoneNumber" : ""
      }
    });
},
```

Listing 6.20 createEntry Method in AppModel

As you can see in the code for the `createEntry` method, we're creating a new property on the model under a separate path reserved for new entries, and we store an object there with empty attributes for a supplier.

Normally, information about how a supplier entity is structured would come from a metadata definition, either from the service itself or from a local resource you create. You could accomplish this easily by using a separate JSON file that holds this data for you. However, because we're only editing a single entity for now, we've written the structure into the `AppModel` code for the sake of simplicity.

When the new method is in place, we'll have an empty entry in the model as soon as the edit view is displayed, so the binding will still work and leave us with some empty fields on the UI side. The visibility of the ID field still needs to be bound—which is why we created the view model. In Edit.view.xml, we'll will add this ID field along with a label and bind the `visible` attribute of the new input to the createMode value stored in the view mode. Conveniently, this is already a Boolean value, so we can bind it directly. The edit view will now contain the code shown in Listing 6.21.

```
<mvc:View
  controllerName="sapui5.demo.mvcapp.controller.Edit" xmlns:mvc=
"sap.ui.core.mvc" xmlns:layout="sap.ui.layout" xmlns:form=
"sap.ui.layout.form" xmlns="sap.m">
  <Page id="page"
    navButtonPress="onNavPress"
    showNavButton="true"
    title="{i18n&gt;detailTitle}">
    <content>
      <form:SimpleForm id="form"
        layout="ResponsiveGridLayout"
        editable="true"
        class="sapUiResponsiveMargin"
        width="auto"
        labelSpanL="3" labelSpanM="3"
        emptySpanL="4" emptySpanM="4"
        columnsL="1" columnsM="1">
        <form:content>
          <Label id="idLabel"
            text="{i18n>Id}"
            visible="{viewModel>createMode}" />
          <Input id="idInput"
            value="{
              path: 'id',
              type: 'sap.ui.model.type.Integer'
            }"
            visible="{viewModel>createMode}" />
          <Label id="nameLabel"
            text="{i18n>Name}" />
          <Input id="nameInput"
            value="{
              path : 'Name',
              type : 'sap.ui.model.type.String'
            }" />
          <Label id="cityLabel"
            text="{i18n>City}" />
          <Input id="cityInput"
            value="{Address/City}" />
          <Label id="countryLabel"
            text="{i18n>Country}" />
          <Input id="countryInput"
            value="{Address/Country}" />
          <Label id="phoneLabel"
            text="{i18n>PhoneNumber}" />
```

```
            <Input id="phoneInput"
              value="{Address/PhoneNumber}" />
          </form:content>
        </form:SimpleForm>
      </content>
      <footer>
        <Toolbar>
          <ToolbarSpacer />
          <Button
            text="{i18n>Save}"
            press="onSave" />
          <Button
            text="{i18n>btnDelete}"
            press="onDelete" />
        </Toolbar>
      </footer>
    </Page>
</mvc:View>
```

Listing 6.21 Code for Edit View

In Listing 6.21, there are two new elements in the view are: the label and the input for the ID of the new supplier. For both elements, the `visible` attribute is now also bound.

We'll also remove the hard-coded label texts from the view and move them over to the i18n folder where they belong.

The complete list of translatable texts in the i18n.properties file now looks like Listing 6.22.

```
appTitle=Suppliers and Products
appDescription=Sample app from the SAPUI5 Comprehensive Guide, showing
  suppliers along with their products
notFoundTitle=Not Found
notFoundText=The resource was not found
backToMaster=Back to Master List

# Master View
suppliersList = Suppliers List
masterViewTitle=Supplier Overview
tableNoDataText=No data
masterTableTitle=Supplier
btnAddSupplier = New supplier
tableIDColumnTitle=ID
tableNameColumnTitle=Name
tablePriceColumnTitle=Price
```

```
# Detail view
detailTitle=Supplier Detail
detailTableHeader=Supplier Products
ID=ID
btnSave=Save
btnDelete=Delete

# Edit View
Id=Id
Name=Name
City=City
Country=Country
PhoneNumber=Phone Number
saveFailed=Saving the supplier failed
```
Listing 6.22 Key-Value Pairs for Edit View in i18n.properties

We now have everything in place to create a new supplier locally on the client, but we still need to send this new entity off to the REST service (Listing 6.23). Go into AppModel once more and enhance the saveEntry method so that it will also process POST requests, not only the PUT requests we've used so far for updating entries. The sLocalPath parameter will only contain information when we update an existing entry, so we can also use it to decide whether a create request when calling the function. Depending on whether this parameter is set or not, we'll set the request type accordingly to either PUT or POST, as shown in Listing 6.23.

```
saveEntry : function(oObject, sUrl, sLocalPath){
  var sType,
      that = this,
      oData;
  // local path indicates whether we are updating an existing object
  // or creating a new one
  if(sLocalPath){
    sType = "PUT";
  } else {
    sType = "POST";
  }
  oData = JSON.stringify(oObject);
  jQuery.ajax({
    type : sType,
    contentType : "application/json",
    data: oData,
    url : sUrl,
    dataType : "json",
```

```
    success : function() {
      //store the new/updated entry in the model
      that._updateModel(sLocalPath, oObject);
      //call createEntry to reset the dummy property to empty values
      that.createEntry("/");
      that.fireRequestCompleted();
    },
    error : function() {
      that.fireRequestFailed();
    }
  });
},
```

Listing 6.23 Enhanced saveEntry Method in AppModel

As mentioned previously, we'll also enhance the `_updateModel` method so that it will store a new entry correctly (see Listing 6.24).

```
_updateModel : function(sLocalPath, data){
  if (sLocalPath){
    //store data for an existing object
    this.setProperty(sLocalPath, data);
  } else {
    //store new object: get all data as array from model, push new
    //entry, set data to the model again
    var aData = this.getData();
    aData.push(data);
    this.setData(aData);
  }
}
```

Listing 6.24 Enhanced _updateModel Method in AppModel

Within the method, we check if there is a local path present. If not, that indicates we're storing an entry that has just been created. Storing this entry requires us to use a little trick: Because `JSONModel` doesn't have an `addProperty` method, we retrieve all the data from the model with the `getData` method (inherited from `sap.ui.model.json.JSONModel`). This method returns the data in an array. We can push the new entry to the array using the array's own push method, and then replace the complete model data with our new array containing the new entry. However, this is only a good idea if you won't handle large amounts of data within your model. If you do, it would be better to extend the model once more and write the functionality to add entries yourself.

Now, we only need to modify the event handler in edit mode that's invoked when a user clicks on the SAVE button (see Listing 6.25).

```
/**
 * Saves changes to the remote service
 * @function
 */
onSave: function(){
  var sLocalPath,
      oRouter = this.getRouter(),
      sPath = this.getView().getElementBinding().getPath(),
      oModel = this.getModel(),
      oObject = oModel.getProperty(sPath),
      oBundle = this.getResourceBundle();

  //check if we're in edit or create mode
  if(!this.getModel("viewModel").getProperty("/createMode")){
    //we're not, so we update an existing entry
    sUrl = "/Suppliers/" + oObject.id;
    sLocalPath = sPath;
  } else {
    sUrl = "/Suppliers";
  }
  oModel.saveEntry(oObject, sUrl, sLocalPath);
  oModel.attachEventOnce("requestCompleted", function(){
    oRouter.navTo("master");
  }, this);
  oModel.attachEventOnce("requestFailed", function(){
    MessageToast.show(oBundle.getText("updateFailed"));
  });
},
```

Listing 6.25 onSave, Reflecting Create Mode in the Edit View

In Listing 6.25, the functionality we added is in bold. This code determines which view mode we're in. According to the outcome, we set and generate the correct path for the URL. In case of a new supplier, we don't want to use the supplier ID (which would be createEntry) in the request URL, so we omit this part of the path.

We also do not pass sLocalPath in this case, so the saveEntry method in the model will know it's dealing with a create operation, not an update.

Now we can create new suppliers and update existing ones—but how about adding functionality to delete a supplier?

6.3.3   Deleting an Entry

You've created a lot of dummy entries during the development process in the last sections, so you may want to have functionality in place to get rid of those. To do so, we'll first add the `Delete` method to the `AppModel`. The `Delete` method parameters only take the local path from the model as well as the URL of the service, which consists of the supplier path plus the ID of the supplier.

This method will again send an Ajax request, this time using the `Delete` method to remove the entry on the server (see Listing 6.26).

```
deleteEntry : function(sUrl, sLocalPath){
  var that = this;
  jQuery.ajax({
    type : "DELETE",
    contentType : "application/json",
    url : sUrl,
    dataType : "json",
    async: true,
    success : function() {
      //store the new/updated entry in the model
      that._updateModel(sLocalPath, null,  true);
      that.fireRequestCompleted();
    },
    error : function() {
      that.fireRequestFailed();
    }
  });
},
```

Listing 6.26 deleteEntry Method in AppModel

We want to update the model accordingly without sending an unnecessary additional read request to all the suppliers afterwards. We therefore invoke the `_updateModel` method, but we also have to modify it because we now want to remove an entry from the model.

We'll add a third parameter to the method, a Boolean parameter named `bDelete`. When we delete something from the server, we call the method with three parameters: `sLocalPath` in order to identify the object to be deleted, no data (`null`), and `true`. The modified `_updateModel` method will now look like Listing 6.27.

```
_updateModel : function(sLocalPath, data, bDelete){
  var aData = this.getData();
  if (sLocalPath && bDelete) {
```

```
    //remove from model
    aData.splice(sLocalPath.substr(1), 1);
    this.setData(aData);
    this.refresh();
  } else if (sLocalPath) {
    //store data for an existing object
    this.setProperty(sLocalPath, data);
  } else {
    aData.push(data);
this.setData(aData);
  }
```

Listing 6.27 Modified _updateModel Method in AppModel

In Listing 6.27, the added code is in bold. When `bDelete` is true, we need to retrieve all data from the model using `getData`. This method will return an array containing all the suppliers. We can use the native JavaScript `Array.prototype.splice` method to remove the entry we want to delete from this array, and then call `setData` on the model again to update it with the remaining suppliers. We then replace the model data with a modified array. We need to use this trick in the implementation because `JSONModel` does not have any public methods we can use to delete a single entry.

The only step left is to alter the edit controller so that it also invokes the `deleteEntry` method on the model. We'll therefore add a DELETE button to the detail view, right next to the EDIT button, so the footer of our page now looks like Listing 6.28.

```
<footer>
  <Toolbar>
    <ToolbarSpacer />
    <Button text="{i18n>btnEdit}" press="onEdit" />
    <Button text="{i18n>btnDelete}" press="onDelete" />
  </Toolbar>
</footer>
```

Listing 6.28 Added Delete Button to Detail View

We'll then implement a handler for the DELETE button, which we'll call `onDelete` (see Listing 6.29).

```
onDelete : function() {
  var oModel = this.getModel(),
      sLocalPath = this.getView().getElementBinding().getPath(),
      oObject = oModel.getProperty(sLocalPath),
      that = this;
```

```
oModel.deleteEntry("/Suppliers/" + oObject.id, sLocalPath);

oModel.attachEventOnce("requestCompleted", function(){
  that.getRouter().navTo("master");
}, this);

oModel.attachEventOnce("requestFailed", function(){
  MessageToast.show(that.getResourceBundle().getText("deleteFailed"));
});
},
```

Listing 6.29 onDelete in Detail Controller

Here, we're again preparing the local path and passing it together with the URL to the service. We then attach to the `requestCompleted` and `requestFailed` events on the model again, and react with a navigation to the master on success. On error, we want to show a message toast again, this time with a different text: DELETE FAILED.

We need to add the text for the DELETE button and the text for the error message to the i18n.properties files:

```
btnDelete=Delete
deleteFailed=Delete failed
```

6.4   Sorting, Filtering, and Grouping in JSON Models

Now that you know how to create, update, and delete entries in your apps, let's look at how to determine the order of suppliers within the master view, how to filter for values that are currently relevant, and how to group entries together depending on a particular property value they have in common.

Because JSON models are client-side models, sorting, filtering, and grouping functionality is completely implemented in JavaScript. For other models, there are also options to invoke, for example, server-side filters.

Currently, when we create new suppliers in our app, they are added to the model and displayed in the table and sorted. However, we want to sort them by the IDs they have on the service. We can define a sorter for our suppliers now for the ID or name.

6.4.1 Sorting

In the master view, we can pass the `sorting` property as an attribute within the control definition of the table control. In particular, we can add a sorter to the binding definition of the items aggregation, as shown in Listing 6.30. Doing this will give the table a fixed sorting order that will be applied both initially and when bindings are refreshed.

```
<Table
  id="table"
  width="auto"
  class="sapUiResponsiveMargin"
  items="{
    path: '/',
    sorter: {
      path: 'id'
    }
  }"
  noDataText="{i18n>tableNoDataText}">
[...]
</Table>
```
Listing 6.30 Sorting Table Items Table in Master View

But what do we do when we want to give users the opportunity to sort the entries in the list themselves—for example, by clicking on a button? In such a situation, we need to have a dynamic sorting function in place that we can invoke when the user triggers this action.

For this example, we'll give the user the option to sort the suppliers by ID, descending and ascending, and add a sorter for the name. We'll also add a Sort button to the corresponding column headers in the products table. To do so, we'll change the column headers so that they contain a `sap.m.Toolbar` control. This toolbar will handle rendering any buttons in the right place. To enable this control, the table code in Master.view.xml should be enhanced as shown in Listing 6.31.

```
<mvc:View controllerName=
"sapui5.demo.mvcapp.controller.Master" xmlns:mvc=
"sap.ui.core.mvc" xmlns="sap.m">
  <Page id="page"
    navButtonPress="onNavBack"
    showNavButton="true"
    title="{i18n>masterViewTitle}">
    <content>
      <Table id="table"
```

```
width="auto"
class="sapUiResponsiveMargin"
items="{
  path: '/',
  sorter: {
    path: 'id'
  }
}"
noDataText="{i18n>tableNoDataText}">
<headerToolbar>
  <Toolbar>
    <Title id="tableHeader"
      text="{i18n>SuppliersList}" />
    <ToolbarSpacer />
    <Button
      icon="sap-icon://add"
      tooltip="[i18n>btnAddSupplier}"
      press="onAddSupplier"></Button>
  </Toolbar>
</headerToolbar>
<columns>
  <Column id="idColumn">
    <header>
      <Toolbar>
        <Text
          text="{i18n>tableIDColumnTitle}"
          id="IDColumnTitle" />
        <Button
          icon="sap-icon://sort"
          press="onSortID" />
      </Toolbar>
    </header>
  </Column>
  <Column id="nameColumn">
    <header>
      <Toolbar>
        <Text
          text="{i18n>tableNameColumnTitle}"
          id="nameColumnTitle" />
        <Button
          icon="sap-icon://sort"
          press="onSortName" />
      </Toolbar>
    </header>
  </Column>
</columns>
<items>
  <ColumnListItem
    type="Navigation"
    press="onListPress">
```

```
          <cells>
            <ObjectIdentifier
              text="{id}" />
            <ObjectIdentifier
              text="{Name}" />
          </cells>
        </ColumnListItem>
      </items>
    </Table>
  </content>
 </Page>
</mvc:View>
```
Listing 6.31 Detail View with Sorting Buttons in Column Headers

The new column headers are highlighted in bold in Listing 6.31. The master view should now look like Figure 6.3.

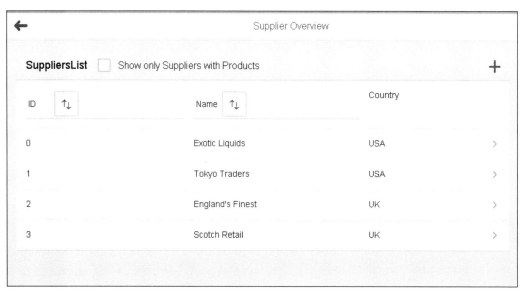

Figure 6.3 Master View with Filter Checkbox: Some Supplier Data Added

When the user clicks on one of our new buttons, we want the sorting to be applied to the list. We hence define additional functions in Master.controller.js that will be invoked via onPress, which will trigger the sorting. We'll initialize the Sorter objects in the onInit event like so:

```
onInit : function () {
this._sorter = new sap.ui.model.Sorter("id", false);
```

```
this._NameSorter = new sap.ui.model.Sorter("Name", false);
},
```

We'll then create a new event handler in the corresponding section of our controller, which will apply the sorting to the table, as shown in Listing 6.32.

```
/**
  * Sorts the products table after ID
  * @function
*/
onSortID:  function(){
  this._IDSorter.bDescending = !this._IDSorter.bDescending;
  this.byId("table").getBinding("items").sort(this._IDSorter);
},
/**
  * Sorts the products table after name
  * @function
*/
onSortName :  function(){
  this._NameSorter.bDescending = !this._NameSorter.bDescending;
  this.byId("table").getBinding("items").sort(this._NameSorter);
},
```

Listing 6.32 Sorting Functions in Master View

The code for both sorters is a bit redundant and could be optimized, but writing it this way makes it easy to see the pattern of what needs to be done.

When you now reload the application, you'll see the new buttons. When a user clicks on one of the buttons, the corresponding function inverts the current sorting direction (descending or ascending) and applies the sorter to the table. Therefore, when you click on one of the new buttons, you should see how the products are sorted on the corresponding column values right away. Because we invert the current value of the bDescending property at the sorter every time a user clicks on the button, the user can switch between ascending and descending sorting with every press.

Note that you can also pass more than one sorter within a binding path, as shown in Listing 6.33.

```
<Table items="{
    path: '/,
    sorter: [{
        path: 'field1',
        descending: false
    }, {
        path: 'field2',
```

```
        descending: true
    }]
  }">
...
</ Table>
```
Listing 6.33 Multiple Sorters

This can be useful if you want to sort by multiple columns—for example, when you have personal data in your application, and you want to first sort by last name and then by first name.

Custom Sorters

You can also write custom sorters, if you want to have some more sophisticated sorting rules then just ascending and descending. A custom sorter is simple to write. You pick the property you want to use for sorting and instantiate the sorter, like so:

```
var oSorter = new sap.ui.model.Sorter("property");
```

Now, you only need to implement the fnCompare function at this sorter. It has to return -1, 0, or +1, depending on whether your algorithm says the current element needs to go before, at the same level as, or after the element it's compared to:

```
oSorter.fnCompare = function(val1, val2) {
if (val1 < val2) return -1;
if (val1 == val2) return 0;
if (val1 > val2) return 1;
};
```

6.4.2 Filtering

The next step will provide users with the ability to filter suppliers. We assume the user wants to see not all suppliers, but only those that have products, so we allow them to filter out the suppliers that do not meet this criterion in the model.

We can implement our own custom filters via the following code:

```
var oFilter = new sap.ui.model.Filter("products");
oFilter.fnTest = function(value) {
return !!value;
};
```

We'll use this approach to define filters in a minute, but first, let's give the user the means to trigger filtering from the UI.

The filter takes a particular path as a parameter to its constructor. In the `fnTest` method we need to implement, a filter simply expects that the test returns true or false, and we can then derive from this if we need to display a supplier in the table or not.

Filters can be invoked on any binding, and you can pass an array of filter options to the filter function like so:

```
oTable.getBinding("items").filter([oFilter1,oFilter2,oFilter3]);
```

We want to apply a filter on user interaction, so we'll add another element to our UI—in this case, `sap.m.Checkbox`. This checkbox will allow the user to decide if he wants to display suppliers without products or not. We'll place this checkbox in the header of the suppliers table in the master view, as shown in Listing 6.34.

```
<Table id="table"
  width="auto"
  class="sapUiResponsiveMargin"
  items="{
    path: '/',
    sorter: {
      path: 'id'
    }
  }"
  noDataText="{i18n>tableNoDataText}">
  <headerToolbar>
    <Toolbar>
      <Title id="tableHeader" text="{i18n>SuppliersList}"/>
      <CheckBox id="cbProducts" text="{i18n>filterSuppliers}"
        select="onFilterSuppliers" />
      <ToolbarSpacer />
      <Button icon="sap-icon://add"
        tooltip="[i18n>btnAddSupplier}"
        press="onAddSupplier"></Button>
    </Toolbar>
  </headerToolbar>
  [...]
```

Listing 6.34 Checkbox for Filter in Supplier's Table Header

We again need to add one more text to the i18n.properties file in order to show the right text next to the checkbox:

```
filterSuppliers=Show only Suppliers with Products
```

Next, we'll initialize the filter in `onInit`. We'll also define the custom filter method that will look for products in the supplier, as shown in Listing 6.35.

```
onInit : function () {
  this._IDSorter = new Sorter("id", false);
  this._NameSorter = new Sorter("Name", false);
  this._suppliersFilter = new Filter({
    path:"products",
    test : function(value) {
      if(value && value.length > 0){
        return true;
      }
    }
  });
},
```

Listing 6.35 Custom Filter Checking a Property's Array Length

Now, we need to invoke this filter on the binding when someone checks the corresponding checkbox in the table header. We'll create a `onFilterSuppliers` method that will contain the necessary code.

At the `oEvent` object that gets passed into this function, we'll find information about whether the control triggering the event has been selected or deselected. We invoke the function `getParameter("selected")` on the object to retrieve this information.

Depending on the returned value, we then either add a new filter and call the filter on the table's binding, or remove the filter again. Because we're simply setting all potential filters to `null`, we need to refresh the table binding, as shown in Listing 6.36.

```
onFilterSuppliers : function(oEvent){
  var oTable = this.getView().byId("table"),
      oTableBinding = oTable.getBinding("items"),
      aFilters = [];
  if(oEvent.getParameter("selected")){
  //the checkbox was selected and we should apply the filter
    aFilters.push(this._suppliersFilter);
    oTableBinding.filter(aFilters);
  } else {
    //the checkbox was unselected, so we unset the filter
    oTableBinding.aFilters = null;
    oTable.getModel().refresh(true);
  }
},
```

Listing 6.36 Applying and Unsetting Filters

Here, we're building an array within the `getParameter("selected")` function, which we then pass to the filter function on the binding. Theoretically, we could use an arbitrary number of filters here, which could go into the `aFilters` array.

Instead of a custom filter, you can also use the predefined filters in SAPUI5, of which there is a whole set. However, like the custom filter we just implemented here, which checks the size of a particular array (the products) at a certain entry (a supplier), the predefined filters have not been preimplemented in the framework.

Instantiating a new filter works like this:

```
new Filter("path", FilterOperator, value1, value2, ));
```

`Path` is the path to the property you want to apply the filter to, `FilterOperator` is one of a list of predefined `sap.ui.model.FilterOperators`, and `value1` and `value2` are property values from the model you can use for comparison. You will not need every parameter for every filter, as you'll see in a minute.

Table 6.1 shows a list of the predefined filters available in SAPUI5.

Filter Operator	Meaning
`sap.ui.model.FilterOperator.BTFilterOperator`	Between, requires two values
`sap.ui.model.FilterOperator.ContainsFilterOperator`	Contains, requires one value
`sap.ui.model.FilterOperator.EndsWithFilterOperator`	Ends with, requires one value
`sap.ui.model.FilterOperator.EQFilterOperator`	Equals, requires one value
`sap.ui.model.FilterOperator.GEFilterOperator`	Greater or equals, requires one value
`sap.ui.model.FilterOperator.GTFilterOperator`	Greater than, requires one value

Table 6.1 Predefined Filter Operators in SAPUI5

You can also influence the way that filters can be combined. By default, when you're using multiple filters, these are combined with an AND conjunction. If you want to use several filters and want an OR conjunction for the different criteria, you need to set the parameter and to false on all filters it should apply to. If you only want the parameter to be applied to a subset of all filters and the rest should be AND conjunctions, you can also specify an array of filters that will be part of this particular OR setting—for example, by invoking the following:

```
sap.ui.model.Filter(aFilters, false);
```

We'll talk more about filtering in Chapter 7, when we discuss OData services in applications.

Let's combine our custom filter with a predefined filter now. We want to a second sap.m.CheckBox element in the table's headerToolbar to allow users to filter for suppliers from within a certain country. If you're living in the United States, for example, you may only want to see US suppliers, because their shipping rates will be usually cheaper.

We can add a second checkbox right next to the first one. Listing 6.37 shows the new table headerToolbar aggregation in the master view.

```
<headerToolbar>
  <Toolbar>
    <Title id="tableHeader" text="{i18n>SuppliersList}"/>
    <CheckBox id="cbProducts" text="{i18n>filterSuppliers}" select=
"onFilterSuppliers" />
    <CheckBox id="cbCountry" text=
"{i18n>filterSuppliersForCountry}" select="onFilterSuppliers" />
    <ToolbarSpacer />
    <Button icon="sap-icon://add" tooltip=
"{i18n>btnAddSupplier}" press="onAddSupplier"></Button>
  </Toolbar>
</headerToolbar>
```
Listing 6.37 Header Toolbar in Master View with New Checkbox

Next, we need functionality in the master controller that will allow us to apply one or both of these filters to the table bindings. We could, of course, just copy and adapt the function from the first filter, but that wouldn't allow us to easily remove a single filter again when we uncheck one box. Another downside of that approach is that it would lead to some redundant code. Hence, we'll need to refactor the code a bit so that most of the functionality can be used for an arbitrary number of filters.

We'll add the new filter to the master view in onInit again, along with another member variable at the view we will call this._aFilters (because it's going to be an array).

The modified onInit will contain the code shown in Listing 6.38.

```
onInit : function () {
  this._IDSorter = new Sorter("id", false);
  this._NameSorter = new Sorter("Name", false);
  this._suppliersFilter = new Filter({
    path:"products",
    test : function(value) {
      if(value && value.length > 0){
        return true;
      }
    }
  });
  this._countryFilter = new Filter({path: "Address/Country", operator:
sap.ui.model.FilterOperator.EQ, value1:"USA"});
  this._aFilters = [];
},
```

Listing 6.38 Modified onInit in Master View Controller to Add Second Filter

The new code is highlighted in bold in Listing 6.38. this._countryFilter uses one of the predefined filter operators—namely, the equals operator. Therefore, the filter will check if the value of any of the entries in the binding under the (Address/Country) path equals the value1 parameter ("USA") given in the filter constructor call.

Now we have the filter instance, but it isn't applied anywhere yet. To apply it, we'll reuse the onFilterSuppliers event handler we implemented previously and enhance it so that it knows which checkbox has just been checked. To do so, we'll check the event source for a particular sId property. In any UI-triggered event in SAPUI5, this parameter will contain the ID of the control that caused the event to be fired.

We can retrieve this ID in the event handler by invoking the getSource method on the event object, which, as previously mentioned, is passed to the handler by default.

Depending on which of the checkboxes is selected or deselected, we want to add or remove the correct filter from the binding.

The new `onFilterSuppliers` function will now contain the code shown in Listing 6.39.

```
onFilterSuppliers : function(oEvent){
  var oFilter,
      bAdd = oEvent.getParameter("selected"),
      oTable = this.getView().byId("table"),
      oTableBinding = oTable.getBinding("items");

  if (oEvent.getSource().sId === this.createId("cbProducts")){
    oFilter = this._suppliersFilter;
  } else {
    oFilter = this._countryFilter;
  }

  this._changeFilters(oFilter, oTableBinding, bAdd);
},
```

Listing 6.39 Modified onFilterSuppliers Method in Master Controller

Here, we want to call a private function (`_changeFilters`) on the controller when a filter is added or removed. We therefore added a Boolean variable, `bAdd`, to the function, which will now provide information about whether a checkbox has been selected or deselected by checking against the event parameter. We pass this information on to the new `_changeFilters` method, along with the filter to be applied and the binding on which the filter will be applied (see Listing 6.40).

```
_changeFilters : function (oFilter, oBinding, bAdd){
  if (bAdd){
    this._aFilters.push(oFilter);
  } else {
  //using the native JavaScript function Array.prototype.filter here:
    this._aFilters = this._aFilters.filter(function (filter) {
      return filter.sPath !== oFilter.sPath;
    });
  }
  oBinding.filter(this._aFilters);
},
```

Listing 6.40 Private _changeFilters Method Adding or Removing Filters from Binding

Within the method, we can decide, depending on the `bAdd` parameter, whether to add or remove a filter. For adding, we simply push our new filter to the `this._aFilters` array. For removal, we use the `Array.prototype.filter` method built into native JavaScript to delete the filter from the array `this._aFilters`. (Please don't confuse the filter method on an SAPUI5 binding with the native filter method on JavaScript arrays.)

Eventually, we have to invoke the filter method on the table binding, again represented in this method by the `oBinding` object.

6.4.3 Grouping

You now know how to sort and filter bindings, but there is also another method you can use to display data in different ways to your users: grouping. With *grouping*, you can have similar entries form groups that will be displayed differently in some SAPUI5 controls—like our table, for example.

Now, let's look at the desired outcome first before we go into the implementation details so that you know in advance why you're doing this (see Figure 6.4).

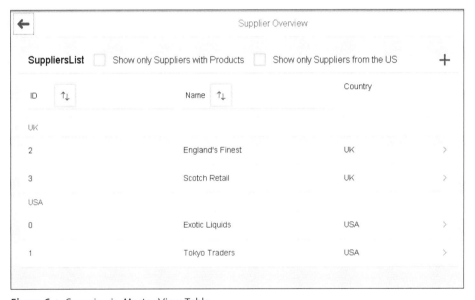

Figure 6.4 Grouping in Master View Table

Figure 6.4 shows how grouping works for the data displayed in the table. In the figure, the suppliers table has received a new column, COUNTRY, and data is grouped by country. `sap.m.Table` will automatically group the entries with the same countries together and will also create group headers.

Note that it is not necessary to display the data you want to group by in a table column; it's sufficient to have the data in the binding. We're displaying the additional column here because it makes it easier to check whether the grouping function has worked correctly.

Initial Grouping

Having data initially grouped by a particular value is easy. Remember how we defined the sort parameter on items binding in the master view? We changed the binding itself within the view, adding the path to sort by.

We can extend this code by now setting an additional group attribute and changing the path of the sorter to the `Address/Country` of our suppliers (see Listing 6.41).

```
<Table
  id="table"
  width="auto"
  class="sapUiResponsiveMargin"
  items="{
    path: '/',
      sorter: {
      path: 'Address/Country',
        group: true
      }
  }"
noDataText="{i18n>tableNoDataText}">
```

Listing 6.41 Sort and Group Table in Master View by Country

This will produce the output you saw back in Figure 6.4. However, when a user now clicks on one of the SORT buttons in the table column headers, the grouping will be discarded and the entries will simply be sorted by the corresponding column's data.

To get the grouping back, we can add another button that will us allow to trigger this behavior dynamically. We'll look at this new button in the next section.

Grouping on a User Input

The new button will go into the header toolbar of the table again, next to the filter buttons (see Listing 6.42).

```
<headerToolbar>
  <Toolbar>
    <Title id="tableHeader" text="{i18n>SuppliersList}"/>
    <CheckBox id="cbProducts" text="{i18n>filterSuppliers}" select=
"onFilterSuppliers" />
    <CheckBox id="cbCountry" text=
"{i18n>filterSuppliersForCountry}" select="onFilterSuppliers" />
    <Button icon="sap-icon://group-2" id="btnGroup" text=
"{i18n>btnGroupByCountry}" press="onGroupByCountry" />
    <ToolbarSpacer />
    <Button icon="sap-icon://add" tooltip=
"{i18n>btnAddSupplier}" press="onAddSupplier"></Button>
  </Toolbar>
</headerToolbar>
```

Listing 6.42 Group Button in Master View

The code for the new button is highlighted in Listing 6.42. We are using the
group-2 icon from the SAP icon font and the text key btnGroupByCountry. The latter still needs to be defined in the i18n.properties file, where we'll add the following line:

```
btnGroupByCountry=Group Suppliers by Country
```

Next, we'll implement the corresponding event handler onGroupByCountry in the
master controller. To make this work, we have to add a new dependency in the
controller's define section: sap.ui.model.Sorter. Because only adjacent entries
with similar properties can be grouped, the entire group functionality is implemented into the Sorter class, not into its own Group class as one might assume
(see Listing 6.43).

```
sap.ui.define([
  "sapui5/demo/mvcapp/controller/BaseController",
  "sap/ui/model/Sorter",
  "sap/ui/model/Filter",
  "sap/ui/model/FilterOperator"
], function (BaseController, Sorter, Filter, FilterOperator) {
```

Listing 6.43 Adding sap.ui.model.Sorter to Master Controller

Now that we have the Sorter class available in the controller, we can start working with it. We'll create a new Sorter here with the parameters "Address/Coun-
try" (the binding path), false (sets descending order to false), and true (sets
grouping to true; see Listing 6.44).

261

```
onGroupByCountry : function(){
  // sort first, as only adjacent rows can be grouped
  var oSorter = new Sorter("Address/Country", false, true);
  this.byId("table").getBinding("items").sort(oSorter);
},
```
Listing 6.44 onGroupByCountry in Master Controller

Note that without the `group` parameter set to `true`, you could also use such a sorter to simply sort entries for some binding without user input or declaring it in a view. Also note that to unset a sorter, you can call the `sort` function on the binding with null as parameter instead of a sorter instance.

6.5   Summary

In this chapter, you learned how to connect to a remote service using `JSONModel` from SAPUI5. You also saw that there's a bit of coding you need to do yourself in order to not send out too many requests, for example, or to store or remove new data simultaneously in the model and on the server. You've also seen how you can handle the data locally, by applying filters and sorting and grouping your model entries.

However, there's another model based on a particular type of REST service that allows you to use a lot more functionality, like filtering and sorting the data when it's loaded from the service by using corresponding parameters in the request. This type of service allows you to lazy load data and only request it when it's needed. This also allows for an elegant paging mechanism we could not easily have achieved in our JSON model.

This particular REST service type is called OData, and it will be covered in the next chapter.

In this chapter, you'll learn all you need to know about OData and how to use it within SAPUI5. This will help you build CRUD applications with an OData backend.

7   Using OData

In the previous chapter, we looked at the principles behind REST and how CRUD operations are performed via HTTP verbs (`POST`, `GET`, `PUT`, and `DELETE`). This knowledge comes in handy when working with OData, because OData is based on REST principles.

In this chapter, we'll discuss some the basics of OData, such as entity types, associations, and navigation properties. Then, we'll walk through why SAP has chosen OData as its preferred protocol to exchange data.

In previous chapters, we looked at the SAPUI5 JSON model and started building small and simple examples to explore all the different possibilities available. Now, we'll do the same with the SAPUI5 OData model. We'll implement similar coding as in the previous chapters. The similarity is intentional: Most of the coding will look familiar to you, but you'll also notice some slight differences. Throughout the rest of this chapter, you'll also notice the built-in convenience from the OData model in areas such as filtering, sorting, and thresholds.

A lot of the details you learned in Chapter 5 are also true for OData, so we'll mainly highlight the differences here. In this chapter, we'll focus on simple examples, but in the next chapter, we'll look at OData applications and explore further possibilities of the OData model.

7.1   OData at a Glance

OData is an open, HTTP-based protocol for consuming, querying, and exposing data on the web. The idea behind OData is to provide a common way to access, query, and modify data without the need to learn new APIs for accessing all the different data sources from all over the web.

OData was initiated by Microsoft in 2007 and is published with an Open Specification Promise, so anyone can build servers, clients, or tools without royalties or restrictions. OData is also an OASIS standard, which define best practices for building and consuming RESTful APIs.

The standardized ways to query OData with a simple yet powerful query language has led to it being called Open Database Connectivity (ODBC) for the Web. *ODBC* is a standard programming language middleware API for accessing *database management systems* (DBMS).

7.1.1   Northwind OData Service

Before we continue with technical details about OData itself, let's dive into an OData service and see it in action. We'll use the publicly available Northwind service. In previous chapters, you worked with some datasets for products and suppliers; now, you'll see where that data originally came from.

Northwind OData Service

You can access this service via *http://services.odata.org/V3/Northwind/Northwind.svc/*.

Figure 7.1 shows an extract from the Northwind service with the relevant data we'll examine. The screenshot was taken from the XOData tool, which is a publicly available tool for exploring OData services. The tool has the Northwind service already set for exploration.

XOData Tool

You can access the XOData tool screen via *http://pragmatiqa.com/xodata/*.

In Figure 7.1, you'll see different objects, like `Product`, `Supplier`, and `Category`. In OData terms, those objects are called *entity sets*.

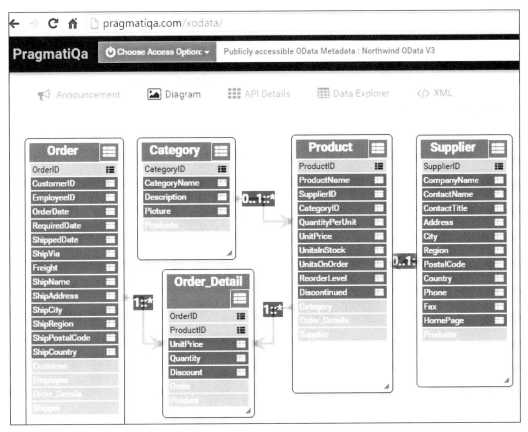

Figure 7.1 Northwind Service in XOData Tool

Figure 7.1 shows the *entity data model* (EDM), which describes the entities with their properties, keys, and their relations to each other (associations and navigation properties).

In the `Product` entity set, you'll see familiar properties like `ProductID`, `Product-Name`, and `UnitPrice`. In the `Supplier` entity set, you'll see other familiar properties, like `SupplierID`, `CompanyName`, and `Address`.

Notice that the connection between `Product` and `Supplier`, which is indicated with an arrow and the text "0..1". This describes the association between those two entries: A product can have zero suppliers or one supplier.

At the bottom of the `Product` entry, we see three entries: `Category`, `Order_Details`, and `Supplier`. The `Supplier` has one entry: `Products`. Those entries are called *navigation properties*. This means that `Product` has some kind of relation to `Supplier` and vice versa. Keep this in mind; we'll see this relationship in action soon.

7.1.2 Service Document

Now that we have a high-level overview of the service, we can start to explore it. Open the Northwind service URL, *http://services.odata.org/V3/Northwind/Northwind.svc/*, in Microsoft Internet Explorer or Google Chrome.

some quirks occur in some browsers when displaying OData services, such as bad formatting when there is too much data (Google Chrome) or not displaying all the data (Firefox). We recommend using Microsoft Internet Explorer for exploring OData services or using the XML Viewer plugin for Google Chrome.

Displaying OData

The simplest way to display OData is with Microsoft Internet Explorer.

You can alternatively use Google Chrome with the XML Viewer plugin.

CRUD Operations

To perform CRUD operations on OData services we can use the Postman or the Advanced REST client Google Chrome plugin. We have listed both in Appendix E.

Figure 7.2 shows part of the Northwind service with the `Product` and `Supplier` entity sets highlighted. This portion is called the *service document*.

The service document tells us when we can browse certain collections, like `Products` or `Suppliers`. The collections are the entity sets you saw in the XOData model (refer back to Figure 7.1). Before we look into these different collections and their data, let's further examine the service itself.

Figure 7.2 Northwind Service Document

7.1.3 Service Metadata Document

We want to know where to find information such as ID or Name for those entity sets in the service. To do so, simply add *$metadata* at the end of the service URL:

http://services.odata.org/V3/Northwind/Northwind.svc/$metadata

In the *service metadata document*, you'll find information about all the properties from an entity set or the associations and navigation properties between entity sets. Figure 7.3 and Figure 7.4 show the metadata from Products and Supplier, respectively.

```
- <EntityType Name="Product">
   - <Key>
       <PropertyRef Name="ProductID"/>
     </Key>
     <Property Name="ProductID"
         xmlns:p6="http://schemas.microsoft.com/ado/2009/02/edm/annotation"
         p6:StoreGeneratedPattern="Identity" Nullable="false" Type="Edm.Int32"/>
     <Property Name="ProductName" Nullable="false" Type="Edm.String" Unicode="true"
         FixedLength="false" MaxLength="40"/>
     <Property Name="SupplierID" Type="Edm.Int32"/>
     <Property Name="CategoryID" Type="Edm.Int32"/>
     <Property Name="QuantityPerUnit" Type="Edm.String" Unicode="true" FixedLength="false"
         MaxLength="20"/>
     <Property Name="UnitPrice" Type="Edm.Decimal" Scale="4" Precision="19"/>
     <Property Name="UnitsInStock" Type="Edm.Int16"/>
     <Property Name="UnitsOnOrder" Type="Edm.Int16"/>
     <Property Name="ReorderLevel" Type="Edm.Int16"/>
     <Property Name="Discontinued" Nullable="false" Type="Edm.Boolean"/>
     <NavigationProperty Name="Category" FromRole="Products" ToRole="Categories"
         Relationship="NorthwindModel.FK_Products_Categories"/>
     <NavigationProperty Name="Order_Details" FromRole="Products" ToRole="Order_Details"
         Relationship="NorthwindModel.FK_Order_Details_Products"/>
     <NavigationProperty Name="Supplier" FromRole="Products" ToRole="Suppliers"
         Relationship="NorthwindModel.FK_Products_Suppliers"/>
  </EntityType>
```

Figure 7.3 Northwind Product Entity Set Metadata

```
- <EntityType Name="Supplier">
   - <Key>
       <PropertyRef Name="SupplierID"/>
     </Key>
     <Property Name="SupplierID"
         xmlns:p6="http://schemas.microsoft.com/ado/2009/02/edm/annotation"
         p6:StoreGeneratedPattern="Identity" Nullable="false" Type="Edm.Int32"/>
     <Property Name="CompanyName" Nullable="false" Type="Edm.String" Unicode="true"
         FixedLength="false" MaxLength="40"/>
     <Property Name="ContactName" Type="Edm.String" Unicode="true" FixedLength="false"
         MaxLength="30"/>
     <Property Name="ContactTitle" Type="Edm.String" Unicode="true" FixedLength="false"
         MaxLength="30"/>
     <Property Name="Address" Type="Edm.String" Unicode="true" FixedLength="false"
         MaxLength="60"/>
     <Property Name="City" Type="Edm.String" Unicode="true" FixedLength="false" MaxLength="15"/>
     <Property Name="Region" Type="Edm.String" Unicode="true" FixedLength="false" MaxLength="15"/>
     <Property Name="PostalCode" Type="Edm.String" Unicode="true" FixedLength="false"
         MaxLength="10"/>
     <Property Name="Country" Type="Edm.String" Unicode="true" FixedLength="false"
         MaxLength="15"/>
     <Property Name="Phone" Type="Edm.String" Unicode="true" FixedLength="false" MaxLength="24"/>
     <Property Name="Fax" Type="Edm.String" Unicode="true" FixedLength="false" MaxLength="24"/>
     <Property Name="HomePage" Type="Edm.String" Unicode="true" FixedLength="false"
         MaxLength="Max"/>
     <NavigationProperty Name="Products" FromRole="Suppliers" ToRole="Products"
         Relationship="NorthwindModel.FK_Products_Suppliers"/>
  </EntityType>
```

Figure 7.4 Northwind Supplier Entity Set Metadata

Let's look at the navigation properties of those two entities. Figure 7.5 shows an extract of the whole metadata file. There you'll see the relationship between a *navigation property* and an *association*. A navigation property is an *implemented association*, which means that you can make use of the association between two entities in order to navigate. In the example application, we'd use this property to navigate to the supplier of a certain product or to show all products of a certain supplier.

```
Products
<NavigationProperty Name="Supplier" FromRole="Products" ToRole="Suppliers"
     Relationship="NorthwindModel.FK_Products_Suppliers"/>

Supplier
<NavigationProperty Name="Products" FromRole="Suppliers" ToRole="Products"
     Relationship="NorthwindModel.FK_Products_Suppliers"/>
```

```
Association
- <Association Name="FK_Products_Suppliers">
      <End Type="NorthwindModel.Supplier" Multiplicity="0..1" Role="Suppliers"/>
      <End Type="NorthwindModel.Product" Multiplicity="*" Role="Products"/>
   - <ReferentialConstraint>
      - <Principal Role="Suppliers">
           <PropertyRef Name="SupplierID"/>
        </Principal>
      - <Dependent Role="Products">
           <PropertyRef Name="SupplierID"/>
        </Dependent>
     </ReferentialConstraint>
  </Association>

Association Set
- <AssociationSet Name="FK_Products_Suppliers"
    Association="NorthwindModel.FK_Products_Suppliers">
      <End Role="Products" EntitySet="Products"/>
      <End Role="Suppliers" EntitySet="Suppliers"/>
  </AssociationSet>
```

Figure 7.5 Relationship between Navigation Property and Association: Shortened metadata.xml File

7.1.4 Accessing Data

Now that you've seen the available entities, their relationships to each other, and their properties, we can start to explore some data. To view the data of a service, we attach the entity type name to the base URL of the service; we find the base URL of the service by accessing the service definition in the browser, as shown in Figure 7.6.

For the Northwind service, the base URL is *http://services.odata.org/V3/Northwind/Northwind.svc/*.

Figure 7.6 Service Base URL

Read Entity Set: Products

When we add the name of the collection—in this case, `Products`—at the end of the base URL, we can display the products data. Enter the following URL in your browser:

http://services.odata.org/V3/Northwind/Northwind.svc/Products

Figure 7.7 shows the data for the entity.

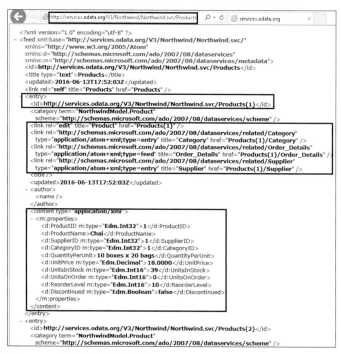

Figure 7.7 Products Entity Set

Let's look at the response and what it means. Table 7.1 lists the different XML nodes and what they mean.

XML Node	Meaning
`<feed></feed>`	`<feed>` contains a collection of zero or more `<entry>` elements.
`<entry ></entry>`	The `<entry>` element contains the data for one element of the feed's collection.
`<id></id>`	Each entry has an ID, which represents the key fields of the entity.
`<link></link>`	The `<link>` elements point to related business data.
`<content></content>`	The `<content>` area contains the actual business data.

Table 7.1 XML Nodes and Their Meanings

The other properties like `<title>`, `<author>`, or `<updated>` remind us that the OData protocol is derived from the Atom specification. The relevant data we are interested in is stored in the `<content>` section of the document. We see the name of properties like `ProductID` and `ProductName` and their corresponding data types.

Read Entity

Now, let's read a single entity. In Figure 7.7, we've seen in the `<id>` and in the `<link>` section that we can read the first entity with `Products(1)`. The `(1)` is the key value of this particular entity. Let's enter this URL in our browser:

http://services.odata.org/V3/Northwind/Northwind.svc/Products(1)

We get only one entity back, which we can see in Figure 7.8.

It's also possible to access a single property of an entity if you add the name of the property to the URL. Let's access the product name of the first product by adding */ProductName* at the end of the URL:

http://services.odata.org/V3/Northwind/Northwind.svc/Products(1)/ProductName

The response in Figure 7.9 shows only information about the product name.

Figure 7.8 First Product Entry

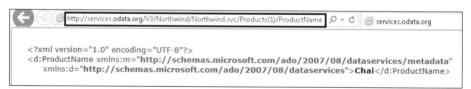

Figure 7.9 Product Name of Product 1

Navigation

Now that we're looking at a certain entity in the dataset, we can navigate to another entity. Figure 7.8 shows that the last `<link>` type points to the supplier for this product. Now, enter the following URL in your browser:

http://services.odata.org/V3/Northwind/Northwind.svc/Products(1)/Supplier

Figure 7.10 shows the corresponding supplier for the product with the ID of 1.

```
  http://services.odata.org/V3/Northwind/Northwind.svc/Products(1)/Supplier    ρ ▾ ℃      services.odata.org

  <?xml version="1.0" encoding="utf-8" ?>
- <entry xml:base="http://services.odata.org/V3/Northwind/Northwind.svc/" xmlns="http://ww
    xmlns:d="http://schemas.microsoft.com/ado/2007/08/dataservices"
    xmlns:m="http://schemas.microsoft.com/ado/2007/08/dataservices/metadata">
    <id>http://services.odata.org/V3/Northwind/Northwind.svc/Suppliers(1)</id>
    <category term="NorthwindModel.Supplier"
      scheme="http://schemas.microsoft.com/ado/2007/08/dataservices/scheme" />
    <link rel="edit" title="Supplier" href="Suppliers(1)" />
    <link rel="http://schemas.microsoft.com/ado/2007/08/dataservices/related/Products"
      type="application/atom+xml;type=feed" title="Products" href="Suppliers(1)/Products" />
    <title />
    <updated>2016-06-13T17:58:53Z</updated>
-   <author>
      <name />
    </author>
-   <content type="application/xml">
-     <m:properties>
        <d:SupplierID m:type="Edm.Int32">1</d:SupplierID>
        <d:CompanyName>Exotic Liquids</d:CompanyName>
        <d:ContactName>Charlotte Cooper</d:ContactName>
        <d:ContactTitle>Purchasing Manager</d:ContactTitle>
        <d:Address>49 Gilbert St.</d:Address>
        <d:City>London</d:City>
        <d:Region m:null="true" />
        <d:PostalCode>EC1 4SD</d:PostalCode>
        <d:Country>UK</d:Country>
        <d:Phone>(171) 555-2222 </d:Phone>
        <d:Fax m:null="true" />
        <d:HomePage m:null="true" />
      </m:properties>
    </content>
  </entry>
```

Figure 7.10 Supplier for Product 1

We can now display all products for this supplier. In Figure 7.10, in the <id> section we see that the supplier also has the ID 1: Supplier(1). In the <link> section, we see the that we can access all products for the supplier with *Supplier(1)/Products*. Now, add this information to the base URL and enter the resulting URL in your browser:

http://services.odata.org/V3/Northwind/Northwind.svc/Suppliers(1)/Products

Figure 7.11 shows all the products for supplier 1.

```
http://services.odata.org/V3/Northwind/Northwind.svc/Suppliers(1)/Products    🔍 ▾ ♂    🌐 services.odata.org    ✕
```
```xml
<?xml version="1.0" encoding="utf-8" ?>
- <feed xml:base="http://services.odata.org/V3/Northwind/Northwind.svc/" xmlns="http://www.w3.org/
    xmlns:d="http://schemas.microsoft.com/ado/2007/08/dataservices"
    xmlns:m="http://schemas.microsoft.com/ado/2007/08/dataservices/metadata">
    <id>http://services.odata.org/V3/Northwind/Northwind.svc/Suppliers(1)/Products</id>
    <title type="text">Products</title>
    <updated>2016-06-13T18:02:10Z</updated>
    <link rel="self" title="Products" href="Products" />
  - <entry>
      <id>http://services.odata.org/V3/Northwind/Northwind.svc/Products(1)</id>
      <category term="NorthwindModel.Product"
        scheme="http://schemas.microsoft.com/ado/2007/08/dataservices/scheme" />
      <link rel="edit" title="Product" href="Products(1)" />
      <link rel="http://schemas.microsoft.com/ado/2007/08/dataservices/related/Category"
        type="application/atom+xml;type=entry" title="Category" href="Products(1)/Category" />
      <link rel="http://schemas.microsoft.com/ado/2007/08/dataservices/related/Order_Details"
        type="application/atom+xml;type=feed" title="Order_Details" href="Products(1)/Order_Details" />
      <link rel="http://schemas.microsoft.com/ado/2007/08/dataservices/related/Supplier"
        type="application/atom+xml;type=entry" title="Supplier" href="Products(1)/Supplier" />
      <title />
      <updated>2016-06-13T18:02:10Z</updated>
    - <author>
        <name />
      </author>
    - <content type="application/xml">
      - <m:properties>
          <d:ProductID m:type="Edm.Int32">1</d:ProductID>
          <d:ProductName>Chai</d:ProductName>
          <d:SupplierID m:type="Edm.Int32">1</d:SupplierID>
          <d:CategoryID m:type="Edm.Int32">1</d:CategoryID>
          <d:QuantityPerUnit>10 boxes x 20 bags</d:QuantityPerUnit>
          <d:UnitPrice m:type="Edm.Decimal">18.0000</d:UnitPrice>
          <d:UnitsInStock m:type="Edm.Int16">39</d:UnitsInStock>
          <d:UnitsOnOrder m:type="Edm.Int16">0</d:UnitsOnOrder>
          <d:ReorderLevel m:type="Edm.Int16">10</d:ReorderLevel>
          <d:Discontinued m:type="Edm.Boolean">false</d:Discontinued>
        </m:properties>
      </content>
    </entry>
  - <entry>
      <id>http://services.odata.org/V3/Northwind/Northwind.svc/Products(2)</id>
      <category term="NorthwindModel.Product"
```

Figure 7.11 Products of Supplier 1

Let's examine the last important navigation property of the products entity. Each product belongs to a certain category, and we'll need this category information later on when we create a new product. You can find information about the category of a certain product by looking at the <link> property:

```
<link rel="http://schemas.microsoft.com/ado/2007/08/dataservices/
related/Category" type="application/atom+xml;type=entry" title=
"Category" href="Products(1)/Category" />
```

To find the category of product 1, enter the following URL in your browser:

http://services.odata.org/V3/Northwind/Northwind.svc/Products(1)/Category

Figure 7.12 shows the category information for product 1. At this point, you've accessed all the data in the browser and gained a basic knowledge of OData, so now we can continue to implement some examples with SAPUI5 and the OData model. While doing this, we'll continue to deepen your knowledge of OData.

```xml
<?xml version="1.0" encoding="utf-8" ?>
- <entry xml:base="http://services.odata.org/V3/Northwind/Northwind.svc/" xmlns="http://www
    xmlns:d="http://schemas.microsoft.com/ado/2007/08/dataservices"
    xmlns:m="http://schemas.microsoft.com/ado/2007/08/dataservices/metadata">
    <id>http://services.odata.org/V3/Northwind/Northwind.svc/Categories(1)</id>
    <category term="NorthwindModel.Category"
      scheme="http://schemas.microsoft.com/ado/2007/08/dataservices/scheme" />
    <link rel="edit" title="Category" href="Categories(1)" />
    <link rel="http://schemas.microsoft.com/ado/2007/08/dataservices/related/Products"
      type="application/atom+xml;type=feed" title="Products" href="Categories(1)/Products" />
    <title />
    <updated>2016-06-13T18:08:00Z</updated>
  - <author>
      <name />
    </author>
  - <content type="application/xml">
    - <m:properties>
        <d:CategoryID m:type="Edm.Int32">1</d:CategoryID>
        <d:CategoryName>Beverages</d:CategoryName>
        <d:Description>Soft drinks, coffees, teas, beers, and ales</d:Description>
        <d:Picture
          m:type="Edm.Binary">FRwvAAIAAAANAA4AFAAhAP////9CaXRtYXAgSW1hZ2UUAUGFpbnQ
      </m:properties>
    </content>
</entry>
```

Figure 7.12 Product 1 Category

7.2   OData Model at a Glance

The OData model is used to consume data from the OData backend. In contrast to the JSON model, the OData model is a server-side model. All of the data is only available on the server; the client only knows the currently visible (and requested) data. All operations like sorting and filtering are done on the server. The client sends the request to the server and receives the corresponding data. Hence, the new SAPUI5 OData v2 model also supports client-side sorting and filtering.

SAPUI5 implements two version of the OData model:

- ▸ `sap.ui.model.odata.ODataModel` (deprecated)
- ▸ `sap.ui.model.odata.v2.ODataModel`

Version *v2* in the later model has nothing to do with OData version 2.0; it only indicates that it's the more advanced OData model version with an improved features set. We recommend using the v2 version, and that's the version we'll use in this book as well.

Note

The OData model currently supports OData version 2.0.

Table 7.2 presents an overview of the differences between the two models. This table was taken from the "Instantiating on OData Model" section of the SAPUI5 documentation.

Feature	v2 ODataModel	Deprecated ODataModel
OData version support	2.0	2.0
JSON format	Yes (default)	Yes
XML format	Yes	Yes (default)
Support of two-way binding mode	Yes; for property changes only, not yet implemented for aggregations	Experimental; only properties of one entity can be changed at the same time
Client-side sorting and filtering	Yes	No
`$batch`	Yes (default); all requests can be batched	Only manual batch requests
Data cache in model	All data is cached in the model	Manually requested data is not cached
Automatic refresh	Yes (default)	Yes
Message handling	Yes	No

Table 7.2 OData Model Differences

When we want to access the backend, we must be aware of the *same-origin policy* security concept, which means that it's not possible to access data from different domains or sites.

When hosting the SAPUI5 application under the same domain as the backend service, we'll have no problems accessing the data. This is the case when we use SAP Gateway as the frontend UI server and when the OData service is also hosted on SAP Gateway.

In our SAPUI5 Northwind example, we are going to access the backend from a different domain. In Appendix B, you'll find detailed instructions on how to access this data and overcome the same-origin policy.

To instantiate an OData model, we need to provide the service URL in the model constructor. There are two ways to instantiate the model; one uses the service URL directly, and the other uses an object. Both options are shown in Listing 7.1.

```
// the mandatory service URL
var sServiceURL = "http://services.odata.org/Northwind/Northwind.svc/";

// instantiation with the service URL directly
var oModel = new sap.ui.model.odata.v2.ODataModel(sServiceURL);

// instantation with the service URL in an object
var oModel = new sap.ui.model.odata.v2.ODataModel({
  serviceUrl: sServiceURL
});
```

Listing 7.1 Instantiation of OData Model

Note

Every OData model is bound to a certain service URL, so if you want to access different services, you have to create multiple OData model instances.

7.2.1 Service Metadata

After instantiating the model with the service URL, a call to the backend is triggered automatically and requests the service metadata:

http://services.odata.org/Northwind/Northwind.svc/$metadata

The service metadata is cached per service URL, so multiple OData models with the same service URL can share the metadata document. Only the first model will trigger a `$metadata` request.

In the OData v2 model, the service metadata document is loaded asynchronously; it's impossible to load it synchronously. You can listen to the event when the metadata has finished loading with the `metadataLoaded` event. You'll need to attach the `metadataLoaded` function event to the model with `attachMetadata-Loaded`. After that, the metadata will be available in the model and can be accessed with `oModel.getServiceMetadata()`:

```
oModel.attachMetadataLoaded(function() {
  var oMetaData = oModel.getServiceMetadata();
  console.log("Service Metadata", oMetaData);
});
```

The opposite event when the metadata loading has failed is called `metadata-Failed` and you can attach to it via the model with `attachMetadataFailed`.

Figure 7.13 shows the output of the console. We expanded some information about the product. You'll see information about the service as you've seen previously in this chapter, but this time in JSON representation.

Figure 7.13 Service Metadata Information in JSON Format

7.2.2   Instantiating the OData Model in the SAP Web IDE

Previously, we mentioned that you must be aware of the same-origin policy (see Appendix B) when accessing the backend. In the SAP Web IDE in the cloud, we have the ability to use the *connectivity service* from SAP HANA Cloud Platform (HCP). This service acts as a proxy server, allowing us to access the data from the backend.

When accessing the backend with the SAP Web IDE, we must keep three things in mind:

1. **Connection to the backend**

   The destination is set up in SAP HCP (Figure 7.14).

Figure 7.14 Northwind Destination in SAP HANA Cloud Platform

   The destination points to *http://services.odata.org*.

2. **Include the destination in** `neo-app.json`

   In `neo-app.json`, the connection to the backend destination must be added as shown in Listing 7.2.

```
{   "routes": [
  ...
  {
      "path": "/destinations/northwind",
      "target": {
        "type": "destination",
        "name": "northwind"
      },
      "description": "northwind"
  } ...
```

Listing 7.2 Northwind Destination in neo-app.json

3. **Change the service URL**

Use the URL path we have defined in the `neo-app.json` to access the backend as shown in Listing 7.3.

```
// we don't access the backend directly
/* var sServiceURL = "http://services.odata.org/Northwind/North-
wind.svc/"; */

// we use the destination instead
var sServiceURL = "/destinations/northwind/V3/Northwind/North-
wind.svc/";
```

Listing 7.3 Accessing the Backend via the SAP HCP Destination Service

- The destination points to *http://services.odata.org*.
- The path in `neo-app.json` is `"/destinations/northwind"`.

The service URL is

`"/destinations/northwind/V3/Northwind/Northwind.svc/"`.

In the end, the final call to the backend should be resolved to this URL:

http://services.odata.org/V3/Northwind/Northwind.svc/

We say should because the call will be sent to the backend via a URL that includes the name of the destination. When your application is deployed to SAP HCP, then the URL looks like this (line breaks have been added for better readability):

https://yourapp-yourtrialaccount.dispatcher.hanatrial.ondemand.com/destinations/ northwind/V3/Northwind/Northwind.svc/

If your app is not deployed, the first part of the URL changes to this:

https://webidetestingdynamicnumber-yourtrialaccount...

We'll see this in action later when we test our application.

Now, let's instantiate the model and check the loading of the metadata from the service. The coding of the whole HTML page is shown in Listing 7.4. We'll deactivate the batch functionality and enable it later again in order to more easily inspect the backend calls, because they are not batched together in one big request; they're sent one by one.

```
<!DOCTYPE HTML>
<html>
<head>
  <meta http-equiv="X-UA-Compatible" content="IE=edge" />
  <meta charset="UTF-8">
  <title>OData Model Init Metadata</title>
  <script id="sap-ui-bootstrap" src="../resources/sap-ui-core.js"
    data-sap-ui-libs="sap.m" data-sap-ui-theme="sap_bluecrystal"
    data-sap-ui-compatVersion="edge"
    data-sap-ui-xx-bindingSyntax="complex">
  </script>
  <script>
    var sServiceURL =
    "/destinations/northwind/V3/Northwind/Northwind.svc/";

    // instantiate the model
    var oModel = sap.ui.model.odata.v2.ODataModel(sServiceURL);

    // don't batch the requests for now
    oModel.setUseBatch(false);

    oModel.attachMetadataLoaded(function() {
      var oMetaData = oModel.getServiceMetadata();
      console.log("Service Metadata", oMetaData);
    });

    sap.ui.getCore().setModel(oModel);
  </script>
</head>
<body class="sapUiBody" role="application">
  <div id="content"></div>
</body>
</html>
```

Listing 7.4 Instantiating OData Model in SAP Web IDE

If you run the application now, you should see metadata logged to the console (Figure 7.15), but the app itself only displays a blue screen. We've expanded only the root property dataServices, the details of which you saw in Figure 7.13.

Figure 7.15 Overview Service Metadata Object in Console

Because we're performing SAPUI5 application development, we'll now use Google Chrome again, because it's the most advanced browser for web development. Open the NETWORK tab and reload the application. Enter "northwind" to filter the requests. Figure 7.16 shows the same metadata information you saw previously in Figure 7.2. You'll also see that the SAPUI5 OData model has automatically triggered the call to the metadata document.

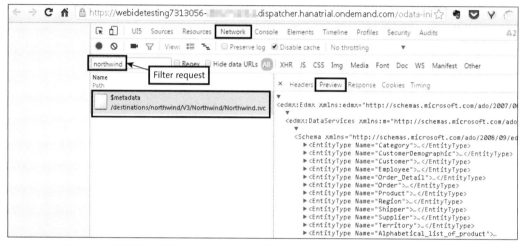

Figure 7.16 Network Request to Metadata Document

We've set up all the prerequisites necessary to access the data, so let's start reading data and enhancing the application.

7.3 Reading Data

Let's enhance our previous example and access some data from the products collection. First, we'll do this manually by coding and reading information about a certain product and logging it to the console. Then, we'll access the data from one certain product in a text field, followed by all other products in a table. We'll use a simple app with one view for that process.

7.3.1 Reading Data Manually

When we want to read data manually, we can use the `read` function from the SAPUI5 OData model. The `read` function triggers a `GET` request to the specified path. The data is returned in a `success` handler callback function. If the request was not successful, you can provide an `error` handler callback function to the `read` function. Listing 7.5 presents an example call.

```
function fnSuccess(oData, oResponse) {
  console.log("Data", oData);
  console.log("Response", oResponse);
}
function fnError(oError) {
  console.log("Error", oError);
}
oModel.read("/Products(1)", {
  success: fnSuccess,
  error: fnError
});
```

Listing 7.5 Reading Data Manually: Separate Success and Error Handlers

Here, we're referencing the `fnSuccess` and `fnError` functions, which are defined elsewhere in the code. It's also possible to define those functions inline as shown in Listing 7.6.

```
oModel.read("/Products(1)", {
  success: function(oData, oResponse) {
    console.log("Data", oData);
    console.log("Response", oResponse);
  },
  error: function(oError) {
    console.log("Error", oError);
  }
});
```

Listing 7.6 Reading Data Manually: Inline Success and Error Handlers

The `success` handler can have the following parameters: `oData` and `oResponse`. As the names indicate, in `oData` you'll receive the data, and in `oResponse` you'll find further information about the request, such as the status. The `error` handler receives an `oError` object with further error information about why the request failed.

Listing 7.7 provides a full example of how to access the data from the first product via the Northwind service with the SAP Web IDE. We'll also trigger a call to a product that doesn't exist to show the error handler in action.

283

```
var sServiceURL = "/destinations/northwind/V3/Northwind/Northwind.svc/";
// instantiate the model
var oModel = sap.ui.model.odata.v2.ODataModel(sServiceURL);
// don't batch the requests for now
oModel.setUseBatch(false);

function fnSuccess(oData, oResponse) {
  console.log("Data", oData);
  console.log("Response", oResponse);
}
function fnError(oError) {
  console.log("Error", oError);
}

oModel.read("/Products(1)", {
  success: fnSuccess,
  error: fnError
});
// this product does not exist
oModel.read("/Products(abc)", {
  success: fnSuccess,
  error: fnError
});
```

Listing 7.7 Reading OData Data Manually inside SAP Web IDE

When you run the code and open the console (Figure 7.17), you'll see the successful request at the top, including the data and the response. At the bottom, you'll see the failed request with a status code of 400, which means that the requested resource does not exist.

We also find the information about successful and failed requests in the NETWORK tab, as shown in Figure 7.18 (filtered for requests to Northwind).

Let's examine one interesting aspect of the data we've received. We know that the product has a relation to the category and the supplier. Because this information is not immediately available to us, the information is *deferred*. We must access it in a separate request, as we did previously when we entered the URL into the browser. Later in Section 7.4, you'll learn how to access such data immediately.

Figure 7.17 Manual Product Request: Console Success and Error Output

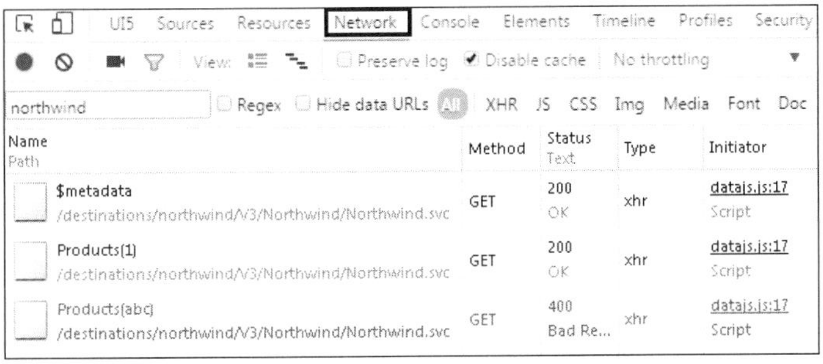

Figure 7.18 Manual Product Request: Network Success and Error Output

In Figure 7.19, we've expanded the category from the product so that you can see the deferred information. The URL has been shortened for the screenshot.

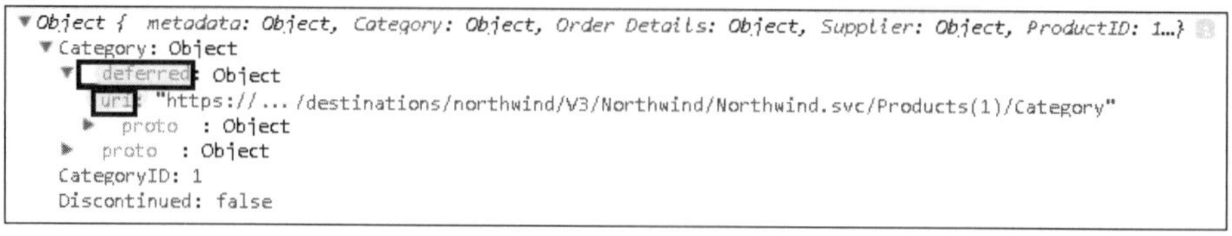

```
▼ Object { metadata: Object, Category: Object, Order Details: Object, Supplier: Object, ProductID: 1…}
  ▼ Category: Object
    ▼ deferred : Object
        url : "https://... /destinations/northwind/V3/Northwind/Northwind.svc/Products(1)/Category"
      ▶ __proto__ : Object
    ▶ __proto__ : Object
    CategoryID: 1
    Discontinued: false
```

Figure 7.19 Deferred Category

After we successfully receive the data, it's stored and cached in the OData model and can now be accessed via the getData() or getProperty() methods from the OData model via the cached entry. Listing 7.8 shows how to access data and the property.

```
function fnSuccess(oData, oResponse) {
  ...
  // accessing the data from the model now
  var oProduct1 = oModel.getData("/Products(1)");
  var oProduct1Name =
    oModel.getProperty("/Products(1)/ProductName");
  console.log("Product 1 from Model", oProduct1);
  console.log("Product 1 name from Model", oProduct1Name);
}

oModel.read("/Products(1)", {
  success: fnSuccess
});
```

Listing 7.8 Accessing OData Model Data with getData and getProperty

If we try to access data that hasn't been loaded yet, we receive no data. There also would be no data requested—meaning that no GET request was sent and that the oProduct2 variable will be undefined:

```
// notice - no GET request will be triggerd
// oProduct2 will be undefined
var oProduct2 = oModel.getData("/Products(2)");
console.log("Data from product 2 (not available)", oProduct2);
```

7.3.2 Accessing Data via Data Binding

When accessing the data from a certain product—like name or ID—we must first make sure that we have a binding context to the products collection or to the corresponding product! Otherwise, we'll see no data, because the backend call to the corresponding entities/entity have not been triggered!

We'll show how to bind the whole view to one product and then display the product name with a relative binding in Listing 7.9. Add the coding from the listing after `sap.ui.getCore().setModel(oModel)` from the previous code snippet.

```
...
sap.ui.getCore().setModel(oModel);

// display the product name
var oText = new sap.m.Text({
  text: "Product name: {ProductName}"
});
oText.addStyleClass("sapUiMediumMargin");

var oPageMaster = new sap.m.Page("masterPage", {
  title: "Product 1 Info",
  content: [oText]
});

// bind the whole page to the product 1
// so that the product name of product 1 wil be shown
oPageMaster.bindElement("/Products(1)");

var oApp = new sap.m.App();
oApp.addPage(oPageMaster);
oApp.placeAt("content");
```

Listing 7.9 Reading Product Data from One Entry

If you run the application now and inspect the network, you'll see that the call to `Product(1)` has been triggered automatically. We again filtered for Northwind requests (see Figure 7.20).

We can now inspect the bindings of the page and the text field with the UI5 Inspector; refer to Appendix B for instructions on how to enable this Google Chrome plugin. Figure 7.21 shows the binding of the page, and Figure 7.22 shows the binding of the text field.

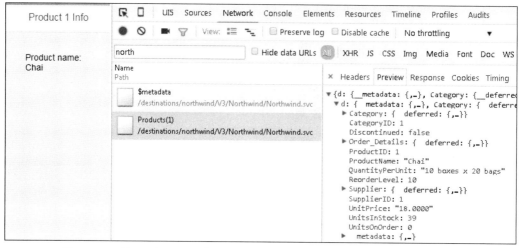

Figure 7.20 Network Request for Product 1

Figure 7.21 Binding Page to Product 1

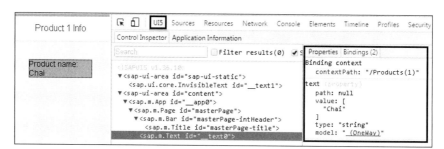

Figure 7.22 Binding Text to Product 1 Name

The whole page has an *absolute binding path*, which always starts with a slash (/)—for example:

- `"/Products"`

- `"/Products(1)"`

- `"/Products(1)/ProductName"`

- `"/Products(1)/Supplier"`

- `"/Products(1)/Supplier/CompanyName"`

We can enter those binding contexts at the end of the base service URL. For the Northwind service, the corresponding URLs are as follows:

- *http://services.odata.org/V3/Northwind/Northwind.svc/Products*

- *http://services.odata.org/V3/Northwind/Northwind.svc/Products(1)*

- *http://services.odata.org/V3/Northwind/Northwind.svc/Products(1)/ProductName*

- *http://services.odata.org/V3/Northwind/Northwind.svc/Products(1)/Supplier*

- *http://services.odata.org/V3/Northwind/Northwind.svc/Products(1)/Supplier/ CompanyName*

Relative binding paths can be resolved with a context, such as `"/Products(1)"`. With such a context, it's possible to resolve relative bindings such as the following:

- `"ProductId"`

- `"ProductName"`

- `"UnitPrice"`

- `"UnitsInStock"`

The preceding relative bindings with the binding context `"/Products(1)"` resolve to the following absolute bindings:

- `"/Products(1)/ProductId"`

- `"/Products(1)/ProductName"`

- `"/Products(1)/UnitPrice"`

- `"/Products(1)/UnitsInStock"`

In the code example in Listing 7.9, we combined absolute and relative binding paths. Listing 7.10 presents a shortened version to highlight the absolute and relative bindings:

```
// relative binding
var oText = new sap.m.Text({
```

```
   text: "Product name: {ProductName}"
});

// absolute binding
oPageMaster.bindElement("/Products(1)");
```
Listing 7.10 Absolute and Relative Bindings

The relative binding "ProductName" will resolve to "/Products(1)/ProductName".

We can also change the binding of the whole page to the products collection. Then, we would have an absolute bind of the text of product 1. Listing 7.11 gives a shortened example of what this binding would look like.

```
// absolute binding
// display the product name
var oText = new sap.m.Text({
   text: "Product name: {/Product(1)/ProductName}"
});

// absolute binding
oPageMaster.bindElement("/Products");
```
Listing 7.11 Absolute Bindings

7.3.3   Best Practices

We can now continue to implement our example with XML views, which are the recommended way to implement views. We'll discuss best practices and use a component, routing, and the Application Descriptor. We'll also make use of the automatic model instantiation from the Application Descriptor.

We'll only highlight important elements in the example, because you're already familiar with the basic concepts and best practices from Chapter 4. The folder structure of the project is presented in Listing 7.12.

When you implement this example on your own, you'll need to use care with the neo-app.json file, which routes to the SAPUI5 resources and the Northwind destination.

```
Odata-model-reading-data-bestpractice
|   index.html
+---webapp
|   |   Component.js
|   |   manifest.json
|   |
|   +---controller
|   |       BaseController.js
|   |       Master.controller.js
|   +---i18n
|   |       i18n.properties
|   |
|   \---view
|           App.view.xml
|           Master.view.xml
|
```

Listing 7.12 Folder Structure for OData: Reading Best Practice

We'll use the master view (`Master.view.xml`) to display the data, the app view (`App.view.xml`) to contain `sap.m.App`, and the router to put the master view in the pages aggregation. Although we won't write any controller code in this example, we'll use the controller in later examples. Therefore, we've set up a controller for the master view that inherits from `BaseController.js`.

Let's look at the most important elements of our files. Let's start with the code of Component.js, which you'll see in Listing 7.13. The code is quite short; all the heavy lifting is done by the Application Descriptor (`manifest.json`). We just reference this file with `metadata: { manifest: "json" }`. Then, we only need to initialize the router.

```
// Comoponent.js
sap.ui.define([
  "sap/ui/core/UIComponent"
], function(UIComponent) {
  "use strict";

  return UIComponent.extend(
    "sapui5.demo.odata.readingdata.bestpractice.Component", {

    metadata: {
      manifest: "json"
    },

    init: function() {
      // call the base component's init function
      UIComponent.prototype.init.apply(this, arguments);
```

```
      // create the views based on the url/hash
      this.getRouter().initialize();
    }
  });
});
```
Listing 7.13 OData Reading Best Practice: Component.js

Next, we'll look at the App Descriptor and its important properties, as shown in
a shortened form in Listing 7.14.

```
// manifest.json - shortened
{ "_version": "1.1.0",
  "sap.app": {
    ...
    "dataSources": {
      "mainService": {
        "uri":
          "/destinations/northwind/V3/Northwind/Northwind.svc/",
        "type": "OData",
        "settings": {
          "odataVersion": "2.0"
        }
      }
    }
  },
  ...
  "sap.ui5": {
    "_version": "1.1.0",
    "rootView": {
      "viewName":
        "sapui5.demo.odata.readingdata.bestpractice.view.App",
      "type": "XML"
    },
    ...
    "models": {
      "": {
        "dataSource": "mainService",
        "settings": {
          "useBatch": false
        }
      },
    ...
    "routing": {
      "config": {
        "routerClass": "sap.m.routing.Router",
        "viewType": "XML",
        "viewPath":
          "sapui5.demo.odata.readingdata.bestpractice.view",
```

```
        "controlId": "app",
        "controlAggregation": "pages"
    },
    "routes": [{
        "pattern": "",
        "name": "master",
        "target": "master"
    }],
    "targets": {
      "master": {
        "viewName": "Master",
        "viewId": "master",
        "viewLevel": 1
      }
    ...
```

Listing 7.14 OData Reading Best Practice: Shortened manifest.json

In the `sap.app` section, we can define `dataSources`, and we've called the service `mainService`. We've defined the type as `OData` and set `oDataVersion` to `2.0`. Those settings correspond to `sap.ui.model.odata.v2.ODataModel`.

In the `sap.ui5` section, there's a dedicated `models` section. We refer to the data source `mainService` that we defined in the `sap.app` section. Again, we set the batch mode to `false` with the `useBatch` property. Listing 7.15 shows part of the `sap.ui5` section for reference.

```
"models": {
  "": {
    "dataSource": "mainService",
    "settings": {
      "useBatch": false
    }
  }
```

Listing 7.15 sap.ui5 Section

In the `routing` part of `sap.ui5`, we've referenced the master view and control ID `"app"`, which is in the app view and is responsible for rendering the pages. The app view is quite small and shown in Listing 7.16.

```
<!-- App.view.xml -->
<mvc:View
  xmlns:html="http://www.w3.org/1999/xhtml"
  xmlns:mvc="sap.ui.core.mvc" xmlns="sap.m"
  displayBlock="true">
```

```
   <App id="app" />
</mvc:View>
```
Listing 7.16 OData Reading Best Practice: App.view.xml

Now, let's look at the master view. Listing 7.17 shows how to set the binding of the page to `Products(1)` and how to access the `ProductName` property in the `Text` field. We also see that the equivalent of `oPage.bindElement("/Products(1)")` is the `binding` property in the XML view.

```
<!-- Master.view.xml -->
<mvc:View
   xmlns:mvc="sap.ui.core.mvc"
   xmlns="sap.m">
   <Page
      title="Product 1 Info"
      binding="{/Products(1)}">
      <content>

        <Text
          text="Product name: {ProductName}"
          class="sapUiMediumMargin">
        </Text>
      </content>
   </Page>
</mvc:View>
```
Listing 7.17 OData Reading Best Practice: Master.view.xml

Finally, we'll use index.html to instantiate the application as shown in in Listing 7.18.

```
// index.html - head script
<script>
  sap.ui.getCore().attachInit(function() {
    new sap.m.Shell({
      app: new sap.ui.core.ComponentContainer({
        height: "100%",
        name: "sapui5.demo.odata.readingdata.bestpractice"
      })
    }).placeAt("content");
  });
</script>
```
Listing 7.18 OData Reading Best Practice: index.html

We haven't shown the code of the controllers here because we don't need to use them yet. If you run the application now, you won't see any difference in the UI, as shown in Figure 7.23. However, we've significantly improved the application's structure and can build upon it from here.

Product 1 Info

Product name: Chai

Figure 7.23 Product Info App

7.3.4 Displaying Additional Product Information

Now, let's enhance the appearance of the view. We'll replace `sap.m.Text` with `sap.m.ObjectHeader`. In this section, we'll add a formatter for the unit price and another for the discontinued status. Both of these can be done via expression binding. For the sake of readability, we hard-coded the texts here, but in a real project, you would use the i18n model. Because the data model has no currency value, we've hard-coded *EUR* into the view.

With the adoption of the view, we want to show that the binding and formatting works the same in the OData model as in the JSON model. Listing 7.19 shows the adapted Master.view.xml file, and Figure 7.24 presents a look at the app now.

```
<mvc:View xmlns:mvc="sap.ui.core.mvc"
  xmlns="sap.m">
  <Page
    title="Product {ProductID} Info"
      binding="{/Products(1)}">
    <content>

      <ObjectHeader
        title="{ProductName}"
        number="{
          parts: [{path:'UnitPrice'},'EUR'],
          type: 'sap.ui.model.type.Currency',
          formatOptions: {showMeasure: false}
        }"
        numberUnit="EUR">
        <attributes>
          <ObjectAttribute
            text="Units in stock: {UnitsInStock}" />
          <ObjectAttribute
            text="Units on order: {UnitsOnOrder}" />
          <ObjectAttribute
```

```
                  text="Reorder Level: {ReorderLevel}" />
            <ObjectAttribute
              text="Quantity per Unit: {QuantityPerUnit}" />
          </attributes>

          <statuses>
            <ObjectStatus text="ID: {ProductID}" />
            <ObjectStatus
              text="{= ${Discontinued}
                ? 'Discontinued' : 'Available' }"
              state="{= ${Discontinued} ? 'Error' : 'Success' }" />
          </statuses>
        </ObjectHeader>

      </content>
    </Page>
</mvc:View>
```

Listing 7.19 Displaying Product Information with an Object Header

```
                        Product 1 Info


          Chai                        18,00
                                        EUR

          Units in stock: 39            ID: 1

          Units on order: 0          Available

          Reorder Level: 10

          Quantity per Unit: 10 boxes x 20 bags
```

Figure 7.24 Product 1 Information with an Object Header

7.3.5   Displaying Navigation Properties

We now want to display information about the category and the supplier, which
are navigation properties from the products. We'll use sap.m.IconTabBar to
switch between those two properties, and we'll display the information with
sap.m.SimpleForm and bind each form to the corresponding navigation property.
We have bound the whole page to the first product with the binding property of
the page:

```
<Page
title="Product {ProductID} Info"
binding="{/Products(1)}">
```

We can now also bind a certain form to a certain navigation property. We can reuse the same binding property, as you'll see in Listing 7.20. All bindings inside the form will be resolved to Category or Supplier, respectively. Those two properties will be resolved relative to the respective Product. When using sap.m.SimpleForm, be sure to declare the namespaces for sap.ui.layout.form and sap.ui.core for the title. You can see the result of the view in Figure 7.25.

```
<mvc:View
  xmlns:mvc="sap.ui.core.mvc"
  xmlns:core="sap.ui.core"
  xmlns:f="sap.ui.layout.form"
  xmlns="sap.m"
  >
  <Page
    title="Product {ProductID} Info"
    binding="{/Products(1)}">
  ...
</ObjectHeader>

<IconTabBar
expanded="true"
class="sapUiResponsiveContentPadding">
<items>
  <IconTabFilter
  icon="sap-icon://activity-items">
   <f:SimpleForm
   binding="{Category}" >
   <core:Title text="Category Information" />
   <Label text="Category ID"/>
   <Text text="{CategoryID}" />
   <Label text="Category Name"/>
   <Text text="{CategoryName}" />
   <Label text="Category Description"/>
   <Text text="{Description}" />
   </f:SimpleForm>
  </IconTabFilter>
  <IconTabFilter
  icon="sap-icon://supplier">
   <f:SimpleForm
   binding="{Supplier}" >

   <core:Title text="Supplier Information" />
   <Label text="Supplier ID"/>
   <Text text="{SupplierID}" />
   <Label text="Company Name"/>
   <Text text="{CompanyName}" />
   <Label text="Address"/>
```

```
        <Text text="{Address}" />
        <Label text="City"/>
        <Text text="{City}" />
        <Label text="PostalCode"/>
        <Text text="{PostalCode}" />
        <Label text="Country"/>
        <Text text="{Country}" />

        <core:Title text="Contact Information" />
        <Label text="Contact Name"/>
        <Text text="{ContactName}" />
        <Label text="Contact Title"/>
        <Text text="{ContactTitle}" />
    </f:SimpleForm>
  </IconTabFilter>
 </items>
</IconTabBar>
```

Listing 7.20 Navigation Property Binding in SimpleForm inside IconTabBar

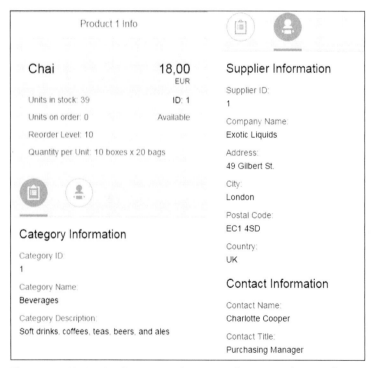

Figure 7.25 Naviagtion Property Binding in SimpleForm inside IconTabBar

When you investigate the network trace of the app, you'll see that separate network requests have been sent for the respective supplier and category (see Figure 7.26). Keep this in mind later when we examine the $expand property to get this data in one request.

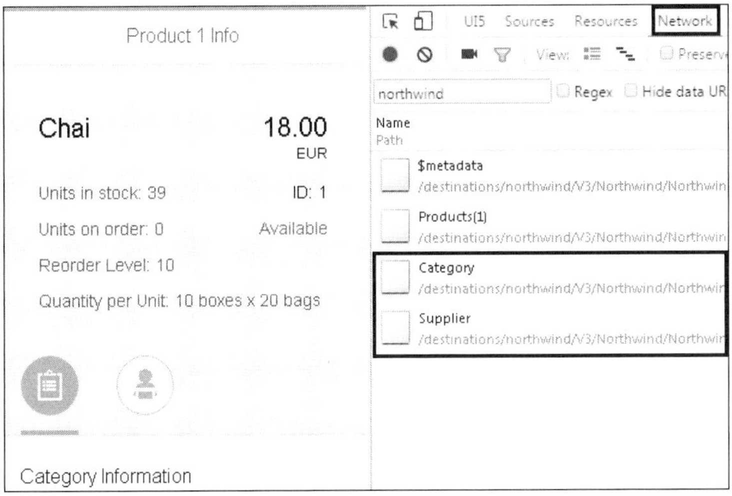

Figure 7.26 Separate Requests for Category and Supplier

7.4   Filter, Sort, Expand, and Group

You've learned a lot about how to display single entries. Now, let's focus on displaying more that one entry. When we're displaying more entries, we can also examine sorting, filtering, expanding, and grouping more easily.

7.4.1   Filtering with $filter

We'll start with filtering and will explore some filter possibilities directly in the browser. To filter entries, the URL parameter $filter is appended with a question mark at the end of the collection, followed by an equals sign and the query. The following example query shows products with a unit price that's larger (gt stands for greater than) than 20:

```
/Products?$filter= UnitPrice gt 35
```

When entering the URL in the browser, the space characters will be replaced with %20. The following is the full URL for the price query:

http://services.odata.org/V3/Northwind/Northwind.svc/Products?$filter= UnitPrice%20gt%2035

When you execute the query (Figure 7.27), you'll see that the first entry from the result set is now the product with the number 8 and a unit price of 40. For filtering, there exist logical, arithmetic, and grouping operators. String, date, math, and type-related functions also are available.

Figure 7.27 Filtering Unit Price Greater Than 35

Table 7.3 lists all the logical operators, which are the most important for querying data. Table 7.4 lists the most important string operators. You can find the full list of all possible operators at *http://www.odata.org/documentation/odata-version-2-0/ uri-conventions/* (search for "$filter").

Operator	Description	Example
eq	Equal	/Suppliers?$filter=City eq 'London'
ne	Not equal	/Suppliers?$filter=City ne 'London'
gt	Greater than	/Products?$filter=UnitPrice gt 20
ge	Greater than or equal	/Products?$filter=UnitPrice ge 10
lt	Less than	/Products?$filter=UnitPrice lt 20
le	Less than or equal	/Products?$filter=UnitPrice le 100
and	Logical and	/Products?$filter=UnitPrice le 200 and UnitPrice gt 3
or	Logical or	/Products?$filter=UnitPrice le 3.5 or UnitPrice gt 200
not	Logical negation	/Products?$filter=not endswith(ProductName,'milk')

Table 7.3 Logical Filtering Operators

Operator	Example
substring	/Products?$filter=substringof('Chai',ProductName)
startswith	/Products?$filter=startswith(ProductName,'Ch')
endswith	/Products?$filter=endswith(ProductName,'Ch')

Table 7.4 Important String Filtering Operators

sap.ui.model.FilterOperator supports certain operations so that we don't have to construct all filter queries ourselves (see Table 7.5).

FilterOperator Operations	OData Filter Equivalent
sap.ui.model.FilterOperator.EQ	eq (equals)
sap.ui.model.FilterOperator.NE	ne (not equal)
sap.ui.model.FilterOperator.GT	gt (greater than)
sap.ui.model.FilterOperator.GE	ge (greater than or equals)
sap.ui.model.FilterOperator.LT	lt (less than)
sap.ui.model.FilterOperator.LE	le (less than or equals)

Table 7.5 sap.ui.model.FilterOperator Operations

FilterOperator Operations	OData Filter Equivalent
`sap.ui.model.FilterOperator.Contains`	`Substring`
`sap.ui.model.FilterOperator.StartsWith`	`Startswith`
`sap.ui.model.FilterOperator.EndsWith`	`Endswith`
`sap.ui.model.FilterOperator.BT`	between one and another value; example for `UnitPrice` from products between 1 and 10: `/Products?$filter=(UnitPrice ge 1 and UnitPrice le 10)`

Table 7.5 sap.ui.model.FilterOperator Operations (Cont.)

When using the `sap.ui.model.FilterOperator.BT` operator with strings, be aware that such usage might not be 100% intuitive. When we filter between *'Chai'* and *'M'* for the product names, the entry *'Chai'* would be included, the entry *'M'* itself (if it exists) will also, and all values in between.

Now that you have the relevant background information about filtering, we can start to implement filtering in the application. We'll adapt Master.view.xml and implement BaseController.js and Master.controller.js. BaseContoller.js will contain only convenience methods, which we could reuse in other controllers as well (see Listing 7.21).

```
// BaseController.js
sap.ui.define([
  "sap/ui/core/mvc/Controller"
], function(Controller) {
  "use strict";

  return Controller.extend("sapui5.demo.odata.filter.sort.
  BaseController", {
    getRouter: function() {
      return sap.ui.core.UIComponent.getRouterFor(this);
    },
    getModel: function(sName) {
      return this.getView().getModel(sName);
    },
    setModel: function(oModel, sName) {
      return this.getView().setModel(oModel, sName);
    },
    getResourceBundle: function() {
      return this.getOwnerComponent().getModel("i18n")
        .getResourceBundle();
```

```
      }
   });
});
```
Listing 7.21 BaseController.js with Convenience Methods

Master.view.xml now contains `sap.m.List` inside the `sap.m.Page` content. Listing 7.22 shows the list with `sap.m.SearchField` inside `sap.m.ToolBar` inside the `headerToolbar` aggregation of the list. The search field has a `search` action that refers to the `onFilterProducts` function.

```
// Master.view.xml
...
<List
  id="productList"
  class="sapUiResponsiveMargin"
  width="auto"
  items="{/Products}">
  <headerToolbar>
    <Toolbar>
      <Title text="Products in Stock" />
      <ToolbarSpacer />
      <SearchField width="50%" search="onFilterProducts" />
    </Toolbar>
  </headerToolbar>
  <items>
    <ObjectListItem
        title="{UnitsInStock} x {ProductName}"
        number="{
          parts: [{path:'UnitPrice'},'EUR'],
          type: 'sap.ui.model.type.Currency',
          formatOptions: {showMeasure: false}
        }"
        numberUnit="EUR">
    </ObjectListItem>
  </items>
</List>
...
```
Listing 7.22 Master.view.xml for Filtering

Master.controller.js will extend the base controller, and we'll contain the `onFilterProducts` method for filtering. The filtering will be done via `sap.m.SearchField`. When the search field is triggered, it throws an event with the `"query"` parameter. With this parameter, we can create a new `sap.ui.model.Filter` element for `ProductName` with `sap.ui.model.FilterOperator`. With this filter, we can manipulate the binding of the product list with the ID `productList` (see Listing 7.23).

```
// Master.controller.js
sap.ui.define([
  "sapui5/demo/odata/filter/sort/controller/BaseController",
  "sap/ui/model/Filter",
  "sap/ui/model/FilterOperator"
], function(BaseController, Filter, FilterOperator) {
  "use strict";

  return BaseController.extend(
    "sapui5.demo.odata.filter.sort.controller.Master", {

    onFilterProducts: function(oEvent) {
      // build the filter array
      var aFilter = [];
      var sQuery = oEvent.getParameter("query");
      if (sQuery) {
        aFilter.push(new Filter(
          "ProductName", FilterOperator.Contains, sQuery));
      }

      // filter the list via binding
      var oList = this.getView().byId("productList");
      var oBinding = oList.getBinding("items");
      oBinding.filter(aFilter);
    }
  });
});
```

Listing 7.23 Master.controller.js for Filtering

If you run the application (Figure 7.28) and filter for "Chocolate", you'll see that the `$filter` parameter substring has been automatically attached to the request. The character `%27` represents the apostrophe. Ignore the `$skip` and `$top` parameters for now; we'll look at them later on. For now, the request that was automatically created looks like this:

```
/Products?$filter=substringof('Chocolate',ProductName)
```

And it represents what we created with the filter:

```
// sQuery = "Choclate";
new Filter("ProductName", FilterOperator.Contains, sQuery));
```

Figure 7.28 Automatic $filter Query Due to sap.ui.model.Filter

7.4.2 Sorting with $orderby

The next step to improve the application is to introduce sorting functionality. You may have noticed that our list is initially sorted by the product ID; a more intuitive choice would be to sort alphabetically by product name.

OData supports sorting with the `$orderby` parameter. It's possible to sort ascending (`asc`) or descending (`desc`); ascending is the default. The `$orderby` parameter is appended at the end of a collection with a question mark:

```
/Products?$orderby=ProductName
```

Here are some examples with fully qualified URLs:

- All products entries returned in ascending order when sorted by the `ProductName` property: *http://services.odata.org/V3/Northwind/Northwind.svc/Products?$orderby=ProductName*

- Same as above, this time with explicit ascending ordering: *http://services.odata.org/V3/Northwind/Northwind.svc//Products?$orderby=ProductName%20asc*

- Products subsequently sorted (in descending order) by the `CategoryName` property of the related category entry: *http://services.odata.org/V3/Northwind/Northwind.svc/Products?$orderby=ProductName,Category/CategoryName%20desc*

Now, let's use these sorting capabilities in the running example application. We can define a sorter inside the XML view. In Listing 7.24, the sorter property is set to `ProductName` for the list in Master.view.xml.

```
<List
  id="productList"
  class="sapUiResponsiveMargin"
  width="auto"
  items="{
    path: '/Products',
    sorter: {
      path: 'ProductName'
    }
  }">
```

Listing 7.24 Master.view.xml Sort by ProductName

It's also possible to set the descending property directly in the XML view:

```
sorter: {
path: 'ProductName',
descending: false
}
```

If you run the application now, you'll see that the list is sorted alphabetically. When you inspect the NETWORK tab, you'll see that the OData model has automatically attached the $orderby property to the request, as shown in Figure 7.29.

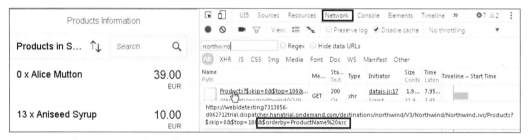

Figure 7.29 Product Information Sorted by ProductName

Now, we want to re-sort the list dynamically. To do so, we'll place a button before the search field in the headerToolbar of the list. When a user clicks on the button, the list will toggle between ascending and descending values. The button will have the onpress handler onSortProductName. Listing 7.25 provides the coding to add the button.

```
<!-- Master.view.xml -->
...
<List ...
```

```
<Toolbar>
  <Title text="Products in Stock" />
  <ToolbarSpacer />
  <Button icon="sap-icon://sort"
    press="onSortProductName"/>
```
Listing 7.25 Adding Sorter Button in Master View

There are two ways to interact with the SAPUI5 sorter. One way is to create a new sorter and not use the initial sorting in the XML view. In our controller, we need to import `sap.ui.model.Sorter`, which is responsible for sorting. In `onInit`, we'll create a new sorter and store the reference to this sorter. In `onSortProductName`, we then toggle the `bDescending` property of the sorter and assign it to the list binding (`getBinding("items")`) via `sort`, as shown in Listing 7.26. When we access the list binding, we get a `sap.ui.model.odata.v2.ODataListBinding` object.

```
// Master.controller.js
sap.ui.define([
  "sapui5/demo/odata/filter/sort/controller/BaseController",
  "sap/ui/model/Filter",
  "sap/ui/model/FilterOperator",
  "sap/ui/model/Sorter"
], function(BaseController, Filter, FilterOperator, Sorter) {
  "use strict";

  return BaseController.extend(
    "sapui5.demo.odata.filter.sort.controller.Master", {

    onInit: function() {
      this._sorter = new Sorter("ProductName", false);
    },
    onSortProductName: function() {
      this._sorter.bDescending = !this._sorter.bDescending;
      this.getView().byId("productList").getBinding("items")
        .sort(this._sorter);
    }, ...
```
Listing 7.26 New sap.ui.model.Sorter in Controller

If we want to reuse the current sorter from the XML view, we can use the coding in Listing 7.27. Here, we're directly accessing the `aSorters` array of `sap.ui.model.odata.v2.ODataListBinding`. Be aware when using the `aSorters` property that currently there is no `getSorters()` method available; this might change in the future. We don't need to import `sap.ui.model.Sorter`, because we don't create a new sorter (see Listing 7.27).

```
// Master.controller.js
onSortProductName : function() {
  // resuse the current sorter
  var aSorter = [];
  var oListBinding =
    this.getView().byId("productList").getBinding("items");
  var aListSorters = oListBinding.aSorters;
  var oSorter;
  if (aListSorters.length > 0) {
    oSorter = aListSorters[0];
    oSorter.bDescending = !oSorter.bDescending;
    oListBinding.sort(oSorter);
  } }, ...
```
Listing 7.27 Reusing Current Sorter in Controller

7.4.3   Expanding with $expand

Before we move on with grouping the list, let's examine another interesting OData option. Previously, when we explored a single product we saw that the `Category` and `Supplier` had deferred properties, which means that the data was not immediately available for us.

When we created `sap.m.IconTabBar` with `sap.m.SimpleForm`, we set the binding property of the form to `Category` and `Supplier` and bound the text and label fields to the corresponding properties of those two entities. This explicit binding was necessary; otherwise, the data from the two entities would not be requested.

Let's review what we have to do when we don't use the `$expand` property; we'll describe `$expand` in a second. We could add `sap.m.ObjectAttribute` to `sap.m.ObjectListItem` in Master.view.xml to display information about the category of the product, as in Listing 7.28.

```
<!-- Master.view.xml -->
<ObjectListItem
    title="{UnitsInStock} x {ProductName}"
    ...
  <attributes>
    <ObjectAttribute
      binding="{Category}"
      text="{CategoryName}" />
```

```
    </attributes>
</ObjectListItem>
```
Listing 7.28 Product Category Name in List without $expand

When you run the application, you'll see that the category name is now displayed below the product name. When you examine the network trace (Figure 7.30) of the application, you'll see a lot of `Category` requests—one request per list entry! You can imagine that so many requests are bad for performance. This is not a good practice within a list with a lot of entries.

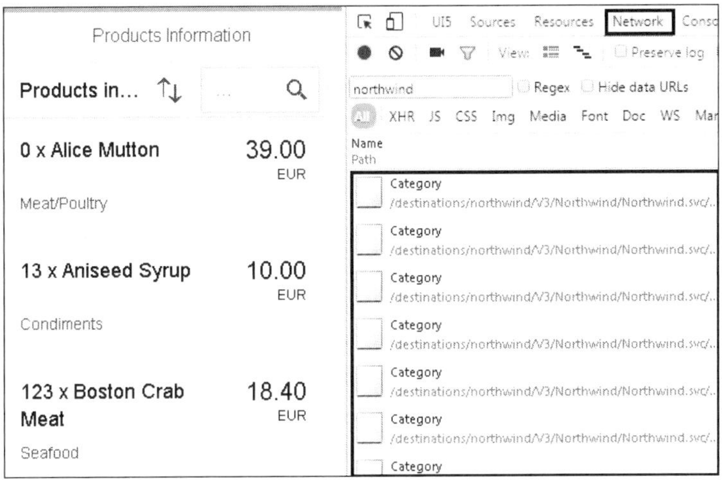

Figure 7.30 Network Requests for Category Name of Product without $expand

With the `$expand` query, we can request the associated navigation properties of the entity with one request. Therefore, instead of using these two requests to get information about the product and its category:

```
/Products(1)
/Products(1)/Category
```

we can request this information with one request:

```
/Products(1)?$expand=Category
```

Let's enter this request into the browser:

*http://services.odata.org/V3/Northwind/Northwind.svc/Products(1)?$expand=
Category*

Look at the result in Figure 7.31. There, you'll see the new `inline` property for the category that contains the corresponding data.

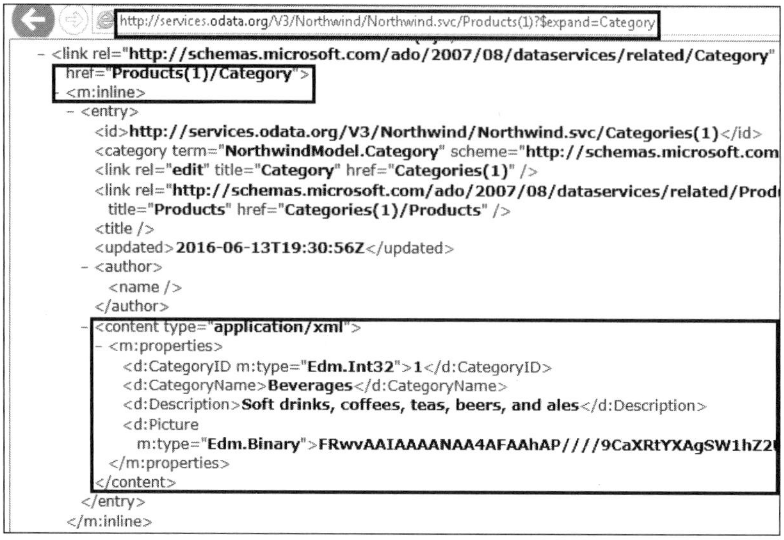

Figure 7.31 Product 1 with Expanded Category

The `$expand` property can be appended at the end of a single entry or at the end of a collection with a question mark. Therefore, this request is also possible:

```
/Products?$expand=Category
```

We can also expand more than one navigation property if we separate the properties with a comma:

```
/Products?$expand=Category,Supplier
```

For each product, the information about the category and the supplier will be displayed inline. There's another interesting option here, too: Imagine we want to get all the product information from a certain category. We would do this as follows:

```
/Categories?$expand=Products
```

We know that each product has a supplier, so we could also expand the supplier information within the product while getting all products in a certain category. Then, we'd separate the navigation properties with a slash, and the resulting queries would look like this:

```
/Categories?$expand=Products/Supplier
/Categories(1)?$expand=Products/Supplier
```

You can look at the `expand` query at the fully qualified URL:

http://services.odata.org/V3/Northwind/Northwind.svc/Categories?$expand=Products/Supplierhttp://services.odata.org/V3/Northwind/Northwind.svc/Categories?$expand=Products/Supplier

Listing 7.29 shows a simplified response to the request. Note the `inline` property inside an `inline` property. One is from the expanded product, and the other is from the expanded supplier of the product.

```
Category(1)
  inline
    Products(1)/Suppliers
      inline
        Supplier content
    Product(1) content
  inline
    ... all the other products with their respecting suppliers
  Category(1) content
Category(2)
...
```

Listing 7.29 $expand of Supplier of a Certain Product within Categories

You can think of `$expand` as like a join for different database tables. You use a join to get data from different sources all at once; in OData terms, you can join entities with their corresponding navigation properties. Now that you've learned about `$expand` options and explored them in the browser, we can move on and use them in the SAPUI5 application.

We can use `$expand` within a binding with the `parameters` object and the `expand` property. Listing 7.30 shows how to add this parameter to the list.

```
<!--- Master.view.xml -->
<List
  id="productList"
  ...
  items="{
    path: '/Products',
    sorter: {
      path: 'ProductName',
      descending: false
    },
```

```
  parameters: {
    'expand' : 'Category'
  }
}">
```

Listing 7.30 $expand inside XML View

You can now change `sap.m.ObjectAttribute` to directly reference the category name within the category:

```
<ObjectAttribute
text="{Category/CategoryName}" />
```

If you run the application now and look at the NETWORK tab (Figure 7.32) and filter for "Northwind", you won't see the `Category` requests anymore; there will be just six requests total. This is for better for performance purposes. However, keep in mind how much data you want to expand for such lists. The more data you expand, the bigger your responses get!

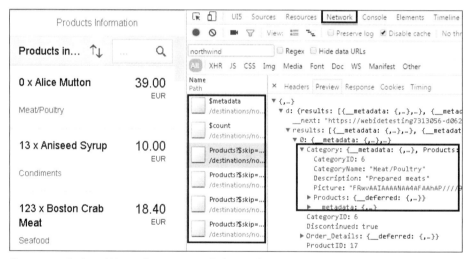

Figure 7.32 Reduced Network Requests with $expand

7.4.4 Grouping with group

Now that we have the information about the category available, we can use it to group products by category. The grouping itself is not a property of OData. The grouping is possible via the list binding. To activate grouping for the category name, we need to set the `group` property of the `sorter` of the list to `true`, as shown in Listing 7.31. Figure 7.33 shows the results.

```
<List
  id="productList"
  ...
  items="{
    path: '/Products',
    sorter: {
      path: 'Category/CategoryName',
      descending: false,
      group : true
    },
    parameters: {
      'expand' : 'Category'
    }
  }">
```

Listing 7.31 Grouping Products List by Category Name

Products Information	
PRODUCE	
15 x Uncle Bob's Organic Dried Pears	30.00 EUR
35 x Tofu	23.25 EUR
26 x Rössle Sauerkraut	45.60 EUR
20 x Manjimup Dried Apples	53.00 EUR
4 x Longlife Tofu	10.00 EUR
SEAFOOD	
31 x Ikura	31.00 EUR

Figure 7.33 Grouping Products List by Category Name

7.5   Paging and Thresholds

Until now, we've always requested the full amount of data from the backend. When we have a lot of data, this can lead to longer response times, and on mobile devices, the user doesn't want to see that much data all at once. OData provides the ability to display only a certain amount of data via the `$top` property. This property is appended at the end of a collection with a question mark, as shown:

```
/Products?$top=5
// SQL equivalent
SELECT * FROM Products LIMIT 5
```

http://services.odata.org/V3/Northwind/Northwind.svc/Products?$top=5

Figure 7.34 shows the result of such a query; the entries have been collapsed so that you can more easily see the five entries.

Figure 7.34 Displaying Top Five Products

The `$top` property also can be combined with `$orderby`—for example:

http://services.odata.org/V3/Northwind/Northwind.svc/Products?$top=5&$orderby= ProductName%20desc

What if we don't want to display the top five entries, but instead want to skip the first five entries? OData supports this out of the box with the `$skip` parameter. When we use `$skip` and a number, that number of entries will be skipped and we'll see the remaining entries (starting at the number + 1). Append the `$skip` parameter at the end of a collection with a question mark and provide a number:

```
/Products?$skip=5
```

Using this syntax in a URL, we get the following result:

http://services.odata.org/V3/Northwind/Northwind.svc/Products?$skip=5

When you execute this query, you'll see that the products returned now start with product ID 6 instead of 1 (see Figure 7.35).

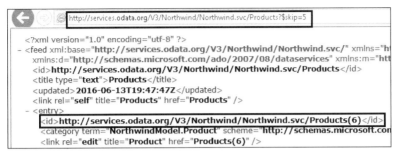

Figure 7.35 Skipping Product Collection Entries

The real power is released when we combine those two parameters! If we can display a limited number of entries (`$top`) and skip a certain number of entries (`$skip`), then we can now navigate through the dataset bit by bit. This ability is called *paging*, and the number of entries we request is called the *threshold*.

SAPUI5 lists and tables support paging and threshold capabilities out of the box:

▶ `/Products?$skip=5&$top=5`
  http://services.odata.org/V3/Northwind/Northwind.svc/Products?$skip=5&$top=5

▶ `/Products?$skip=5&$top=5&orderby=ProductName`
  *http://services.odata.org/V3/Northwind/Northwind.svc/Products?$skip=5&$top=5&
  orderby=ProductName*

Let's extend the running example application with those features. Note that paging and threshold features work whether grouping is enabled or not. Listing 7.32 shows the adapted list. The property for enabling the growing feature is `growing` and must be set to `true`. The `growing` property helps when your content is too large to be loaded or shown at once. It breaks the content into smaller pieces, called *pages*, which are then shown one after the other. With `growingThreshold`, you can specify the number of entries you'd like to see.

```
<List
id="productList"
class="sapUiResponsiveMargin"
width="auto"
items="{
  path: '/Products',
  sorter: {
    path: 'Category/CategoryName',
    descending: false,
```

```
    group : true
  },
  parameters: {
    'expand' : 'Category'
  }
}"
growing="true"
growingThreshold="5"
>
```

Listing 7.32 Growing Feature in List

When you run the app, you'll now see that only the first five entries are displayed (Figure 7.36). If you inspect the network trace, you'll see that the OData request contains the $skip and $top parameters. For the initial call, $skip is zero, because we're starting from the beginning. The $top parameter is set to 5, set via growing-Threshhold.

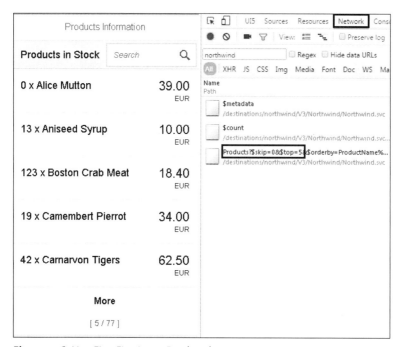

Figure 7.36 List: First Five Items Displayed

After you click in the MORE area, you'll see that a second request has been fired (Figure 7.37). With this request, the first five entries are skipped and the $top parameter stays the same. The result of this query was automatically appended to the list.

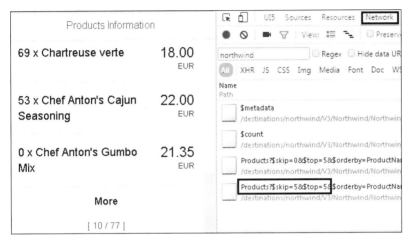

Figure 7.37 List: Next Five Items Displayed

Table 7.6 lists the available parameters for the `growing` feature. We used the `growing` feature in `sap.m.List`; when using `sap.m.Table`, the settings are the same, because both controls inherit from `sap.m.ListBase`, and `ListBase` is the control with those properties.

Property	Description
growing	Boolean; turn the growing feature on or off.
growingScrollToLoad	Boolean; if this is set to true, the next entries will be fetched automatically when the user reaches the end of the list. If this is set to false or not set at all, the user has to click the MORE button. Default value is 20.
growingThreshold	Integer; the number of entries that should be requested initially and each time the list expanded.
growingTriggerText	String; by default, the text MORE is shown, but this text can be overwritten via this property.

Table 7.6 Growing Feature Properties

When using a table that does not inherit from `sap.m.ListBase`, like `sap.ui.table.Table`, then there is only one property, which is called `threshold`.

7.6 Batch Mode

In previous examples, we disabled batch mode with `useBatch=false` for educational purposes, because it makes it easier to inspect the network trace. In a real application, you will always aim to enable batch mode, because it results in far fewer network requests. Batch mode essentially combines network requests into one request, which results in fewer total requests. These requests can combine read and write access.

When we enabled `growing` in the list and looked at the network requests in Figure 7.36, we could also see that two requests were sent for accessing data. One request was `$count`, and the other was to request the first five entries.

Note

We didn't cover `$count` before now. With `$count`, you can get the number of entries, but it's not possible to display this number for the list directly. We'll cover an alternative option in Chapter 8 when we take a deeper look at applications.

Let's enable batch mode for the application now in the manifest.json file, as shown in Listing 7.33. We can set `useBatch` to `true`, or we can delete the whole parameter, because the default setting is `true` in the SAPUI5 OData v2 model.

```
"sap.ui5": {
  ...
  "models": {
    "": {
      "dataSource": "mainService",
      "settings": {
        "useBatch" : true
      }
    },  ...
```
Listing 7.33 Enabling Batch Mode

Run the application now and inspect the network request for `$batch`, as shown in Figure 7.38. Notice that there is now a request payload sent with the request. The number you see in `--batch_NUMBER` was created automatically, so it might differ in your request. The payload closes with `--batch_NUMBER--`.

When you now look at the response (Figure 7.39), you'll also see that the response is sent back with `--batchresponse` information; the number in `--batchresponse_NUMBER` was created automatically and might differ in your response. The response closes with `--batchresponse_NUMBER--`.

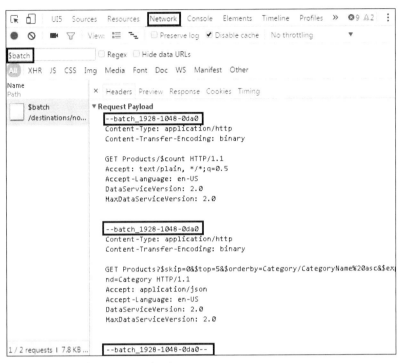

Figure 7.38 Batch Request Payload

Figure 7.39 Batch Response

7.7   One-Way and Two-Way Bindings

You learned about one- and two-way binding in Chapter 5, and the same principles you learned there apply to OData. The default binding for the SAPUI5 OData model is one-way binding. To manipulate the data inside the model with one-way binding, we must use the `setProperty` method of the OData model.

To explore the different binding options, we'll create a simple example in which we'll edit the properties of one product. The example is based on `odata-model-reading-data-bestpractice`, in which we had a view bound to the first product.

7.7.1   One-Way Binding

In the view, we'll use `sap.m.Text` to display the product name. Then, we'll use an `sap.m.Input` field to edit the product name. Those two controls are inside `sap.m.Panel` to enhance the visual display. At the bottom, we'll have two `sap.m.Button` instances, one to apply the changes and the other to reset the changes. Keep in mind that the changes won't be submitted to the backend. The page and the input now also get IDs so that we can more easily access them in the controller. Listing 7.34 shows the coding for the view.

```
<!-- Master.view.xml -->
<mvc:View
  controllerName=
"sapui5.demo.odata.readingdata.bestpractice.controller.Master"
  xmlns:mvc="sap.ui.core.mvc" xmlns="sap.m">
  <Page
    binding="{/Products(1)}"
    id="productInfo"
    title="Product {ProductID} Info">
    <content>
      <Panel>
        <Text
          text="Product Name: {ProductName}" />
        <Input
          id="newProductName"
          maxLength="40"
          placeholder="New product name" />
      </Panel>
    </content>
    <footer>
      <Bar>
        <contentRight>
          <Button
```

```
                    icon="sap-icon://undo"
                    press="onReset"
                    text="Reset Changes"/>
                <Button
                    icon="sap-icon://accept"
                    press="onChange"
                    text="Change Product Name"
                    type="Accept"/>
            </contentRight>
        </Bar>
    </footer>
  </Page>
</mvc:View>
```

Listing 7.34 View for One-Way Data Binding

In the controller coding we're accessing the binding path of the view—which is /Products(1)—by accessing the binding context of the page in the _getPathInfo function. We don't do this in the onInit function, because at this time, the binding information of the view is not available. To get the current model, we use the getModel() function, which inherited from BaseController.js; see Listing 7.21 for details.

In onChange, we're accessing the value from the input field directly. If there is no value, we leave the function. (This could also be solved with a JSON model.) Then, we set the new value for the product name with the setProperty method (we didn't name this function onSave because we're not writing to the backend). Next, we log to the console if the model has changes (which should be true) and then log those changes. In onReset, we reset the changes with resetChanges([sPath]). When you call this method without an array, all models are reset, so be careful! We again log if the model has changes (which should be false this time) and then log the changes (which should now be an empty object; see Listing 7.35).

```
sap.ui.define([
  "sapui5/demo/odata/readingdata/bestpractice/
    controller/BaseController"
], function(BaseController) {
  "use strict";

  return BaseController.extend(
"sapui5.demo.odata.readingdata.bestpractice.controller.Master", {

    _getPathInfo: function() {
```

```
      if (!this._sPath) {
        var oPage = this.getView().byId("productInfo");

        // "/Products(1)/ProductName
        this._sPath = oPage.getBindingContext()
          .getPath() + "/ProductName";
      }
      return this._sPath;
    },
  onEdit: function() {

    var oModel = this.getModel();
    var sPath = this._getPathInfo();
    var sNewValue = this.getView()
      .byId("newProductName").getValue();

    if (!sNewValue) {
      return;
    }
    oModel.setProperty(sPath, sNewValue);

    console.log("After setProperty: Model has pending changes:",
      oModel.hasPendingChanges());
    console.log("Pending changes:",
      oModel.getPendingChanges());
  },
  onReset: function() {

    var oModel = this.getModel();
    var sPath = this._getPathInfo();
    oModel.resetChanges([sPath]);

    console.log("After reset: Model has pending changes:",
      oModel.hasPendingChanges());
    console.log("Pending changes:",
      oModel.getPendingChanges());
  }
 });
});
```

Listing 7.35 Controller for One-Way Data Binding

Now, run the application and open the console. Change the name of the product, then click on the CHANGE PRODUCT NAME button. You'll see that the text in the text field above the input field also changes. When you click on the RESET CHANGES button, the text will change again back to what it was originally. In the console (Figure 7.40), you can see the expected outputs for the pending changes.

Figure 7.40 Pending and Reset Changes from OData Model

Now, let's move on to the two-way binding example. In the previous SAPUI5 OData model, this binding method was only experimental, but with the new OData v2 model, two-way binding is now supported.

7.7.2 Two-Way Binding

We can now adapt the view to display a `sap.m.SimpleForm` control instead of the text and input field before. Doing so will enhance the look of the app. We'll edit the name of the product and information about the quantity per unit. As before, we'll display this information in a text field above the input field. We don't need a button to apply the changes now; instead, we'll check the data inside the model to see if there are changes and what they are.

We'll enable the two-way binding within the Application Descriptor in which we defined the model. The property is called `defaultBindingMode`, as shown in Listing 7.36.

```
// manifest.jsonn
"sap.ui5": {
  ...
  "models": {
    "": {
      "dataSource": "mainService",
        "settings": {
          "useBatch": false,
          "defaultBindingMode": "TwoWay"
        }
    }, ...
```

Listing 7.36 Enabeling Two-Way Binding inside manifest.json

Listing 7.37 provides the shortened code of the view. We have set the `value-LiveUpate` property of the input fields to `true` so that the changes are reflected immediately.

```
<!-- Master.view.xml -->
<mvc:View
  ...
  xmlns:f="sap.ui.layout.form"
  xmlns:core="sap.ui.core"
  xmlns="sap.m">
  <Page id="productInfo" binding="{/Products(1)}">
    ...
    <Panel>
      <Text
        text="Product Info: {ProductName}, {QuantityPerUnit}">
      </Text>
      <f:SimpleForm>
        <core:Title
          text="Product Information" />
        <Label text="Product Name"/>
        <Input
          maxLength="40"
          value="{ProductName}"
          valueLiveUpdate="true"/>
        <Label
          text="Quantity per Unit"/>
        <Input
          maxLength="20"
          value="{QuantityPerUnit}"
          valueLiveUpdate="true"/>
      </f:SimpleForm>
    </Panel>
  </content>
  <footer>
    <Bar>
      <contentRight>
        <Button ...
        <Button
          icon="sap-icon://display"
          type="Accept"
          press="onCheck"
          text="Check changes"/>
      </contentRight> ...
```
Listing 7.37 View for Two-Way Binding

In the controller code, we've created the new `onCheck` function and adapted it to display the model data, as shown in Listing 7.38.

```
onCheck: function() {
  var oModel = this.getModel();
  var sPath = this._getPathInfo();
  var oData = oModel.getData(sPath);

  console.log("Model data:", oData);
  console.log("Model has pending changes:", oModel.hasPendingChanges());
  console.log("Pending changes:", oModel.getPendingChanges());
}, ...
```
Listing 7.38 Controller for Two-Way Binding

Let's run the app, open the console and apply the changes, and then reset them (Figure 7.41). Notice while you're typing that the text field now immediately displays the changes in the model. This is possible because we've used two-way binding. If your input field did not have the `valueLiveUpate` set to `true`, then you would have to tab to the next field or click on a button to see the changes.

Figure 7.41 Changing Data with Two-Way Binding

7.8 Writing Data

Before we start writing—that is creating, updating, and deleting—data with SAPUI5 and the OData model, let's explore those functions with the Postman plugin for Google Chrome. With the Postman plugin, you can send any kind of HTTP requests and you can also manipulate the headers. You can also use the Advanced REST client Google Chrome plugin as well.

Northwind v2 vs. v3

For the rest of this chapter, we'll switch to a lower version of the Northwind OData service—namely, to v2. Until now, we've used version v3 of the service, which is suitable for read scenarios and has more data to explore and play around with.

The SAPUI5 OData model currently supports only v2, but reading data from a v3 service was no problem. The next supported OData version from SAPUI5 is expected to be the new OData 4.0.

Let's run our first experiment with Postman with the familiar OData v3 service and request some data from the Products collection. Open the tool and enter the following URL:

http://services.odata.org/V3/Northwind/Northwind.svc/Products

In the Headers section, enter the following:

```
Accept: application/json
```

Make sure you're sending a GET request, and then click on the SEND button. Now, you should see that the data we get in response is JSON data (see Figure 7.42).

When the SAPUI5 OData v2 model requests data, it also gets JSON as a response by default, in contrast to XML for queries with Microsoft Internet Explorer. It's also possible to get JSON data with the URL parameter *http://services.odata.org/V3/Northwind/Northwind.svc/Products?$format=json*.

When you enter this URL into Microsoft Internet Explorer, the browser wants to download a JSON file. Therefore, it's better to use this URL in Google Chrome or Postman. The only resource you can't access as JSON is the metadata! Feel free to try out queries like $skip, $top, or $orderby in the tool that we previously looked at in the browser.

Figure 7.42 Getting Data as JSON via Postman

Now that you've played around a bit with the tool, let's get familiar with a Northwind service that has write capabilities enabled. There's a dedicated service for that purpose with only three entities (products, categories, and suppliers), and they contain only few properties. The only thing we need to be careful of is to note that the property names have changed slightly,—for example, from `ProductName` to `Name`.

Northwind OData Write Support

The Northwind OData service also provides a service with write support. To access it, just enter this URL into your browser:

http://services.odata.org/V2/(S(readwrite))/OData/OData.svc/

This will automatically create a random token that replaces the term *readwrite*. The result would look something like this:

http://services.odata.org/V2/(S(bpm4sqei3ponguqtna253n1a))/OData/OData.svc/

The service stores the data only for your current session! If you run into a problem and can't access your data anymore, just request a new session.

You can find more information about the service and supported actions at *http://www.odata.org/odata-services/*.

Figure 7.43 shows an overview of the service; here, we put the URL of the service including */$metadata* into the previously mentioned XOData online tool. One interesting point to note is the presence of the complex type, a reusable data structure inside the service to model complex data—address data, for example. Figure 7.44 shows an extract of the metadata from the service with the complex address type and how it's linked within the supplier. The whole namespace of the complex address is `"ODataDemo.Address"`, but when using it inside the supplier via the `Address` property, we can access the data like in Listing 7.39.

Figure 7.43 Northwind v2 Write-Enabled Service Overview

```
// access the whole address:
/Supplier(1)/Address
// access parts of the address
/Supplier(1)/Address/Street
/Supplier(1)/Address/City
```

Listing 7.39 Address Property

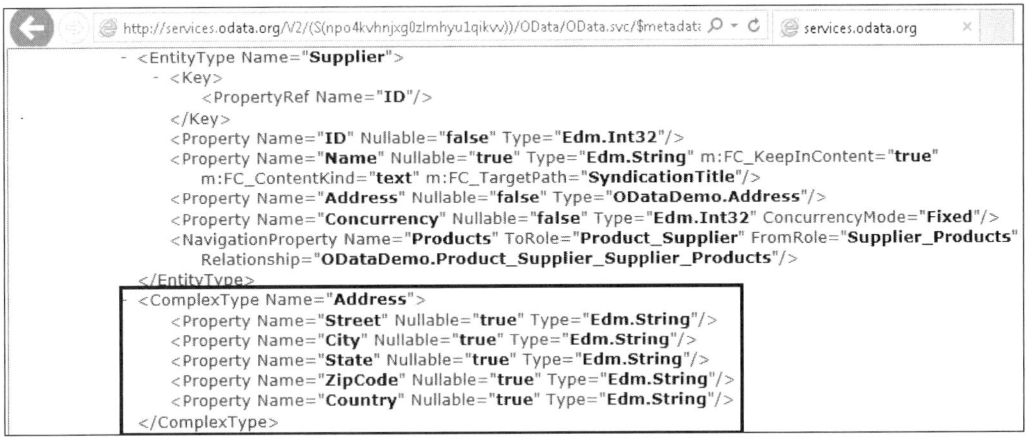

Figure 7.44 Supplier Complex Type for Address

Now that we have access to a backend in which we can manipulate some data, we can try it out within Postman. In the following sections, we'll look at creating, updating, and deleting an entry.

7.8.1 Creating an Entry

In this section, we'll start with the CREATE operation. You'll need the following information:

- Action: `Create`
- HTTP Method: `Post`
- Sent to: Collection
- Payload: Yes

Let's start by creating a supplier. The easiest way to do so is to first request an existing supplier, then copy and manipulate the response, and then create a new supplier. Enter the following URL into Postman, replacing bold section with your own session information:

*http://services.odata.org/V2/(S(**your-session-token**))/OData/OData.svc/Suppliers(1)*

Make sure that you have set the header as follows:

```
Accept: application/json
```

Ensure that you have selected a GET request. The result of this query is shown in Figure 7.45. Copy the response in the BODY area.

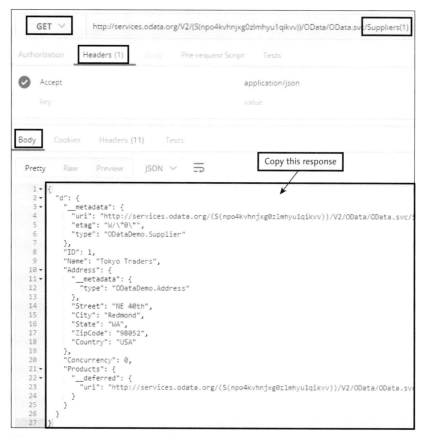

Figure 7.45 Response to GET Supplier 1 in Postman

The equivalent of this request in SAPUI5 would look like Listing 7.40.

```
oModel.read("/
Suppliers(1)", {success: fnSuccessHandler, error: fnErrorHandler});
function fnSuccessHandler(oData) {
  console.log("Data", oData);
} ...
```

Listing 7.40 Equivalent GET Request

Now, switch to a POST request and enter an additional header property (shown in bold):

```
Accept: application/json
Content-Type: application/json
```

Switch to the BODY tab next to the HEADER tab and select the RAW option. We chose this option because we don't send the data via a URL parameter or via a form. You should see JSON (APPLICATION/JSON) selected; this property comes from the Content-Type header. Figure 7.46 shows these settings.

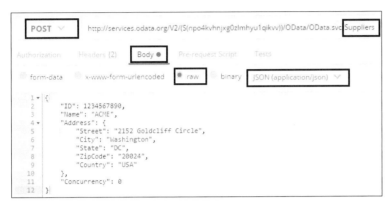

Figure 7.46 Settings in Postman to Create New Supplier

The data we will send is called a *payload*. Enter data like that in Listing 7.40; feel free to modify it.

```
{
  "ID": 1234567890,
  "Name": "ACME",
  "Address": {
    "Street": "2152 Goldcliff Circle",
    "City": "Washington",
    "State": "DC",
    "ZipCode": "20024",
    "Country": "USA"
  },
  "Concurrency": 0
}
```

Listing 7.41 Payload for Creating New Supplier

> **Note**
>
> In a real-life scenario, we wouldn't create the ID on the client side; this should be handled by the backend!

Let's compare this payload with the data we've received (Figure 7.45); both sets of data are listed in Table 7.7. We eliminated the "d" property; we also got rid of the two "__metadata" properties. The first one told us the URL of the supplier, which we don't need when we create a new supplier. The second one described the type of the address, which we don't need to send when we're creating data. We also deleted the "Products" object. If you refer back to Figure 7.43, you'll see that the product has a zero-to-many relationship with the supplier. Therefore, we don't need to define this relationship when we are creating a supplier.

POST Payload	GET Payload
| ```
{
  "ID": 1234567890,
  "Name": "ACME",
  "Address": {
    "Street":
      "2152 Goldcliff
      Circle",
    "City":
      "Washington",
    "State": "DC",
    "ZipCode": "20024",
    "Country": "USA"
  },
  "Concurrency": 0
}
``` | ```
{
  "d": {
    "__metadata": {
      "uri": "http://
services.odata.org/V2
/OData/OData.svc/Suppliers(1)",
      "etag": "W/\"0\"",
      "type": "ODataDemo.Supplier"
    },
    "ID": 1,
    "Name": "Tokyo Traders",
    "Address": {
      "__metadata": {
        "type": "ODataDemo.Address"
      },
      "Street": "NE 40th",
      "City": "Redmond",
      "State": "WA",
      "ZipCode": "98052",
      "Country": "USA"
    },
    "Concurrency": 0,
    "Products": {
      "__deferred": {
        "uri": "http://
services.odata.org/V2
/OData/OData.svc/Suppliers(1)/
Products"
      }
    }
  }
}
``` |

Table 7.7 Differences between the POST and GET Payloads

Last, but not least, change the URL as follows, replacing the bold section with your own session information:

*http://services.odata.org/V2/(S(**your-session-token**))/OData/OData.svc/Suppliers*

When we want to create an entry, we must POST it to the collection—in this case, /Suppliers (and not to an individual entry, like /Suppliers(1)). When the creation of an entry is successful, you should see an HTTP status of 201 and the data of the new entry should be returned, as shown in Figure 7.47.

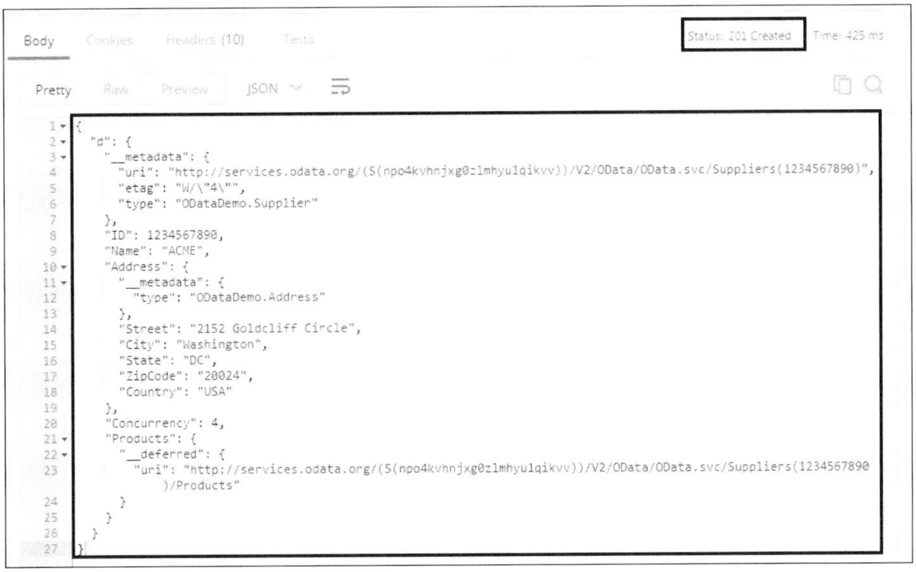

Figure 7.47 Successful Creation of New Supplier

You can now also access the data of the new supplier when you send a GET request to the new supplier URL:

*http://services.odata.org/V2/(S(**your-session-token**))/OData/OData.svc/Suppliers(1234567890)*

The SAPUI5 equivalent of creating such an entry is shown in Listing 7.42.

```
var oData ={
  "ID": 1234567890,
  "Name": "ACME",
  "Address": {
    ...
```

```
  },
  "Concurrency": 0
};
oModel.create("/Suppliers ", oData, {success: fnSuccessHandler,
  error: fnErrorHandler});
```
Listing 7.42 SAPUI5 OData Model: Create

7.8.2   Updating an Entry

When we want to update the data in OData, there are a few options; we can use the HTTP verbs PUT, PATCH, or POST. When using PUT, we have to send the whole modified dataset back; when using PATCH or POST (with merge), we only need to send the changes. The Northwind v2 service only supports PUT and POST, and the SAPUI5 OData v2 model uses the POST method.

You'll need the following information:

▸ Action: Update

▸ HTTP Method: PUT/PATCH/POST (with merge)

▸ Sent to: Entry

▸ Payload: Yes

Let's explore the different options via the Postman tool; we'll use the response from the newly created supplier to update the name. Let's start with the PUT method. Set the following Headers:

```
Accept: application/json
Content-Type: application/json
If-Match: *
```

The If-Match property has to do with concurrency control (called Etag). When we set it to *, we tell the service to overwrite the current stored properties of the service with our data; we're doing this here for demonstration purposes only! In Section 7.10, we'll provide an example of how to handle concurrency, because we don't want to force overwriting of the data in case another person has updated it as well. The SAPUI5 OData model manages the Etag handling automatically.

Enter the payload in Listing 7.43 into the BODY • RAW area (as we did when we created the supplier).

```
{
  "ID": 12347890,
  "Name": "ACME Inc.",
```

```
  "Address": {
    "Street": "2152 Goldcliff Circle",
    "City": "Washington",
    "State": "DC",
    "ZipCode": "20024",
    "Country": "USA"
  },
    "Concurrency": 0
}
```

Listing 7.43 Payload for Updating Supplier with PUT

The URL for the service should point to the supplier we'd like to edit:

*http://services.odata.org/V2/(S(**your-session-token**))/OData/OData.svc/Suppliers
(1234567890)*

A successful update returns the HTTP status `204 No Content`, and we don't get any payload content back, as you can see in Figure 7.48.

Figure 7.48 Successful Response for Updating a Supplier

The `PUT` method seems cumbersome, because we always have to send the complete data to the backend to update a property. It's more convenient to send only the data we want to change. We can enable this for the HTTP method `POST` with the header property `x-http-method` and set it to `MERGE`. This means that the changes we send will be merged in the backend. Let's add this setting into the header section:

```
Accept: application/json
Content-Type: application/json
If-Match: *
x-http-method: MERGE
```

Change the HTTP method to `POST` and provide this payload:

```
{
  "Name": "ACME"
}
```

Keep the previous URL:

http://services.odata.org/V2/(S(your-session-token))/OData/OData.svc/Suppliers (1234567890)

After you send the data, you should receive the same 204 response you saw in Figure 7.48. The SAPUI5 equivalent of this request would look like Listing 7.44.

```
var oData ={
  "Name": "ACME Super Inc."
};
oModel.update("/Suppliers(1234567890)", oData, {success:
  fnSuccessHandler, error: fnErrorHandler});
```

Listing 7.44 SAPUI5 OData Model: Update

7.8.3 Deleting an Entry

To delete an entry, we need to send a DELETE request to the corresponding entry. You'll need the following information:

- ▶ Action: Delete
- ▶ HTTP Method: DELETE
- ▶ Sent to: Entry
- ▶ Payload: No

Set the following headers:

```
Accept: application/json
Content-Type: application/json
If-Match: *
```

Do not put any payload in the BODY • RAW area, and point to the following URL:

http://services.odata.org/V2/(S(your-session-token))/OData/OData.svc/Suppliers (1234567890)

After you have sent the request, you should receive the same 204 response that you saw in Figure 7.48. Figure 7.49 shows the settings for sending the DELETE request.

The SAPUI5 equivalent of this request would look like this:

```
oModel.remove("/Suppliers(1234567890)", {success: fnSuccessHandler,
error: fnErrorHandler});
```

Figure 7.49 Settings for Deleting an Entry

In the source code folder *odata-model-write-edit-delete-supplier* of this chapter, we've provided a minimalistic example in which you can see examples of everything in this writing data section in action. You only need to adapt the session token in the manifest.json file. Feel free to explore the NETWORK tab when you're manipulating the data in the SAPUI5 app, and also explore the data in the Postman tool at the same time. In Chapter 8, we will provide additional, full-fledged applications, including information on how to use the OData model in a real application.

7.9   Function Imports

The OData protocol allows you to call functions. You can use this ability to request data, which would be tedious if you put together a query every time. It's also useful when you want to update the status of a leave request that would otherwise trigger a lot of other actions (workflow scenarios).

The write-enabled Northwind service we used in the previous section also provides a function import, which we'll explore now. You can access information about the function imports that a service provides from the metadata of the services, accessed by appending */$metadata* at the end of the service's root URL. Figure 7.50 shows information for the `GetProductsByRating` function import. Note the `httpMethod`, which you need for calling the function, and the parameters you need to provide. For this example, we need `GET` and to provide a `rating` parameter. You can also see that we'll get a collection of entries back.

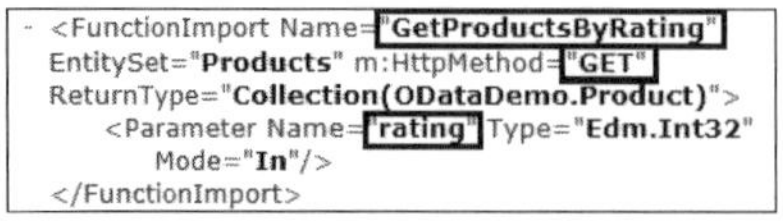

```
- <FunctionImport Name="GetProductsByRating"
  EntitySet="Products" m:HttpMethod="GET"
  ReturnType="Collection(ODataDemo.Product)">
    <Parameter Name="rating" Type="Edm.Int32"
      Mode="In"/>
  </FunctionImport>
```

Figure 7.50 Function Import Metadata Information

Because this is a simple `GET` request, we can handle it easily in our browser by entering the following information into the browser (enter your own session token):

http://services.odata.org/V2/(S(your-session-token))/OData/OData.svc/GetProducts-ByRating?rating=3

You should now see a few entries that fulfill the rating criteria, which we've set to 3 (Figure 7.51).

Figure 7.51 Calling GetProductsByRating Function Import in Browser

An equivalent SAPUI5 request would look like this:

```
oModel.callFunction("/GetProductsByRating",{method:"GET",
urlParameters:{"rating":3}, success:fnSuccess, error: fnError});
function fnSuccess(oData) { ... } ...
```

Currently, only the `"IN"` parameters of a function import are supported. When we're only accessing data with GET, no data will be updated, so the data in the OData model will not change! When we perform data manipulation—with POST, for example—the model will update automatically. When we send the request with callFunction, we can access the result in the success handler, put this data into a JSON model, and display it in a list. You'll find such an example in the source code folder *odata-model-function-import* from this chapter; just change your session token for the service in manifest.json. Listing 7.45 shows an extract of the view, and Listing 7.46 shows an extract from the corresponding controller.

```
<!-- Master.view.xml -->
<List
  class="sapUiResponsiveMargin"
  width="auto"
  items="{viewModel>/Products}">
  <headerToolbar>
    <Toolbar>
      <Title text="Products: GetProductByRating" />
      <ToolbarSpacer />
      <SearchField width="50%"
        placeholder="Rating"
        search="onGetProductsByRating" />
    </Toolbar>
  </headerToolbar>
  <items>
    <ObjectListItem
      title="{viewModel>Name}"
      number="{viewModel>Rating}" >
    </ObjectListItem>
  </items>
</List>
```

Listing 7.45 View for Calling Function Import

We used a named model, called viewModel, and the property /Products to display the data in the list. In the controller, you'll see that this is a JSON model initialized in the onInit function. When you press [Enter] in the search field or click on the magnifying glass, onGetProductsByRating is called and the rating number we've entered is passed to the function. The data for the list is set after we have successfully called the function import.

```
sap.ui.define([
  "sapui5/demo/odata/function/import/controller/BaseController",
  "sap/ui/model/json/JSONModel"
], function(BaseController, JSONModel) {
```

```
  "use strict";

  return BaseController.extend(
"sapui5.demo.odata.function.import.controller.Master", {

    onInit: function() {
      var oModel = new sap.ui.model.json.JSONModel();
      this.getView().setModel(oModel, "viewModel");
    },

    onGetProductsByRating: function(oEvent) {
      var oODataModel = this.getModel();
      var sQuery = oEvent.getParameter("query");
      var mParameters = {
        "rating": sQuery
      };

      oODataModel.callFunction("/GetProductsByRating", {
        method: "GET",
        urlParameters: mParameters,
        success: fnSuccess.bind(this),
        error: fnError.bind(this)
      });

      function fnError(oError) {
        console.log("error", oError);
      }

      function fnSuccess(oData, oResponse) {
        if (oData) {
          var oViewModel = this.getModel("viewModel");
          oViewModel.setData({
            Products: oData.results
          }); ...
```

Listing 7.46 Controller for Calling Function Import

Figure 7.52 shows the result of the running application.

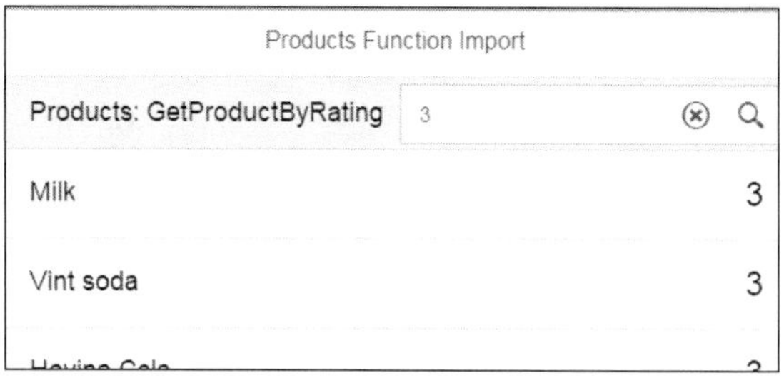

Products Function Import			
Products: GetProductByRating	3	⊗	🔍
Milk			3
Vint soda			3
Havina Cola			3

Figure 7.52 Running Function Import Application

7.10 Concurrency Control

When we updated a supplier entry in Section 7.8, we touched on the topic of concurrency, which we'll now explain further. REST is a stateless protocol, so there's no ability to lock certain data when one person is editing the data. If we could lock the data, this would be called *pessimistic concurrency*; you may be familiar with this concept from ABAP Logical Unit of Work (LUW). What we can achieve with OData is *optimistic concurrency*, in which the client is responsible for holding the temporary data rather than locking it.

To implement optimistic concurrency, we use the so-called `Etag`. This functionality can be provided for each entity type. In our write-enabled Northwind example, the supplier entity is capable of `Etags`.

When receiving an entry, the server returns an opaque `Etag` value. The location of the `Etag` value can differ, so we have listed them below:

- When requesting several entries, the `Etag` is included in the `metadata` section of the entry.
- When a single value is requested, the `Etag` is returned in the response header called `Etag`, and the server also may include it in the body for reasons of consistency.
- During `POST`, `PUT`, and `MERGE` operations, the server should compute a new `Etag` and return it in a response header.

When sending a `POST`, `PUT`, `MERGE`, or `DELETE` request, the client needs to send the `Etag` in the `If-Match` HTTP header. Based on the values of the `Etag` from the client and on the server the requests will be successful or not, based on the following:

- If it's acceptable for a client to overwrite any version of the entry on the server, then the value * can be used instead of the current `Etag`.
- If the `Etag` of the client and the `Etag` of the server are different, the request will fail with a `Precondition Failed` response. If no `Etag` was provided, the request will fail with a `Missing If-Match header` message.
- When the modification of the entry succeeds, we'll receive a `204` response with no content.

341

We can produce such a conflict behavior in the Postman tool to produce a `Pre-condition Failed` response. Let's create a new supplier like we did in Section 7.8. In the response, we'll receive an `Etag`, which we'll copy (see Listing 7.47).

```
{  "d": {
    "__metadata": {
      "uri": "http://services.odata.org/(S(your-session-token))/V2/
ODataData/OData.svc/Suppliers(1234567890)",
      "etag": "W/\"3\"",
      "type": "ODataDemo.Supplier"
    }, ...
```
Listing 7.47 Etag Response Creation of Supplier

When copying the `Etag` value, please note that the \ is there as an escape character; we don't need it. You can copy the value more easily from the response header, as shown in Figure 7.53.

Figure 7.53 Response Header with Etag after Creating Supplier

Now, let's update the name of the supplier with a `POST` request with `MERGE` enabled. Put the settings we just copied into the request header (your `Etag` may be different):

```
Accept: application/json
Content-Type: application/json
If-Match: W/"3"
x-http-method: MERGE
```

You should receive a successful `204` response. If not, double-check the value of the `Etag`. You'll also receive a new `Etag` in the response header, as you can see in Figure 7.54.

Figure 7.54 Response Header with Etag after Updating Supplier

Note this new `Etag`. We can already simulate a concurrency problem; we just need to send the same request again—with the old `Etag`! Because the value of the `Etag` on the server is different from the value we sent from the client, we now have a problem, which results in a `Precondition Failed` response, shown in Figure 7.55.

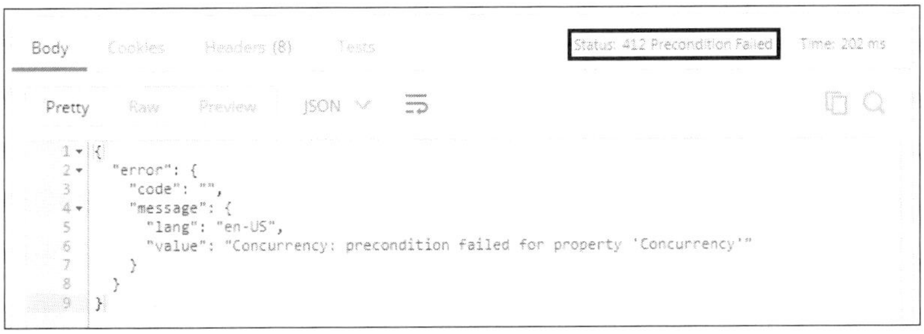

```
1 {
2   "error": {
3     "code": "",
4     "message": {
5       "lang": "en-US",
6       "value": "Concurrency: precondition failed for property 'Concurrency'"
7     }
8   }
9 }
```

Figure 7.55 Etag Conflict

In real life, this will happened if, say, User 1 changes the name of the supplier, and then User 2 also tries to change the name. Both changes would send the same `Etag`, but after the successful modification of User 1, a new `Etag` was created, and thus the `Etag` of User 2 was no longer valid. User 2 would now need to request the new `Etag` and modify his request.

To solve the conflict, we need to provide the correct `Etag` we noted earlier and send the request again. We should now get a `204` and a new `Etag` in the response header: `W/"5"`.

If instead we want to overwrite whatever value is stored on the server for this entry, we can set our request header as follows:

```
If-Match: *
```

You can also simulate such a conflict if you modify your entry with Postman and then try to modify the value in your SAPUI5 app. Postman would be User 1 in this situation, and your SAPUI5 app would be User 2. You need to create a new supplier inside Postman, modify it there, and then try to modify it in the SAPUI5 app.

The `Etag` functionality is supported by SAP Gateway SP 09/SAP NetWeaver 7.4 SP 08. It is not supported in the SAPUI5 MockServer. (You'll learn more about MockServer in Chapter 11.)

7.11 Summary

In this chapter, we started with the basics of OData and explored how we can interact with such a service via a browser. You learned about the service document and the service metadata document, which help us understand which entities are contained in the service, if and how we can navigate between them, and which properties they contain.

We were able to filter, sort, and expand the displayed data, access only a certain amount of data, or skip certain entries via URL parameters. You learned how to execute the same operations with the SAPUI5 OData model and how specific SAPUI5 controls such as list implement such operations.

Next, you modified data in the OData service, first with a REST client and later on via SAPUI5 coding. You also learned about batch mode, which is able to combine multiple requests into one request.

We explained the differences between one- and two-way data binding when working with OData and SAPUI5. Two-way data binding is now officially supported as of the SAPUI5 OData v2 model, which makes application coding much easier. Finally, we looked at how to call function imports from OData services and how concurrency handling is implemented.

In the coding examples for this chapter, there are many small examples that highlight all the different aspects we talked about. We encourage you to try them out and to look at the network requests that are sent and their responses. Also play around with the Northwind service with a REST client and try to modify data with it. When you use the write-enabled service, make sure to update your session token, as we discussed in Section 7.8.

It's crucial to understand OData when developing SAPUI5 applications, because most data will be exchanged and modified via OData. We hope we have given you a broad overview of this topic and how to handle OData within SAPUI5. Chapter 8 will address how to build more sophisticated applications, and it will be easy for you to expand those applications with more functionality and OData operations, like modifying or deleting data.

Application development in general must close the gap between technological feasibility and the best possible support for a given usage scenario. Therefore, we must not only know about technology but also have a deep understanding of user requirements and constraints. In this chapter, we'll approach the topic of application patterns from both design and technical perspectives.

8 Application Patterns and Examples

Application development with SAPUI5 benefits from the well-defined design patterns and overall application concepts found in the SAP Fiori design guidelines, available at *https://experience.sap.com/fiori-design/*. From a design perspective, this information provides clear guidance on how to structure your content, define usage patterns, and define interaction flows, allowing you to concentrate on your specific scenario implementation, building on top of best practices. From an application developer's point of view, SAPUI5 supports the implementation of these guidelines by providing controls and the right APIs that are built based on the overall design requirements.

Although it's been said that good user experience can never be achieved simply by technology alone, technical aspects and decisions do play an important role. As previously stated, SAP Fiori design concepts and SAPUI5 grew up together. While SAP Fiori emphasized the implementation of small, single-purpose applications, SAPUI5 served as the tailored technology for these application.

For us, this means that we should always try to build individual and focused applications. For example, in a scenario in which our users can create, approve, and analyze leave requests, we should create three applications.

In this chapter, we'll explore general application concepts and patterns found in SAPUI5. We'll start with general application layouts, then dig deeper and explore more detailed floorplans. Finally, we'll look into specific application types and explore shared application features. We'll always start from a design perspective and build knowledge for use cases and underlying assumptions. Then, we'll start to explore technical assets like controls that are provided by SAPUI5 and that ease the implementation of these design patterns.

In the final section of this chapter, you'll learn how SAP Fiori Launchpad serves as the central access point for SAPUI5 applications in many scenarios and will gain some hands-on experience with its developer features.

8.1 Layouts

Laying out applications generally happens at different levels. Think of a grid used to cut the screen into pieces that will later be assigned individual content. This concept is common in web development.

When building full-blown applications, you might still use a grid-based approach. However, you should first think about the general cut of your application, meaning the overall number of content areas you'll need to leverage to enrich user experience and to streamline the tasks your users will have to complete using the application you build. Therefore, the first decision you make should be simply whether you want to build a *full-screen* or *split-screen application*. Differentiating between full-screen and split-screen options might seem like a no-brainer at first glance, but we'll discuss these difference to a greater extent in this section. The choice isn't as simple as it may seem initially.

These applications can be derived from the task, sequence of usage, and target group of your application. This first decision will ultimately help you understand the underlying usage scenario of your application in greater detail. We'll outline the important questions to ask when choosing a layout in this section, and then we'll build example implementations using SAPUI5 controls. To begin, we'll use a simple application skeleton that can be generated from a template in the SAP Web IDE.

The generation of templates in the SAP Web IDE is covered in Appendix D of this book. Please look up the general wizard functionality there. What we want to generate now is the SAPUI5 APPLICATION template (see Figure 8.1).

This template provides the right folder structure and all the files needed to build our first prototypes. Most of it should look familiar from the previous examples in the book. We use this template frequently to test new controls or even to test complex patterns isolated from the actual project we're working on. With some small changes, it can also serve as a base for application development.

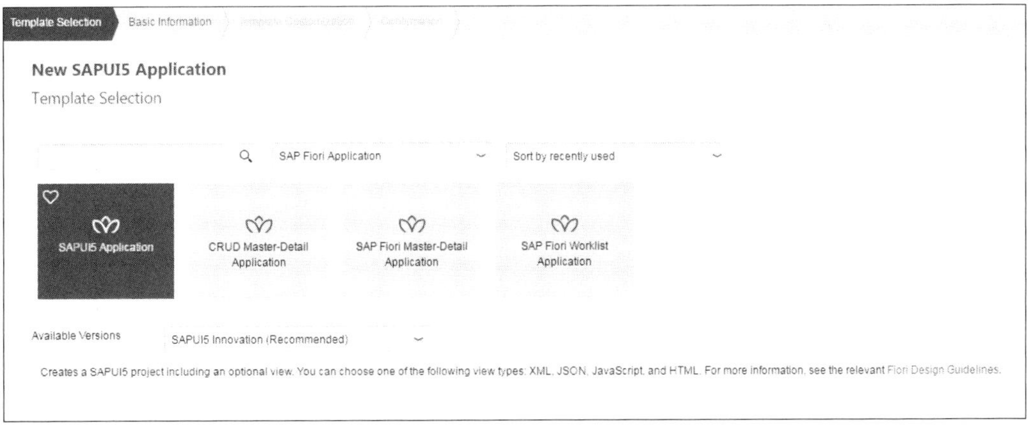

Figure 8.1 SAPUI5 Template in Template Wizard

Let's first look into the Main.view.xml file in the *view* folder of the project. This is defined as the `rootView` in manifest.json and will therefore be loaded at application startup (see Listing 8.1).

```
<mvc:View
  controllerName="my.app.controller.Main"
  xmlns:html=http://www.w3.org/1999/xhtml
  xmlns:mvc="sap.ui.core.mvc"
  xmlns="sap.m">
  <App>
    <pages>
      <Page title="{i18n>title}">
        <content></content>
      </Page>
    </pages>
  </App>
</mvc:View>
```

Listing 8.1 Initial Main.view.xml

The app control serves as a root control for the template application. However, it already has a `sap.m.Page` element prefilled in its `pages` aggregation. In application development, we use routing in SAPUI5 to display individual views and can therefore delete the page and all its content. In addition, we'll add an ID to the root control that we can use later in the routing configuration (see Listing 8.2).

```
<mvc:View
  controllerName="my.app.controller.Main"
  xmlns:html=http://www.w3.org/1999/xhtml
  xmlns:mvc="sap.ui.core.mvc"
  xmlns="sap.m">
  <App id="rootControl"/>
</mvc:View>
```
Listing 8.2 Main.view.xml: Adapted

We still need to set up some basic routing configuration to enable the dynamic display of content in the root control. For this, we'll add a routing block into the sap.ui5 namespace in manifest.json (see Listing 8.3). This block should hold the ID of the root control and some generic settings, such as controlAggregation and the path to the root view. Refer back to Chapter 4 for more details.

```
"sap.ui5": {
  "_version": "1.1.0",
  "rootView": {
    "viewName": "my.app.view.Main",
    "type": "XML"
  },
  "routing": {
    "config": {
      "routerClass": "sap.m.routing.Router",
      "controlId": "rootControl",
      "controlAggregation" : "pages",
      "viewPath": "my.app.view",
      "viewType": "XML",
      "async": true
    }
  },
```
Listing 8.3 Basic Routing Configuration

Although the SAPUI5 controls from the sap.m library we will use come with built-in support for different form factors, like mobile and desktop devices, we still have to tell the toolkit for what device it should optimize the display. This will happen dynamically based on what the sap.ui.Device API has identified. To enable this functionality, we'll add the check shown in Listing 8.4 to the onInit event of the main controller.

```
onInit : function() {
  var sContentDensityClass = "";
  if (jQuery(document.body).hasClass("sapUiSizeCozy") || jQuery(documen
t.body).hasClass("sapUiSizeCompact")) {
    sContentDensityClass = "";
```

```
  } else if (!Device.support.touch) {
    sContentDensityClass = "sapUiSizeCompact";
  } else {
    sContentDensityClass = "sapUiSizeCozy";
  }
  this.getView().addStyleClass(sContentDensityClass);
}
```

Listing 8.4 Content Density Check in Main.controller.js

Finally, we'll add a configuration for the creation of a `sap.ui.model.odata.v2.`
`ODataModel` instance that uses an SAP NetWeaver demo OData service provided
by SAP as `dataSource` into manifest.json. We'll use this model later to display real
data when building the floorplans and example applications. For now, it will be
created silently without any effect.

```
{
  "sap.app" : {
    "dataSources": {
      "mainService": {
        "uri": "/destinations/ES4/sap/opu/odata/IWBEP/GWSAMPLE_BASIC/",
        "type": "OData",
        "settings": {
          "odataVersion": "2.0"
        }
      }
    }
..},
  "sap.ui5":{
    "models": {
      "": {
        "dataSource": "mainService",
        "settings": {
          "metadataUrlParams": {
            "sap-documentation": "heading, quickinfo"
          }
        }
      }
    }
  }
}
```

Listing 8.5 Excerpt from manifest.json with OData Model Creation

The result should now look like Figure 8.2: a simple, letterboxed `sap.ui.core.`
`UIComponent` display that's still unspectacular. However, with this foundation in

place, we're well prepared to later implement specific layouts and floorplans and then start the real application development.

Figure 8.2 Application Starter Template Display

In the following two subsections, we'll look at guidelines for creating both a full-screen and a split-screen layout.

8.1.1 Full-Screen Layout: sap.m.App

Naturally, full-screen apps make use of the entire screen. You can still decide if you want to have your app in a letterboxed display or not (see Section 8.3.4 for details), but the main characteristic of a full-screen layout from a programming point of view is that it contains a single content area.

The term *content area* might need some explanation. Just think of one, single-purpose area on your screen. This could be a list of items that is displayed, for example, or details about a specific item. This will become clearer when you learn more about the split-screen layout in Section 8.1.2.

For the full-screen layout, it's important to understand that there should be only one purpose per screen (like the display of object details), although this could still mean that you mix information from different data sources and even use different types of display. This can include charts, textual information, and even a list of related items. Therefore, a full-screen layout is clearly purpose-oriented and has nothing to do with data origin or media.

The following are some guiding questions you should ask yourself when using a full-screen layout:

- Do I want to display a high number of facets related to a single entity with minimal navigation?
- Does the content require maximal space (e.g., charts or images)?
- Do I want to display a list in combination with complex filtering options?

Technically, a full-screen layout uses the `sap.m.App` control as a root control. Based on the routing configuration, different views can be placed into its `pages` aggregation. Because the `sap.m.App` control inherits from `sap.m.NavContainer`, transitions are fully supported, and routing-specific events can be attached and handled based on the existing API.

Pay attention to *responsive behavior* for full-screen applications. Later, you'll see that the control used as a root control for the split-screen layout introduces some responsiveness out of the box. This is not the case for the app control, however, because of the single content area. That's why we will have to take care of enabling responsive behavior directly for the full-screen layout. Luckily, SAPUI5 provides controls that include the necessary intelligence to handle different form factors, which is why we'll use pages from `sap.m.semantic` when building applications. For this example, we'll use `sap.m.semantic.FullscreenPage`, which provides overflow handling for header and footer areas in the full-screen layout. We'll revisit headers and foots in Section 8.3.5.

Let's now enhance the starter application by adding a first view and additional routing configuration so that it can serve as a first, simple, full-screen-layout application (see Listing 8.6 and Listing 8.7). This results in a simple full-screen display as in Figure 8.3.

```
<mvc:View
  controllerName="my.app.controller.Main"
  xmlns:html=http://www.w3.org/1999/xhtml
  xmlns:mvc="sap.ui.core.mvc"
  xmlns="sap.m"
  xmlns:semantic="sap.m.semantic">
  <semantic:FullscreenPage title="Fullscreen">
    <!-- Enough space for your content here -->
  </semantic:FullscreenPage>
</mvc:View>
```

Listing 8.6 webapp/view/Home.view.xml

```json
"routing": {
  "config": {
    "controlId": "rootControl",
    "controlAggregation" : "pages",
    "viewPath": "my.app.view",
    "viewType": "XML"
  },
  "routes": [{
    "name" : "home",
    "pattern": "",
    "target": ["home"]
  }],
  "targets": {
    "home": {
      "viewName": "Home"
    }
  }
},
```

Listing 8.7 Simple Full-Screen Routing Configuration in manifest.json

Figure 8.3 Simple Full-Screen Layout

This is obviously not rocket science: You could easily build upon this foundation with what you've learned in this book already and extend this view now with controls and content.

Now, let`s look at what floorplans, defined by the SAP Fiori design guidelines, make use of the full-screen layout:

- **Initial page**
  Single object display based on user input (search, barcode scanning).

- **Worklist**
  See Section 8.2.1.

- **List report**
  Multi-object display with extended filtering/sorting capabilities.

8.1.2 Split Screen Layout: sap.m.SplitApp

Now, let's turn our attention to the split-screen layout in SAPUI5. A split screen consists of at least two content areas displayed side by side. However, this does not mean that the two areas are separate from each other; in fact, both content areas need to be orchestrated such that they're dependent on each other. One frequently used and well-established floorplan in SAP Fiori is the master-detail pattern. The selection in the master list determines the display of details of the selected item in the object view. We will look into this pattern in more detail in Section 8.2.2.

One use case that benefits the most from using a split-screen layout is one in which you expect your application users to review a high number of items—for example, in approval scenarios. In this case, you generally want to assure that users do not have to execute a high number of back and forth navigations and therefore want to display the list to select from next to the details to review, all on one screen. Most of us use this pattern on a daily basis; for example, it's a default setting in most of the local email clients available.

The general build-up of a split-screen layout is similar to what you've already seen for the full-screen layout in Section 8.1.1, with some slight modifications. We can again make use of the application starter template we created in Section 8.1.

We'll start by using a different root control and some other slight modifications down the line. First, we'll use the `sap.m.SplitApp` control in Main.view.xml (see Listing 8.8).

```
<mvc:View
  controllerName="my.app.controller.Main"
  xmlns:html=http://www.w3.org/1999/xhtml
  xmlns:mvc="sap.ui.core.mvc"
  xmlns="sap.m">
  <SplitApp id="rootControl"/>
</mvc:View>
```

Listing 8.8 Main.view.xml for Split-Screen Layout

The `sap.m.SplitApp` control is a pretty clever composite control that provides two `sap.m.NavContainer` elements internally as hidden aggregations that can be populated by making use of two public aggregations: `masterPages` and `detailPages`. We can therefore use the routing configuration to handle the placement of views into these aggregations and again use routing events if needed. The `masterPages` and `detailPages` are derived from the internal navigation containers that are wrapped and exposed by the `sap.m.SplitApp` control. Before we look into the routing configuration in detail, let's first create two views. For the split screen with `sap.m.SplitApp`, we can use specific semantic page controls—one for the `masterPages` aggregation (see Listing 8.9), and one for `detailPages` (see Listing 8.10).

```
<mvc:View
  xmlns:html=http://www.w3.org/1999/xhtml
  xmlns:mvc="sap.ui.core.mvc"
  xmlns="sap.m"
  xmlns:semantic="sap.m.semantic">
  <semantic:MasterPage title="Master">
    <!-- Enough space for your content here -->
  </semantic:MasterPage>
</mvc:View>
```

Listing 8.9 Master.view.xml with sap.m.semantic.MasterPage

```
<mvc:View
  xmlns:html=http://www.w3.org/1999/xhtml
  xmlns:mvc="sap.ui.core.mvc"
  xmlns="sap.m"
  xmlns:semantic="sap.m.semantic">
  <semantic:DatailPage title="Detail">
```

```
    <!-- Enough space for your content here -->
  </semantic:DetailPage>
</mvc:View>
```
Listing 8.10 Detail.view.xml with sap.m.semantic.DetailPage

Now, let's modify and enhance the existing routing configuration. We want to ensure that both Master.view.xml and Detail.view.xml are displayed in the respective aggregations of the root control when the application is started.

To achieve this, let's quickly revisit what you learned in Chapter 4, Section 4.7 about how routing works in SAPUI5. The routing configuration is built up by configuring the router globally in the `config` setting and can then be enriched for specific routes and targets. In that sense, the configuration for targets is more specific than the one for routes, and configuration options can even be overridden. For the current scenario, we'll therefore have specific targets that define their own aggregations to address the two content areas in `sap.m.SplitApp` accordingly. Compared to the routing configuration for the full-screen layout, we'll have two additional targets for every route. Here, the sequence makes a difference. This is because `sap.m.SplitApp` handles the display of views based on the current screen size and therefore includes responsiveness across form factors out of the box. Figure 8.4 shows that the control displays differently across device types.

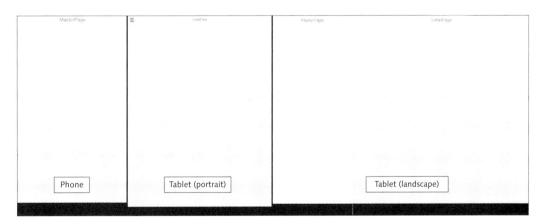

Figure 8.4 Responsiveness of sap.m.SplitApp

You can influence this control behavior with the routing configuration. To do so, define the targets per route in the right sequence with the target you want to have displayed on a phone, on which only one content area will be displayed, for this route in the array of targets. For the default route, with an empty hash, you'll most likely choose the master view. In that case, on a tablet in portrait mode, you'll see the details view and a button in the header; clicking on that button will slide in the master view (see Listing 8.11).

```
"routing": {
  "config": {
    "controlId": "rootControl",
    "viewPath": "my.app.view",
    "viewType": "XML"
  },
  "routes" : [
    {
        "pattern" : "",
        "name" : "main",
        "target" : ["detail", "master"]

    }
  ],
  "targets" : {
    "master" : {
      "viewName" : "Master",
      "controlAggregation" : "masterPages"
    },
    "detail" : {
      "viewName" : "Detail",
      "controlAggregation" : "detailPages"
    }
  }
},
```

Listing 8.11 Routing Configuration in manifest.json

---

sap.m.SplitAppModes

In addition to its default behavior, `sap.m.SplitApp` offers four different modes for handling the `masterPages` aggregation display on mobile devices. The `mode` property can be set either as static on the declaration of the control in the XML or as dynamic in JavaScript using the default setter. The modes include the following:

► `ShowHideMode` **(default)**
Master hidden in portrait mode

► `StretchCompressMode`
Master in a compressed version in portrait mode

► `PopoverMode`
Master shown in a popover in portrait mode

▸ `HideMode`
  Master initially hidden in portrait and landscape

In SAPUI5, there are several controls that can be used to create an application with more than one content area. Most of these examples are part of the `sap.ui.layout` library:

▸ `sap.ui.layout.Splitter`

▸ `sap.ui.layout.DynamicSideContent`

▸ `sap.ui.layout.ResponsiveSplitter`

In this section, we walked through the split-screen layout. In the next section, we'll use the skeleton layouts of our full- and split-screen layouts in floorplans.

8.2 Floorplans

In this section, we'll take the layout skeletons we built in Section 8.1 and extend them to match their respective floorplans with all the needed functionality. We'll actually take this one step further and build two applications that we can later use in Section 8.4 to integrate into SAP Fiori Launchpad and make use of some of the features the launchpad provides for cross-application navigation.

In Section 8.2.1, we'll build a worklist that displays data from `SalesOrder` entitySet in a demo service. Because each `SalesOrder` item is associated with a specific `BusinessPartner` in the service, we'll also build a business partner address book in Section 8.2.2 using the master-detail layout.

> **Note**
>
> In the following sections, we outline the most important features and cornerstones of SAPUI5 application development. Because application development with SAPUI5 could easily fill more than a single chapter, we'll only give examples of certain application patterns here. We'll also describe some shared application features in Section 8.3. Here is a list of application best practices that should be followed but could not be described or used in the scope of this chapter:
>
> ▸ **Usage of i18n texts**
>   Do not use hard-coded strings in XML or JavaScript to be displayed in the view. Always use texts that can be translated centrally.

> ► **Usage of fixed IDs for controls**
> Always add a fixed ID to all controls that are not used as templates in aggregations.

8.2.1 Worklist

In this section, we'll take the full-screen layout we created in Section 8.1.1 and extend the coding to match the worklist floorplan. The *worklist floorplan* can be used for all applications that should display a number of work items. *Work items* are items that need to be processed by the user. For example, stock management is a use case in which users have to ensure a balanced stock level and can trigger actions on individual items. Applications should display the most relevant information in a list of all items on the first screen, allow users to review more detailed information per item on a second screen, and generally offer processing options. If we stay with the stock management use case, these processing options could include reordering or discontinuing items. The SAPUI5 Demo Kit includes a tutorial covering how to build this use case.

We'll now lay the foundation for a worklist by creating the views and adding the essential controls.

Worklist Table

The actual worklist is technically a responsive table (`sap.m.Table`). We'll add the table to the *Home.view.xml* file created in Section 8.1, but will rename it to Worklist.view.xml. The user should be offered additional options to limit or refine the results displayed in the worklist. This can be achieved by using filters, search, or sorting capabilities, which can be triggered by controls displayed via `sap.m.Toolbar`. `sap.m.Toolbar` can be added to the `headerToolbar` aggregation of the responsive table.

For a nice display, we'll also add a `responsive-margin-css` class provided by SAPUI5 and bind it to `SaleOrderSet` in the OData service. To have a minimal footprint on the screen, we'll also show some bound properties via `sap.m.ColumnListItem` and add a custom action to the table using `sap.m.Button`.

The simple version shown in Listing 8.12 leads to the display shown in Figure 8.5.

Note

Custom actions on the worklist are an optional way to provide direct access to commonly used functionality for the user. You can decide to add the actions directly on the list based on whether the information available initially justifies an action to be triggered. Another option is to require actions to be performed initially in every case.

```
<Table
  id="table"
  class="sapUiResponsiveMargin"
  width="auto"
  items="{
    path : '/SalesOrderSet'
  }">
  <headerToolbar>
    <Toolbar>
      <Title
        Id="title"
        text="Manage Sales Orders"/>
      <ToolbarSpacer/>
      <SearchField
        width="auto"/>
      <OverflowToolbarButton icon="sap-icon://filter"/>
      <OverflowToolbarButton icon="sap-icon://sort"/>
    </Toolbar>
  </headerToolbar>
  <columns>
    <Column>
      <Text text="Customer"/>
    </Column>
    <Column>
      <Text text="Net Amount"/>
    </Column>
    <Column/>
  </columns>
  <items>
    <ColumnListItem vAlign="Middle">
      <cells>
        <Link text="{CustomerName}"/>
        <Text text="{NetAmount}"/>
        <Button text="Create Incoive"/>
      </cells>
    </ColumnListItem>
  </items>
</Table>
```

Listing 8.12 sap.m.Table as Worklist

Figure 8.5 Simple Worklist Page

Now, let's add two more things to the application in this step: an item count in the list indicated next to the table title and search functionality.

Item Count in Table Title

Here, we need to update the displayed item count number whenever the binding of the responsive table is updated. Luckily, this event exists on the table control, and we can simply attach to it by adding `updateFinished="onTableUpdateFin-ished"` to the control constructor in the view. We can then implement the handler function on the controller, as shown in Listing 8.13. Here, we can receive the total count of items available on the backend based on the current filter as a parameter from the argument of the callback. With this information, we can update the title control.

To achieve a nice display, as shown in Figure 8.6, we need two numbers here. In addition to the total number of items available in this collection, we also can display the number of items currently displayed on the screen. This makes sense if the growing feature of the list is enabled and if your users most likely will have to deal with a high number of items.

```
onTableUpdateFinished : function(oEvent) {
  var sTitle = "Sales Orders",
      oTable = this.getView().byId("table");
  //catch cases where the backend is not supporting remote count
  if(oTable.getBinding("items").isLengthFinal()) {
    var iCount = oEvent.getParameter("total"),
        iItems = oTable.getItems().length;
    sTitle += " (" + iItems + "/" + iCount + ")";
  }
  this.getView().byId("title").setText(sTitle);
}
```

Listing 8.13 Event Handler Function to Set Number of Items

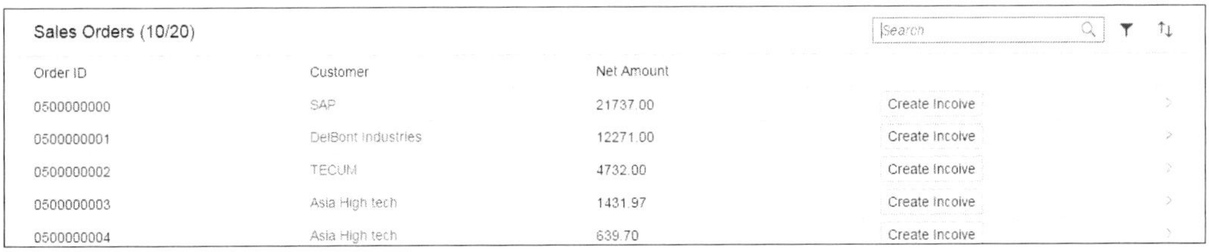

Sales Orders (10/20)			Search		
Order ID	Customer	Net Amount			
0500000000	SAP	21737.00	Create Incoive	>	
0500000001	DelBont Industries	12271.00	Create Incoive	>	
0500000002	TECUM	4732.00	Create Incoive	>	
0500000003	Asia High tech	1431.97	Create Incoive	>	
0500000004	Asia High tech	639.70	Create Incoive	>	

Figure 8.6 Item Count with Two Numbers

Handle Search Input and Filter the Table

Search capabilities give users the feeling of direct control over the displayed list. To increase the effect of this capability even more, we'll use the liveSearch event that sap.m.SearchFiled provides and will pass a handler function to it by adding liveChange="onSearch" to the constructor in the XML. Technically, we'll use filtering on the binding in this handler function. These work equally as well as simply implementing a predefined filter with the buttons directly.

In the handler function to be implemented on the controller (see Listing 8.14), we'll receive the query string entered and instantiate a new sap.ui.model.Filter object that will get this query string, a sap.ui.model.FilterOperator element of choice and the property to be filtered against. Because it's likely that application users do not want to search on only one column, we'll create a filter that will perform a search on several columns. The buildup is a little more complex, but it's really nothing more than wrapping several sap.ui.model.Filter objects into one, which is later handed over to the filter function on the binding. For this filter function, we can also choose between the filter modes. In Figure 8.15, we'll set it to `Application`, which will come at the cost of an additional round-trip to the server with every new filter request. This can be costly, especially when live search is used, and might lead to a bad user experience, especially for applications mostly used on mobile devices. The alternative method is to use `Client`, which would trigger only local filtering. The result is shown in Figure 8.7.

```
onSearch : function(oEvent) {
  var sSearchValue = oEvent.getSource().getValue(),
  aFilters = [];
  if(sSearchValue.length > 0) {
    var oFilterName = new Filter("CustomerName", sap.ui.model.
      FilterOperator.Contains, sSearchValue);
    var oFilterID = new Filter("SalesOrderID", sap.ui.model.
      FilterOperator.Contains, sSearchValue);
    aFilters.push(new Filter({
      filters : [oFilterID, oFilterName],
      And : false}));
  }
  this.getView().byId("table").getBinding("items").filter(aFilters,
    "Application");
}
```

Listing 8.14 Handler Function for Search Functionality

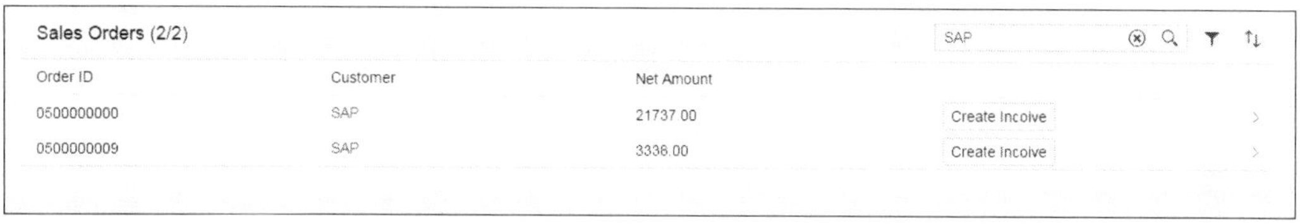

Sales Orders (2/2)			SAP	⊗ Q ▼ ↑↓
Order ID	Customer	Net Amount		
0500000000	SAP	21737.00	Create Incoive	›
0500000009	SAP	3336.00	Create Incoive	›

Figure 8.7 Search Handling in Worklist

Now that we've added the worklist table functionality for the worklist floorplan, in the next section, we'll provide functionality for navigation to the detail view.

Navigation and Detail View

In general, a worklist can offer two different types of navigation: *Inner-application navigation*, triggered by clicking on one of the list items, which brings the user to a second screen within the application that shows details for the selected item; and *cross-application navigation*, which can jump to a second application. We'll look into cross-application navigation in more detail in Section 8.4. Jumping to an external website triggered by clicking a link can be a valid use case for a worklist, but this functionality should not be seen as mandatory and should be implemented based on user requirements.

Now, let's build a simple second screen and set up the routing to ensure that navigation within the application based on a click as well as deep links is possible. We've covered how to do this in code multiple times up to this point throughout the book. However, we'll now perform these functions based on the Descriptor Editor provided by the SAP Web IDE. This tool offers UI-based configuration of the manifest.json file and opens by default when opening any manifest.json file in the SAP Web IDE. Based on the work we've done already, when you open the Descriptor Editor and click on the ROUTING tab, the Descriptor Editor should look like Figure 8.8.

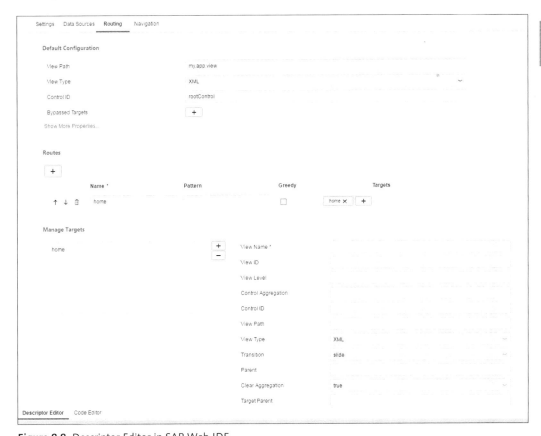

Figure 8.8 Descriptor Editor in SAP Web IDE

First, let's add a new route. To do so, click on the + button in the ROUTES section, and a new route will appear. Change the name for the new route; let's call it salesOrder. Because we want to have deep link capabilities for the new route, we'll also define a pattern here. Any string would work here, but we suggest making the link transparent to the user and calling it SalesOrder/{SalesOrderID}. The identifier in curly brackets now will be used to identify the distinct sales order to be displayed and handed over to the navigation step. This route now needs a target.

> **Note**
>
> The number of identifiers used in application patterns is determined by the number of identifiers defined in the metadata for the specific entity set. Otherwise, single entities cannot be addressed correctly.

In the MANAGE TARGETS section (refer to Figure 8.8), click on + and a popup will open (see Figure 8.9) in which you can define the name for the new target. Let's call it salesOrder.

Figure 8.9 Add Target

This target is created instantly, so we can configure it now. Here, all we have to do is define the VIEW NAME (SalesOrder) and we're done. Finally, we need to associate this target with the route. To do so, click on + in line with the route; a popup will open, and you can select salesOrder (see Figure 8.10).

Figure 8.10 Target Assignment in the Descriptor Editor

Now, save the changes and run the application with a hash like so: #SalesOrder/ 4711. You'll see an error in the console indicating that SalesOrder.view.xml could not be loaded, which tells us that we did everything correctly and have to create the view now.

We've performed similar tasks related to navigation in previous chapters (see Chapter 4), so we don't want to repeat the individual steps here; instead, try to implement it on your own. When doing so, please keep in mind to separate concerns. The navigation step in particular may tempt you to build a close interaction between the two controllers. Use the router here to abstract the interaction by calling the navTo function on one controller and attaching two patternMatched events on the other controller. The complete code can be found in the Git repository that accompanies this book. Here's a brief outline of the steps to follow:

1. Create a new view called SalesOrder.view.xml in the *view* folder, and add some controls and relative binding. Don't forget to add BACK button handling.

2. Attach the patternMatched event in the controller for this view and bind the view to the SalesOrderID in the hash. Ensure that the metadata is already loaded (use metadataLoaded promise on the OData Model; see Listing 8.15).

```
this.getOwnerComponent().getRouter().getRoute("salesOrder").attachPa
tternMatched(function(oEvent) {
    var that = this;
    var sSalesOrderID =
  oEvent.getParameter("arguments").SalesOrderID;
    this.getView().getModel().metadataLoaded().then(function(){
    var sObjectPath =
  that.getView().getModel().createKey("SalesOrderSet", {
        SalesOrderID : sSalesOrderID
    });
    that.getView().bindElement({
        path : "/" + sObjectPath,
        parameters : {
            expand : "ToLineItems"
        }
    });
  });
}.bind(this));
```

Listing 8.15 Handling Binding on the SalesOrder.controller.js

3. Implement a press handler function that triggers navigation when an item in the worklist is clicked on.

Figure 8.11 shows how the final result looks like, based on the coding in the Git repository. Still, there are lots of variations possible, and the service we're using allows for displaying lots of related and additional information. For example, you could display the list of products associated in the sales orders here, the geo information of the supplier, and much more.

Figure 8.11 Worklist and SalesOrder Views

8.2.2 Master-Detail

In this section, we'll extend the split-screen layout we built in Section 8.1.2 and extend it to a master-detail floorplan. The master-detail floorplan, because of its different dependent content areas, is complex to implement, and its details and pitfalls could fill an entire book on its own. Therefore, we'll only explore its complexity and learn how to overcome some trouble areas of the master-detail floorplan—just enough to get a better understanding of SAPUI5 application development for this complex pattern overall. If you want to build a master-detail application in one of your projects, we highly recommend using the template available in the SAP Web IDE. The SAP Web IDE covers best practice implementation for all these little, but sometimes annoying details.

Before we dive deeper into the technical details for this floorplan, let's first discuss valid use cases in which master-detail should be your floorplan of choice. The buildup is pretty simple: We always have a list in the master section that displays a set of items. Based on what's selected in this list, a detail area provides more relevant information for the selected item. If you think of software you use on a daily basis, you'll find some examples of master-detail floorplans in action.

Think of email clients, local as well as web-based: Most of them have a list of emails on the left showing the most important information, and when one email is selected, the entire email text appears in a bigger content area on the right. Or, if you're an iPad user, you can see the master-detail pattern at work in your device settings.

From these examples, we can derive some golden rules for deciding when to use master-detail floorplans in applications. First, master-detail is helpful in cases that require minimal navigation, such as when you want your application users to be able to quickly switch between different business objects while always keeping the overview of the complete set of objects available.

However, this makes only sense if the amount of data displayed on the details screen is easy to consume. In the email client, the email content displayed upon selection is something a user can handle. The user clicks on an email stub and sees the entire email displayed. This pattern would simply not work if not only this email but six other related emails were displayed at once. This means that we should only use the master-detail floorplan if the amount of data to be displayed on the details side is strongly related to the content to be displayed on the master list.

Master List

Now, let's move into some hands-on work with the master-detail floorplan by creating the master list. We'll start by creating the controllers for the master view and the detail view, then we'll register them in the view, and then add the files to the controller folder. (We created the application skeleton with a `sap.m.SplitApp` control and basic routing that displays the empty master and detail pages in Section 8.1.)

In this section, we'll first concentrate on the master list and extend Master.view.xml (see Listing 8.16) with `sap.m.List` that we'll bind to `BusinessPartnerSet` in the OData service. `sap.m.List` offers several modes for single or multi select and some that affect general appearance. We'll use `sap.m.List` as `SingleSelectMaster`, the optimized mode for single selection on desktop devices. Individual items in this list will be displayed using `sap.m.ObjectListItem` to show a minimal set of details per item in a nice, card-like display. We'll also add a search field in the `subHeader` of the semantic page. (We covered search handling in Section 8.2.1.) Listing 8.14 provides the binding and event handlers.

```
<semantic:subHeader>
  <Bar id="headerBar">
    <contentMiddle>
    <SearchField id="searchField" search="onSearch"
      width="100%"/>
    </contentMiddle>
  </Bar>
</semantic:subHeader>
</semantic:content>
<List
  id="list"
  selectionChange="onItemPressed"
  mode="SingleSelectMaster"
  growing="true"
  growingScrollToLoad="true
    items="{
      path: '/BusinessPartnerSet'
    }">
  <items>
    <ObjectListItem
      title="{CompanyName}"
      intro="{WebAddress}"/>
  </items>
</List>
</semantic:content>
```

Listing 8.16 Master List with Binding and Event Handlers in Place

Object View

For Detail.view.xml, we'll opt for a minimal display for now and will add `sap.m.ObjectHeader` with one bound property, which we'll bind later to the model relative to the selected item. Doing this requires one simple line of code in the content aggregation of `sap.m.semantic.SemanticDetailPage`: `<ObjectHeader title="{CompanyName}"/>`.

Synchronize Master and Detail

Because we now have some basic content for our two content areas in place, we need to orchestrate these two content areas in such a way that any selection in the master view reflects the content that is displayed in the detail view. To do so, we need to implement three features: handling of master list selections, full support for deep links, and handling of the default route. Finally, we have to follow some steps to ensure the master-detail floorplan can function for mobile scenarios as well.

Handling of Master List Selections

Currently, the application has a master list with data, but no visible details about this data and no selectable content. In this section, we'll add some depth to the master list by providing details for its data upon selection. The first thing we want to do is create a new route, called `detail`, which will use a pattern from which we can extract the item ID later (see Listing 8.17). The targets we established previously can be reused; only the sequence is important. In Section 8.1.2, you learned that the first target defined in routes that are used with `sap.m.SplitApp` is to be displayed on mobile devices. It can be assumed that a user opening an application with a deep link wants to see the details page and not the master page first, so we'll add the detail target first and the master target second into the array.

```
{
  "name": "detail",
  "pattern": "BusinessPartner/{BusinessPartnerID}",
  "greedy": false,
  "target": ["master", "detail"]
}
```

Listing 8.17 Master-Detail Route for Deep Links

We will now add the function (`onItemPressed`) to handle selections in Master.controller.js (see Listing 8.18). We've done something similar several other times in this book (see Chapter 4). One particular function of the `selection-Change` event that we're using now is that you get the list item that was pressed as a parameter in the callback argument instead of calling `oEvent.getTarget()`. From this list item, we get the entity ID from the binding context and trigger navigation to the detail route that gets this ID as a parameter.

```
onItemPressed : function(oEvent) {
  var oItem = oEvent.getParameter("listItem");
  var sID = oItem.getBindingContext().getProperty("BusinessPartnerID");
  this.oRouter.navTo("detail", {
    BusinessPartnerID : sID
  }, false);
},
```

Listing 8.18 Handling of Press Event on Master List

We'll now attach to the `patternMatched` event in the Detail.controller.js and bind the view based on the parameter we just received (see Listing 8.19). Because `sap.ui.model.OData.V2.ODataModel` offers some functionality to create the key that can be used to bind the view (which is handy, especially for entity sets with more than one key), we can use this function. You just have to be aware that the actual key generated is dependent on the metadata.xml file already loaded and processed. We can use a promise provided by `sap.ui.model.OData.V2.OData-Model` here to secure this.

```
onInit : function() {
  this.oRouter = this.getOwnerComponent().getRouter();
   this.oRouter.getRoute("detail").attachPatternMatched(this.
     onDetailRouteHit.bind(this));
},

onDetailRouteHit : function(oEvent) {
  var sID =  oEvent.getParameter("arguments").BusinessPartnerID;
  this.getView().getModel().metadataLoaded().then(function(){
    var sObjectPath =
  this.getView().getModel().createKey("BusinessPartnerSet", {
    BusinessPartnerID : sID
    });
    this.getView().bindElement({
      path: "/" + sObjectPath,
    });
  }.bind(this)
}
```

Listing 8.19 Binding of Detail.view.xml Based on Navigation

Full Support for Deep Links

If you run what we have so far, it will appear as if nothing has changed. The master list appears with all the items, and no details are displayed. However, once you select an item in the list, the detail content area will be updated and will display what we have bound to the list item. We can even see in the URL that the pattern we defined before is filled, and the ID of the selected object is included there. If you now click REFRESH in the browser, the detail matching the browser is displayed, but the focus on the master list for the selected item is not set. Now, let's select any item again. It becomes even more obvious that we missed something if we change the browser hash manually (e.g., from *#/BusinessPartner/0100000000* to *#/BusinessPartner/0100000004*). The detail changes, but the selection on the master list stays the same.

This is awkward for the user, but luckily we can fix this problem in the Master.controller.js. Here, we'll attach to the `patternMatched` event of the detail route and handle it in a function we'll call `onDetailRouteHit`. Because we'll have to handle different cases now and some exceptions, let's build our example up step by step. First, we'll create the functions described previously, (`patternMatched` and `onDetailRouteHit`) plus one additional function that we'll use to search items based on the key to review all the items the list (see Listing 8.20). The idea is now to call `selectAnItem` once the detail route is hit in order to support a deep link.

```
onInit : function() {
  // reuse variables
  this.oList = this.byId("list");
  this.oRouter = this.getOwnerComponent().getRouter();

  this.oRouter.getRoute("detail").attachEvent("patternMatched",
    this.onDetailRouteHit.bind(this));
},
onDetailRouteHit : function(oEvent) {
  var sBusinessPartnerID =
 oEvent.getParameter("arguments").BusinessPartnerID;
  this.selectAnItem(sBusinessPartnerID);
}
selectAnItem : function(sBusinessPartnerID) {
  var sKey = this.getView().getModel().
    createKey("BusinessPartnerSet", {
      BusinessPartnerID : sBusinessPartnerID
  });
  var oItems = this.oList.getItems();
    oItems.some(function(oItem) {
    if (oItem.getBindingContext() && oItem.getBindingContext().
      getPath() === "/" + sKey) {
      this.oList.setSelectedItem(oItem);
      return;
    }
  }, this);
},
```

Listing 8.20 Handling Simple Deep Links: First Try

We should now expect that the deep links should work. However, when we start the application to test it with a deep link (e.g., *#/BusinessPartner/0100000000*), the deep link doesn't work. An analysis with the F12 tools in your browser and adding a breakpoint to the `selectAnItem` function uncovers that when we call this function, there are no items in the list yet (see Figure 8.12). This is rather interesting and offers more insight into the lifecycle of routing itself. When the event triggered, the list binding had not yet been resolved. Therefore, the list had no items to select from.

Figure 8.12 Analysis of Item-Selection Failure

We'll need to ensure that `sap.m.List` resolves its binding and that items are available to select from before the event is thrown. The easiest way to do this is to hook into an event called `updateFinished` that we can attach to. This event is thrown once the list binding update has completed. Therefore, we can be sure that there are items in the list by that point:

```
this.oList.attachEventOnce("updateFinished", function() {
this.selectAnItem(sBusinessPartnerID);
}.bind(this));
```

With this change, the deep links should work. However, we'll still run into issues later when we want to handle errors or "not found" cases, because we do not have this error as a status we can request at any time. We can solve this issue using a *JavaScript promise* (see Listing 8.21). This becomes a little complex, because we have to ensure two things now: First, that the view already has its binding, for which we'll use `eventDelegate` functionality to attach to an event of the parent control; and second, that the `dataRequest` event can be used to identify error cases. Now, we also can react when no data could be loaded for any reason. We'll implement this later in Section 8.3.2. Add the code in Listing 8.21 to the `onInit` method of Master.controller.js now.

```
var that = this;
this.oListBindingPromise = new Promise(
  function(resolve, reject) {
    that.getView().addEventDelegate({
      onBeforeFirstShow: function() {
        that.oList.getBinding("items").attachEventOnce("dataReceived",
          function(oEvent) {
            if(oEvent.getParameter("data")){
              resolve();
            } else {
              reject();
            }
          }
      }, this);
    }.bind(that)
  });
}
);
```

Listing 8.21 Promise to Decouple Navigation from Events

We now simply select an item programmatically once oListBindingPromise has resolved. However, changing the hash manually does not change the selection. We'll need to add some more logic to the onDetailRouteHit function to get this right.

We'll now handle these three cases individually. First, we'll handle the case in which a user selects an item manually. In this case, we simply do nothing. In the second case, the classical deep link scenario, we select an item once the binding has resolved. For all other cases, mainly the manual hash change is handled here, and we can simply select the item straight away (see Listing 8.22).

```
onDetailRouteHit : function(oEvent) {
  var sBusinessPartnerID =
 oEvent.getParameter("arguments").BusinessPartnerID;
  var oSelectedItem = this.oList.getSelectedItem();
  if (oSelectedItem && oSelectedItem.getBindingContext().
    getProperty("BusinessPartnerID") === sBusinessPartnerID) {
    return;
  } else if (!oSelectedItem) {
    this.oListBindingPromise.then(function() {
      this.selectAnItem(sBusinessPartnerID);
    }.bind(this));
  } else {
    this.selectAnItem(sBusinessPartnerID);
  }
},
```

Listing 8.22 Optimized Detail Route Handling

Handling the Default Route: Empty Pattern

As a last step, we want to cover the *empty pattern route*. An empty pattern route is hit whenever an application starts without a hash. In such a case, the current application doesn't display anything, which is not preferred; the preferred option is to display the first list item details. In addition, we'll also show that the first item is selected. Most of the code in Listing 8.23 should make sense by now and the function will be called once the master route was hit. Again, we have to ensure that the promise is resolved before we can determine the first item and trigger the navigation for the detail.

```
onMasterRouteHit : function() {
  this.oListBindingPromise.then(function() {
    var oItems = this.oList.getItems();
    this.oList.setSelectedItem(oItems[0]);
    this.oRouter.navTo("detail", {
      BusinessPartnerID : oItems[0].getBindingContext().
        getProperty("BusinessPartnerID")
    });
  }.bind(this));
},
```

Listing 8.23 Empty Pattern Route Handling

Support for Mobile Devices

For desktop devices and tablets in landscape mode, our application should work fine. Still, we also have to plan for devices that do not offer enough real estate to fit an entire master-detail layout on one screen. To do so, we'll make use of dynamic expressions in XML and the `sap.ui.Device` API that identifies device type, touch support, and much more on application startup.

If you now run this application in device emulation mode in Google Chrome with an empty hash, you'll see that it instantly jumps to the detail screen for the first item, which is not our intent. We want it to stay on the master list if the main route is hit. The following simple return statement that only comes into play on mobile devices in the function that handles the main route will fix this problem:

```
if(sap.ui.Device.system.phone){ return; }
```

If you rerun the application in Google Chrome now, you'll land on the master list. If you select an item in the master list, the navigation brings you to the detail screen.

Everything seems to work, but from the detail screen there is no easy way to get back to the master list page. We have to add a BACK button to Detail.view.xml and ensure that it will only be displayed on phones. Again, we'll use the `sap.ui.Device` API, this time as a dynamic expression directly in XML and based on the same path we used previously in the `return` statement:

```
showNavButton="{= ${device>/system/phone}}"
navButtonPress="onNavButtonPressed"
```

We've also added the name of a handler function that will navigate back to the master list; we'll will implement this function in Detail.controller.js like this:

```
onNavButtonPressed : function(){
this.oRouter.navTo("master");
}
```

If you click on the BACK button in the top left of the detail view now, you're returned to the master list. However, one slightly unfortunate detail is that the last item selected is still selected in the master list. This makes no sense, because we don't have something that reflects the selection on the detail side of the screen. We can suppress this selection in the list by using a different `listMode`. We now have `listMode` set to `SingleSelectMaster`. We'll also use another expression to set `listMode` to `None` on mobile devices, like so:

```
mode="{= ${device>/system/phone} ? 'None' : 'SingleSelectMaster'}"
```

This change will make some more changes necessary, because the `listMode` set to `None` will also result in the `selectionChange` event no longer being thrown. So far, we've used this event to handle clicks on list items. Now, we'll have to add a `press` handler for individual list items instead. It's possible to handle clicks on mobile devices differently from clicks on desktop devices by simply defining two handler functions. However, in the case, the same function will work for both types of devices. We also have to dynamically set the type of the list items to `Active` on mobile devices to make the items clickable, like so:

```
type="{= ${device>/system/phone} ? 'Active' : 'Inactive'}"
press="onItemPressed"
```

We need to make one more adaption to the handler function. Because the `selectionChange` event returns the list and the item as a parameter and the `press` event on an individual item returns itself as the source of the event, we'll have to cover both cases in the handler:

```
var oItem = oEvent.getParameter("listItem") || oEvent.getSource();
```

One last feature we want to handle differently on mobile devices is the way the user can refresh the master list. For desktop devices, we already display a REFRESH button in the SEARCH field, but for touch-supported devices, we should to use a pull-to-refresh feature to handle refreshing the master list. This feature is fairly simple to add. On `sap.m.SearchField`, we can add a dynamic expression that will set the `showRefreshButton` property for us:

```
showRefreshButton="{= !${device>/support/touch} }"
```

We'll also add a `sap.m.PullToRefresh` control to the content aggregation of the semantic page. Again, we'll let a dynamic expression handle the visibility for us:

```
<PullToRefresh id="pullToRefresh"
refresh="onRefresh"
visible="{device>/support/touch}"/>
```

To make `sap.m.PullToRefresh` work, we have to do two more things:

1. Hide the control once the refresh is over (ideally in the `updateFinished` event on the list), like so:

   ```
   this.byId("pullToRefresh").hide();
   ```

2. Perform the actual refresh on the list binding (in the refresh event handler), like so:

   ```
   this.oList.getBinding("items").refresh();
   ```

> **Note**
>
> `sap.m.PullToRefresh` has to be used as the first element in the content aggregation of the first `sap.m.ScrollContainer` on the page. Otherwise, you might experience severe rendering issues that might break the usability of your application completely.
>
> The control also could be used on nontouch devices, resulting in the display of a clickable REFRESH area.

8.3   Additional Application Features

Independent from any floorplan, the apps within certain layouts generally have some qualities or features that are always needed. Application users take most of these features for granted. We have to confess that if we put ourselves into the position of application users—which we are, in fact, on a daily basis—we would expect, for example, to be notified if something goes wrong in an app. Many of us would associate this with some technical error—for example, when writing data to the backend—whereas others may first think about some deep link that could not be resolved as expected. Error handling and "not found" handling only form the tip of the iceberg.

However, there is much more to be considered in application development in general—not only ensuring that applications work as expected from a technical perspective, but also ensuring that they provide the user with the best possible support to fulfill daily routines.

In the following sections, we provide a quick rundown of technical and user experience-related shared application qualities and how SAPUI5 offers support in their implementation.

8.3.1 Not Found Handling

Error code 404 may be the only status code that even casual users understand. Many websites and web apps tend to spit out this technical information on the screen whenever the page a user wants to access is not available. Although there has been a trend in recent years to enrich these "not found" pages with funny designs, the numeric code seems never to disappear.

In this section, you'll learn about "not found" handling within the master-detail floorplan. Since version 1.28, SAPUI5 has provided a page to be displayed in not found cases, which is `sap.m.MessagePage`; it should be used as a single control in a view, like so:

```
<mvc:View xmlns:mvc="sap.ui.core.mvc" xmlns="sap.m">
<MessagePage/>
</mvc:View>
```

Figure 8.13 shows the default display of this page.

Admittedly, its design is very business-like, but it's fit for its purpose. We'll learn how to tweak it a bit later, but first, let's look at some use cases.

On websites, you will typically have only one `notFound` page that handles all links that can't be resolved. When using business applications, more precise feedback for the user is desirable, and with a well-defined, single-purpose application, it's easy to narrow down cases to be handled. We'll look at how to do so in the following subsections.

No matching items found.
Check the filter settings

Figure 8.13 sap.m.MessagePage with Default Settings

BusinessPartnerNotFound Scenario

In routing with SAPUI5, you can define routes that have specific patterns that should be reflected in the URL. That's what we call a *deep link*.

Because these patterns often hold the ID that matches a specific data set that could later be used to bind it to a view (for a master-detail example, see Listing 8.24), we have to handle all those cases in which individual IDs can't be found in the database. The aim is to show a not found page that gives some details about what went wrong and offers a link back to the application in a valid state whenever the user enters the application with a deep link to a business partner that does not exist.

```
{
  "name": "detail",
  "pattern": "BusinessPartner/{BusinessPartnerID}",
  "greedy": false,
  "target": ["master", "detail"]}
```
Listing 8.24 Route with ID in Pattern

Now, let's define a target that should be displayed when a specific business partner can't be found. We'll need a new view to handle these cases (see Listing 8.25). We'll reference a new view in the route and call it BusinessPartnerNotFound.view.xml.

```
"businessPartnerNotFound": {
  "viewName": "BusinessPartnerNotFound",
  "controlId": "rootControl",
  "controlAggregation": "detailPages"
},
```

Listing 8.25 Target for ObjectNotFound Scenarios

We'll create this view accordingly and also customize sap.m.MessagePage a little to create a nice display (see Listing 8.26). Because the view will be displayed in the detailPages aggregation, we again have to make sure that navigation back is possible on mobile devices and must use an expression to show a button for such navigation.

```
<mvc:View
  controllerName="my.app.controller.Main"
  xmlns:mvc="sap.ui.core.mvc"
  xmlns="sap.m">
  <MessagePage
    icon="sap-icon://doctor"
    navButtonPress="backToHome"
    showNavButton="{device>/system/phone}"
    text="BusinessPartner not found"
    title="Something went wrong">
    <customDescription>
        <Link text="click here to get back to main page"
            press="backToHome"/>
    </customDescription>
  </MessagePage>
</mvc:View>
```

Listing 8.26 BusinessPartnerNotFound.view.xml

We'll simplify a bit by using the existing Main.controller.js file to implement the handler functions for not found cases. In a real application, it might make sense to have an shared controller for these cases. For the back navigation, we'll use the same logic as in Section 8.2.2. To achieve this behavior and the resulting display, shown in Figure 8.14, we have to add some logic to Detail.controller.js, in the DetailRouteHit function. We'll use events of the binding to implement the back navigation and extend the call of bindElement with the change event. We'll then display the `BusinessPartnerNotFound` target whenever no `bindingContext` is set on the view, indicating some error, as in Listing 8.27.

```
this.getView().bindElement({
    path: "/" + sObjectPath,
    events: {
        change: function(){
          var oView = this.getView();
          if(!oView.getElementBinding().getBoundContext())){
            this.oRouter.getTargets().display("businessPartnerNotFound");
            }
        }.bind(this)
    }
});
```

Listing 8.27 Handling Business Partner Not Found Scenario

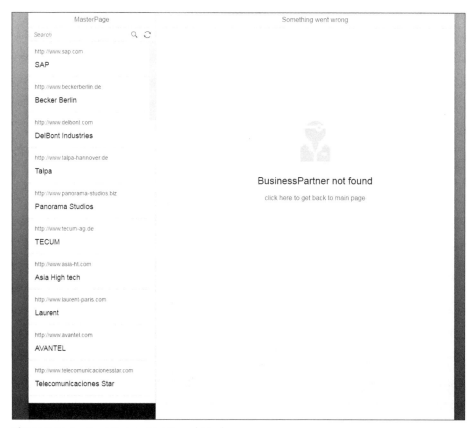

Figure 8.14 Business Partner Not Found Display

catchAll Scenario

The second situation we have to handle is generic not found cases, also referred to as `catchAll` cases. These are cases in which the user has tried to enter the application with a URL that does not match any pattern defined in the routing configuration. Luckily, this scenario is easier to implement than the previous scenario because it's not dependent on the application data from the backend. SAPUI5 routing provides a generic `bypassed` route for `catchAll`. The target(s) that should be displayed in all these cases can simply be handed over to the `config.bypassed` property in the routing configuration, as in Listing 8.28. The target that will be declared for bypassed has to be created as well. This can be done as in Listing 8.25, but we recommend using a different target and view for generic cases. This will help the user differentiate between the two situations.

```
"routing": {
  "config": {
    "bypassed": {
      "target": ["notFound", "master"]
    }
  }
}
```

Listing 8.28 Bypassed Configuration for Generic notFound Cases

Finally, we need to handle existing selections on the master list. Imagine someone manipulating the hash manually to something that is not defined in any pattern. The correct not found page will be displayed, but the selected item remains the same. To handle this deselection, attach to the `bypassed` event routing provided, and release the selection on the master list (see Listing 8.29). The result should then be as shown in Figure 8.15.

```
this.oRouter.attachEvent("bypassed", function() {
  this.oList.removeSelections(true);
}.bind(this));
```

Listing 8.29 Handling of List Selections for Bypassed Cases

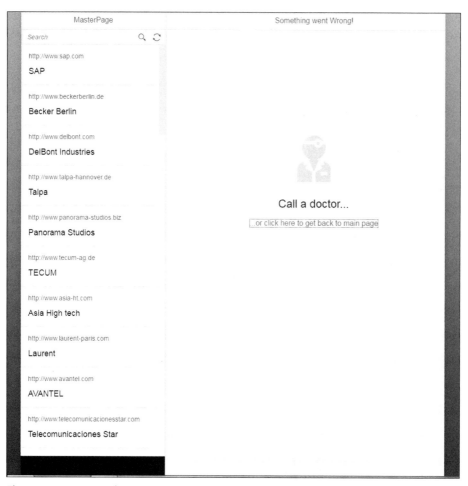

Figure 8.15 Customized sap.m.MessagePage for catchAll Cases

8.3.2 Error Handling

You've seen that not found cases and error cases have to be differentiated, and now we'll draw a clear line between them. In *error cases*, a technical error occurs that leads to the application no longer being usable. This also means that the notification for the user should occur in a more disruptive way. Best practice would be to make sure there is a clear indication that they should reload the application. Therefore, we will use a modal dialog for notifying the user. SAPUI5 provides `sap.m.MessageBox` as a convenient API that wraps `sap.m.Dialog` and additional controls. We'll handle two cases in the following subsections, but both will be displayed in the same `sap.m.MessageBox`. Therefore, we'll use a function to bring up the notification and reuse it for both cases (see Listing 8.30). We'll implement this function in the Component.js file of our application. Please note that there may be more than one error raised by the application. To ensure that there will be only one `sap.m.MessageBox` displayed, we'll use a simple flag that indicates that a notification is already present.

```
_showServiceError: function(sDetails) {
  if (this._bMessageOpen) {
    return;
  }
  this._bMessageOpen = true;
  MessageBox.error("An Error Occurred",
    {
      details: sDetails,
      actions: [MessageBox.Action.CLOSE],
      onClose: function() {
        this._bMessageOpen = false;
      }.bind(this)
    }
  );
}
```

Listing 8.30 Generic Error Notification Function

Error Response Specification

In SAP NetWeaver and SAP Gateway OData services, there is an SAP-specific response protocol that ensures that all server messages are returned with predictable formatting. This function is handled by `sap.ui.model.odata.ODataMessageParser`, and all messages can then be accessed through `sap.ui.core.message.MessageManager`. Because these functions currently cover validation-related messages only, generic handling for error messages cannot be described at this point in time; such handling might vary based on your service implementation and other factors.

We'll also disable the automatic closing of dialogs on the router target handler, which could be controversial. However, because we will display dialogs and specific pages, and because it's not possible to synchronize the two events (routing and data requests), disabling automatic dialog closing is a valid option for most of use cases. Disable automatic dialog closing as follows:

```
this.getRouter().getTargetHandler().setCloseDialogs(false);
```

Handling Metadata Errors

For SAPUI5 applications built on top of OData services, there will always be cases in which a metadata call did not result in a success. Let's handle such cases now. We can simply attach to the `metadataFailed` event provided by `sap.ui.model.V2.ODataModel` and display a message box showing details. Let's also display the generic not found page:

```
this.getModel().attachEvent("metadataFailed", function(oEvent) {
  this._showServiceError(oEvent.getParameters().getResponse);
  this.getRouter().getTargets().display("notFound");
}.bind(this));
```

Handling Service Errors

For service errors, we'll need some more logic, although the overall pattern remains the same. We'll again attach to a model event—in this case, the `request-Failed` event. However, because this event is thrown for cases we already handled using the not found implementation, we'll have to exclude such cases. Therefore, we'll make the following assumptions based on the error code the event provides as part of the parameters: All 404 cases (not found) and all 400 cases (parsing error on the server) will not be handled by the error handling, because they're already covered by the not found handling, resulting in the handler function in Listing 8.31.

```
this.getModel().attachRequestFailed(function(oEvent) {
  var oParams = oEvent.getParameters();
  if (oParams.response.statusCode !== "400" &&
 oParams.response.statusCode !== "404") {
    this.getRouter().getTargetHandler().setCloseDialogs(false);
    this.getRouter().getTargets().display("notFound");
    this._showServiceError(oParams.response);
  }
}, this);
```
Listing 8.31 Handling Request Errors

8.3.3 Busy Handling

As a user, *busy handling* gives you the feeling that the hard work is done for you by showing a busy indicator. Busy handling is not only the real work an application is doing but also the responses you get in general regarding the state your application is currently in. We bet there are more apps out there that fake actual busy time just to display nice busy animations than you might imagine. The reason for this may be that the screen flickers if the actual request only takes milliseconds, and the busy indicator will be shown and hidden again instantly. In SAPUI5, there is a default `busyIndicatorDelay` property on all controls that defaults to 500 milliseconds; we should keep it that way instead of delaying the response artificially.

Busy handling is important for the perceived performance of an application, especially at startup. It's good to assume your user has a slow Internet connection. A busy indicator showing the user that there is some work being done behind the scenes will keep him patient.

Handling the Metadata Call

As for error handling, we can differentiate two cases or, more precisely for this section, two phases of loading data. First, the OData metadata.xml file is requested. During this time, the application is not ready to work at all. We'll therefore set the outer view (Main.view.xml) as busy during this phase. The easiest way to do so is to set busy as the default behavior in the XML (`busy="true"`) for our root control, and later, when the metadata is loaded or loading failed, simply call `setBusy(false)`, as in Listing 8.32.

```
// handling the good case
this.getOwnerComponent().getModel().metadataLoaded()
  .then(function() {
    oRootControl.setBusy(false);
  });
// handling the bad case
this.getOwnerComponent().getModel().attachMetadataFailed(
  function() {
    oRootControl.setBusy(false);
});
```

Listing 8.32 Metadata Request: Busy Handling

Handling Calls on Individual Controls

While the metadata call is happening, individual requests are triggered only once at application startup, but binding refresh will occur multiple. Therefore, we should ensure that busy handling for these cases is in place.

For `sap.m.List` and `sap.m.Table`, busy handling is already implemented as a default, so we don't have to do anything for these controls. For all other controls, we should use the appropriate events to manage busy handling. However, individual requests are triggered only once at application startup, but binding refresh will occur multiple. One rule of thumb for determining this information is to have all controls bound against the same entity. If we look at the master-detail example, this entity would be the entire detail page in the current state. However, in real applications, you would most likely fill up the detail screen and may even expand the displayed data to a related entity in the service. Possibilities for the service we've been using in this example are shown in Figure 8.16. Now, let's assume we want to display a list of sales orders next to the business partner details on the details page. In this case, we would handle the busy state for this area within the screen separately from the sap.m.ObjectHeader element in which we're displaying the business partner details currently.

```
<Property Name="BusinessPartnerRole" Type="Edm.String" Nullable="false" MaxLength="3" sap:lab
<Property Name="CreatedAt" Type="Edm.DateTime" Precision="7" sap:label="Time Stamp" sap:creat
<Property Name="ChangedAt" Type="Edm.DateTime" Precision="7" ConcurrencyMode="Fixed" sap:labe
<NavigationProperty Name="ToSalesOrders" Relationship="/IWBEP/GWSAMPLE_BASIC.Assoc_BusinessPa
<NavigationProperty Name="ToContacts" Relationship="/IWBEP/GWSAMPLE_BASIC.Assoc_BusinessPart
<NavigationProperty Name="ToProducts" Relationship="/IWBEP/GWSAMPLE_BASIC.Assoc_BusinessPart
</EntityType>
<EntityType Name="Product" sap:content-version="1">
  ▼<Key>
    <PropertyRef Name="ProductID"/>
    </Key>
```

Figure 8.16 Related Entities to Business Partners

For handling the busy state, technically, we'd use binding events, as previously stated. The most appropriate choice would be to set the control to busy once data is requested and release the busy state once data is received by the control. An example implementation for this setup can be found in Listing 8.33. Here, we've implement the functions in the controller for the view that declares the controls and added the handler functions to the controls at declaration in XML. The actual implementation for this minimal example in master-detail is in Listing 8.34.

```
onDataRequested: function(oEvent) {
  oEvent.getSource().setBusy(true);
},
onDataReceived: function(oEvent) {
  oEvent.getSource().setBusy(false);
}
```

Listing 8.33 Generic Busy Handling

```
this.getView().bindElement({
  path: "/" + sObjectPath,
```

```
    events: {
      change: function(){
              if(!this.getView().getElementBinding().getBoundContext()){
                 this.oRouter.getTargets().display("businessPartnerNotFo
und");
              }
      }.bind(this),
      dataRequested: function() {
        this.getView().setBusy(true);
      },
      dataReceived: function() {
          this.getView().setBusy(false);
      }
    }
});
```

Listing 8.34 Master Detail Busy Handling: Minimal Example

8.3.4 Letterboxing

Letterboxing is a term often associated with filming to ensure the original aspect ratio when transferring video material across screens with different ratios. This is achieved by using black bars, mostly displayed on the top and bottom of the screen to narrow the actual screen and fill the spaces that aren't covered by the film itself.

In application development, letterboxing has become a good practice for all cases when content is limited. Think of a simple master-detail application that only displays some details for a selected item. In such a case, it's much easier to ensure good design for the content on the screen if you can rely on a fixed content area, even on big screens. In addition, your application users will gain a more focused view.

The application examples we've presented so far have always run in sap.m.Shell, which uses a letterboxed display for applications to center the content by default. However, letterboxing can be disabled, because it's reflected in a property called appWidthLimited in the shell. This letterbox option provides a width of 1,280 px reserved for the content, and the rest of the screen displays the default application background. This background can be customized based on either the theme used or settings in the shell itself.

In order to change the behavior as shown in Figure 8.17, configure the properties on instantiation in sap.m.Shell, as shown in Listing 8.35.

Figure 8.17 Letterboxing and Custom Background on sap.m.Shell

Unfortunately, there is no Explored app example for the control. Additional options include `backgroundImage`, `backgroundRepeat`, and `backgroundOpacity`.

```
// not letterboxed
new sap.m.Shell({
  appWidthLimited : false,
  app: new sap.ui.core.ComponentContainer({
    height : "100%",
    name : "myCompany.myApp"
  })
}).placeAt("content");

// custom background
new sap.m.Shell({
  backgroundColor : "rgb(0,153,204)",
  app: new sap.ui.core.ComponentContainer({
    height : "100%",
    name : "myCompany.myApp"
  })
}).placeAt("content");
```

Listing 8.35 Appearance Configuration for sap.m.Shell

8.3.5 Headers and Footers

Headers and footers generally provide access to certain functionality for applications users. This functionality can impact entire content areas. For example, if your application view contains a form, the button to save the form content to the backend should be displayed in the footer. This also ensures applications have focused content areas, so you're not tempted to overload your screens.

In SAPUI5, headers and footers are mainly part of `sap.m.Page` or other related controls. In this chapter, we've mainly used pages from `sap.m.semantic`, but we haven't yet looked into the main benefit they deliver: predefined buttons, so-called actions that implement design guidelines like predefined icons, texts, tooltips, and even overflow handling (also clustering on the screen according to their distinct usage). For example, the BACK navigation button is left in the header, and all actions related to collaboration (e.g., `SendEmailAction`) are hidden in an overflow and display upon clicking the OVERFLOW INDICATOR button in a popover. Certain actions like `PositiveAction` are displayed in the app, making use of semantic colors. This highly improves development routines when designing new screens and ensures minimal distraction from implementing underlying functionality. Each action has a `press` handler that points to the controller for the view and fires the matching function there, just like it's always handled in SAPUI5.

In addition, you can add custom content in the headers and footers of the semantic pages, because they offer the `customHeaderContent` and `customFooterContent` aggregations and a `subHeader` aggregation for ambitious projects. There is even a `customShareMenuContent` aggregation that allows you to add custom actions into the popover described previously.

Let's now look at a sample `sap.m.semantic.FullscreenPage` installation with some actions and custom content; this page could be used for a simple shopping cart checkout page (Figure 8.18).

Figure 8.18 Header and Footer Options with Semantic Page

The XML to achieve this setup is pretty simple. You might have to get used to the high number of aggregations that are used here, making the API a little superfluous overall, but once you've adjusted to it, it works very well (see Listing 8.36).

```
<mvc:View
  xmlns:html=http://www.w3.org/1999/xhtml
  xmlns:mvc="sap.ui.core.mvc"
  xmlns="sap.m"
  xmlns:semantic="sap.m.semantic">
  <semantic:FullscreenPage
    title="Shopping Cart Checkout"
    showNavButton="true">
    <semantic:subHeader>
      <Toolbar>
        <ToolbarSpacer/>
          <Text text="6 Items ready for checkout"/>
          <ToolbarSpacer/>
      </Toolbar>
    </semantic:subHeader>
    <semantic:sendEmailAction>
      <semantic:SendEmailAction press="onSendMailPressed"/>
    </semantic:sendEmailAction>
    <semantic:printAction>
      <semantic:PrintAction press="onPrintPressed"/>
    </semantic:printAction>
    <semantic:positiveAction>
      <semantic:PositiveAction text="Checkout Cart" press=
"onCheckoutPressed"/>
    </semantic:positiveAction>
    <semantic:negativeAction>
      <semantic:NegativeAction text="Discart Cart" press=
"onDiscartPressed"/>
    </semantic:negativeAction>
    <semantic:customShareMenuContent>
      <OverflowToolbarButton icon="sap-icon://message-popup" text=
"send IM" press="onPress"/>
    </semantic:customShareMenuContent>
  </semantic:FullscreenPage>
</mvc:View>
```

Listing 8.36 XML Declaration for Header and Footer Options with Semantic Page

The additional application features described in the current section allow you to control errors and wait times and to implement letterboxing and adjust headers and footers.

In the next section, we'll look at how to run apps in SAP Fiori Launchpad.

8.4   Running Apps in SAP Fiori Launchpad

In this chapter, you've learned that building application families that distribute functions across single-purpose-based apps is better than building one large, monolithic, multipurpose app. We have successfully built at least the outline of two small, single-purpose applications.

SAP Fiori Launchpad offers user management, application provisioning, navigation and integration of new applications, and maybe even third-party technologies. The launchpad's main purpose is to provide access to several applications and application types via one simple user interface. What sounds like a link list at first is actually a challenge not only from a technological standpoint but also from a user experience perspective. Just think of the challenge to support older technologies like Web GUI transactions as well as modern web applications like the ones we build with SAPUI5.

For our SAPUI5 applications, SAP Fiori Launchpad offers tight integration, because SAP Fiori Launchpad is itself based on SAPUI5 technology. SAP Fiori Launchpad offers a lot of functionality, not only for application users but also for application developers. Cross-application navigation from one application to another and the ability to programmatically create bookmarks that reflect a certain application state are just two features that come to mind. It soon becomes obvious that integration of at least a sandboxed SAP Fiori Launchpad early on during implementation will pay off later.

In this section, we'll start with the implementation of a simple standalone SAP Fiori Launchpad sandbox demo application and then extend it to include more than one application together in one sandboxed SAP Fiori Launchpad. From there, we'll add simple cross-application navigation using SAP Fiori Launchpad's API. Finally, we'll try out productive usage when we deploy our app to SAP HCP via the SAP Web IDE.

8.4.1   SAP Fiori Launchpad Sandbox

SAP Fiori Launchpad, when used productively, has several backend dependencies that can't be simulated in the context of single app development easily. That's why an SAP Fiori Launchpad sandbox is available that offers the most widely used features with a minimal footprint but still allows for testing during development. The display can be seen in Figure 8.19.

Figure 8.19 Generic SAP Fiori Launchpad Sandbox UI

There are several options to run your application in an SAP Fiori Launchpad sandbox. It's important to understand that within SAP Fiori Launchpad, you will not need a dedicated HTML file per application anymore; you'll simply register your application to the sandbox itself.

In this section, we'll look at running an application in a sandbox SAP Fiori Launchpad via the SAP Web IDE and in a custom-built sandbox SAP Fiori Launchpad.

SAP Fiori Launchpad Sandbox Runner in SAP Web IDE

The most convenient option to run your application in the SAP Fiori Launchpad sandbox is to use the built-in component runner provided by the SAP Web IDE. This feature offers a simple SAP Fiori Launchpad sandbox in which you can currently run one application component at a time. To do so, right-click on COM-PONENT.JS, and the context menu opens as shown in Figure 8.20; then select RUN • RUN AS • SAP FIORI COMPONENT ON SANDBOX, and your component will be launched in a minimal sandbox, as shown Figure 8.19. Here, you can test that the application still runs within SAP Fiori Launchpad. The scope of this option is still limited, and integrations such as cross-application navigation are not supported.

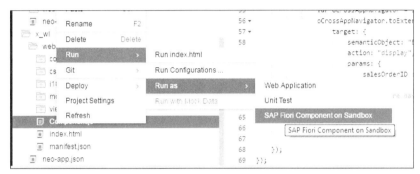

Figure 8.20 Usage of SAP Fiori Launchpad Sandbox Component Runner

Custom-Built SAP Fiori Launchpad Sandbox: Experimental

To test cross-application features in the SAP Web IDE, you can bootstrap your own sandbox. Note that this approach should be used for testing purposes only; any productive usage is not encouraged. However, this is a simple way to avoid deploying every change. Be sure to test early in the process directly in the workspace.

To do create a custom sandbox, we'll first create a new folder in our workspace. In this folder, we'll add a new HTLM file called FLPSandbox.html. In this file, we'll place a script block that will handle the SAPUI5 bootstrap as we did for all runnable files before (see Listing 8.37). In addition, we'll add some configuration for the SAP Fiori Launchpad sandbox and load an additional bootstrap script. The only important point to note here is to pay attention to the application's property block within the configuration. We'll add more here to register the application components to the sandbox in the next step.

```
<!DOCTYPE HTML>
<html>
  <head>
  <meta http-equiv="X-UA-Compatible" content="IE=edge" />
```

```
    <meta charset="UTF-8">
    <title>FLP Sandbox</title>
    <script>
      window["sap-ushell-config"] = {
        defaultRenderer : "fiori2",
        renderers: {
          fiori2: {
          componentData: {
            config: {
            search: "hidden"
            }
          }
        }
      }
    },
    applications: {};
</script>

<script src="../test-resources/sap/ushell/bootstrap/sandbox.js" id=
"sap-ushell-bootstrap"></script>
<!-- Bootstrap the UI5 core library -->
<script id="sap-ui-bootstrap"
  src="../../resources/sap-ui-core.js"
  data-sap-ui-libs="sap.m, sap.ushell, sap.collaboration"
  data-sap-ui-theme="sap_bluecrystal"
  data-sap-ui-compatVersion="edge">
</script>

<script>
  sap.ui.getCore().attachInit(function() {
  // initialize the ushell sandbox component
  sap.ushell.Container.createRenderer().placeAt("content");
  });
</script>
</head>

<body class="sapUiBody" id="content"/>
</html>
```

Listing 8.37 SAP Fiori Launchpad Sandbox Initialization

In the same folder, we'll create a new folder for every app we want to run within the custom SAP Fiori Launchpad sandbox and give each one a meaningful name. Into these folders, we'll copy the respective *webapp* folders of the applications we want to run—for example, for the *Sales Orders* and *Business Partners* applications we created in Section 8.2.

Let's now register our applications to the sandbox. To do so, we'll add a new key referencing an object for every application to the applications settings block you've seen before. This key serves as the hash to be resolved by the SAP Fiori Launchpad on navigation later. The settings for each application should be easy to understand: We need to give the component a namespace, a type, and a relative URL for where to find the component. The title can be chosen freely and will later be displayed on a tile. The coding to add the Sales Orders and Business Partners applications is found in Listing 8.38.

```
"SalesOrder-display": {
  additionalInformation: "SAPUI5.Component=sales.order.app",
  applicationType: "URL",
  url: "./SalesOrders/webapp/",
  title: "Sales Orders"
},
"BusinessPartner-display": {
  additionalInformation: "SAPUI5.Component=business.partner.app",
  applicationType: "URL",
  url: "./BusinessPartners/webapp/",
  title: "Business Partners"
}
```

Listing 8.38 Registering Applications to SAP Fiori Launchpad Sandbox

If you run the registered applications now, they should look like Figure 8.21. You can test the application, and if you click on the individual tiles, the applications should open and be displayed as we left them.

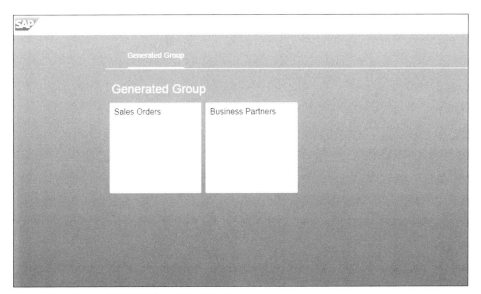

Figure 8.21 Custom SAP Fiori Launchpad Sandbox

8.4.2 Cross-Application Navigation

With the custom-built SAP Fiori Launchpad sandbox, we can now test the cross-application navigation function as a simple feature example for what the SAP Fiori Launchpad generally provides. When someone clicks on the link to one business partner in the Sales Orders application worklist screen, the Business Partner application should open with the chosen business partner selected.

Let's first look at the Sales Order application that triggers the navigation. For this, we'll add a click handler to the link on the worklist table like so:

```
<Link text="{CustomerName}" press="onCustomerPressed"/>
```

The matching event handler (see Listing 8.39) in Worklist.controller.js should then make use of the navigation service provided by SAP Fiori Launchpad and call the `toExternal` function with some parameters. We'll use the settings we just made in Listing 8.38 (`BusinessPartner-display`) to identify the application during navigation. We'll also hand over the ID of the business partner we want to navigate to as an additional parameter.

To retrieve the ID, we have to think outside the box a little. Because we can't use the ID of the `SalesOrder` we're currently using, we have to retrieve the `Business-PartnerID` to properly handle the navigation on the other app. Therefore, we'll add an `expand` parameter to the binding of the table—parameters : { expand : 'ToBusinessPartner'}—and add the ID of the `BusinessPartner` as custom data in the link itself—data:id="{ToBusinessPartner/BusinessPartnerID}. Then, we can retrieve the ID in the handler directly from the element itself (see Listing 8.39).

```
onCustomerPressed: function(oEvent) {
  var BusinessParnterId = oEvent.getSource().data().id;
  var oCrossAppNavigator =
 sap.ushell.Container.getService("CrossApplicationNavigation");
  oCrossAppNavigator.toExternal({
    target: {
      semanticObject: "BusinessPartner",
      action: "display",
      params: {
        BusinessPartner : BusinessParnterId
      }
    }
  });
}
```

Listing 8.39 Cross-Application Navigation Handler

If you click on the BUSINESS PARTNER link in the Sales Order application now, navigation to the Business Partners application is triggered and it hits the master route. In the URL, the ID is visible as a parameter. We now only have to handle the selection based on the parameter we handed over on the other side. To do so, we'll retrieve the ID as `startupParamters` on the instance of the application component.

We'll add additional logic to the resolving promise in the handler of the master route that then checks for the existence of startup parameters and navigates to the matching detail if startup parameters are available, as in Listing 8.40.

```
var aBusinessPartner = this.getOwnerComponent().getComponentData().
  startupParameters.BusinessPartner;
var sId;
if (aBusinessPartner) {
    sId = aBusinessPartner[0];
} else {
    sId = this.oList.getItems().getBindingContext().
      getProperty("BusinessPartnerID");
}
this.selectAnItem(sId);
this.oRouter.navTo("detail", {
 BusinessPartnerID: sId
});
```

Listing 8.40 Handling Cross-Application Navigation in Target

8.4.3 Register and Run in Production

With all the pieces in place and working in the sandbox, we can deploy the two applications straight out of the SAP Web IDE into SAP HCP. However, first we have to locate each application in the root of our workspace again. Use the context menu triggered by right-clicking on the application root folder and select DEPLOY • DEPLOY TO HANA CLOUD PLATFORM. First, we'll deploy the Business Partner application. In the popup (see Figure 8.22), you can set some details and also see the application status and whether it's already deployed. We do not need to make any changes here; simply click DEPLOY. For more details on deploying and managing application versions, see Appendix D.

After a while, you'll see a success notification with a prominent button marked REGISTER TO SAP FIORI LAUNCHPAD. Click on this button, and a dialog opens in which you can perform all the needed steps to set up your application in SAP Fiori Launchpad.

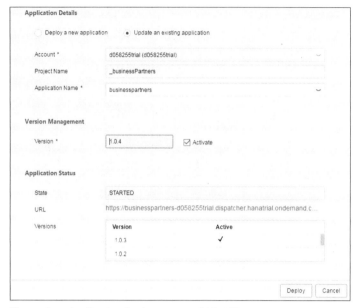

Figure 8.22 Application Deployment on SAP HCP

On the first screen (see Figure 8.23), we will mainly set up the navigation to this application within the SAP Fiori Launchpad in the INTENT settings; we defined these settings in Listing 8.39 when we set up the cross application. We have to use the same settings now again for the SEMANTIC OBJECT and the ACTION. Then, click on NEXT.

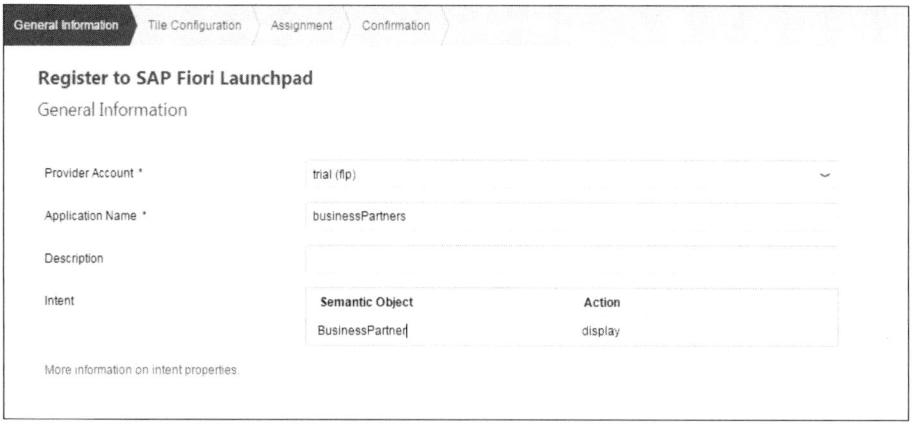

Figure 8.23 Set Up Navigation within SAP Fiori Launchpad

On the next screen (see Figure 8.24), we can set up the appearance of the tile for this application in the SAP Fiori Launchpad. You can choose between two different tile types (static and dynamic), define an icon, and set a title and subtitle to be displayed. We'll just change the title here and delete the placeholder for the subtitle. Again, proceed by clicking on NEXT.

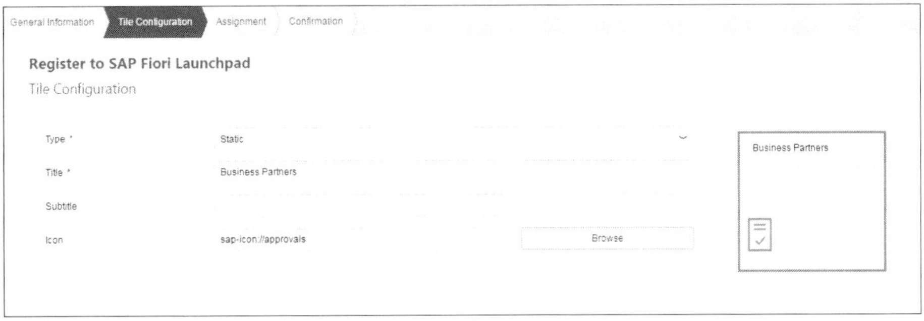

General Information	Tile Configuration	Assignment	Confirmation

Register to SAP Fiori Launchpad
Tile Configuration

Type *	Static	⌄	Business Partners
Title *	Business Partners		
Subtitle			
Icon	sap-icon://approvals	Browse	☰ ✓

Figure 8.24 Set Up Tile Appearance within SAP Fiori Launchpad

In the last step (see Figure 8.25), we'll finally assign this new tile that represents the application and allows the user to open it to our launchpad. We can only cover some basics here, so we don't want to get into the details of these settings. SAP Fiori Launchpad as an entry point to applications uses roles to provide access, while the allocation of applications is done via catalogs. This means that a business role like—for example, for procurement—has one or many catalogues assigned. Each of these catalogues consists of a set of applications. An administrator can then assign catalogues to a role, and each employee is assigned to a role as well. This then defines what applications are to be part of their SAP Fiori Launchpad. Let's keep the default settings and click on NEXT.

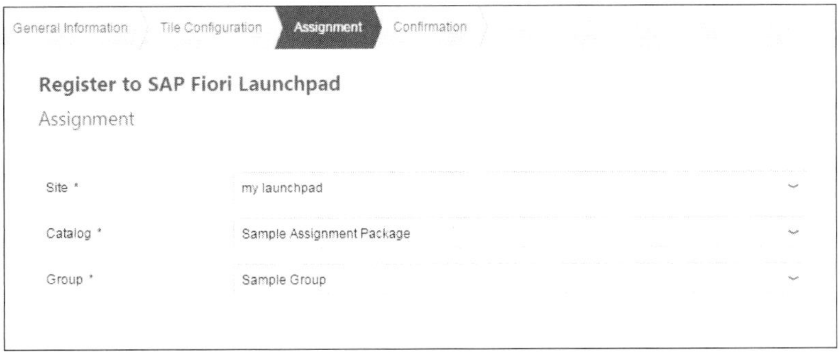

General Information	Tile Configuration	Assignment	Confirmation

Register to SAP Fiori Launchpad
Assignment

Site *	my launchpad	⌄
Catalog *	Sample Assignment Package	⌄
Group *	Sample Group	⌄

Figure 8.25 Assign Application to the SAP Fiori Launchpad

We'll now perform the same tasks for the Sales Orders application. Based on your settings, the final result should look like Figure 8.26. If all intents are set to match our cross-application navigation settings, it should now be possible to perform the navigation between the two apps as implemented in Section 8.4.2.

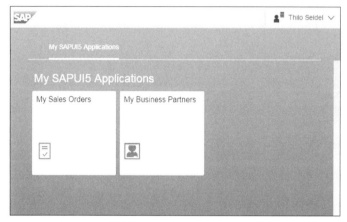

Figure 8.26 Application in SAP Fiori Launchpad at SAP HCP

8.5 SAP Fiori Reference Apps

So far, we've explored application development from different angles: In Section 8.2, we created application skeletons, and we refined them in Section 8.3. However, thus far we have not built full-blown applications but have only gained an understanding of the different building blocks that matter in application development.

In this section, we want to look at the SAP Fiori reference applications that can be evaluated directly in the SAP Web IDE. Specifically, we'll look at the Manage Products and Shop apps.

All applications are built using best practices for SAP Fiori development. This means they are component-based, come with an SAP Fiori sandbox set up, and make use of controls from the sap.m library. However, note that these application are built on SAPUI5 version 1.28, and therefore, for example, manifest.json isn't used. For the full list of applications available, see Figure 8.27. You can open this wizard by clicking FILE in the menu bar, then NEW, and then PROJECT FROM SAMPLE APPLICATION.

Figure 8.27 SAP Fiori Reference Apps in SAP Web IDE

8.5.1 Manage Products App

The Manage Products application (see Figure 8.28) uses the master-detail floorplan. The master list is implemented as in Section 8.2.2, but comes with additional filtering, sorting, and grouping functionality. In the detail content area are `sap.m.ObjectHeader` and two `sap.m.Panel` controls displaying different types of data within static forms related to the selected item. Footer buttons are added that allow you to switch from detail view to edit mode. You also can delete or copy any selected item.

The Manage Products application is a good example of how to build an application designed to change, add, or delete business objects. It makes good use of the master-detail floorplan; you can quickly navigate between the different products. In addition, the display on the details side is highly sorted and not overloaded.

From a coding perspective, you can see that several helper files are needed, most of them dealing with CRUD operations. Because the coding is extensively documented using inline comments, we won't go into details here.

Figure 8.28 Manage Products Reference Application

8.5.2 Shop App

The SAP Fiori reference Shop application is built on top of the worklist floorplan. The scenario that is implemented here is a simple Shop application where a user can browse different items and add them to a shopping cart. In Figure 8.29, you can see that it looks familiar to what we created in Section 8.2.1.

In the worklist, an action is implemented where the user can add items to their shopping cart straight out of the item list without browsing any details. One additional control that is used here to refine the items to be displayed is a `sap.ui.comp.smartfilterbar.SmartFilterBar`. We will provide more details about the capabilities of smart controls in SAPUI5 in Chapter 9.

The navigation in the Shop application has two additional views displaying the items in the shopping cart as well a view that is used to place an order once the user is ready to checkout.

Figure 8.29 Shop Reference Application

It is interesting to see how items are to be added to this cart. One might assume that there is an additional model involved here. However, there is actually a function import on the OData model being used in this scenario. We have already learned about this OData feature in Chapter 7. Here, OData can be used for adding items to a shopping cart as well as for placing an order.

8.6 Summary

In this chapter, you've seen the complexity of application development first-hand. SAPUI5 helps to build applications, and SAP Fiori Launchpad launches applications into an environment that eases their orchestration and provisioning. Beyond just looking at the technical aspects of application patterns, it's important not to forget the needs of your application users. Therefore, within this chapter we spent some time on the general layout of applications, explained how to make use of existing application floorplans, reviewed user experience best practices, and outlined some of the most important nonfunctional application capabilities every user expects. During this process, you built two application skeletons and learned how all the technical concepts explained in the previous chapters can be used in combination.

With this chapter, we've concluded the chapters on the pure basics in SAPUI5; in the next chapter, we'll look into more advanced concepts that build on top of what you've learned so far.

For more advanced applications, this chapter explains how OData annotations can be used to feed smart controls or factory functions, how application developers can extend SAPUI5 functionality by writing their own controls, and how code can be shared easily across applications by using fragments.

9   Advanced Concepts

In this chapter, we'll provide insight into several of the more advanced concepts that can be used when writing SAPUI5 applications. We'll start by looking at how to develop custom controls for an application. We'll then shed light on another reusable view element in SAPUI5: fragments. Finally, we'll take a closer look at how OData services can be enhanced with annotations, and how smart controls and templates can be used with these annotations.

9.1   Writing Your Own Controls

You've used a lot of preexisting controls throughout this book. In this section, we'll explore how controls work internally, and what you can do when a control is missing in SAPUI5. As you'll see, you can write your own controls rather easily.

There are numerous reasons why writing your own controls may be preferable:

▶ When you need a control to wrap external resources in, so you can benefit of SAPUI5 data binding in it.

▶ For a combination of controls you are using time and again, where controls belong together semantically and need to respond to changes in the other controls in the group. Here, you also benefit from the fact that you can internally change details about the implementation—for example the rendering—without the need to change anything in the application.

▶ When a new layout is required and it should be reusable, not just copied from view to view.

For any of these instances, it's not complicated to build your own controls. Whenever you find yourself using the same control configuration or combination time and again throughout your applications, it makes sense to create your own control that can be reused across applications. You can even package your own custom controls into a reusable control library! You can also add single custom controls to your application just like any other resource.

In this section, we'll begin by looking at the basic structure of controls in SAPUI5. Then, we'll dive into implementing composite controls.

9.1.1 SAPUI5 Control Structure

Each control in SAPUI5 has the same code structure. This structure is shown in the skeleton code in Listing 9.1.

```
sap.ui.define([
  "sap/ui/core/Control"
], function (Control) {
  "use strict";
  return Control.extend("sapui5.demo.mvcapp.controls.myCustomInput", {
    metadata : {
    },
    init : function () {
    },
    onBeforeRendering : function(){
    },
    onAfterRendering : function(){
    },
    exit: function() {
    },
    renderer : function (oRM, oControl) {
    }
  })
});
```

Listing 9.1 Control Skeleton

You can see that just as in previous instances of SAPUI5 classes we've used, controls also make use of the `define` syntax. In the first part, all dependencies are declared. The array parameter for the dependencies contains at least the basic control class from SAPUI5, `sap.ui.core.Control`. This base class is extended here to create a new control.

Note that controls can also be based on other existing controls, which can be extended. In such a case, the control that's extended needs to be loaded as a dependency instead of `sap.ui.core.Control`.

In the following subsections, we'll start with the definition of the control metadata, which form the API. Then, we'll turn to the behavior implementation of the control. Last, we'll create the functionality which will render the control into the DOM.

Metadata

In the second parameter of the `define` call, you'll see a factory function. In this case, it extends a control instead of a controller. The factory function creates the constructor for the control and returns this constructor. Here, we find the *metadata* for the control, in which all the properties and aggregations are declared. The metadata defines the API of the control and can contain properties, aggregations and associations, and events fired by the control.

When you design an API, you should consider how properties and aggregations are named, what types they are, and what default values they will have. This is one of the most important technical parts of designing a control. As soon as you have published a control and its API and there is more than one application using it, it's hard to change anything about the API again without causing regressions and potentially breaking apps. If you're unsure about the naming, refer back to Chapter 3, Section 3.1. You can also look at existing controls—for instance, in the `sap.m` library—to get a feel for how APIs are designed there.

Properties

A property definition consists of a name, type, and default value, if desired. For a simple text property, which we will call `myProperty` of the type string, the metadata will look like this:

```
metadata : {
    properties : {
      "myProperty": {
      type: "string",
      defaultValue: "your default value goes here"}
  }
}
```

If you do not need a default value or any further settings, you can also simply assign a type to the name of the property, like so:

```
metadata : {
  properties : {
    "myProperty": "string"
  }
}
```

You can also use SAPUI5-specific types here, like so:

```
metadata : {
  properties : {
    "myCSSProperty": {
      type : "sap.ui.core.CSSSize",
        defaultValue : '100%'},
      }
    }
}
```

Aggregations

As you already know from Chapter 3, complex controls can be parents for other controls. These controls are usually aggregated into the parent control. To define such aggregations for child controls, you need to extend the metadata as highlighted in Listing 9.2.

```
metadata : {
  properties : {
   "myProperty": "string"
  },
  aggregations : {
    content : {type : "sap.ui.core.Control", multiple : true,
singularName : "content"}
  }
}
```

Listing 9.2 Adding an Aggregation to Control Metadata

Aggregation definitions again consist of an aggregation name and a type, which is either a particular control or the core control class if every control type is accepted.

The `multiple` parameter determines what relationship the aggregation has to its parent. If it is set to `true`, the relationship is of type 0..n, which means an arbitrary number of children can be aggregated. If it is set to `false`, the result is a 0..1 relationship, so there can be never more than one control in this aggregation.

As mentioned in Chapter 3, aggregated controls take part in the lifecycle of their parents. Aggregations will be instantiated and destroyed along with their parents. Due to this fact, a particular control instance can never be in more than one aggregation at a time.

The parameter `singularName` is optional. You know from Chapter 2 that the `sap.ui.core.Control` class inherits from `sap.ui.base.MangedObject`. From this parent, it gets functionality such as all the getter and setter methods for properties, aggregations, and associations. These getters and setters are usually typed, meaning, there are methods created for each property that will contain the property name. A property with the name `sampleProperty` will automatically have a getter method named `getSampleProperty` and a setter named `setSampleProperty`.

For aggregations, the same holds true, except that the aggregation name is usually transformed into a plural form for the getter method, if the aggregation allows for multiple children. In the definition, when you name your aggregation, it is conventional to specify the name as singular, even if multiple children are expected, like so:

```
listItem : {type : "sap.ui.core.Control", multiple : true}
```

This will result in a getter named `getListItems`.

If you do not want to have the plural form of your aggregation name in the getter method because you're using a name that doesn't allow for it—like *content*—you need to set the `singularName` parameter and specify explicitly which name to use for the getter method.

In the case of the content aggregation definition, we'll have a getter method called `getContent`, as expected.

Default Aggregations

If you want to omit the aggregation tag in an XML view, you can specify a default aggregation that child controls should go into automatically if no other target aggregation is specified in the view.

A default aggregation needs to be defined in the control metadata, as highlighted in Listing 9.3.

```
metadata : {
  properties: {
```

```
[…]
  },
  defaultAggregation : "content",
  aggregations : {
    content : {type : "sap.ui.core.Control", multiple : true,
      singularName : "content"}
  }
[…]
```

Listing 9.3 Defining a Default Aggregation in Control Metadata

Associations

Remember that associations create a relationship between two controls that are otherwise independent from each other. They do not share a lifecycle, so if one is instantiated or destroyed, the associated control might not be. An aggregation stores the reference to the child control's instance, whereas an association only stores the ID. Associations can be defined as controls similarly to aggregations, like so:

```
associations : {
myAssociationName: {type : "sap.ui.core.Control", multiple : false}
}
```

You can also define a `singularName` parameter, as you would do for aggregations.

Events

Events fired by a control you're implementing also need to be specified in the metadata so that applications can attach to or detach from them. Like with the getters and setters for properties, aggregations, and associations, the named attach and detach methods are automatically generated for you by the framework. In the metadata, events are defined like so:

```
events : {
press : {}
}
```

Mostly, events are just specified as empty objects. You can also specify an optional `allowPreventDefault` parameter if you want to give the application the ability to cancel the event. In that case, the metadata for the event would look like this:

```
events : {
press : {"allowPreventDefault" : true}
}
```

However, abstract controls currently are rather static and only consist of elements; they have no behavior and do not fire any events.

Control Behavior

The control behavior consists of the implementation of the lifecycle methods as needed and any additional methods you want to define for the control functionality, including event handlers. All lifecycle methods do not necessarily need to be implemented for each control. It's up to you as the developer to decide which of the methods mentioned ahead are required.

The control lifecycle provides some hooks that allow you to define what should happen at certain lifecycle phases of the control. For the control, you can implement methods corresponding to these lifecycle hooks.

In the `init` method of the control, the control constructor, everything necessary for the control to do its work is initialized. This method is called only once, when the control is instantiated.

The `onBeforeRendering` method will be called every time the control is (re-)rendered. Anything functionality you would like to include to prepare the output properly goes in here. For example, `sap.m.Dialog` uses this lifecycle hook to determine whether it needs to display its own scrollbar or if its content is scrollable itself. Because this information is not available in the `init` phase, this is the only hook in which checking for this content feature is possible.

In the `onAfterRendering` method, which will be called after each (re-)rendering of a control, the control has already been rendered and is hence also already part of your application's DOM. This can be an important phase if you want to run animations, for instance, which rely on a DOM reference for the control.

Finally, in the `exit` method, you can do all kinds of clean-up work. This method is invoked when the control is destroyed, and it should take with it all resources no longer required by your application. If you have any resources in your control that are not managed by SAPUI5, you should destroy them here.

Control Rendering

The `renderer` method tells the `RenderManager` at the `core` how it should be displayed on screen. This is where you tell SAPUI5 what information and what

DOM elements to create in the browser. This is a static method that gets the control instance itself and the global `RenderManager` instance passed in.

For `RenderManager`, there are some predefined methods to use for the renderer implementation. We will use most of them in our example control in the next subsection, so bear with us for a few minutes to learn which methods there are and how they're used.

Now that you know about the structure of a control, it's time to tap into the real world and create a control.

9.1.2   Implementing a Composite Control

In this section, we'll extend the `sap.ui.core.Control` class as we implement a composite control. We'll create a combination of an icon and an input field, so we can use this combination in any form we have in our application.

We suggest picking up the main sample application we developed throughout the majority of the previous chapters where we last left it, before we dove into the different application patterns. The current app is the version from the end of Chapter 7. If you do not have the app in this state anymore or want to start fresh, you can always refer to Appendix E in order to find the right starting point in the GitHub repository.

We'll create a new folder in the sample app, called *controls*. Within this folder, we'll create a new file called *myCustomInput.js*.

Structure, Metadata, and Dependencies

Next, we'll create a skeleton for the custom control. This skeleton will look like Listing 9.1. The metadata will contain two properties for the new control:

```
properties : {
"value": {type: "string", defaultValue: ""},
"iconURI": {type: "URI", defaultValue: ""}
},
```

When this control is rendered, we want the icon to be there first, and then the text next to it. We'll therefore tell the renderer to use a layout in the control. To be able to use a layout, we have to declare the corresponding dependency.

Let's work with `sap.ui.layout.Grid` again, because it's the most flexible column-based layout SAPUI5 provides. The grid lets us align multiple controls in one row.

We need to declare the dependency right at the top of the control, just like we do when we want to load a dependency in a controller. We also need `sap.m.Input` and `sap.ui.core.Icon`. We also want to define some additional layout data for these controls so that they cover the right number of grid columns. For this layout data, there is a special class for the grid: `sap.ui.layout.GridData`. The dependencies will be enhanced as in Listing 9.4.

```
sap.ui.define([
  "sap/ui/core/Control",
  "sap/ui/layout/Grid",
  "sap/ui/layout/GridData",
  "sap/m/Input",
  "sap/ui/core/Icon"
], function (Control, Grid, GridData, Input, Icon) {
```

Listing 9.4 Defining Dependencies for New Control

The dependencies that were added to the original skeleton are highlighted in Listing 9.4.

Because we want the layout to become a full member of the control, we not only instantiate the layout in the `init` method, but also declare it as an internal, "hidden" aggregation at the control. That way, it will automatically take part in the control lifecycle, so it will be instantiated when the parent control is and will be destroyed along with the custom control. The inner child control can also still automatically inherit the model from its parent (the layout), and the layout in turn will get access to the model of its own parent (the custom control).

Add the following code to the control metadata, right below the `properties` object:

```
aggregations:{
"_layout" : {type : "sap.ui.layout.Grid", multiple: false,
visibility : "hidden"}
}
```

By setting the visibility to `hidden`, we exclude the aggregation for the layout from being exposed via our control API. We do this because we don't want an application to overwrite the layout with any other layout control, so we don't want to expose a corresponding setter for the aggregation. Because we also want to indicate this properly in our code, we prefix this private aggregation name with an underscore.

Constructor

Now, we need to think about where the child controls for the new control should be instantiated. We can't handle this in the `renderer`, because the child control would be instantiated anew every time the control is re-rendered. The only point in time when instantiating the child controls makes sense is in the `init` phase of the new control.

First, we'll instantiate the input and the icon, as in Listing 9.5.

```
init : function () {
  this._oInput = new Input({
    value: this.getValue(),
    layoutData : new GridData({
      span : "L11 M11 S11"
    })
  });

  this._oIcon = new Icon({
    src: this.getIconURI(),
    layoutData : new GridData({
      span : "L1 M1 S1"
    })
  });
  this._oIcon.addStyleClass("sapUiSmallMarginBegin");
},
```

Listing 9.5 Instantiating the Member Controls for the Composite Control

You can see that we're adding two members to the new control, one for each of the child controls we want to integrate. We created the instances of these controls here, because we need to put them into the grid layout later but still want to have the references to these controls, because we'll manipulate their values later on.

We'll assign additional layout data to the input and the icon. The layout data tells the grid layout which of its 12 columns should be covered by which child control.

In the layout data constructor call, we'll set the `span` property for the controls. The pattern `L11 M11 S11`, for example, tells the grid that the input should cover 11 of 12 columns on all kinds of screen sizes. Correspondingly, we set the value to L1 M1 S1 at the icon to adjust for screen size.

We'll also add a style class to the icon, which will cause some small padding at the beginning of the control. In a right-to-left direction, this class adds space on the left of the icon. This style class and others are provided by SAPUI5. See Appendix E for a link to the class details and a list of all the available classes.

Next, we'll create the layout, using the setAggregation method the control inherits from the ManagedObject class. We'll add the setAggreation method below the other two controls in the init method, as shown in Listing 9.6.

```
init : function () {
  this._oInput = new Input({
    value: this.getValue(),
    layoutData : new GridData({
      span : "L11 M11 S11"
    })
  });

  this._oInput.addStyleClass("sapUiSmallMarginEnd");
  this._oIcon = new Icon({
    src: this.getIconURI(),
    layoutData : new GridData({
      span : "L1 M1 S1"
    })
  });
  this._oIcon.addStyleClass("sapUiSmallMarginBegin");

  this.setAggregation("_layout",
   new Grid({
    content: [
      this._oIcon,
      this._oInput
    ],
    hSpacing: 0,
    vSpacing: 0
  });
},
```

Listing 9.6 Setting Hidden Aggregation in init Method of the Custom Control

We're also adding the previously prepared child controls to the content aggregation of the grid.

Control Behavior Methods and Events

Next, we'll overwrite the setters for our properties. Until now, when an application called `setValue` at the control, it was not reflected in the actual child control, the input. We need to create this connection now, as follows:

```
setValue : function(sValue){
this.setProperty("value", sValue, true);
this._oInput.setValue(sValue);
},
```

We'll define a `setValue` function and overwrite the method coming from `ManagedObject`. Within the function, we call the `setProperty` method available at the `Control` class. It takes the property name (in our case, value), the actual value we want to set, and a third, Boolean parameter as arguments. We're setting the third parameter in this function call to `true` to tell the framework that this property change should not cause any automatic re-rendering. We do this because in the next line, we also set the value of that child control to what was passed in to the method, which will trigger a re-rendering anyway.

Next, we need to create a similar setter method for the other child control, the icon, like so:

```
setIconURI : function(sURI){
this.setProperty("iconURI", sURI, true);
this._oIcon.setSrc(sURI);
},
```

When the application now calls these two methods, either explicitly or automatically when creating the binding, we've made sure that properties set at the custom control itself also transfer their values to the internal child control.

However, we also need the data to flow in the opposite direction. When a user types data into the input field on the screen, the value property at the input is automatically set. This value should then also go into the property of the custom control. We also want the icon belonging to the input to change color when someone provides a value for an input. To do this, we need to attach to the change event of the input control within the `init` method.

In the event handler we're creating, we can capture the value the user has provided. We can then set the value property for the custom control to the same value. Depending on whether the input field is now filled or emptied (i.e., the user just deleted what was already there), we'll toggle a style class for the icon.

When the input is filled, the icon's color will turn to green; otherwise, the icon will be black. The `init` method will now look like Listing 9.7.

```
init : function () {
  var that = this;
  this._oInput = new Input({
    value: this.getValue(),
    layoutData : new GridData({
      span : "L11 M11 S11"
    })
  });

  this._oInput.addStyleClass("sapUiSmallMarginEnd");
  this._oIcon = new Icon({
    src: this.getIconURI(),
    layoutData : new GridData({
      span : "L1 M1 S1"
    })
  });
  this._oIcon.addStyleClass("sapUiSmallMarginBegin");
  this.setAggregation("_layout",
    new Grid({
      content: [
        this._oIcon,
        this._oInput
      ],
      hSpacing: 0,
      vSpacing: 0
    }));

  this._oInput.attachChange(function(){
    that._oIcon.toggleStyleClass("sapThemePositiveText",
      that._oInput.getValue()!=="");
    that.setValue(that._oInput.getValue());
  });
},
```

Listing 9.7 init Method and Custom Control with Change Handler for Input

In Listing 9.7, the bold segments show which code we've added. In the anonymous event handler function reacting on the change event at the input, we retrieve the instance of the icon control and toggle a style class that's available across all themes shipped with SAPUI5. We're using this class to make sure that the color will always fit the theme and also will not cause any issues when a user sets the theme to high-contrast black. The theme itself defines the exact color behind this class. The class is called sapThemePositiveText, and it does not necessarily turn anything green.

You could also write custom CSS for your control, of course, and load it as an additional resource in your manifest, as highlighted in Listing 9.8.

```
[…]
"sap.ui5": {
  "_version": "1.1.0",
  "rootView": {
  "viewName": "sapui5.demo.odata.readingdata.bestpractice.view.App",
      "type": "XML"
    },
  "dependencies": {
    "minUI5Version": "1.30.0",
    "libs": {
      "sap.ui.core": {},
      "sap.m": {},
      "sap.ui.layout": {}
    }
  },
  "resources": {
    "css": [
      {
        "uri": "/webapp/controls/css/style.css"
      }
    ]
  },
  "contentDensities": {
    "compact": true,
    "cozy": true
    },
[…]
```

Listing 9.8 Excerpt from Manifest Loading Additional CSS

However, for colors, this is usually not a good idea, because you have to ensure your color will remain compatible with whatever theme a user may pick, and will, for example, also not be themeable with the UI Theme Designer. More on theming and the UI Theme Designer will be covered in Chapter 10.

As you can see, within this control, we're not making use of the onBeforeRendering and onAfterRendering hooks, because they're not required in this use case. To complete the control's lifecycle, however, we need to implement one more method: exit. In the exit, as mentioned, we can perform all kinds of cleanup tasks. In this case, we specifically need to destroy the two child controls stored at the custom control as member variables. We will therefore implement the exit method as shown:

```
exit : function() {
this._oInput.destroy();
this._oIcon.destroy();
},
```

Note that we do not need to destroy the hidden aggregation "_layout", because everything that is a property or an aggregation of the custom control shares the same lifecycle and will be destroyed along with it. However, this does not apply to the two controls we just stored at member variables of the custom control.

Renderer

Our control is instantiated correctly, its content is created, the data flux between internal controls and properties is established, and we've set up the cleanup. What's still missing is the renderer, which will tell the framework what DOM elements to create.

As previously mentioned, the renderer is a static function that takes two parameters: the instance of the render manager, and the control itself that should be rendered. Both are required to define what is rendered—the render manager for rendering methods, and the control providing the data to render.

For the render manager, there are several methods available that you need in order to get the right information on screen. Let's look at what the renderer of the control should look like and go through the methods and examine what they do (see Listing 9.9).

```
renderer : function (oRenderManager, oControl) {
  oRenderManager.write("<div");
  oRenderManager.writeControlData(oControl);
  oRenderManager.addClass("myListItem");
  oRenderManager.writeClasses();
  oRenderManager.write(">");
  oRenderManager.renderControl(oControl.getAggregation("_layout"));
  oRenderManager.write("</div>");
}
```
Listing 9.9 Custom Control Renderer

The simplest method at RenderManager is the write method. This method simply adds to the buffer that contains what's written to the DOM whatever string you pass it. Most controls have a DIV element surrounding their content, so let's start by opening the corresponding tag.

In the second line of the renderer, we call a `writeControlData` function and pass the control instance to it. This function outputs all relevant control data, like an ID or any properties that need to be directly attached.

The next line adds a style class (using `addStyleClass`). You can add multiple style classes by invoking this method several times; when all classes you need are assembled, call the method `writeClasses` so that they are also written to the control. We then invoke the `write` function again, closing the `DIV` tag.

Next in line is the child control that we want to see in the view. We can render any additional controls by calling renderControl at the render manager and passing the instance of the control to be rendered in as a parameter.

Finally, we need to add the closing tag for the `DIV`, so we can use the write function again.

There is one more important function that isn't shown here: the `writeEscaped` function. This function takes a string as a parameter and escapes it properly. We use this for everything that needs to be rendered and can be influenced by user input.

Using a Control in the App

Now that we've completed the custom control, we can use it in our application. If you've picked up the sample app from the point we suggested (the end of Chapter 7), you should have a master view with `SimpleForm` in it. There are several instances of regular inputs of type `sap.m.Input` already there. We can replace some of them and see what happens. To include a control from your own web application in your XML views, you need to define a new namespace pointing to the directory your control is in.

Let's define this namespace at the top of the view, as highlighted in Listing 9.10.

```
<mvc:View  controllerName=
"sapui5.demo.odata.readingdata.bestpractice.controller.Master"
  xmlns:mvc="sap.ui.core.mvc"

  xmlns:f="sap.ui.layout.form"
  xmlns:core="sap.ui.core"
  xmlns="sap.m"
  xmlns:my="sapui5.demo.odata.readingdata.bestpractice.controls">
```
Listing 9.10 Defining New Namespace for the Custom Control

In Master.view.xml, replace as many of the input instances in `SimpleForm` with your custom control, like so:

```
<Label text="Supplier ID"/>
<my:MyCustomInput value="{ID}" iconURI="company-view" />
```

Don't forget to provide the control with an icon URI. The icons can be found in the Explorer app from the SAPUI5 Demo Kit, as discussed in Chapter 1.

After completing these tasks, your form will look like Figure 9.1.

Figure 9.1 Custom Control in Action

As you can see, all the inputs now have icons in front of them, nicely turning green when you type something in. Next, we'll investigate what you can do when you want to use control combinations, which do not need the specific functionality and behavior of a custom control, but should be displayed in combination at more than one place in your app.

9.2   Using Fragments

In this section, we'll look at another reusable element you can easily create yourself: a fragment. A *fragment* is not dissimilar to a custom control, but it resembles a view in terms of functionality—but it's more lightweight. A fragment consists of one or multiple controls. It's defined similarly to a view, so you can create Java-Script fragments, HTML fragments, and, of course, XML fragments. In this section, we'll concentrate on the latter: using XML fragments.

Fragments can be embedded in views, and their content can be reused in different views this way. Once embedded in a view, a fragment does not leave any trace of its existence at runtime. Unlike a view, fragment content is not encapsulated in the surrounding DIV tags. In fact, the controls a fragment contains become normal members of the surrounding view. Because of this, a fragment also does not need (and actually cannot have) its own controller. It can access the controller functionality of the view that embeds the fragment, and its content can also access the model of the embedding view. We'll look into this further later in Section 9.2.3.

Fragments are useful whenever you want to use a particular combination of controls in several views in or across your applications, or when you want to easily switch from displaying one set of controls to another—if you have an edit mode and a display mode for some data, for example.

In this section, we'll look at this second use case (switching from displaying one set of controls to another) and implement it in the sample application. We have a form in which we can create a new supplier, and when the supplier is successfully created, we want to switch from displaying the form to displaying sap.m.Panel with the supplier data we've just created.

9.2.1 Creating Fragments

We'll create two fragments, one containing the SimpleForm control we already have in our sample application, and one for displaying the data. The fragment files will go into the *view* folder.

Fragment for SimpleForm

Let's start with the fragment for the form. We'll call the file *EditSupplier.fragment.xml*.

Fragment Suffix

Note that all fragments, by convention, carry the fragment suffix in their file names. XML fragments will thus end with fragment.xml, and JavaScript fragments will end with fragment.js, for example.

The code for the *fragment definition* looks like this:

```
<core:FragmentDefinition
xmlns:core="sap.ui.core">
</core:FragmentDefinition>
```

You can see that the `Fragment` class is not located in the `sap.ui.core.mvc` namespace, but instead directly in the core. The rest of the code is similar to a view: You open the fragment definition with the corresponding tag, add the namespaces you need for the controls inside and the one for the core to get the namespace for the fragment definition itself, and then place all the controls you want the fragment to contain inside the fragment.

Let's cut `SimpleForm` and its content from the master view and place it in this fragment; it will look like Listing 9.11.

```
<core:FragmentDefinition
  xmlns="sap.m"
  xmlns:core="sap.ui.core"
  xmlns:f="sap.ui.layout.form"
  xmlns:my="sapui5.demo.advanced.fragments.controls">
  <f:SimpleForm>
    <core:Title text="Supplier Information" />
    <Label text="Supplier ID"/>
    <my:MyCustomInput value="{ID}" iconURI="company-view" />
    <Label text="Company Name"/>
    <my:MyCustomInput value="{Name}" iconURI="company-view" />
    <Label text="Street"/>
    <my:MyCustomInput value="{Address/Street}" iconURI="building" />
    <Label text="City"/>
    <my:MyCustomInput value="{Address/City}" iconURI="addresses" />
    <Label text="ZipCode"/>
    <my:MyCustomInput value="{Address/ZipCode}" iconURI="addresses" />
    <Label text="Country"/>
    <my:MyCustomInput value="{Address/Country}" iconURI="world" />
    <Label text="Concurrency"/>
    <Input value="{Concurrency}"  />
  </f:SimpleForm>
</core:FragmentDefinition>
```
Listing 9.11 Edit Fragment for Supplier

As you can see, the fragment really only contains the form that used to be part of the master view. The remainder of the master view now looks like Listing 9.12.

```
<mvc:View
controllerName="sapui5.demo.advanced.fragments.controller.Master"
  xmlns:mvc="sap.ui.core.mvc"
```

```
xmlns:f="sap.ui.layout.form"
xmlns:core="sap.ui.core"
xmlns="sap.m">
<Page
  id="supplierInfo"
  title="{i18n>SupplierTitle}">
  <content>
    <Panel/>
  </content>
  <footer>
    <Bar>
      <contentRight>
        <Button
          icon="sap-icon://undo"
          press="onReset"
          text="{i18n>ResetChanges}" />
        <Button
          icon="sap-icon://save"
          type="Accept"
          press="onSave"
          text="{i18n>SaveChanges}" />
      </contentRight>
    </Bar>
  </footer>
</Page>
</mvc:View>
```

Listing 9.12 Remainder of Master View without the Form

The only control left in the `Page` content is an empty `Panel`.

Fragment to Display Data

Next, let's create the second fragment. It will contain controls that will only *display* the data from the supplier, rather that provide the data in an editable form. We'll call this fragment *DisplaySupplier.fragment.xml*.

DisplaySupplier.fragment.xml will contain controls of type `sap.m.Label` and `sap.m.Text` for the supplier data and will be grouped in layout controls of type `HBox` and `VBox`, which allow for horizontal and vertical groupings of their content (see *https://sapui5.hana.ondemand.com/explored.html#/entity/sap.m.FlexBox/samples* for the details of these controls). The fragment will look like Listing 9.13.

```
<core:FragmentDefinition
    xmlns="sap.m"
    xmlns:core="sap.ui.core">
  <HBox>
    <VBox class="sapUiSmallMarginEnd">
      <Label text="{i18n>SupplierID}"/>
      <Label text="{i18n>CompanyName}"/>
      <Label text="{i18n>Street}" />
      <Label text="{i18n>City}" />
      <Label text="{i18n>ZipCode}" />
      <Label text="Country"/>
    </VBox>
    <VBox>
      <Text text="{ID}" />
      <Text text="{Name}" />
      <Text text="{Address/Street}" />
      <Text text="{Address/City}" />
      <Text text="{Address/ZipCode}"/>
      <Text text="{Address/Country}" />
    </VBox>
  </HBox>
</core:FragmentDefinition>
```

Listing 9.13 Fragment for Displaying Supplier Data

Now that we've created the two fragments we need, let's look at how we can integrate their content into the master view.

9.2.2 Embedding Fragments into Views

If you only want to embed a fragment into a view, you can do this as you would with any control, or with a nested view. Put the tag for the fragment into the place in your view that you want the fragment content to be rendered at runtime.

We could, for example, embed EditSupplier.fragment.xml into the master view as shown in Listing 9.14.

```
<mvc:View  controllerName=
"sapui5.demo.advanced.fragments.controller.Master"
  xmlns:mvc="sap.ui.core.mvc"
  xmlns:f="sap.ui.layout.form"
  xmlns:core="sap.ui.core"
  xmlns="sap.m">
  <Page
    id="supplierInfo"
    title="{i18n>SupplierTitle}">
    <content>
```

```
        <Panel id="SupplierPanel">
          <core:Fragment fragmentName="sapui5.demo.advanced.fragments.
            view.EditSupplier" type="XML" />
        </Panel>
      </content>
      <footer>
  [...]
      </footer>
    </Page>
  </mvc:View>
```

Listing 9.14 Fragment Declaratively Embedded in XML View

This is a perfectly valid approach to embed a fragment. However, when you want to embed different fragments depending on some condition or another, you need to implement the fragment differently. In such a case, you do not want to declaratively instantiate the fragment, but instantiate it in the controller, depending on whether your particular conditions are met.

For this sample application, this means that within our controller we need to set and check for two different modes: Either we're editing/creating a new supplier, or we're only displaying supplier data. Depending on whether we're in the first mode or the second, we'll display the corresponding fragment. Furthermore, we'll have a new button, the EDIT button, with which we can navigate from display mode to edit mode. Finally, we only want to have this button visible when we're not already in edit mode. The SAVE button and the REJECT button of our application should also only be visible when we're in edit mode.

From Chapter 5, we know that we can use a simple JSON model to keep track of the mode we're in and make this mode information bindable for our button's visibility. Therefore, let's create such a model in the `onInit` method of the master controller (see Listing 9.15).

```
onInit: function() {
  var oModel = new JSONModel({
    edit: true
  });
  this.setModel(oModel, "viewModel");
  this.getRouter().getRoute("master").attachPatternMatched(this
    .onAdd, this);
  this.getOwnerComponent().getModel().metadataLoaded()
    .then(this._onMetadataLoaded.bind(this));
},
```

Listing 9.15 Modified onInit of Master Controller

The new model information is highlighted in bold in Listing 9.15.

We now need methods that will instantiate the fragments for us and set them as content in the panel containing the supplier data. We'll create two private methods, _showDisplay and _showEdit, in the controller code. Both will lazy load their respective fragments; _showDisplay will load the DisplaySupplier fragment, and _showEdit will load the EditSupplier fragment. This means that we must first check if there is already a reference to the fragment stored at the controller. If not, we instantiate the fragment content, using a particular factory function. Either way, we retrieve the fragment content by the end of the method, as you can see in Listing 9.16.

```
_showEdit: function(){
  if (!this._editFragment){
    this._editFragment = sap.ui.xmlfragment("sapui5.demo.advanced.
      fragments.view.EditSupplier");
  }
  this._supplierPanel.removeAllContent();
  this._supplierPanel.addContent(this._editFragment);
},

_showDisplay: function(){
  if (!this._displayFragment){
    this._displayFragment = sap.ui.xmlfragment("sapui5.demo.advanced.
      fragments.view.DisplaySupplier");
  }
  this._supplierPanel.removeAllContent();
  this._supplierPanel.addContent(this._displayFragment);
},
```

Listing 9.16 Fragment Lazy Loading in Master Controller

You can see that we're first checking whether the fragment has already been instantiated. If not, we invoke the factory function sap.ui.xmlfragment (hence, no new keyword here). We then want to set the fragment content as content in the remaining panel. Before we add the content, we make sure the panel is empty and does not contain the other fragment anymore, so we invoke the removeAll-Content method on the panel before we call addContent and pass the current fragment content in.

For this to work, there's one more prerequisite: We need to make sure that this._supplierPanel contains a reference to the panel. To achieve this, we need to add an `ID` to `Panel` within the view so that we can retrieve the panel instance in the controller. Let's give the `Panel` the ID `"SupplierPanel"`, like so:

```
<Panel id="SupplierPanel" />
```

Next, because we need this reference in more than one method, we'll create it in the `onInit` method of the controller. Add this line to `onInit`:

```
this._supplierPanel = this.byId ("SupplierPanel");
```

Now, we need to make sure the new methods for loading the fragments are invoked at the right points in the code. We want the app to start in edit mode, so we add another line to the `onInit` method, making sure that in the beginning the fragment containing the form is shown. We'll call the new _showEdit method at the end of the `onInit` method, like so:

```
this._showEdit();
```

When a user edits data and clicks on the SAVE button, he will be presented with the fragment that displays the data. To achieve this, we need to add the _showDisplay method invocation to the `onSave` method in the controller. We also want to make the new mode we entered known to the view model. The `onSave` method now looks like Listing 9.17.

```
onSave: function() {
  var oModel = this.getModel();
  // submit changes to server
  oModel.submitChanges();
  this.getModel("viewModel").setProperty("/edit", false);
  this._showDisplay();
},
```

Listing 9.17 Setting the View to Display Mode

We're still missing is some means to return to the edit mode. Let's add the new EDIT button to the view, and while we're working on the buttons anyway, let's also bind the visibility of the buttons so that they're not all shown at all times. Remember, we want the EDIT button to disappear in edit mode and the other two buttons to disappear when in display mode.

Add the new button to the master view like so:

```
<Button
  icon="sap-icon://edit"
  press="onEdit"
  text="{i18n>Edit}"
  visible="{= !${viewModel>/edit}}"/>
```
Listing 9.18 Edit Button in the Master View

The binding for the visible attribute is an expression binding; you should be familiar with expression bindings from Chapter 5. This expression in particular returns true if the edit property of the view model is *not* true.

The other buttons get bindings for their visibility properties, which simply point to the edit property of the model. If true, the buttons show up; if not, they don't (see Listing 9.19).

```
<Button
  icon="sap-icon://undo"
  press="onReset"
  text="{i18n>ResetChanges}"
  visible="{viewModel>/edit}" />
<Button
  icon="sap-icon://save"
  type="Accept"
  press="onSave"
  text="{i18n>SaveChanges}"
  visible="{viewModel>/edit}" />
```
Listing 9.19 Binding Button Visibility to View Model

We've assigned the EDIT button an onEdit function, which will handle the press event. Let's implement it now, setting the edit property at the view model back to true, and invoking the _showEdit method to switch back to the form again, as shown:

```
onEdit: function(){
  this.getModel("viewModel").setProperty("/edit", true);
  this._showEdit();
},
```

When you now rerun the application, you can enter data, and, once you click on SAVE, you'll see the screen shown in Figure 9.2.

Figure 9.2 Display Mode for Supplier

9.2.3 Using Dialogs in Fragments

We now can switch between the two modes in the view by using two different fragments. When we click on the SAVE button, we see the display mode, and with the EDIT button, we can return to the form in which we can edit supplier data. We can also reset any changes we've entered into the supplier form so long as we haven't saved those changes.

However, we would also like to have a popup which asks users to confirm if they really want to reset. After all, a user could click the wrong button. Because a confirmation dialog might be something we'd like to reuse in an application, we can put it into a fragment as well.

However, there are some additional facts to know when you're using fragments in dialogs. The most important difference from other fragments is that dialogs do not become part of the view DOM. Because they're rendered in a separate area of the DOM by the framework, the so-called *static area*, their controls are not get registered by the framework as part of a particular view. This means that the content of such a fragment also does not automatically take part in the view's lifecycle, which means that these controls do not get access to the view's models.

However, you can change this by making such a dialog a dependent of a view. In this section, we'll show you how to do so. Let's build the dialog fragment first.

We'll use a normal `sap.m.Dialog` element and create it with a text and two buttons: one to reset the data and one to cancel the `reset` action and close the popup without touching the data. The fragment we'll put the dialog in will be called *ConfirmDialog.fragment.xml*, and, as always, it will go into the *view* folder. The code within the fragment will look like Listing 9.20.

```
<core:FragmentDefinition
  xmlns="sap.m"
  xmlns:core="sap.ui.core">
  <Dialog title="{i18n>confirmTitle}"
    type="Message">
    <content>
      <Text text="{i18n>ConfirmText}" />
    </content>
    <beginButton>
      <Button text="{i18n>btnReset}"
        press="onReset" />
    </beginButton>
    <endButton>
      <Button text="{i18>btnCancel}"
        press="onCancel" />
    </endButton>
  </Dialog>
</core:FragmentDefinition>
```

Listing 9.20 Fragment Containing a Dialog

This fragment can now be instantiated in the controller of the view that requires the fragment, just like any other fragment. When someone clicks on the RESET button, we will lazy load the fragment. This fragment is different from those we've used previously, because not only does it not get part of the view, but also has some behavior of its own. As you know, fragments cannot have their own controllers, but we can give them access to the functionality of the controller of their parent view. We can pass the controller instance to the fragment when the latter is instantiated. Because we need functions reacting on the button press events within the dialog, we'll implement these functions into the controller of the master view and pass the controller instance to the dialog fragment, as shown in Listing 9.21.

```
onResetRequested: function (){
  if(!this._oConfirmDialog){
    this._oConfirmDialog =
 sap.ui.xmlfragment("sapui5.demo.advanced.fragments.view.ConfirmDialog"
, this);
    this.getView().addDependent(this._oConfirmDialog);
  }
  this._oConfirmDialog.open();
},
```
Listing 9.21 Lazy Loading Dialog from Fragment

As you can see, when the RESET button is clicked on, we want to check whether the dialog already exists at the controller. Note that the fragment factory function returns the fragment contents for us. Because the fragment is a single-rooted fragment, which means that there is only one control at its root, we get the instance of this control back directly when we invoke the factory function.

If we don't have the dialog instance yet, we create it, passing the controller instance as second parameter into the fragment factory, and set it to the private member variable at the controller. Then, we use a new method at the view, called addDependent, and pass the dialog in there. This makes it possible for controls inside of the fragment to access the models of the surrounding view and take part in the lifecycle of the view. When this is done, we open the dialog by calling its open function.

As you can see, in Listing 9.22, we've called the event handler opening the dialog onResetRequested, because this is the method we want to call when someone clicks on the RESET button in the master view.

We'll keep the onReset function, because this is what will be invoked when the reset is confirmed. However, we need to point the press event of the RESET button in the master view to our new function now, like in Listing 9.22.

```
<Button
  icon="sap-icon://undo"
  press="onResetRequested"
  text="{i18n>btnResetChanges}"
  visible="{viewModel>/edit}" />
```
Listing 9.22 Press Event of the Reset Button

In the highlighted portion of the code, you can see that we're using the new function now, which triggers the dialog when the RESET button is clicked on.

There's now only one function missing in the controller, and that's the `onCancel` function for the dialog, which is attached to the CANCEL button in the dialog. This function does nothing more than closing the button, like so:

```
onCancel: function(){
  this._oConfirmDialog.close();
}
```

This is all it takes to use a dialog in a fragment. You could now either copy the code from one controller to others to reuse the same dialog, or you could also transfer the code into a separate file, creating an object that performs the lazy loading of the fragment and the handling of button events.

For details on how to do transfer the code to a separate file, we recommend looking at the corresponding walkthrough chapter in the SAPUI5 Demo Kit: *https://sapui5.hana.ondemand.com/#docs/guide/(19453962b8074b7399372c65cbe05370.html.)*

So far, you've learned how to create your own controls and how to create a particular, reusable set of controls that can be shared across your applications. In the next section, you'll learn all about SAP OData extensions and how they can be used to automatically instantiate controls and control combinations via smart controls and smart templates.

9.3 SAP OData Annotations

Standard OData metadata was not fully capable of describing all the additional information about the data that's available in the SAP backend. SAP wanted to provide information like label texts, if an entity is updateable, if you can filter it, and so on. Luckily, the OData standard provides a capability to enhance the service with such information: *annotations*.

The first OData version SAP used was OData 2.0. Those annotations differ from OData 4.0. In this section, we'll look at OData 2.0 and OData 4.0 annotations and at the differences between them.

9.3.1 Custom SAP OData 2.0 Annotations

The AtomPub format, on which OData is based, allows you to extend the service document with elements and attributes from a custom XML namespace. The SAP namespace values are identified by the `sap:` namespace prefix. Figure 9.3 shows the definition of the namespace `xmlns:sap="http://www.sap.com/Protocols/SAPData"` at the top of the XML document, along with annotations like `sap:label` or `sap:createable`.

```
<?xml version="1.0" encoding="UTF-8"?>
<edmx:Edmx xmlns:sap="http://www.sap.com/Protocols/SAPData"
xmlns:m="http://schemas.microsoft.com/ado/2007/08/dataservices/metadata"
xmlns:edmx="http://schemas.microsoft.com/ado/2007/06/edmx" Version="1.0">
  - <edmx:DataServices m:DataServiceVersion="2.0">
    - <Schema xml:lang="en"
      xmlns="http://schemas.microsoft.com/ado/2008/09/edm" sap:schema-
      version="1" Namespace="/IWBEP/GWSAMPLE_BASIC">
      - <EntityType sap:content-version="1" Name="BusinessPartner">
        - <Key>
            <PropertyRef Name="BusinessPartnerID"/>
          </Key>
          <Property Name="Address" Nullable="false"
            Type="/IWBEP/GWSAMPLE_BASIC.CT_Address"/>
          <Property Name="BusinessPartnerID" Nullable="false" Type="Edm.String"
            sap:updatable="false" sap:createable="false" sap:label="Business Partner
            ID" MaxLength="10"/>
          <Property Name="CompanyName" Nullable="false" Type="Edm.String"
            sap:label="Company" MaxLength="80"/>
```

Figure 9.3 SAP OData Annotations

These annotations can be created automatically—for example, by SAP Gateway— depending on properties of certain attribute fields or entity types. We won't discuss how to create these annotations in the backend.

SAP OData 2.0 Annotations

For more information on OData 2.0 annotations in SAP, please visit *http://scn.sap.com/docs/DOC-44986*.

Table 9.1 lists some common annotations for an entity set.

Annotation	Meaning	Description
`sap:creatable`	Creatable	The `createable` property indicates if the creation of an entity type is supported. For example, a new product can be created.
`sap:updatable`	Updatable	The `updateable` property indicates if it is possible to update an entity type. For example, it's possible to update a product with the number 100000.

Table 9.1 Common Annotations for Entity Types

Annotation	Meaning	Description
sap:deletable	Deletable	The deletable property indicates if it's possible to delete an entity type. For example, it's possible to delete a product with the number 100000.
sap:pageable	Pageable	The pagable property indicates if client-side paging is supported with $top and $skip.
sap:requires-filter	Requires filter	The requires-filter property indicates if a filter is needed to access the data. This makes sense when the provided dataset is very large.
sap:addressable	Addressable	The addressable property indicates if the entity can be accessed directly, like Products, or if you have to use a navigation property, like SalesOrders('1')/Items (for the items).

Table 9.1 Common Annotations for Entity Types (Cont.)

Table 9.2 lists some common annotations for attributes.

Annotation	Meaning	Description
sap:creatable	Creatable	The createable property is used when creating an entry. This annotation is typically set to true, except for fields that are supposed to be filled by the backend, like ProductID or SalesOrderID.
sap:updatable	Updatable	The updateable property is used when an entry is updated and indicates if a property can be changed. This property is usually in line with the creatable annotation. It's set to true for attributes like ProductDescription or NetPrice. For fields that are updated by the backend, like NetSum or ChangeTimeStamp, the property is set to false.
sap:sortable	Sortable	The sortable property indicates if the attribute can be used in an $orderBy query option, like $orderBy=ProductName.

Table 9.2 Common Annotations for Attributes

Annotation	Meaning	Description
sap:filterable	Filterable	The filterable property indicates if the attribute can be used in a $filter query operation, like $filter=ProductNumber eq '100000'.
sap:label	Label	This property provides short, human-readable text suitable for labels and captions in the UI.

Table 9.2 Common Annotations for Attributes (Cont.)

Annotations inform the developer about the various options for the service, but they don't force any behavior. If the property sap:updateable is set to false for a certain attribute, you could still send this data along with your request, although it's not needed. Another important aspect is that annotations are also machine readable.

9.3.2 OData 4.0 Annotations

The drawback of OData 2.0 custom annotations is that non-SAP client libraries ignore custom annotations. SAP had to use custom annotations to express business semantics, but this reduced some of the benefits of an open and standards-based protocol.

With OData 4.0, this semantic information can be expressed in a standardized way with annotations. All OData 4.0-compliant OData client libraries are capable of parsing annotations and will pass them along to the consuming applications. The OData standard itself provides a set of vocabulary components: core, capability, and measures. The core vocabulary contains terms which are needed to write own vocabulary. Examples can include descriptions or if values are immutable or computed. In the capability vocabulary, there are terms which describe whether a service is filterable, supports batch, and if it is possible to update or insert data. The measures vocabulary contains terms for describing monetary amounts and measured quantities. These are just examples; for the full definition go to *http://www.odata.org/vocabularies/*.

OData 4.0 Annotations

You can find out which OData 4.0 annotations are supported by SAP Gateway at *http://scn.sap.com/community/gateway/blog/2013/10/07/vocabulary-based-annotations*.

Listing 9.23 shows the difference between OData 2.0 and OData 4.0 annotations.

```
<!-- SAP v2 OData annoations -->
<Property Name="StockQuanity" Type="Edm.Int16" sap:unit="StockUnit" />
<Property Name="StockUnit" Type="Edm.String" sap:semantics="unit-of-
measure" />

<!-- OData v4 annoations -->
<Property Name="StockQuanitty" Type="Edm.Int16">
  <Annotation Term="Measures.Unit" Path="StockUnit" />
</Property>
<Property Name="StockUnit" Type="Edm.String" />
```

Listing 9.23 Example OData 2.0 and 4.0 Annotations

All annotations are expressed via an `<Annotation>` node. This node can be directly attached to the corresponding element, or it can be defined in a dedicated `<Annotations>` section, which you'll see in Section 9.4. Another important aspect is the `Term`, which defines the type of the annotated element. In Listing 9.23, we defined that `Term` is a `Unit` from the `Measures` vocabulary.

It's also possible to define custom terms and describe them in a machine-readable way. The custom terms are described in the same way as the standard terms.

Now that you've seen a rough overview of annotations, let's look at how they're used in smart controls.

9.4   Smart Controls

During the development of SAPUI5 applications, there are some recurring patterns like value helps, sorting, and filtering that involve a bunch of UI frontend coding. This approach is error-prone, as every developer might implement functionally slightly differently.

Therefore, SAP invented *smart controls*, which provide functionality like filtering, sorting or value helps out of the box in a standardized way. The controls are called smart because they get all the information they need out from the OData metadata and annotations. As of the writing of this book (July 2016), smart controls are only part of SAPUI5, not OpenUI5.

Let's look at a concrete example of smart controls in action. The coding for the example is in the source code folder on the products webpage at *www.sap-press.com/3980*. This example uses a smart table and an annotated OData service, which is mocked by the SAPUI5 mock server. `sap.ui.comp.smarttable.SmartTable` automatically creates all of its necessary columns based on annotations. You'll see a code example of a smart table in Listing 9.24 and the rendered table in Figure 9.4. The magic of the table happens because it's bound to the `Products` entity.

```
<mvc:View ...
  xmlns:smartTable="sap.ui.comp.smarttable">
  <smartTable:SmartTable
    id="smartTable_ResponsiveTable"
    tableType="ResponsiveTable"
    editable="false"
    entitySet="Products"
    useVariantManagement="false"
    useTablePersonalisation="false"
    header="Products"
    showRowCount="true"
    useExportToExcel="false"
    enableAutoBinding="true">
  </smartTable:SmartTable>
```

Listing 9.24 Smart Table Example

Phones and Tablets			
Products (8)			
Product ID	Name	Category Description	Color
1	iPhone 6S Plus 16GB	Phone	Silver
2	iPhone 6S 16GB	Phone	Space Gray
3	iPhone SE 16GB	Phone	Gold

Figure 9.4 Smart Table without Personalization

As you can see, there was almost no frontend coding necessary to display a full-fledged table. Also, the text of the column headers was created automatically. Listing 9.25 shows an extract of the OData metadata document with the annotations for the product. The labels for the columns have been taken from the `sap:label` annotations.

```
<EntityType Name="Product">
  <Key>
    <PropertyRef Name="ProductId" />
  </Key>
  <Property Name="ProductId" Type="Edm.String" Nullable="false"
    sap:updatable="false" MaxLength="20" sap:label="Product ID" />
  <Property Name="Name" Type="Edm.String" Nullable="false"
    MaxLength="30" sap:label="Name" />
  <Property Name="Category" Type="Edm.String"
    sap:label="Category Description"
    sap:filterable="true" />
  <Property Name="Description" Type="Edm.String" MaxLength="256"
    sap:label="Description" />
  <Property Name="Price" Type="Edm.String" Nullable="false"
    sap:unit="CurrencyCode" MaxLength="3" sap:label="Price"/>
  <Property Name="CurrencyCode" Type="Edm.String" Nullable="true"
    MaxLength="3" sap:label="Currency"
    sap:semantics="currency-code"/>
  ...
</EntityType>

<!-- annotations for the Smart Table inital columns -->
<Annotations Target="com.sap.smart.controls.Product"
  xmlns="http://docs.oasis-open.org/odata/ns/edm">
  <Annotation Term="com.sap.vocabularies.UI.v1.LineItem">
    <Collection>
      <Record Type="com.sap.vocabularies.UI.v1.DataField">
        <PropertyValue Property="Value" Path="ProductId" />
      </Record>
      <Record Type="com.sap.vocabularies.UI.v1.DataField">
        <PropertyValue Property="Value" Path="Name" />
      </Record>
      <Record Type="com.sap.vocabularies.UI.v1.DataField">
        <PropertyValue Property="Value" Path="Category" />
      </Record>
      <Record Type="com.sap.vocabularies.UI.v1.DataField">
        <PropertyValue Property="Value" Path="Color" />
      </Record>
    </Collection>
  </Annotation>
</Annotations>
```

Listing 9.25 Product Metadata for Smart Table

The SAP-specific annotation term com.sap.vocabularies.UI.v1.LineItem displays the initial table columns with the different record types, with com.sap.vocabularies.UI.v1.DataField referring to the fields. You can also see that the product entity has other properties, like `description` and `price`. It's also possible to display these attributes in the table when table personalization is enabled.

When the `useTablePersonalisation` property from the smart table is set to `true`, the gear icon for the table settings is made visible, as shown in Figure 9.5. When you click on the table settings it is possible to add/hide columns and change their order (Figure 9.6). It is also possible to sort (Figure 9.7) or filter (Figure 9.8) the entries. You can also group the table rows (Figure 9.9).

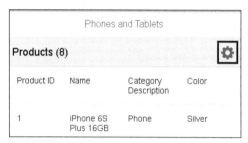

Figure 9.5 Smart Table Personalization Settings Icon

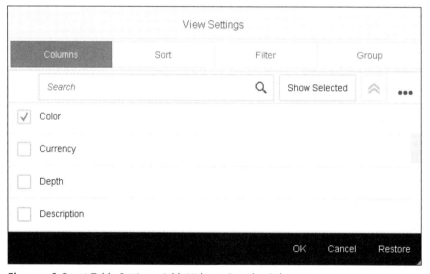

Figure 9.6 Smart Table Settings: Add, Hide, or Reorder Columns

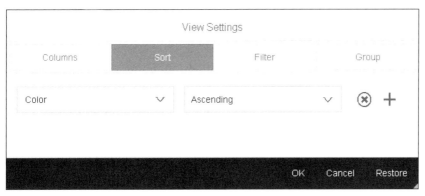

Figure 9.7 Smart Table Settings: Sort Entries

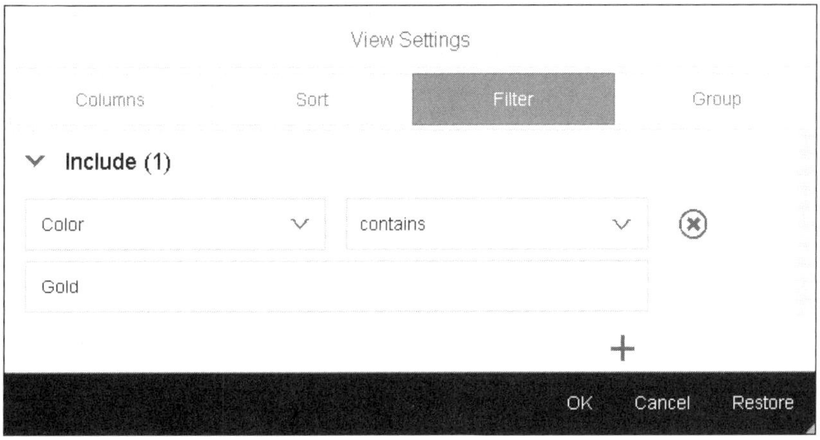

Figure 9.8 Smart Table Settings: Filter Entries

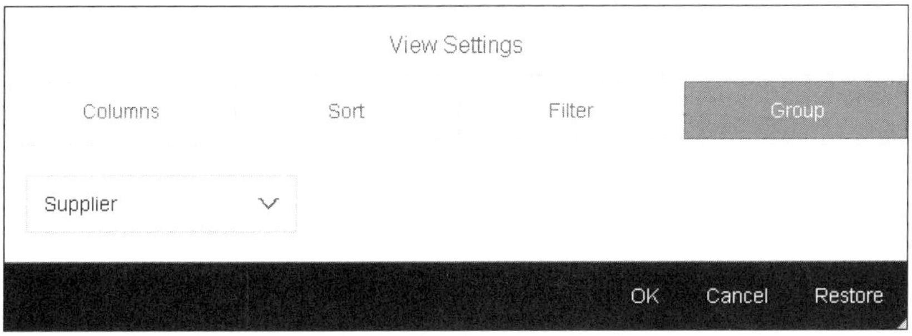

Figure 9.9 Smart Table Settings: Group Entries

You've seen a lot of personalization setting dialogs for the smart table, like filtering and sorting, and no frontend UI coding was necessary. Everything works out of the box, which is a big benefit of the smart controls.

When you change the appearance of the smart table and restart your application in the SAP Web IDE or on your local web server, all personalization will be gone. In a real-life scenario, all your changes should be stored in the backend via SAPUI5 Flexibility Services.

> **SAPUI5 Flexibility Services**
>
> Learn more about saving personalizations, variant management, and UI adaptation via SAPUI5 Flexibility Services at *https://sapui5.hana.ondemand.com/*. Once at the URL, navigate to DEVELOPER GUIDE • DEVELOPING APPS • SAPUI5 FLEXIBILITY SERVICES.

The smart table example should have given you a glimpse into the benefits of smart controls and how they can be used. As you've seen, the creation of the UI is much more driven by the information available in the backend (annotations) than by the frontend. Table 9.3 provides an overview of the currently available smart controls.

Control	SAPUI5 Type
Smart field	`sap.ui.comp.smartfield.SmartField`
Smart label	`sap.ui.comp.smartfield.SmartLabel`
Smart group	`sap.ui.comp.smartform.GroupElement`
Smart form	`sap.ui.comp.smartform.SmartForm`
Smart filter bar	`sap.ui.comp.smartfilterbar.SmartFilterBar`
Smart table	`sap.ui.comp.smarttable.SmartTable`

Table 9.3 Available Smart Controls

For the remainder of this section, we'll highlight some of the controls shown in Table 9.3 and their various use cases. There are dedicated examples in the book's source code for the different controls.

9.4.1   Smart Tables and Smart Filters Bar

A smart table can be combined with a smart filter bar, which allows users to easily look up table data (see Figure 9.10).

Figure 9.10 Smart Table and Smart Filter Bar

Figure 9.11 shows the filter dialog for the category filter.

The smart table and smart filter bar also provide options for variant management, although variant management is only enabled when SAPUI5 Flexibility Services is available. For the purposes of this example, we've mocked this functionality.

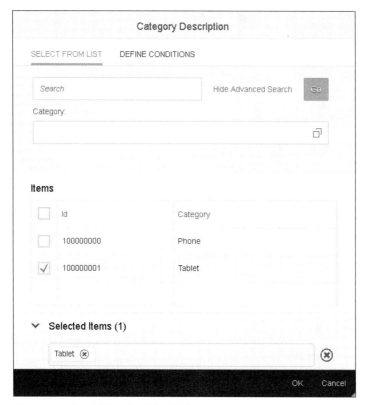

Figure 9.11 Smart Filter Bar Filter Settings

After we changed some table settings (in this case, we added the SUPPLIER column), you can see in Figure 9.12 that the standard variant became dirty, which is indicated by *. Click on the dropdown icon next to STANDARD * to open the variant settings and choose SAVE AS (see Figure 9.13).

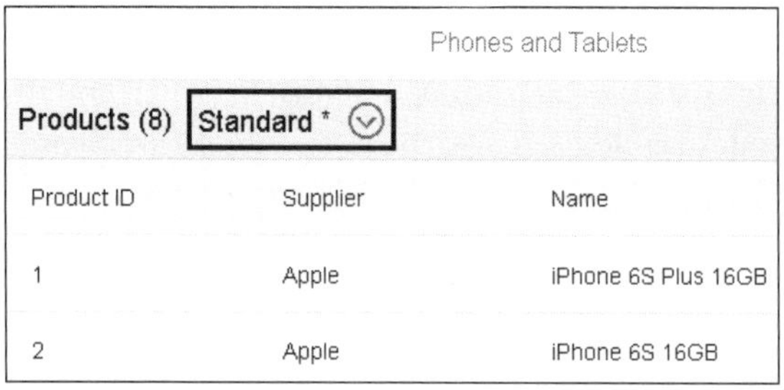

Figure 9.12 Smart Table Variant with Dirty Indicator

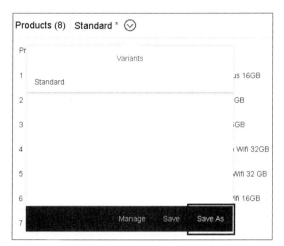

Figure 9.13 Smart Table Variants Dropdown

Let's name this variant "Supplier", as shown in Figure 9.14; then, click on OK. After that, you'll see the new SUPPLIER variant (see Figure 9.15).

Figure 9.14 Smart Table: Save New Variant

Figure 9.15 Smart Table: New Variant Selected

9.4.2 Smart Form and Smart Fields with Value Help

The smart form is capable of rendering field labels automatically. The smart fields take care of accurately rendering fields as an input field, checkbox, or date picker. A smart label could be used to just render the label of a field, then you would have to manually provide the input field. The smart group is capable of rendering a group title and is also used for grouping fields into logical sections.

Figure 9.16 shows an example of a smart form, with the button for the edit mode highlighted.

Figure 9.16 Smart Form with Edit Mode Button

The smart field is also capable of providing a value help, as shown in Figure 9.17, when you're in edit mode.

Figure 9.17 Smart Form with Value Help and Display Mode Button

9.5   Smart Templates

In the previous sections, you learned about OData annotations and how they empower smart controls. The next evolution of this concept is the smart template. We won't cover smart templates in much detail here because they're a code-free way to create applications mainly driven by backend annotations. Nevertheless, we want to give you an overview of this technology.

The SAP Web IDE provides templates for creating smart template–based applications. We have created some source code examples, which you find in the books source code examples.

When creating smart template-based apps, there are some recurring patterns, like a smart filter bar at the top, a smart table at the bottom, and navigation to an object page. The object page itself also has some smart capabilities and some dedicated UI annotations.

You can see a smart table and list report example in Figure 9.18, and an object page in Figure 9.19 and Figure 9.20.

Figure 9.18 Smart Template with Smart Table

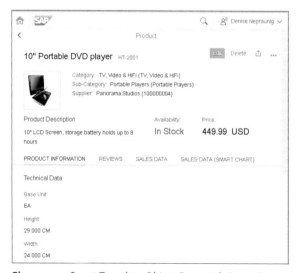

Figure 9.19 Smart Template Object Page with Smart Form

Figure 9.20 Smart Template Object Page with Chart

The other interesting smart template is the overview page, which provides business information in a card layout. The overview page does not replace SAP Fiori launchpad. An overview page is a dedicated SAPUI5 application created for a certain use case. You can see an example of an overview page in Figure 9.21.

Figure 9.21 SAPUI5 Overview Page

> **SAPUI5 Overview Page**
>
> You can learn more about the SAPUI5 overview page at *http://scn.sap.com/docs/DOC-68528*.

There are also patterns for editing, creating, and deleting data within smart templates. The idea of smart templates is to create a lot of apps quickly with the same look and feel. The apps should behave in a consistent way. SAP introduced smart templates for this very purpose: consistency. This does not mean that manually created SAPUI5 applications—so-called freestyle applications—will become unimportant; both types of apps have their benefits and strengths.

Freestyle applications provide a lot of freedom but can be time-consuming to create. Smart template apps are mainly driven by backend annotations, and all the apps look the same. They are quite inflexible, and provide the possibility to create breakouts and insert custom coding. Another benefit of the smart templates is that when certain UI patterns change, the applications are updated automatically.

> **Smart Templates: openSAP**
>
> To learn more about smart templates and smart controls, check out the openSAP course "Develop your own SAP Fiori App in the Cloud—2016 Edition," week 3, unit 3, at *https://open.sap.com/courses*.

9.6   Summary

In this chapter, you learned how to create reusable pieces of code for your views and applications. You now know how to use fragments for combinations of particular controls, and you've seen how fragments can also be used for dialogs when they only contain a single root control. These dialogs can then be used easily in multiple views of an application.

You also learned how you can create your own custom controls, in case some control you need is missing or when you find yourself creating a combination of multiple controls that are closely tied together by a certain behavior in the combination. For the latter case, we looked at how to create composite controls, combining several single controls into one.

Finally, you saw how to create controls and complete views automatically, generating them out of annotations for an OData service. You've also seen in detail what configuration options are available as annotations for a SAP Gateway-based OData service.

This chapter presented a combination of the more advanced techniques of SAPUI5 application implementation. In the next chapter, you'll learn how to put the finishing touches on your applications, making them enterprise grade with theming capabilities, adding accessibility features, speeding up performance building, and using the component preload.

PART III

Finishing Touches

This chapter explains key enterprise features like theming, security, performance, and accessibility in SAPUI5 applications. It shows pitfalls to avoid in theming and why and how you should care about more than just an appealing design.

10   Making Applications Enterprise-Grade

In the last chapter, you learned about some of the more advanced concepts in SAPUI5. Reusing artifacts like fragments or custom controls, or smart controls and smart templates, have already taken your application to the next level. In this chapter, you'll see how to make your apps truly enterprise-grade by incorporating the features required in an enterprise environment. You'll see how to theme, secure, speed-up, and optimize your app for all potential users.

Let's start by investigating how you can theme an application according to your needs and what you can do to ensure that it can be re-themed by a customer using, for example, the UI Theme Designer. Then, we'll dive into security issues that can occur before segueing into performance and optimization topics. In the final section, we'll discuss how to make apps accessible to all users.

10.1   Theming

Themes play an important role in designing applications. A *theme* provides a consistent appearance and should support an application's users while not distracting from its functions. The main building blocks of theming involve selection of coordinated colors—the *color palette*—and the design of individual elements like buttons or list items and their overall arrangement on the screen.

In SAPUI5, the default theme is called *base* and provides just enough CSS to display individual controls. We can examine this theme by adding the `sap-ui-theme` URL parameter to the URL, assigning it the value `base`, and running the application. For example, if we use the base theme with the Master-Detail app created in

Chapter 8, then the display will look like Figure 10.1 on the right; you can compare it directly to the SAP Blue Crystal theme, which is deployed on the left of the screen.

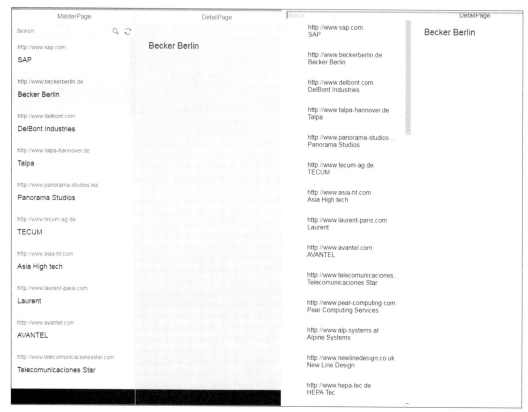

Figure 10.1 Base Theme vs. Blue Crystal

Because theming involves general application design and options to customize the appearance of individual apps, we'll try to cover both stages manual restyling and styling via the UI Theme Designer. First, we'll discuss how to manually restyle applications, and then we'll address how to modify entire themes or even create new ones.

10.1.1   Manual Restyling

It's important to note that manual restyling risks losing the dependency for the used theme overall. This could lead to critical issues, because themes in SAPUI5 are generally built to be changed or even exchanged with different themes over time. SAPUI5 offers three ways to achieve custom styling, which we'll cover in the following subsections.

Custom CSS

Of the three manual restyling options, custom CSS is probably the most issue-prone. We can quickly create one example that highlights this method's flaws by adding a custom CSS class to `sap.m.ObjectListItem`, used in the master-detail application created in Chapter 8, like this:

```
class="customHover"
```

We then add a new resource to the application in manifest.json in the `sap.ui5` namespace, in which we reference a file for the custom CSS like this:

```
1"resources": {
  "css": [{
    "uri": "css/style.css"
  }]
}
```

There, we'll define a CSS rule for this custom class that should change the styling for hovered-over list items—like this:

```
.customHover:hover {
  background-color : white;
}
```

The objective of this example was clear: We wanted to suppress the hover styling for the list items—and this might still be reasonable. As you can see in Figure 10.2, once we change the theme, the custom style might have some unwanted side effects. In a high-contrast theme, the list item text could be white and once hovered over, the item will no longer be readable.

> **Additional Information**
>
> If you need to use custom CSS in your applications, there's a resource summary of common pitfalls and how to overcome them in the SAPUI5 Demo Kit. We won't get into the details here, but recommend that you visit *https://sapui5.hana.ondemand.com/#docs/guide/9d87f925dfbb4e99b9e2963693aa00ef.html*.

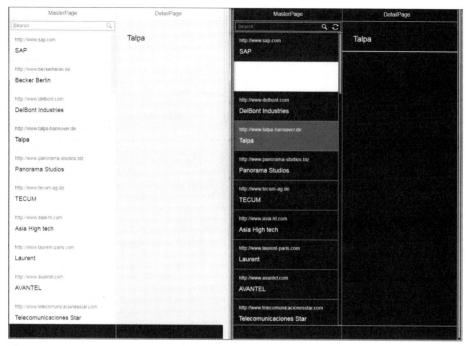

Figure 10.2 Custom CSS Issues on Different Themes

Of course, this example seems a little contrived at first sight, but I think we all know what's possible when technology meets requirements.

Theme-Dependent CSS Classes and Theme Parameters

To restyle applications in a theme-dependent way, SAPUI5 comes with a set of predefined CSS classes and parameters that can be used while still staying dependent on the styling provided by the theme. These classes can be identified by the common prefix `sapTheme` and have been developed mostly due to the need to connect custom-built controls, as in Chapter 9.

> **Note**
>
> Both theme classes and theme parameters come with a certain semantic structure for their names and should be used accordingly. Although it might be tempting to use a parameter called `@sapUiDarkestBorder` as a text or background color, it should be used in a way that matches the given semantic meaning of its name only.

These classes will be rebuilt with every build of the theme itself, and therefore the latest changes to the theme will be reflected. A list of these classes can be found in a consumable way in the SAPUI5 Demo Kit (*https://sapui5.hana.ondemand.com/explored.html#/sample/sap.ui.core.sample.ThemeCustomClasses/preview*). There, you can even examine theme classes across different themes. The theme-dependent parameters, on the other hand, can also be used in applications directly. To give some background here, theme parameters generally are used when a theme is created from scratch or an existing theme is modified. We'll get some hands on experience with parameters when we will work with UI Theme Designer in Section 10.1.2. However, we can also use some parameters in our coding directly. For this purpose, a set of parameters has been defined that reflects RGB color values as used in the current theme.

You could fetch the parameter you want to use by simply calling `var color = sap.ui.core.theming.Parameters.get("sapUiDarkestBorder")`, which would then return an actual color value. You could then set this value for one of your controls received before by the ID (e.g., `var myControl = this.byId("controlID")`) and then assign it to the control's DOM element, like this: `$(myControl).css("border-color", color);`.

Margin and Padding Classes

Some other requirements that are less theme-dependent but are still important are the placement of controls relative to their neighboring controls. On HTML pages for browser-based applications, as you develop applications with SAPUI5 you make use of the CSS box model. The CSS box model implements HTML elements in a content box wrapped by boxes that describe the margin, padding, and borders. When using the CSS box model, you have to style wisely. For example, just think of adjoining margins collapsing on one another! This gets especially problematic when you use SAPUI5 controls where you do not control the individual boxes. Wrong adjustments can easily break your layout.

Luckily, SAPUI5 provides standard classes for *margins* and *paddings*. These classes are implemented in such a way so that there are no surprises if, for example, the styling of SAPUI5 standard controls changes over time. Since this content is covered extensively in the SAPUI5 Demo Kit, we will not go into any further detail here.

So far, we've looked at methods for manual restyling. In the next section, we'll look at using the UI Theme Designer.

10.1.2   UI Theme Designer

In the previous section, we learned how to manually restyle applications and introduced some general information on the themes provided by SAPUI5 out of the box. In this section, we'll now look at how we can directly change the entire appearance of an application by directly modifying a theme and saving it. We can do this via a simple-to-use UI-based tool, the UI Theme Designer. With its integration with SAP HANA Cloud Platform (HCP) and the SAP Web IDE it is also very convenient when restyling deployed applications.

In the following subsections, we'll walkthrough the basic setup for the UI Theme Designer. Then, we'll dive into steps for manipulating themes. Finally, we'll look at what it takes to deploy custom themes to SAP HCP.

Setup

Technically, the UI Theme Designer is nothing more than an HTML5 application on SAP HCP that we can subscribe to.

To set up the UI Theme Designer, follow these steps:

1. Go to the SAP HCP cockpit and select the SUBSCRIPTIONS link.

2. After selecting this link, click the NEW SUBSCRIPTION button.

3. The NEW HTML5 SUBSCRIPTION popup will open (see Figure 10.3) where we can select the PROVIDER ACCOUNT, APPLICATION, and finally give a SUBSCRIPTION NAME (enter "themedesigner" for all three). Select SAVE when complete.

Figure 10.3 UI Theme Designer Subscription Settings

4. Now, launch the UI Theme Designer by calling this URL: *https://themedesigner-USERNAME.dispatcher.hanatrial.ondemand.com*.

Excellent! Let's now begin using the tool.

Manipulating Themes

With the tool now open, let's look at restyling one of our already deployed applications. Let's look at the Master-Detail app from Chapter 8 again. For our example, all we have to do here is to add a route (see Listing 10.1) to the UI Theme Designer HTML5 applications into the neoapp.json file in the project.

```
{
  "path": "/td",
  "target": {
    "type": "application",
    "name": "themedesigner"
  },
  "description": "Route for UI theme designer"
}
```

Listing 10.1 Route to Enable UI Theme Designer for the Application

Now, deploy this change to SAP HCP (see Appendix D for details) and then open the application with the path */td* added to it (e.g., *https://APPNAME-USERNAME.dispatcher.hanatrial.ondemand.com/td/*). The UI Theme Designer will open (see Figure 10.4).

In the UI Theme Designer, select the theme you want to modify (e.g., SAP BLUE CRYSTAL) and click the OPEN button.

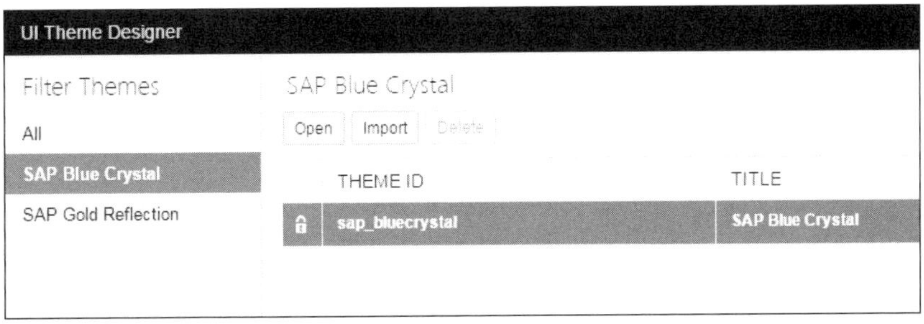

Figure 10.4 Theme Selection

463

The UI Theme Designer then loads our Master-Detail app. We can now begin playing with our app in the UI Theme Designer!

Generally, the UI Theme Designer offers two modes and several additional options to change your theme. For our purposes, we can just use the low-level functionality provided by QUICK mode (see Figure 10.5), which is the default setting.

QUICK mode provides access to global settings for element colors, font colors, and brand imaged. These settings enable you to manipulate some central parameters that are modeled to change the application's appearance while keeping the theme intact. These settings allow you to influence the color palette.

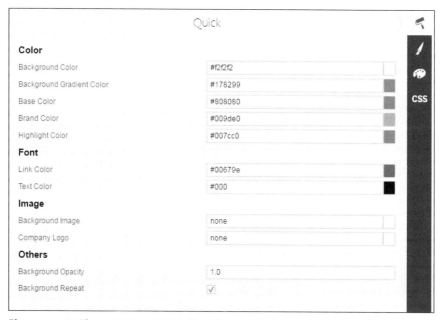

Figure 10.5 UI Theme Designer Quick Mode

For more drastic changes, there is an EXPERT mode (you can switch between the modes and additional options in the tool area on the top right of the screen). This mode allows you to manipulate low-level parameters directly as well. You can also mix in additional parameters or even custom CSS. These are expert features that can lead to unstable results if you are not careful, so proceed with caution. However, they can be fun to play around with!

Let`s now start restyling our app. Once you begin, you will realize that there are certain dependencies between the different color options. For example, the background color and the text color should have a certain contrast ratio between them. The tool here just follow your input, so you will have to play around a little before finalizing your results.

In Figure 10.6, you can see from the settings that we created a new basic color palette based on a light olive green.

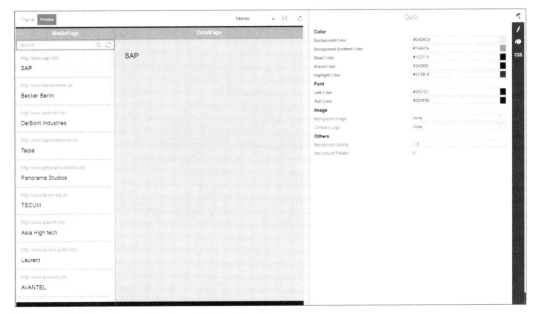

Figure 10.6 Custom Theme Based on SAP Blue Crystal

Deploying a Custom Theme to SAP HANA Cloud Platform

As a next step, we need to run our newly generated theme with our application on SAP HCP. Unfortunately, we cannot do this directly out of the UI Theme

Designer. Instead we have to export our theme and import it into the SAP Web IDE for deployment to SAP HCP. This involves a few manual steps:

1. Let's begin with the export process. First, save the newly created theme. To do this, click on MENU • SAVE DRAFT.

2. The SAVE DRAFT popup will appear. On this popup, we can set the THEME ID, which will be the technical name for our theme. Additionally, we will set a TITLE (e.g., retro green theme) and then confirm by clicking OK.

3. Next, we click on MENU • EXPORT. A popup appears that looks like Figure 10.7. Because we have already made all the relevant settings we will simply confirm which will then trigger the download of our package as zip.

   In order to explore and deploy the content we will do the import in SAP Web IDE now.

Figure 10.7 Export Settings for Modified Theme

4. Switch to the SAP Web IDE and click on the root of our workspace, then on FILE • IMPORT • FROM FILE SYSTEM. The result should look like Figure 10.8.

Figure 10.8 Theme Folder Structure

We see that the UI Theme Designer tool created three folders and three configuration files for us. The first folder is called BASE. In this folder, you will find some

.less files containing all the changes we have made to customize our theme. The second folder is called UI5, which holds the entire new theme that can be used with our SAPUI5 applications. In this folder, you will find the CSS that already includes all your changes. Finally, the third folder is called UR. This folder is pretty interesting. The UI Theme Designer is not only creating a theme based on your configuration for the SAPUI5 application, but also one for other SAP front-end technologies like WDA applications.

Let's now deploy the theme and see it in action. For this we will deploy it to SAP HCP. See Appendix D for the details.

Once this is done, we will have to make some slight modifications to our application. For our Master-Detail app, first add a new route to the theme into the neo-app.json file (see Listing 10.2). In this code, we are defining a path to our custom theme that we can later address when registering it to the application.

```
{
  "path": "/retrogreen",
  "target": {
    "type": "application",
    "name": "retrogreen"
  },
  "description": "Route for custom theme"
}
```
Listing 10.2 Destination for Custom Theme Deployed on SAP HCP

We first set the technical theme name created above as the theme to be loaded and then set the path where to find this theme to our SAPUI5-related theme parts in our new theme (see Listing 10.3).

```
<script id="sap-ui-bootstrap"
  src="../../resources/sap-ui-core.js"
  data-sap-ui-libs="sap.m"
  data-sap-ui-theme="retrogreen"
  data-sap-ui-theme-roots='{"retrogreen" : "/retrogreen/UI5/"}'
  data-sap-ui-compatVersion="edge"
  data-sap-ui-resourceroots='{"business.partner.app": ""}'>
</script>
```
Listing 10.3 Bootstrap for Loading a Custom Theme

You've successfully deployed the theme!

Theming is a great way to customize apps for enterprise users. In this section, we looked at how to employ both manual restyling and restyling via the UI Theme Designer. In the next section, we'll turn our attention to another important enterprise-grade feature: security.

10.2 Security

This section will give you an overview of the most important security issues to avoid when creating SAPUI5 applications.

10.2.1 Input Validation

Although there are mechanisms to validate certain data features on the client side, this doesn't mean that you as an application developer don't have to make sure that data is also validated on the server. This is fairly obvious; data could be intercepted and changed on its way from the client to the server and corrupt the server.

Using model types in combination with a two-way binding allows you to use automatic input validation on the client (as far as types go) and get any messages you need for validation from the service.

When you develop your own controls, you must address input validation on control properties. It's important to assign the right types to these properties and also to check whether the input value fits the assigned type. When you create a renderer, take special care to use the `writeEscaped` method from the render manager in order to correctly escape special characters that may come from a user input.

10.2.2 Cross-Site Scripting

Cross-site scripting (XSS) is a technique used to inject script code into your application. This script code can then be executed from within the application scope to access information just like normal applications can, and it can even send requests to the backend service, harming or corrupting data there.

In order to make your SAPUI5 applications as secure as possible against XSS attacks, you need to make sure that user data sent from the server to the client is properly escaped and is used to assemble the actual HTML page. As a precaution, always assume that user data is unescaped and implement the necessary escape mechanisms.

When you write your own custom controls, however, you as an application developer need to make sure that your controls have escape mechanisms in place as well for any user input.

10.2.3 URLs and Whitelist Filtering

SAPUI5 provides methods to validate URLs, in terms of checking whether they're well-formed and valid. There's also an API that allows you to whitelist particular URLs.

Some controls in SAPUI5 use the URL whitelist to check whether a particular URL is allowed to go into their content. For example, if a user can enter a URL for his profile on several platforms, you may want to allow URLs for LinkedIn, Monster, and Facebook. In this case, you can create a whitelist of the corresponding URLs, and URLs that aren't in the whitelist can be removed. In next two subsections, we'll look at the API used with the URL whitelist and the process of validating URLs.

URL Whitelist API

The API for URL whitelisting provides the following methods:

- `jQuery.sap.addUrlWhitelist`
- `jQuery.sap.clearUrlWhitelist`
- `jQuery.sap.getUrlWhitelist`
- `jQuery.sap.removeUrlWhitelist`

To add a URL to your whitelist, you need to call the `addUrlWhitelist` method, which takes the following parameters:

```
jQuery.sap.addUrlWhitelist(protocol, host, port, path);
```

Note that none of the parameters are mandatory. You can add your own domain, for example, no matter what protocol it uses, to a whitelist like so:

```
jQuery.sap.addUrlWhitelist(null, "www.yourdomain.com");
```

Or you can limit to a particular protocol, like so:

```
jQuery.sap.addUrlWhitelist("https", "www.mydomain.com");
```

Validating a URL

URLs can be validated against the whitelist using `jQuery.sap.validateUrl`:

- ► `jQuery.sap.validateUrl("http://www.yourdomain.com"); // =>` true
- ► `jQuery.sap.validateUrl("https://www.yourdomain.com"); // =>` true
- ► `jQuery.sap.validateUrl("ftp://www.mydomain.com"); // =>` false, wrong protocol

If you have not created a whitelist in your application, the `jQuery.sap.valida-teUrl` method will do some basic validation for you, checking whether the URL is well-formed.

A whitelist for URLs can also be configured at a central whitelist service. This can be useful as a prerequisite for the next technique we'll discuss, which prevents click jacking.

10.2.4 frameOptions and Central Whitelisting

The `frameOptions` configuration allows you to configure several parameters. For instance, you can define whether your application is allowed to be embedded within an IFrame.

Valid values for the `frameOptions` are `default`, which will allow the SAPUI5 application to be embedded anywhere; `deny`, which denies embedding for all origins; and `trusted`. When you use `trusted`, you can configure a whitelist service against which the embedding URL is validated. If no whitelist service is configured, the `trusted` option allows for embedding the app from same-origin URLs.

If the application should not run in any frame, regardless of the embedding URL, set `frameOptions` to `deny`, like so:

```
<script id='sap-ui-bootstrap'
src='resources/sap-ui-core.js'
data-sap-ui-frameOptions='deny'>
</script>
```

If you want to create your own whitelist service, take care that it can return a JSON object in the response, which adheres to the structure shown in Listing 10.4.

```
{
    "version" : "1.0",
    "active"  : true | false, //
 defines if entry is active (if not, framing will be allowed per defaul
t)
    "origin"  : "<same as passed to service>",
    "framing" : true | false //
 if active, describes if framing should be allowed (see FrameOptions)
}
```

Listing 10.4 Create Whitelist Service

You can then configure SAPUI5 to use this whitelist service for URL validation (see Listing 10.5).

```
<script>
window["sap-ui-config"] = {
  whitelistService: 'url/to/whitelist/service',
  frameOptions: 'trusted'
};
</script>
<script id='sap-ui-bootstrap'
  src='resources/sap-ui-core.js'
  [...]>
</script>
```

Listing 10.5 Configuring Whitelist Service for frameOptions

> **Additional Information**
>
> For more information on securing SAPUI5 applications, please refer to the SAPUI5 security guidelines here: *http://help.sap.com/saphelp_uiaddon10/helpdata/en/91/f3d8706f4d1014b6dd926db0e91070/content.htm*.
>
> There's also a great video resource created by Jens Himmelrath, one of the SAPUI5 core developers, which we highly recommend watching: *https://youtu.be/uNDKXgsF2BI*.

10.3 Performance

In this section, we'll look at the use of bundling, Component-preload.js, minification, and uglification for enhancing the performance of application.

10.3.1 Bundling and Component Preload

SAPUI5 applications are built with the MVC pattern and therefore consist of multiple files, like views or controllers. With fragments, it's possible to split up parts of views even further into smaller logical units (see Chapter 9 for more information on using fragments).

Although having a lot of different files based on their functionality is good during development, it's bad when running on a production server. Every necessary file fires a separate network request. You have to wait until all network requests are completed before the app is usable. You may not notice this delay in your corporate network with a fast Internet connection, but you'd notice it on a mobile phone with a moderate connection speed.

To solve this issue, you can package different files into a single file, a process called *bundling*. Through bundling, your app only has to load a single file instead of all the separate files, which speeds up the loading time of your application because your app only has to wait only for a single file to load.

In SAPUI5, this single file is called *Component-preload.js*. This file contains all the code of your application in a minified version. *Minification* means removing all unnecessary whitespace and comments, which also decreases the file size. In addition, the JavaScript source code is also uglified. *Uglification* means that your source code will not be as readable as before.

In the next section, we'll look at an overview and example of minification and uglification in action.

10.3.2 Minification and Uglification

As noted, Component-preload.js can contain code in minified and uglified versions. An example of uglifying occurs when variable names are shortened to save characters, which reduces the file size. The variable names are no longer as telling or verbose as before, which also obscures the functionality of the code for humans, but for a machine the code is still readable. Listing 10.6 shows an example of JavaScript source code before minifying and uglifying.

```
sap.ui.define([
  "sap/ui/core/mvc/Controller"
], function(Controller) {
  "use strict";
```

```
return Controller.extend("test.minification.controller.View1", {

  /**
   * The onInit function of the Controller
   * @public
   */
  onInit: function() {
    /* This is a comment which describes
    the functionallity of my code in a
    lot of words. */

    var sMySuperLongVariableName = "a text value";

    var sAnotherSuperLongVariableName = "another text value";

    var sConcatenatedString = sMySuperLongVariableName +
      sAnotherSuperLongVariableName;

    /* now we log out the concatenated text */
    console.log(sConcatenatedString);
  }
  });
});
```
Listing 10.6 JavaScript Source Code before Minifying and Uglifying

Listing 10.7 shows the same code from Listing 10.6, but now minified and uglified. All unnecessary whitespace, line breaks, and comments have been removed. Long variable names like `sMySuperLongVariableName` also have been replaced with short names like `e`. Obviously, the code is no longer readable, but it's compact and short. One popular library for minimizing JavaScript files is `UglifyJS`.

```
sap.ui.define(["sap/ui/core/mvc/Controller"],function(e){
"use strict";return e.extend("test.minification.controller.View1",{
onInit:function(){var e="a text value",t="another text value",
n=e+t;console.log(n)}})});
```
Listing 10.7 JavaScript Source Code after Minifying and Uglifying

In the following sections, we'll look at how to use minification and uglification to optimize the performance of SAPUI5 apps. When we want to minify and uglify a SAPUI5 application, we have two possibilities: First, we can perform this work manually via a Grunt task on a local machine. Second, we can use SAP Web IDE. In the SAP Web IDE, the minification/uglification process happens automatically when deploying an application to SAP HCP.

Minification via a Grunt Task Runner

You can minify your SAPUI5 application source code via a Grunt task. The Grunt task called `openui5_preload` is in an Node Package Manger (NPM) package called `grunt-openui5`. We'll look at how to use this in the subsequent sections.

Grunt is a task runner based on node.js. A *task runner* can run certain tasks, like linting, minification, bundling, executing unit tests, or compiling SASS/LESS files into CSS. The idea behind a task runner is to automate repetitive work. Another popular task runner is *Gulp*. Grunt can also watch file changes and trigger certain tasks automatically. There are several plugins available for different Grunt tasks so that you don't have to write functionality for tasks like copying files or cleaning directories yourself. Grunt is a package for the Node.js package manager NPM.

Node.js Setup

Node.js is a JavaScript runtime built on Google Chrome's V8 JavaScript engine. With Node.js, you can run JavaScript code server-side. Node.js is event-driven and has a nonblocking I/O model, which makes it efficient. Node.js itself is single-threaded, which makes it easy to program. Big companies like Netflix, Paypal, Facebook, and Walmart use Node.js, just to name a few. SAP uses Node.js for its SAP HANA XS Advanced (XSA) engine. SAP HANA XSA is a small, lightweight application server. Its predecessor, SAP HANA XS, was based on the Mozilla SpiderMonkey JavaScript runtime.

When running JavaScript on the server side, it's possible to read and write files from the file system and you can create web servers, talk to databases, create REST APIs, handle real-time communication via WebSockets, and so on. Those are just a few examples of what's possible with Node.js.

Another great advantage of Node.js is its package manager NPM. There are over hundreds of thousands of packages available. As mentioned earlier, Grunt is such a package. NPM is the largest code registry in the world. There are packages available for simplifying HTTP requests, functional programming helper libraries (`underscore` and `lodash` are very popular), handling asynchronous coding, date parsing, handling authentication, and so on. Check out the most starred NPM packages at *https://www.npmjs.com/browse/star*. You know the saying, "there's an app for that"; now, you could say "there's a package for that." All the required packages for a certain Node.js project are listed in the package.json file.

We highly recommend that you look further into these technologies, because they open up a whole new set of use cases and possibilities for JavaScript. For example, there are even microcontrollers available that are programmable with Node.js *(https://tessel.io/)*, which means that you can now program hardware with JavaScript.

Setting up Node.js is pretty straightforward:

1. Navigate to *https://nodejs.org/* and download Node.js. In this book, we used the version 4 of Node.js.

2. Follow the installer instructions. You can test the installation by opening your command line and typing node -v, which should show you the version number of your node installation (Figure 10.9).

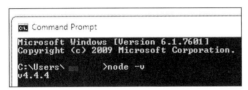

Figure 10.9 Check Node.js Version in Command Line

You can also check your NPM version with the following command: npm -v.

NPM is installed automatically with Node.js.

Grunt Setup

Now you can install the Grunt command-line tool NPM package globally (-g parameter stands for globally) from the command line by typing the following:

```
npm install -g grunt-cli
```

If you run into problems during installation, check your proxy settings. For Microsoft Windows, you can set them in the command line as follows:

```
@SET HTTP_PROXY=http://proxy:8080
@SET HTTPS_PROXY=http://proxy:8080
@SET FTP_PROXY=http://proxy:8080
@SET NO_PROXY=localhost,127.0.0.1,.mycompany.corp
```

After running the `install` command, you should see a similar output as that shown in Figure 10.10. That completes the Node.js and Grunt setup.

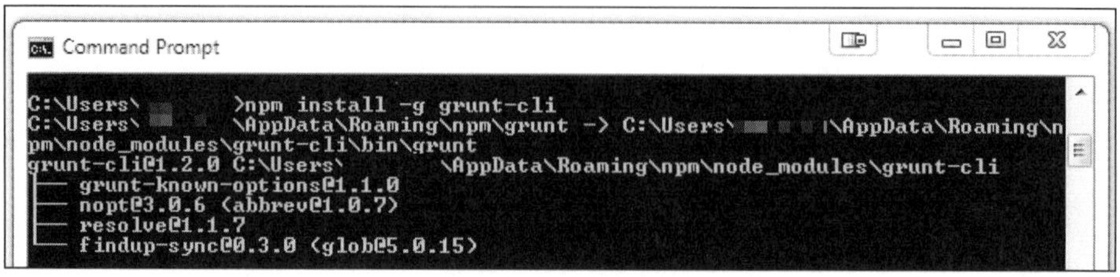

Figure 10.10 Global Installation of Grunt Command-Line Tool

Notes

Learn more about Node.js, the server-side JavaScript runtime, at *https://nodejs.org/*.

Learn more about the package manager NPM, which is included with Node.js, at *https://www.npmjs.com/*.

Learn more about the task runner Grunt at *http://gruntjs.com/*.

Learn more about SAP HANA XSA, a SAP HANA application server based on Node.js, at *http://scn.sap.com/community/developer-center/hana/blog/2015/12/08/sap-hana-sps-11-new-developer-features*.

Learn more about OpenUI5 Grunt tasks, including `openui5_preload` for minification, at *https://github.com/SAP/grunt-openui5*.

Read an SCN blog post on optimizing SAPUI5 applications at *http://scn.sap.com/community/developer-center/front-end/blog/2015/02/18/optimizing-openui5-apps*.

Now that you know about the Grunt task runner and Node.js, let's dive into an example to see the task runner in action.

Grunt-Based Minification Example

To follow this exercise, you must have Node.js and the Grunt command-line tools (`grunt-cli`) installed on your local machine. In the source code for this example, you'll find a master-detail SAPUI5 application (see Chapter 8 for more details on the Master-Detail app). The structure of the application is shown in Listing 10.8; also note the Gruntfile.js and package.json files. *Gruntfile.js* contains the task for minifying the SAPUI5 application, and *package.json* contains all the required modules.

```
Gruntfile.js
package.json
\---webapp
    |   Component.js
    |   index.html
    |   manifest.json
    |
    +---controller
    |       App.controller.js
    |       BaseController.js
    |       Detail.controller.js
    |       ErrorHandler.js
    |       ListSelector.js
    |       Master.controller.js
    |
    +---css
    |       style.css
    |
    +---i18n
    |       i18n.properties
    |
    +---localService
    |       metadata.xml
    |       mockserver.js
    |
    +---model
    |       formatter.js
    |       grouper.js
    |       GroupSortState.js
    |       models.js
    |
    \---view
            App.view.xml
            Detail.view.xml
            DetailNoObjectsAvailable.view.xml
            DetailObjectNotFound.view.xml
            Master.view.xml
            NotFound.view.xml
            ViewSettingsDialog.fragment.xml
```

Listing 10.8 Master-Detail SAPUI5 Application Files

When you run this application and look at Google Chrome's Network tab, you'll see that the Master-Detail application files are requested separately (Figure 10.11).

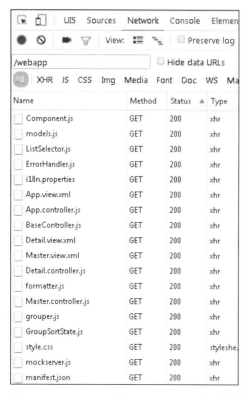

Figure 10.11 Separate Network Requests for SAPUI5 Master-Detail App

Gruntfile.js

Now, let's look at Gruntfile.js, shown in Listing 10.9. You don't have to understand all the details, but you should get a high-level overview of the process.

```
'use strict';
module.exports = function(grunt) {
  grunt.initConfig({
    dir: {
      webapp: 'webapp',
      dist: 'dist'
    },
    copy: {
      dist: {
        files: [{
          expand: true,
          cwd: '<%= dir.webapp %>',
          src: [
            '**',
```

```
              '!test/**'
        ],
        dest: '<%= dir.dist %>'
      }]
    }
  },
  clean: {
    dist: '<%= dir.dist %>/'
  },
  openui5_preload: {
    component: {
      options: {
        resources: {
          cwd: 'webapp',
          prefix: 'sapui5/demo/md/example',
          src: ['**/*.js',
            '**/*.fragment.html',
            '**/*.fragment.json',
            '**/*.fragment.xml',
            '**/*.view.html',
            '**/*.view.json',
            '**/*.view.xml',
            '**/*.properties',
            '**/*.json',
            '**/*.css'
          ],
        },

        dest: 'dist',

      },
      components: 'sapui5/demo/md/example'
    }
  }
});

grunt.loadNpmTasks('grunt-contrib-clean');
grunt.loadNpmTasks('grunt-contrib-copy');
grunt.loadNpmTasks('grunt-openui5');

// Build task
grunt.registerTask('build', ['openui5_preload', 'copy']);

// Default task
grunt.registerTask('default', ['clean', 'build']);
};
```

Listing 10.9 Gruntfile.js

Inside `grunt.initConfig` is one configuration object, `dir`, which refers to the name of the *webapp* folder and the name of the destination folder, *dist*. Then there are three tasks: `copy`, `clean`, and `openui5_preload`. The `copy` task is responsible for copying all the files to the *dist* folder. Notice that any files inside a test folder won't be copied because of `'!test/**'`. The `!` indicates that this folder should be ignored. The `clean` task removes all the files inside the *dist* folder.

The actual minification of the SAPUI5 application happens inside `openui5_preload`. To configure this task, you need to provide the namespace of the application with the `prefix` setting and the name of the component with the `components` setting. The `cwd` property defines the root directory of your application.

We've listed the default settings for `src` in Listing 10.10). When you want to include additional files or exclude certain files, you have to set the `src` property and list all your desired settings. If you use the `src` property, the default settings of the `src` property will be ignored. This means that if you forget to list `'**/*.view.xml'`, then the view files won't be minified anymore.

```
[  '**/*.js',
  '**/*.fragment.html',
  '**/*.fragment.json',
  '**/*.fragment.xml',
  '**/*.view.html',
  '**/*.view.json',
  '**/*.view.xml',
  '**/*.properties']
```
Listing 10.10 openui5_preload Task, src Default Settings

`grunt.loadNpmTasks` loads various plugins, like `grunt-contrib-clean` for cleaning directories or `grunt-openui5` to minify the application. Those tasks expect different configuration settings, like `openui5_preload: { ... }`, which we previously defined inside `grunt.initConfig({ ... })`.

At the end, you'll see `grunt.registerTask`. Here, we register two tasks: `build` and `default`. The `default` task runs when you type "grunt" inside the command line. To execute the build task, you must type "grunt build".

Package.json

Listing 10.11 shows the content of the package.json file. We've listed dependencies like `grunt-openui5` or `grunt-contrib-clean` inside the `devDependencies` setting. This means that those packages are only needed during development of the application and not when running in production mode. Other packages you would only need during development are packages for unit testing or linting. Also note that versions of the desired packages are listed, like `^0.4.5`. You can learn more about the package.json file and the version specifications at *https://docs.npmjs.com/files/package.json*.

When you need packages during the runtime of a Node.js application, they'll need to be listed as `dependencies`. Such packages include those for accessing databases, WebSocket connections, or asynchronous coding.

```
{
  "name": "test-minification-md",
  "version": "1.0.0",
  "description": "",
  "devDependencies": {
    "grunt": "^0.4.5",
    "grunt-openui5": "^0.9.0",
    "grunt-contrib-clean": "^0.6.0",
    "grunt-contrib-connect": "^0.10.1",
    "grunt-contrib-copy": "^0.8.0"
  },
  "scripts": {
    "test": "echo \"Error: no test specified\" && exit 1"
  },
  "author": "Denise Nepraunig",
  "license": "ISC"
}
```

Listing 10.11 Package.json

Now, open the command line and switch to the *test-infrastructure-md* directory, which you'll find in the source code for this chapter. Inside the command line and type "npm install". As you can see in Figure 10.12, all the required dependencies are installed; note that packages like `grunt` have dependencies to other modules like `eventemitter`, `dateformat`, `which`, and so on. If you run into problems installing packages due to an `EACCES` error, visit *https://docs.npmjs.com/getting-started/fixing-npm-permissions*.

Now, all the listed dependencies inside package.json are installed in the *node_modules* folder, as you can see in Figure 10.13.

```
Node.js command prompt

C:\Users\         \git\test-minification-md>npm install
npm WARN package.json test-minification-md@1.0.0 No description
npm WARN package.json test-minification-md@1.0.0 No repository field.
npm WARN package.json test-minification-md@1.0.0 No README data
npm WARN deprecated graceful-fs@1.2.3: graceful-fs v3.0.0 and before will fail o
n node releases >= v7.0. Please update to graceful-fs@^4.0.0 as soon as possible
. Use 'npm ls graceful-fs' to find it in the tree.
grunt-contrib-clean@0.6.0 node_modules\grunt-contrib-clean
  └── rimraf@2.2.8

grunt-contrib-copy@0.8.2 node_modules\grunt-contrib-copy
  ├── file-sync-cmp@0.1.1
  └── chalk@1.1.3 (escape-string-regexp@1.0.5, supports-color@2.0.0, ansi-styles@2
.2.1, has-ansi@2.0.0, strip-ansi@3.0.1)

grunt@0.4.5 node_modules\grunt
  ├── eventemitter2@0.4.14
  ├── dateformat@1.0.2-1.2.3
  ├── which@1.0.9
  ├── async@0.1.22
  ├── colors@0.6.2
  ├── getobject@0.1.0
  ├── lodash@0.9.2
  ├── rimraf@2.2.8
  ├── hooker@0.2.3
  ├── grunt-legacy-util@0.2.0
  ├── exit@0.1.2
  ├── nopt@1.0.10 (abbrev@1.0.7)
  ├── coffee-script@1.3.3
  ├── iconv-lite@0.2.11
  ├── underscore.string@2.2.1
  ├── minimatch@0.2.14 (sigmund@1.0.1, lru-cache@2.7.3)
  ├── glob@3.1.21 (inherits@1.0.2, graceful-fs@1.2.3)
  ├── grunt-legacy-log@0.1.3 (grunt-legacy-log-utils@0.1.1, lodash@2.4.2, undersco
re.string@2.3.3)
  ├── findup-sync@0.1.3 (lodash@2.4.2, glob@3.2.11)
  └── js-yaml@2.0.5 (esprima@1.0.4, argparse@0.1.16)

grunt-contrib-connect@0.10.1 node_modules\grunt-contrib-connect
  ├── connect-livereload@0.5.4
  ├── opn@1.0.2
  ├── async@0.9.2
  ├── portscanner@1.0.0 (async@0.1.15)
  └── connect@2.30.2 (cookie@0.1.3, bytes@2.1.0, utils-merge@1.0.0, cookie-signatu
re@1.0.6, content-type@1.0.2, fresh@0.3.0, parseurl@1.3.1, on-headers@1.0.1, pau
se@0.1.0, response-time@2.3.1, vhost@3.0.2, cookie-parser@1.3.5, basic-auth-conn
ect@1.0.0, depd@1.0.1, qs@4.0.0, connect-timeout@1.6.2, http-errors@1.3.1, serve
-favicon@2.3.0, method-override@2.3.5, debug@2.2.0, morgan@1.6.1, finalhandler@0
.4.0, express-session@1.11.3, type-is@1.6.12, serve-static@1.10.2, multiparty@3.
3.2, csurf@1.8.3, compression@1.5.2, errorhandler@1.4.3, body-parser@1.13.3, ser
ve-index@1.7.3)

grunt-openui5@0.9.0 node_modules\grunt-openui5
  ├── slash@1.0.0
  ├── connect-inject@0.4.0
  ├── url-join@0.0.1
  ├── pretty-data@0.40.0
  ├── async@1.5.2
  ├── cors@2.7.1 (vary@1.1.0)
  ├── multiline@1.0.2 (strip-indent@1.0.1)
  ├── serve-static@1.10.2 (escape-html@1.0.3, parseurl@1.3.1, send@0.13.1)
  ├── connect-openui5@0.6.0 (extend@3.0.0, http-proxy@1.13.2, glob@6.0.4)
  ├── uglify-js@2.6.2 (async@0.2.10, uglify-to-browserify@1.0.2, source-map@0.5.6,
yargs@3.10.0)
  ├── maxmin@1.1.0 (figures@1.6.0, chalk@1.1.3, gzip-size@1.0.0, pretty-bytes@1.0.
4)
  └── less-openui5@0.2.0 (object-assign@4.1.0, less@1.6.3)

C:\Users\         \git\test-minification-md>
```

Figure 10.12 Running NPM install Command

Figure 10.13 Installed Node Modules

Running Grunt

Now, type "grunt" inside the command line to start the minification process (Figure 10.14). When you look inside your project, you'll now see the *dist* folder, which contains the Component-preload.js file, as shown in Figure 10.15.

```
Node.js command prompt

C:\Users\█▄▗▝▘\git\test-minification-md>grunt
Running "clean:dist" (clean) task
>> 0 paths cleaned.

Running "openui5_preload:component" (openui5_preload) task
File dist\Component-preload.js created with 20 files (56.77 kB → 26.94 kB)

Running "copy:dist" (copy) task
Created 7 directories, copied 24 files

Done, without errors.

C:\Users\█▄▗▝▘\git\test-minification-md>
```

Figure 10.14 Running grunt Command

```
test-minification-md
  dist
    controller
    css
    i18n
    localService
    model
    view
    Component-preload.js
    Component.js
    index.html
    manifest.json
  node_modules
  webapp
  Gruntfile.js
  package.json
```

Figure 10.15 dist Folder with Component-preload.json

Optimized Network Requests

If you run the application again from the *dist* folder and inspect the network trace again in Google Chrome (Figure 10.16), you'll see that Component-preload.json is loaded instead of all the separate files shown in Figure 10.11. Keep in mind that you should run this application locally via a web server; you can use any web server you like. We recommend the http-server npm module because you now have Node.js installed. Please refer to *https://www.npmjs.com/package/http-server* to learn how to set up and use this web server.

When you look at Figure 10.16, take note: It's not recommended to package your style sheets into the Component-preload.json file, and it's also not supported currently. It's also not recommended to package your manifest.json file, which also is not supported currently.

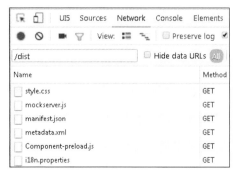

Figure 10.16 Reduced Network Requests Due to Component-preload.json

Even though we had one properties file in this application—the generic i18n.properties—SAPUI5 itself tried to load more language-specific versions, like i18n_de_DE.properties or i18n_en.properties and even the i18n.properties file. This is the current default behavior of SAPUI5, but ultimately SAPUI5 used the translation that had been taken from the Component-preload.json file. You can test this if you rename or delete the translation file from the *dist* folder.

The mockserver.js file was still requested, because it was defined inside index.html, and this request is fired earlier than the request to the Component-preload.json.

Listing 10.12 shows an excerpt of the Component-preload.js file, in which all the application files are listed as modules and included in the minified source code. We've included an example of the minified source code from Component.js.

```
jQuery.sap.registerPreloadedModules({
    "version": "2.0",
    "name": "sapui5/demo/md/example/Component-preload",
    "modules": {
"sapui5/demo/md/example/Component.js": "sap.ui.define([\"sap/ui/core/
UIComponent\",\"sap/ui/Device\",\"sapui5/demo/md/example/model/models\
",\"sapui5/demo/md/example/controller/ListSelector\",\"sapui5/demo/md/
example/controller/ErrorHandler\"],function(e,t,s,o,i){\"use strict\
";return e.extend(\"sapui5.demo.md.example.Component\
",{metadata:{manifest:\"json\"},init:function(){this.oListSelector=
new o,this._oErrorHandler=
new i(this),this.setModel(s.createDeviceModel(),\"device\
"),this.setModel(s.createFLPModel(),\"FLP\
```

```
"),e.prototype.init.apply(this,arguments),this.getRouter().initialize()
},destroy:function(){this.oListSelector.destroy(),this._
oErrorHandler.destroy(),e.prototype.destroy.apply(this,arguments)},getC
ontentDensityClass:function(){return void 0===this._
sContentDensityClass&&(jQuery(document.body).hasClass(\"sapUiSizeCozy\
")||jQuery(document.body).hasClass(\"sapUiSizeCompact\")?this._
sContentDensityClass=\"\":t.support.touch?this._sContentDensityClass=\
"sapUiSizeCozy\":this._sContentDensityClass=\"sapUiSizeCompact\
"),this._sContentDensityClass}})}]);",
        "sapui5/demo/md/example/controller/App.controller.js":
          "sap.ui.define ...",
        "sapui5/demo/md/example/controller/BaseController.js":
          "sap.ui.define ...",
        "sapui5/demo/md/example/controller/Detail.controller.js":
          "sap.ui.define ...",
        ...
```

Listing 10.12 Content of Component-preload.json

Minification in SAP Web IDE

You've seen that the setup and configuration for minification and uglification is a rather long and tedious process. The SAP Web IDE automates this process when you're deploying an application to SAP HCP.

When you create a new SAPUI5 application with a template and deploy the application to SAP HCP, the minified files are created automatically and stored in a *dist* folder, as you can see in Figure 10.17. The files stored in the *dist* folder are then deployed. Note that all the files are deployed, because it's possible that not all files have been minified and included inside Component-preload.js. This could be the case for pictures, for example, or for non-SAPUI5-specific files like YAML (YAML Ain't Markup Language) configuration files. You can learn more about app deployment in Appendix C, in which we'll walk you through the whole process of creating an application with a template, deploying the application, and looking at the minified files. As of the time of writing (July 2016), the SAP Web IDE does not uglify the files and the source code comments are not removed.

We've given you a broad overview of the whole optimization process of your SAPUI5 application with minification and uglification and an idea of how this process can increase the performance of your application.

Figure 10.17 Minified Source Code in SAP Web IDE

Now that we've walk through theming, security, and performance, let's turn to the final enterprise-grade feature: accessibility.

10.4 Accessibility

In this section, we'll talk about accessibility features in online SAPUI5 applications. We'll take a closer look at the motivation behind creating accessible apps, including the desire to exclude no one from using your applications and legal regulations that demand a certain level of accessibility—for example, when software is used in a public context. We'll also see what SAPUI5 does for you in this respect. Finally, we'll examine which tasks are left to you as an application developer. We'll see what you need to do in your application to provide screen reader support and support for different zoom levels, font sizes, and levels of contrasts for users with visual impairments.

10.4.1 Importance of Inclusion and Accessibility

The most obvious reason for caring about accessibility in your applications is that you don't want to exclude interested parties from using your applications. Why would you prevent anyone with, say, a visual impairment from becoming a user of your apps?

However, accessibility often is not highly prioritized in the development phase, and other features—an appealing visual design, enhanced functionality—are valued higher. To stress why this is the wrong approach, let's look at the target group we'd be excluding if we didn't care about their needs, and let's also examine how even users who don't belong to the typical accessibility target group can benefit from an app built with an eye to this topic.

Who Needs Accessibility Features?

As an application developer, it's both your job and to your benefit to make your apps as accessible as possible for as many users as possible. To do this, you must take your users' needs into consideration. When we talk about accessibility for web applications, we usually think of users with visual impairments or other disabilities that want to provide access for. This includes different visual or text cues, elements that can be scaled in size, and a general layout that allows display at different zoom levels.

To better grasp what users we're speaking of, let's create some personas of people who use web applications in their daily work and detail their issues with existing applications.

Mary

Mary is a 42-year-old sales accountant and was born blind. She uses the web daily and has mastered finding web sites that are compatible with her nonvisual browser, which uses JAWS, a screen reader, to access the data on any website. Although accessibility has greatly improved over recent years, Mary still encounters a lot of pages on the web that omit essential information for her screen reader, so she sometimes has to make guesses about context. Any forms without the necessary text cues for her screen reader are inaccessible for her. Fortunately, her employer has ensured that the apps she needs in her daily work are built in such a way that screen readers can deliver all the information Mary needs in an audible form.

Mary also doesn't use a mouse to navigate her PC. She relies on the keyboard and depends on the focus being correctly set when she enters a web page and being able to reach all elements within the page by using the [Tab] key on her keyboard or activating elements by pressing [Space].

Marcus

Marcus is 26 and suffers from Deuteranopia (red-green color blindness). This means that his eyes do not have any cones that allow for processing the wavelengths of green color tones. Marcus belongs to a group of about 6% of all males worldwide who either have Deuteranopia or the milder form, Deuteranomaly. Marcus has problems distinguishing different red and green hues from each other. This can cause issues with apps that rely on colors alone to indicate certain information.

Although red is a warning color for any trichromatic person (people who have three different types of cones for color detection and thus see what we consider the visible color spectrum), it isn't very noticeable for Marcus.

Figure 10.18 shows how a Google Maps control with the prominent red marker looks to Markus.

Figure 10.18 Google Maps Control for Person with Deuteranopia

As you can see, the red marker suddenly has remarkably little contrast with its background. On a larger map on which the marker is not centered, it will be hard to find!

Imagine how Marcus responds to a web application in which red and green are used as colors to indicate the status of processing items and red is used to show that something is blocked or significantly going wrong and needs to be acted on as quickly as possible. It would be hard for Marcus to do his job well if there were no other indicators for statuses.

Helen

Helen is 42 and works in a travel agency. She needs to use web applications to create bookings for her customers. Helen has worn glasses since she turned 25, when she realized she was getting ever-more short-sighted.

Even when she's wearing her glasses, Helen is used to scaling the font on her PC to a convenient size. She benefits from websites with layouts that do not become distorted when a user zooms in.

This is only a small selection of representatives of user groups for which accessibility is particularly. Certainly, this list is by no means meant to be exhaustive.

Accessibility Benefits Everyone

We need to think past the user groups described previously, though, when we want to get a grasp of who we're implementing for. We could come up with a ton of examples in which sticking to accessibility guidelines makes websites more usable and more pleasant for everyone.

You may have come across websites that present multimedia content in a way that allows you to toggle the volume and speed of the audible information. This can be important for people who are using hearing aids, for whom volume is important, as well as clarity of sound. However, it can be equally important for people with a cognitive disability, who may not be able to process information as fast as it was recorded for a video, or for non-native speakers of the language the video was recorded in. The option to see subtitles for such videos can also help communicate information to your users.

Using sharper contrasts in a web application and making the visual elements adapt correctly to different zoom levels can help people whose sight deteriorates as they get older, but they can also help anyone when their displays or the circumstances under which they view an application (broad sunlight, darkness inside a house) are not optimal.

Adapting the size of interactive elements correctly can compensate for a hand tremor when users operate a mouse, but it can also help any user who wants to use a web app on a mobile device, on which a finger press may not be as precise as the mouse pointer.

Being able to navigate through a web application using the keyboard is not only useful for people with visual impairments, but also is extremely useful for professional users who need to record data in a form quickly. When you watch them go, they hardly move their hands away from the keyboard. Every additional move over to the mouse costs time and interrupts the writing flow. These are the types of users who are willing to use function keys frequently when it spares them from using the mouse, and you can make them happy when you don't disrupt their workflow by requiring mouse interaction.

As you can see, designing an application with accessibility guidelines in mind can help every user of your apps.

Legal Regulations

Last but not least, there are also a variety of legal regulations in different countries across the world that stipulate accessibility requirements that have to be met when you want to sell your applications to the public sector.

These regulations mostly follow the recommendations of the Worldwide Web Consortium (W3C)—in particular the Web Accessibility Initiative (WAI) in the W3C. The WAI has a lot of helpful and interesting resources on accessibility at their website, which can be found at *https://www.w3.org/WAI*.

The SAP User Experience Community also has a lot of valuable guidance on accessibility topics; visit *https://experience.sap.com/basics/accessibility-user-experience/*.

From these general considerations, let's move on to the technical requirements of an accessible web application. There are some prerequisites that SAPUI5 provides, and some tasks you as an application developer need to carry out yourself. Let's first look at what's automatically delivered by the framework.

10.4.2 SAPUI5 Accessibility Features

There are a number of accessibility features provided by SAPUI5. The subsections that follow look at some of the most important features.

Screen Reader Support

The following SAPUI5 libraries currently have built-in screen reader support:

- `sap.m`
- `sap.suite.ui.commons`
- `sap.tnt`
- `sap.ui.commons`
- `sap.ui.comp`
- `sap.ui.core`
- `sap.ui.generic`
- `sap.ui.layout`
- `sap.ui.suite`
- `sap.ui.table`
- `sap.ui.unified`
- `sap.ui.ux3`
- `sap.uxap`
- `sap.viz`

As of the time of writing (July 2016), this means in particular that the controls within these libraries have been tested using JAWS version 16 with Internet Explorer 11 on a Windows 7 operating system. Therefore, for this combination of products and OS, the corresponding controls provide all properties that need to be set for screen readers to convey meaningful text about what information controls hold and how they can be used.

When you test your applications for accessibility, we recommend using this same combination of software and versions—and we definitely do recommend testing your applications before shipping.

High-Contrast Black Theme

For users requiring a higher contrast, SAP has created a High-Contrast Black theme that users can switch to. They can do so by appending the following URL parameter to any SAPUI5 application URL:

`sap-ui-theme=sap_hcb`

Currently, the following libraries support the High-Contrast Black theme:

- `sap.m`
- `sap.me`
- `sap.ui.commons`
- `sap.ui.comp`
- `sap.ui.layout`
- `sap.ui.suite`
- `sap.ui.table`
- `sap.ui.unified`
- `sap.ui.ux3`
- `sap.viz`

Keyboard Handling in SAPUI5 Controls

Most SAPUI5 controls provide keyboard handling out of the box, which can speed up processing information and improves the accessibility of applications.

You can find an overview of the current keys that are enabled and used in SAPUI5 applications here:

http://help.sap.com/saphelp_nw74/helpdata/de/3e/631addc9094499a74242cba38e6def/content.htm

This information is particularly useful if you want to create your own custom controls.

Automatically Added ARIA Attributes

When you're using certain properties at controls, these properties will automatically trigger the corresponding ARIA attributes to be added to the controls in the DOM by the render manager.

Table 10.1 shows which control properties translate to which ARIA attributes:

Control Property	ARIA Attribute
editable	aria-readonly
enabled	aria-disabled
visible	aria-hidden
required	aria-required
checked	aria-checked
selected	aria-selected

Table 10.1 Control Properties and Corresponding ARIA Attributes

10.4.3 Making Your Applications Accessible

There are some tasks left for you to do as an application developer, mostly to do with the correct application of accessibility features and properties that are already present in the framework, but need to be set and combined correctly.

Using Roles

Roles in web pages are meant to specify *landmarks*, which are a type of navigational anchor in a page and also have a semantic meaning. There is one role that does not exactly fit into this scheme, but is still important to SAPUI5 applications. This particular role is the application role, which represents the Rich Internet Applications (RIA). In an SAPUI5 application, for the roles, it's best set to the body tag of the application, like so:

```
<body class="sapUiBody" role="application">
```

Note that when you're running in a container like SAP Fiori Launchpad, the container is supposed to handle this setting for you.

Screen readers on Windows devices have different modes to access information in a web page. They access the DOM of the page directly and parse it, creating a kind of copy they operate on. This allows the screen reader to prevent some key press events from invoking their usual behavior in a web page, for instance, to allow navigating through the content using the cursor keys or using shortcut keys built into the screen reader. When you're creating RIAs in which keyboard handling is supposed to be under the control of the widgets in your page, you can force the screen reader to drop out of the virtual cursor mode. For some further information about the different modes of screen readers, we recommend the following blog post:

http://tink.uk/understanding-screen-reader-interaction-modes/

Creating Correct Labels

When you're using controls in your applications that need a label, you need to make sure that the connection between the control and its label is made. At controls of type `sap.m.Label`, you have a `labelFor` association that can be set for this purpose. It expects the control that the label should describe, or the respective control ID in an XML view, like so:

```
<Label text="MyLabelTextHere" labelFor="MyInput" />
<Input id="MyInput" />
```

You can also specify the `ariaLabelledBy` association at the control you want to label. This association can reference a control that provides descriptive text.

This can be particularly useful when you have several inputs that share the same label, because you can't simply use the `labelFor` property at the label in such a case. It can also be useful when you don't have the descriptive text visible somewhere on your screen. In such a case, you can use a control of type `sap.ui.core.InvisibleText` to provide the labeling text. This text will not be displayed on screen, but will still be accessible by screen readers.

Another association called `ariaDescribedBy` can take in any control(s). This association is supposed to provide longer descriptive texts for the control that specified the association.

Both the `ariaLabelledBy` and the `ariaDescribedBy` associations are translated to the corresponding ARIA attributes when rendered.

Creating Alternative Texts and Tooltips

Currently, tooltips are disabled for all controls except for images and buttons without texts. However, there are still options to create alternative texts. For images, you can use the `alt` property, for instance. In general, all images and icons on the screen should have a textual description for screen readers. This also means that you need to provide an alternative description when you use semantic colors. A color blind user may not be able to distinguish a red price in your shop as indicating a special sale if it isn't mentioned elsewhere. The same applies for users who are blind or have a low vision.

Titles for Titles

Use the `sap.m.Title` control when you need to set a title. Depending on the level property you set, the title will be rendered as an `<Hn>` tag in the DOM, where `n` is the title level. This helps identify the text as a real header for the section below the title.

Using Colors

As we mentioned, providing sufficient contrast in your web applications is important so that users with certain visual impairments can still see what's going on in your app, to which end SAP provides a High-Contrast Black theme.

In order to use this theme correctly and not break anything within your application, it's important not to use any hard-coded colors in your custom CSS. Hard-coded colors can lead to strange and undesirable effects when someone changes the theme, to the point that you could potentially have a black font on a black background. See more on this topic in Chapter 12.

Using Sizes

Another feature that should never be hard-coded with a fixed value is size. You always need to consider that your application should still work even when a user sets the zoom level of an application to 200%. Any styling setting that sets a fixed width or height therefore should be avoided. You should also not set CSS styling that disables zoom completely. It's therefore also important to test your application across different zoom levels.

10.5 Summary

In this chapter, you learned how to theme an application according to your needs or a customer's brand without losing the option to theme the app with the UI Theme Designer. You've read about potential security issues in apps and how SAPUI5 provides you with options to avoid these issues.

You also learned how to speed up the performance of your applications using the component preload, and you know how to minify and uglify your code. We also talked about accessibility in web applications, and you learned how important it is to consider this topic while creating your applications. With these factors in mind, it will be easy to make your applications truly enterprise-grade.

In the next chapter, you'll learn how to test your app properly so that you can safely make changes later in its lifecycle, guaranteeing that these changes don't break anything. We'll talk about finding errors and creating unit tests and acceptance tests for applications in SAPUI5 and how you can ensure the desired code quality by linting your code.

In this chapter, you'll learn how to debug applications and set up proper tests for all parts of an application. We'll look at how to write QUnit tests and One-Page Acceptance (OPA5) tests, and how to mock data to guarantee client test stability even when the service behind an application isn't available.

11   Debugging and Testing Code

In order to keep your applications stable and easy to maintain, it probably goes without saying that proper testing is mandatory. In this chapter, you'll learn how to achieve adequate test coverage for all the SAPUI5 assets you're using. Figure 11.1 shows the suggested testing pyramid for SAPUI5 applications.

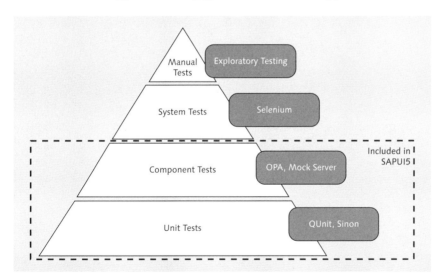

Figure 11.1 Testing Strategy Pyramid

As you can see, the application testing pyramid consists of both parts that are included in SAPUI5 and others that can be used on top of SAPUI5. Selenium, however, is a complex testing framework on its own and won't be covered in this book; we won't talk about how to perform manual testing properly either, because it's not specific to SAPUI5 apps. Instead, we'll concentrate on the two lowest steps in the pyramid: component tests and unit tests. Unit tests in SAPUI5 are written with QUnit and Sinon.JS, two open source testing frameworks that are available on the web and have been incorporated into SAPUI5. We'll take a closer look at both of these to write our first tests. Then, we'll look at OPA tests in SAPUI5 and how they can be written using the OPA5 plugin for QUnit.

As a prerequisite, let's first examine what you can do to make it easier to find bugs in your code if one of your future tests does fail.

11.1 Debugging

This section will provide some of the basics on how to track down errors in your SAPUI5 applications. There are some built-in tools you can use and some techniques that are useful to know.

11.1.1 Tricks to Know

In Chapter 10, you learned how resources can be minified for SAPUI5 applications. This technique is also applied to the SAPUI5 libraries when they're built. In order to make it easier for application developers to trace errors in their applications (or even in the framework, because the developers are humans too), SAPUI5 provides debug resources for every library it ships. These debug resources are not minified and show the plain code as it was written by the respective framework developer.

If you want to switch to the debug resources, there are several ways to do so. You can add a parameter to the URL for your application, like so:

http://your-url-here.tld/?sap-ui-debug=true#maybeSomeHashHere

Or you can use the support tools described in Section 11.1.2 to toggle debug sources. Note that loading the nonminified sources will lead to a higher number of files that need to be loaded too, so don't be surprised when your app suddenly takes longer to load.

Note that there are also other useful URL parameters you can use to test your applications. If you want to test an app in a different language, you can use the URL parameter `sap-ui-language` to change the language, like so:

http://your-url-here.tld/?sap-ui-language=de#maybeSomeHashHere

And you can use the `sap-ui-theme` parameter to switch from one theme to another, like so:

http://your-url-here.tld/?sap-ui-theme=sap_yourdesiredthemename#maybeSome-HashHere

The most important tools for debugging your applications are built into your browser and usually referred to as *developer tools*. When you're on a Windows machine, we recommend using Google Chrome to debug any general, non-browser-specific errors, because we believe that Google Chrome has the most powerful debugging capabilities and is the easiest to handle.

Figure 11.2 shows the menu path for reaching the developer tools in Google Chrome. As shown, you can also press Ctrl+Shift+I or F12.

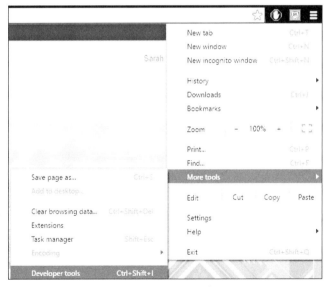

Figure 11.2 Google Chrome Developer Tools Navigation

After selecting Developer Tools, by default, the right side of your browser screen will appear as shown in Figure 11.3. You can change the side on which the tools appear or undock them to display them in a different window using the SETTINGS button in the upper right corner, next to the closing X.

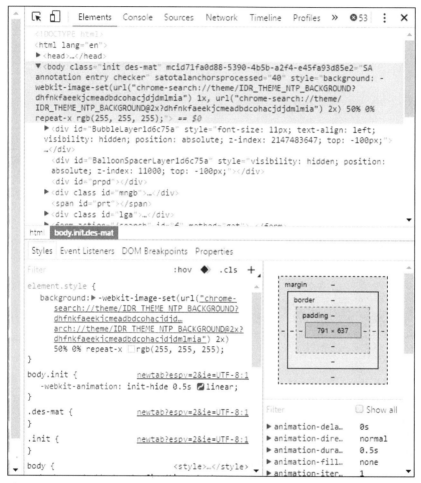

Figure 11.3 Developer Tools

If you prefer any other browser supported by SAPUI5, you're of course also welcome to use it instead.

If you're not familiar with debugging applications in Google Chrome and would like to see some tips and tricks in action, we recommend watching a video by two of the core developers of SAPUI5 on debugging SAPUI5, available at *https://www.youtube.com/watch?v=CmIXJldq8J4*.

11.1.2 Debugging Support Tools

There are three tools you can use for debugging and finding issues besides the ones that are built into your browser: The SAPUI5 Technical Information dialog, the SAPUI5 Diagnostics window, and the Chrome UI5 Inspector.

The Technical Information dialog is built into the framework itself and is available on all SAPUI5 applications. The latter is an open source project, and the developers have created a useful plugin for Google Chrome you can easily install from the Google Chrome Web Store.

SAPUI5 Technical Information

The Technical Information dialog can be brought up on screen by pressing [Alt]+[Shift]+[Ctrl]+[P]. This dialog allows you to quickly see which SAPUI5 version you're using, toggle debug sources, and even try loading your application with a different SAPUI5 version, if it's available and configured for you (see Figure 11.4).

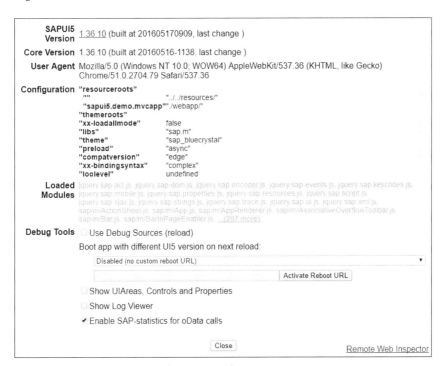

Figure 11.4 SAPUI5 Technical Information Dialog

501

The SAPUI5 Technical Information dialog works well on both desktop and mobile devices.

SAPUI5 Diagnostics

The SAPUI5 Diagnostics window is a popup with a broader functionality than the Technical Information dialog, but it only works well on desktops. You can open it by pressing $\boxed{Alt}$+$\boxed{Shift}$+$\boxed{Ctrl}$+$\boxed{S}$. Why this combination? It was mainly chosen because it's unlikely to interfere with any system shortcuts or any shortcuts that applications would use for their functionality. The S in the combination stands for the word *support*.

When you press this key combination, the popup shown in Figure 11.5 opens. This popup has a lot of functionality that allows you to quickly find the most common issues in an application.

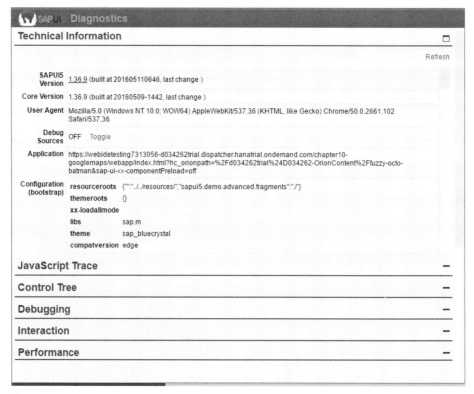

Figure 11.5 SAPUI5 Diagnostics (Support) Popup

The TECHNICAL INFORMATION panel at top, when toggled open, shows you some information about the SAPUI5 version being used by the application. This makes it easy to track down whether an app is on an outdated version and may be facing issues that have already been fixed.

From here, you can also switch debug resources usage on and off by clicking on the TOGGLE link in the DEBUG SOURCES area. Note that you need to reload your application after changing this setting for it to take effect.

Within this panel, when you scroll down, you can also see details about the current configuration and which libraries and resources are loaded. At the very bottom of the panel, when you scroll all the way down, you can also switch on an END-TO-END TRACE.

The next interesting panel is CONTROL TREE, which allows you to investigate how the different SAPUI5 controls and views are nested. When you pick one of the controls or elements shown, you can look up and modify their current property values (see Figure 11.6) or what binding path is defined for them, for example (see Figure 11.7).

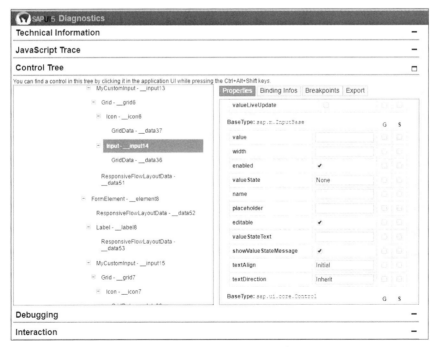

Figure 11.6 Looking Up Control Values in Diagnostics Window

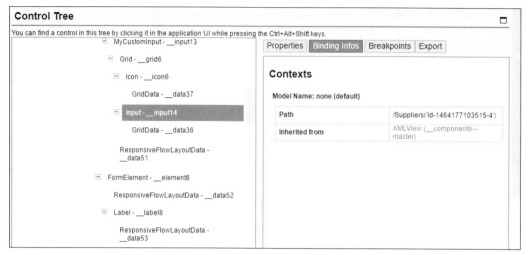

Figure 11.7 Looking Up Binding Info in Diagnostics Window

The control you click on in the CONTROL TREE section is also briefly highlighted in green in your application (see Figure 11.8).

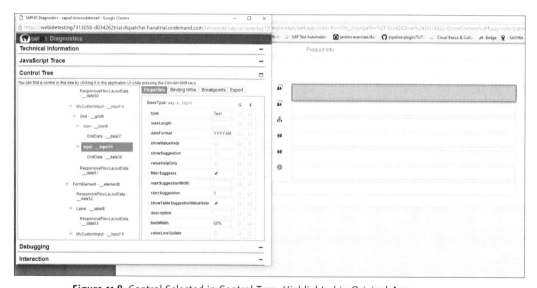

Figure 11.8 Control Selected in Control Tree, Highlighted in Original App

When you switch to the BREAKPOINTS tab in the right pane of the CONTROL TREE, you can even select a method out of those available at the control and set a breakpoint automatically when the selected method is called for the selected control only.

On the next panel in the DIAGNOSTICS window, you can access even more debugging functionality. You can load the application with a different SAPUI5 version to test whether everything would be OK with your app if it ran on a newer version, for example. You also can pick any class from a list of SAPUI5 classes in the left dropdown, add it by clicking on the ADD button next to the dropdown, and then choose from all the available methods in the right pane and set a breakpoint on a method. The difference between this process and the one from the control tree is that now the breakpoint is set for all instances of this class, not for one instance only (see Figure 11.9).

Figure 11.9 Setting Breakpoints in Diagnostics Window

Note that you need to have a debugger opened (e.g., Google Chrome developer tools) so that the breakpoint is taken into account. Within the debugger, you need to go one step up in the call stack in order to get to the method you want to debug, because the debugger always stops in a `methodHook` function that prevents the script from running on.

In the last two panels, you can even do performance and interaction recordings from the Diagnostic window. See more documentation for this functionality at:

- *https://sapui5.hana.ondemand.com/#docs/guide/6ec18e80b0ce47f290bc2645b0c c86e6.html*

- *https://sapui5.hana.ondemand.com/#docs/guide/616a3ef07f554e20a3adf749c11 f64e9.html*.

UI5 Inspector

The UI5 Inspector is an open source Google Chrome plugin you can install from the Google Chrome Web Store at *https://chrome.google.com/webstore/detail/ui5-inspector*. When installed, it will add a new tab to your developer tools in Google Chrome: the UI5 tab (see Figure 11.10).

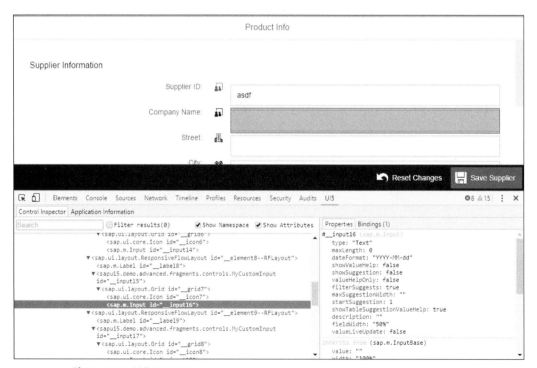

Figure 11.10 UI5 Inspector

In the left pane, the UI5 Inspector will show the tree of all the controls in the current page. When you select a particular control, you can see it highlighted in the app, like in Figure 11.10. In the right pane, you can see the properties of the selected control; switching to the BINDINGS tab in this pane will also show you which path a control property is bound to. This is extremely useful for finding invalid binding paths, which would make your controls appear empty.

With the UI5 Inspector, you do not need to switch between the developer tools and the DIAGNOSTICS Window to debug.

Now that you know which tools are available for debugging your SAPUI5 applications, let's discuss how to write tests to find errors for you.

11.2   Writing Unit Tests

QUnit is a test framework that was originally developed as part of jQuery. As of 2009, it's a standalone framework with its own name and API and is widely used for unit tests in JavaScript-based applications.

When we talk about unit testing in JavaScript, we need to define what a *unit* is first. In many web pages, JavaScript is distributed throughout a page, in particular when there's no special framework used to handle the DOM abstraction. However, because we're using SAPUI5, it's not hard to identify units that can be tested separately; most of the code is encapsulated in separate functions anyway. We use QUnit to test control behavior, and we can also use it to test functions written by an application—for instance, in a formatter or in a controller. QUnit is less helpful when it comes to user integration testing, which should be handled by the SAPUI5 OPA framework.

QUnit allows you to define test modules that have their own start and teardown phases. In these phases, you create the prerequisites for all the tests in one module and clean up what needs to be thrown away before successive modules run. Within your tests, you can call the functions you want to test and check the outcome using assertions. *Assertion types* include, for instance, `equals`, `ok`, or `strictEquals`. These functions can be used to compare or check values returned by your functions called within your test. For each test, you can use one or more assertions. For a test to pass, all assertions must have been met.

All tests usually run within a test page; you'll see in a minute how to create one. The tests run once the page is loaded and will display whether they have run through successfully or if they've encountered any errors.

The typical result you get will look like Figure 11.11.

Figure 11.11 Results from Multiple Unit Tests

What you can see here is that all tests that have run on this page are "green" (you can see this by looking at the small bar below the page title UNIT TESTS FOR TEST, *test* being the application name here). This means that all tests ran successfully. When you click on one of the tests, you can toggle it open to see the assertions in the tests with their results, as shown for test 12 in Figure 11.11.

Before you start writing your first tests, if you're not familiar with QUnit, we recommend checking out the extensive documentation on the project website:

▸ **Getting Started**
  http://qunitjs.com/intro/

▶ **API documentation**
https://api.qunitjs.com/

▶ **The Cookbook**
http://qunitjs.com/cookbook/

11.2.1 Setting up a QUnit Test Page

In this section, we'll rely on the state of the code as found in the *chapter10-google-maps* subdirectory in our repository, which is where we last created the Google Maps control in Chapter 10.

In general, all your applications should have a set of their own tests, which by convention go into your *webapp/test* directory. Within this directory, we usually separate unit tests and acceptance tests into subfolders, so that the structure of your test assets will look like Figure 11.12.

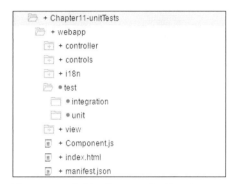

Figure 11.12 Folder Structure for Test Assets

We'll now create an HTML page to load the basic QUnit files all our tests will need. The code for this page will allow us to load all required dependencies and run our tests. We'll call the file *unitTests.qunit.html* and create it in the *test/unit* folder. Its code will look like Listing 11.1.

```
<!DOCTYPE html>
<html>
  <head>
    <title>Unit tests for [App Name Goes Here]</title>
    <meta http-equiv='X-UA-Compatible' content='IE=edge'/>
    <meta charset="UTF-8">
    <script id="sap-ui-bootstrap"
      src="../../../../resources/sap-ui-core.js"
```

```
        data-sap-ui-libs="sap.m"
        data-sap-ui-resourceroots='{
        "test": "../../",
        "test/unit": "./",
        "sapui5.demo.advanced.testing": "../../"
        }'>
    </script>
    <script>
        jQuery.sap.require("sap.ui.qunit.qunit-css");
        jQuery.sap.require("sap.ui.thirdparty.qunit");
        jQuery.sap.require("sap.ui.qunit.qunit-junit");
        jQuery.sap.require("sap.ui.qunit.qunit-coverage");
        QUnit.config.autostart = false;
        sap.ui.require(
          ["test/unit/allTests"],
          function() {
            QUnit.start();
          }
        );
    </script>
  </head>
  <body>
    <div id="qunit"></div>
    <div id="qunit-fixture"></div>
  </body>
</html>
```

Listing 11.1 Start Page for QUnit Tests

Here, we're first bootstrapping SAPUI5 and defining three namespaces in the `resource-roots` attribute at the bootstrap for convenience: one for the general test resources, one for the unit test resources, and the last one is to access the application resources. Note that we've also changed the `src` attribute at the bootstrap: Because we're now two folders down the structure, we need to adapt the path accordingly so that it still looks up the SAPUI5 resources that are two folders further up. We then loading four files that need to be present before we can start running tests using `jQuery.sap.require`. These files contain some styling for the output in the *qunit-css* file; the basic QUnit functionality in the *sap.ui.third-party.qunit* file; a plugin exporting test results in XML style to use in post-build tools like Jenkins, for example, in *qunit-junit*; and a means to allow you to measure code coverage while creating and running your tests in *qunit-coverage*.

When we've made sure all files are loaded, we set the `autostart` value at the global QUnit configuration to `false`. This will ensure that tests won't run before we tell them to using `QUnit.start`. Because the tests will be separated into different test files, as you'll see in a minute, we want to only start the tests when all the test files have been loaded.

Loading the individual test files is done by requiring another file here, which we'll create in the *test/unit* folder and will call *allTests.js*. This file will contain nothing more than an object requiring all the individual test files we create, and could look like Listing 11.2.

```
sap.ui.define([
  "test/unit/model/formatter",
  "test/unit/controller/App.controller",
  "test/unit/controls/myControl"
], function() { "use strict"; });
```
Listing 11.2 allTests.js File Containing List of All QUnit Test Files for the Application

As you can see, this leaves us with an easily maintainable list of test files. When we want to integrate or run them from somewhere other than the unitTests.qunit.html page, we can do so easily by loading the allTests.js file.

Now, let's create the first actual unit tests. We'll start by testing the behavior of one of the custom controls we created in Chapter 9. In this chapter, we implemented our own version of an input combined with an icon, and now we want to test whether all the features work properly.

11.2.2 Writing a Unit Test for a Custom Control

The structure of files and folders within the unit folder should resemble the assets we want to test, because this makes it easy to find a particular test later on. We'll therefore create a new folder in the *unit/test* folder and call it *controls*, just as in the application. Within this folder, we'll create the actual test file and name it like the control the tests are for: *MyCustomInput.js*.

The skeleton of such a test file contains always the same sections. We start creating a new module by using the `sap.ui.define` method and loading the dependencies we need for the test, as shown in Listing 11.3.

```
sap.ui.define([
  //dependencies go here
], function (dependency1, dependency2) {
    "use strict";
    QUnit.module("name of the (first) qunit module");
```

```
  // tests and any functions used across tests go here
  }
);
```
Listing 11.3 QUnit Test Skeleton

For our particular control, this means the code will need to load the control itself as a dependency. The module will be named "MyCustomInput–Behavior Tests". For the module, we want to create a new instance of `MyCustomControl`, and destroy the control again after the test has run. We'll use the QUnit methods `beforeEach` and `afterEach` in the module definition. These two methods will be invoked before and after every test. The test file now looks like Listing 11.4.

```
sap.ui.define([
  "sapui5/demo/advanced/testing/controls/MyCustomInput"
], function (MyCustomInput) {
  "use strict";

  QUnit.module("MyCustomInput – Behavior Tests", {
    beforeEach: function() {
      this.oCustomInput = new MyCustomInput("customInput", {
        "iconURI": "arrow-up"
      });
    },
    afterEach: function() {
      this.oCustomInput.destroy();
    }
  });
});
```
Listing 11.4 Unit Test with Module Setup for MyCustomInput

To create a test with optimal test coverage, we'll create a control instance and test all functionality we've defined ourselves at the control. It's not necessary to test generic getters and setters or any functions that are just inherited; we can rely on the framework for extensively testing those.

For our custom control, this means we want to check the following:

- We have a grid layout containing an icon and an input when the control is instantiated and rendered
- When we set a value for the custom control property, the value is passed correctly to the input inside the custom control

▸ When we set a value directly for the input (to simulate user input), this value is correctly reflected at the corresponding custom control property

▸ When a value is set for the input, the color change for the icon is correctly invoked

Let's start with a test for the constructor of the control.

Testing the Constructor Outcome

In order to check whether we get the right elements on screen, we'll check if we find an instance of the control with the right ID first. Because this instance is created before each test runs, we should already have it at this point in time.

We access the core instance by calling `sap.ui.getCore()` and then ask this instance whether the control is registered there, retrieving the control with the `byId` method at the core.

Next, we'll create our first assertion. The assert object passed into a QUnit test is an object from QUnit itself and is automatically passed into the method; we don't need to do anything for this apart from specifying the parameter name under which we want to access the assert object. We're calling it `assert` to easily recognize what it's for.

The first assertion will be a Boolean check, because we want to test if the control we've tried to instantiate is there or not, so we'll use the `assert.Ok` method. `assert.OK` takes two parameters, the first of which is (or can be interpreted as) a Boolean expression. In the case of our control, the fact that the object exists and is neither null nor undefined can be interpreted as true. The second parameter is the text we want to show in the running test when this assertion has returned its outcome. This test will now look like Listing 11.5.

```
QUnit.test("Should see a Grid containing an icon and an input", functio
n (assert) {
  var oCustomInput = sap.ui.getCore().byId("customInput");
  assert.ok(oCustomInput, "Control Instance was created");
});
```

Listing 11.5 Unit Test with First Assertion

We said we wanted to test not only whether the control is there, but also if its children are correctly instantiated; therefore, we have to add some more assertions to this test. Let's check for the existence of the _layout aggregation, the icon, and the input it should contain. The extended unit test will then look Listing 11.6.

```
QUnit.test("Should see a Grid containing an icon and an input", functio
n (assert) {
  var oCustomInput = sap.ui.getCore().byId("customInput");
  assert.ok(oCustomInput, "Control Instance was created");
  assert.strictEqual(oLayout.getMetadata().getName(), "sap.ui.layout.Gr
id", "Found a Grid control within the custom control");
  assert.strictEqual(this.oCustomInput.getIconURI(), oLayout.getAggrega
tion("content")[
0].getSrc(), "Icon URI was correctly set at control and inner control")
;
  assert.strictEqual(oLayout.getAggregation("content")[
1].getMetadata().getName(), "sap.m.Input", "Found a sap.m.Input inside
the custom control");
});
```

Listing 11.6 Unit Test Checking for Presence of All Child Controls

We're now using the assert method `strictEqual`, which expects three parameters: the first and second are values to compare to each other, and the third is again the text displayed for this test. `strictEqual` only returns `true` if the value of the two compared parameters is equal and if they are also of equal type. Comparing values like `5` and `"5"` with this method would return `false`.

We use this assertion for all the child controls of `MyCustomInput`. We first check for the aggregation, using the `getAggregation` method with the `_layout` aggregation name at the `MyCustomInput` instance. We can test whether the right layout control has been instantiated by asking the `_layout` aggregation for its metadata via `getMetadata()`, and asking the metadata in turn for the control's name.

For the grid, this should return a string with the name `"sap.ui.layout.Grid"` in it (this string is the second parameter).

We can then successively test if in turn the `_layout` aggregation has the correct children. We check for the icon, which should be the first child in the `_layout` aggregations content. We can do so by asking the layout for its content aggregation. This will return an array, and we can pick the first item within this array with [0] as the index.

When we find the icon, we check directly whether the `src` attribute at the icon is the same as the `iconURI` attribute at our `MyCustomInput`, because it should be passed to the icon.

Finally, we check for the inner input, which should be at `index=1` in the content aggregation of the layout. We again check for the control name, and this time we expect it to be `"sap.m.Input"`.

Testing the Setters

Next, we'll check the setters for `MyCustomInput` by adding a new test below the first one. Let's test if user input into the inner input control would be propagated correctly to the `value` property of the `MyCustomInput` instance. We simulate the user input by setting its value directly with the `setValue` method, and then we need to fire the `change` event at the inner input, which would only happen when the user presses ⌷Enter⌷ or the focus leaves the field.

After this, the values of the inner input and the `input` property at the `MyCustom-Input` instance should be the same, so we can test again using the `assert.strict-Equal` method, comparing both values (see Listing 11.7).

```
QUnit.test("Should set the input value at the inner control and at the
custom control", function (assert) {
  // simulate user input by setting the value
  // directly at the inner control:
  this.oCustomInput._oInput.setValue("Hello World");
  this.oCustomInput._oInput.fireChange();
  assert.strictEqual(this.oCustomInput._oInput.getValue(), this.
    oCustomInput.getValue(), "Value property of MyCustomInput has
    the same value as the inner input control");
});
```
Listing 11.7 Test for Setting the Value at Inner Input

We can now be sure that setting and propagating the data in this direction—from the inner input to the value property at the `MyCustomInput` instance—works well. How about writing a test for the other direction?

We want to check whether the value set at `MyCustomInput`—for example, created through a binding—will also be set as the value for the inner input. We can check this by setting a value for `MyCustomInput` and then testing whether the value at the inner input will be the same, as shown in Listing 11.8.

```
QUnit.test("Should set the value from the custom control property at
the inner input control", function (assert) {
  this.oCustomInput.setValue("Hello Unit Test");
  assert.strictEqual(this.oCustomInput._oInput.getValue(),
```

```
      "Hello Unit Test", "value property of MyCustomInput was
      correctly also set at the inner input");
});
```
Listing 11.8 Test for Setting the Value at MyCustomInput Instance

Finally, we want to test if the icon turns green—indicating the correct CSS class is attached—when a user inputs data and if it turns black again—indicating the CSS class has been removed—when the input is emptied again. We can check this by using the `hasStyleClass` method on the icon. We set a new value on `MyCustom-Input` and test with `assert.ok` whether the style class is there. Then we remove the value again and use `assert.notOk` to see whether the `hasStyleClass` method now returns `false` (see Listing 11.9).

```
QUnit.test("Icon should turn green when the input is not empty,
and black again if emptied again", function (assert) {
  this.oCustomInput.setValue("Hello Icon");
  assert.ok(this.oCustomInput._oIcon.
    hasStyleClass("sapThemePositiveText"), "Icon has the appropriate
    style class and is now green");
  this.oCustomInput.setValue("");
  assert.notOk(this.oCustomInput._oIcon.
    hasStyleClass("sapThemePositiveText"), "Icon has no additional
    style class and is now black again");
});
```
Listing 11.9 Test for Color Change of the Icon When Value Is Set

When you run the unit test HTML page now, all tests should be green.

Like this, you can safely edit the code in your custom control—for example, if you need to fix something—and can always check that your code change hasn't broken anything.

We've tested a control now, but our application code certainly does not consist of controls only. Now, let's look at how to create unit tests for other resources in your app.

11.2.3 Unit Tests for Apps

In this section, we'll examine how you can write unit tests for other functionality that is not directly placed on screen and requires user interaction. In the examples, we'll look in particular at how to test functions in a controller. The principles can also be applied for testing formatters, for example.

To ease the writing process of such tests, SAPUI5 makes use of another test framework: Sinon.JS.

Sinon.JS

If you've been bearing with us throughout the previous chapters, the name *Sinon.JS* should ring a bell for you: We used it implicitly in Chapter 6 to simulate a REST service. We didn't look at all its features back then, but we'll do so in this chapter. Sinon.JS ships with SAPUI5, so it's easy to include in your tests. It provides an enhanced testing functionality, including *spies*, *stubs* and *mocks*, *fake timers*, and *fake XMLHTTPRequests*. Spies, stubs, and mocks all belong to a category called *test doubles*, because they act as doubles for real functions we use in tests. We'll see some test doubles in action in a minute, but let's cover some theory first.

Spies

Spies are functions that record several values from function calls. In particular, these are arguments passed to a function, the `this` context, exceptions if any are thrown, and the return value.

With spies, it's easy to write tests for callback functions (whether they are called and with which arguments, for example), because you can simply pass a spy as a callback. When spying on an existing function, the spy will behave like the normal function, but will also give you access to some test data, such as how many times a function was called. Use a spy if you want to make sure something has really happened in your code.

Stubs

Stubs are a special kind of spies with a preprogrammed behavior. They can be used to replace an original function on an object. You use them when you want to create a test that tests a specific code path. This means that when you need a predictive outcome for particular functions, you can stub them to see whether successive functions then return the right value. This comes in handy when you want to test error cases and you need a particular error as prerequisite for a test. It can also be helpful if you want to test functions that would normally trigger a request to a remote service, because you don't need to rely on the request coming back successfully (or, in the case of error handling tests, unsuccessfully). Any code that relies strongly on external factors (like a service) to behave in a particular way can be stubbed in a test.

Mocks

Mocks should be handled with care. You usually use a mock when you would otherwise use a stub, but you need to have multiple assertions checking for the right outcome. In a mock, you can state your expectations upfront, which makes tests easier to read and to maintain. However, because mocks are powerful and give you thorough control over your tested expectations, you can also overuse mocks, making a test less valuable, because the conditions you're testing may be overly specific.

Fake Timers

Fake timers give you more control over how time proceeds in your tests. The clock object you can create makes it possible for you to simulate a certain time passing, and it can also be helpful if you want to create specific Date objects that require a certain time delivered by the now() function for your tests. When you use fake timers, you need to keep in mind that there is a downside: For the test, time will *not* proceed if you don't tell the clock to tick.

Fake XMLHTTPRequests

Sinon allows us to create fake responses to XMLHTTPRequests in our tests also. This is why we used Sinon in Chapter 6; we needed a local instance acting like a real service in order to write our CRUD functions.

When using this functionality, you can decide which requests should be faked and also what result such a request should return. This makes it easy to write functionality like FakeRest (see Chapter 6), which can automatically create responses from JSON data provided, but it can also be useful if you want to test how your application reacts on errors returned from a service. Because you can even decide how long it should take until a fake response is returned, you can also think of tests that require a timeout from a service or throttling the connection, or—thinking in a different direction—when you know your real service is rather slow, you can speed up your tests by letting Sinon deliver the desired response immediately.

Using fake XMLHTTPRequests also decouples your tests from the reliability and availability of a real service, elements that should really be tested elsewhere.

The mock server, which will be covered in Section 11.4 in this chapter, also uses fake XMLHTTPRequests coming from Sinon internally.

Extensive documentation on all of Sinon's features can be found at *http://sinonjs.org/docs/*. We also recommend a great blog post written by Jani Hartikainen that explains comprehensively when to use spies, stubs, and mocks: *https://semaphoreci.com/community/tutorials/best-practices-for-spies-stubs-and-mocks-in-sinon-js*.

Setting Up Sinon.JS

For the next samples, we rely on the state of the code as found in the *Chapter11-unitTests* subdirectory in our repository, which is where we left off when unit testing the custom control.

To integrate Sinon.JS into our test page, we simply need to load some more scripts. However, because Sinon ships as a third-party module with SAPUI5, we don't need to download anything. We can just load Sinon as a dependency into the test page we'll create now; there's no real setup required.

Testing Controller Functionality

Remember that in the application from Chapter 9, we created two fragments. We're displaying the `EditSupplier` fragment when the app starts and the `DisplaySupplier` fragment after an edit has been saved. Now, we want to test if both fragments are instantiated and integrated into the view correctly.

Testing controller functionality that checks whether a function is called or not can be a bit tricky at times, because we have a lot of related functionality to stub in order to get the controller running. This is why we also have some more dependencies this time. Listing 11.10 shows the skeleton for the controller tests.

```
sap.ui.define([
  "sapui5/demo/advanced/testing/controller/Master.controller",
  "sap/ui/core/Control",
  "sap/ui/model/json/JSONModel",
  "sap/m/Panel",
  "sap/ui/thirdparty/sinon",
  "sap/ui/thirdparty/sinon-qunit"
], function(MasterController, Control, JSONModel, Panel) {
  "use strict";
```

```
//Tests go here
});
```
Listing 11.10 Test Skeleton for Master Controller Unit Test

As you can see, we're loading the controller we want to test as a dependency, just like we did with the custom control in the last unit test.

To stub functionality that the controller depends on but which is not coming from itself, we need some more SAPUI5 assets. The view this controller belongs to will neither be rendered nor even instantiated anywhere, in order to be able to isolate the controller test as best as possible from the surrounding functionality.

We're adding dependencies for the `sap.ui.core.Control` class, which we can use to stub the actual view; `JSONModel`, which we can stub the `ODataModel` with; and `sap.m.Panel`, which would include the fragments in the view, so we can stub this container for the fragments, too.

The two functions we want to test in the controller are `_showEdit` and `_showDisplay`. To see whether they're called under the right circumstances, we need to create all the stubs the controller needs to successfully run through its `onInit` function. We do this in the `beforeEach` function, which is the setup for the test module. The setup will look like Listing 11.11.

```
QUnit.module("Show fragments", {
  beforeEach: function() {
    //create the objects returned when stubbing
    this.oViewStub = new Control();
    this.oPanel = new Panel("SupplierPanel");
    this.oComponentStub = new Control();
    this.oRouterStub = new sap.m.routing.Router();
    this.oRouterStub.getRoute = function(){
      return {
        attachPatternMatched: jQuery.noop
      };
    };
    this.fnMetadataThen = jQuery.noop;
    var oODataModelStub = new JSONModel();
    oODataModelStub.metadataLoaded = function() {
      return {
        then: this.fnMetadataThen
      };
    }.bind(this);
    oODataModelStub.submitChanges = function(){
      return {};
    };
```

```
    this.oComponentStub.setModel(oODataModelStub);

    this.oMasterController = new MasterController();

    //
 tell sinon which method calls from the master controller it should stu
b and what to return
    sinon.stub(this.oMasterController, "getView").returns(this.oViewStu
b);
    var oByIdStub = sinon.stub(this.oMasterController, "byId");
    oByIdStub.withArgs("SupplierPanel").returns(this.oPanel);
    sinon.stub(this.oMasterController, "getOwnerComponent").returns(thi
s.oComponentStub);
    sinon.stub(this.oMasterController, "getRouter").returns(this.oRoute
rStub);
    sinon.stub(this.oMasterController, "getModel").returns(oODataModelS
tub);
    sinon.config.useFakeTimers = false;
},
```

Listing 11.11 beforeEach Implementation for Test Module

As you can see, we're only stubbing methods that would otherwise rely on the presence of a view instance, an owner component, a router at this owner component, and a model at the same component. We first create the objects we want the stubs to use, create an instance of the master controller, and then tell Sinon, via the `sinon.stub` method, when to use the stubs, defining what method on the master controller should return the stub instead of invoking the real method.

When we want to limit this behavior to a function call with specific parameters, we can add this limitation using Sinon's `withArgs` method. Note that for some reason, as of the time we're writing this book, we can't chain this method to the `stub` method and the `returns` method. Therefore, we can't write `sinon.stub(something).withArgs("someArg").returns(someStub)`, because Sinon has some issues resolving this correctly, although the correct objects are returned by each function to allow chaining. We can get past this stumbling block by first initializing the stub and then calling the functions `withArgs` and `returns` in a new statement.

Finally, set `faketimers` to `false`, because we want time to proceed normally in this test.

We'll restore the stubbed methods to their original functions and destroy the stub objects in the `afterEach` function of the test module, as shown in Listing 11.12.

```
afterEach: function() {
  this.oMasterController.getView.restore();
  this.oMasterController.byId.restore();
  this.oMasterController.getOwnerComponent.restore();
  this.oMasterController.getRouter.restore();
  this.oMasterController.geModel.restore();
  this.oPanel.destroy();
  this.oViewStub.destroy();
  this.oComponentStub.destroy();
  this.oRouterStub.destroy();
}
```

Listing 11.12 Cleaning Up in afterEach Method of Test Module

Now we can write the actual tests, which are not as complicated. Let's start with the first fragment—the EditSupplier fragment—and see whether the method _showEdit is correctly called (see Listing 11.13).

```
QUnit.test("Should display the edit fragment", function(assert) {
  this.spy(this.oMasterController, "_showEdit");
  this.oMasterController.onInit();

  assert.ok(this.oMasterController._
showEdit.calledOnce, "showEdit was called once");
    assert.strictEqual(this.oMasterController.byId("SupplierPanel").getC
ontent()[
0].getMetadata().getName(), "sap.ui.layout.form.SimpleForm", "Panel con
tains a form");

  this.oMasterController._showEdit.restore();
});
```

Listing 11.13 Testing if EditSupplier Fragment Is Shown

Here, we're creating a spy on the _showEdit method at the master controller. Next, we need to initialize the controller, so we call its onInit method.

With the first assert, thanks to the spy, we can now check if the showEdit function has been called once. The test will run green when this condition is true.

The second assert is used to check whether the correct fragment has been placed in the panel stub. We know that the fragment we want to see has a SimpleForm element in its content, as opposed to the DisplaySupplier fragment, which has a different layout. We can check if we have the right fragment in the panel by asking it for the first control in its content and checking if it's of the right type by using getMetadata().getName() again, as in the custom control unit test.

Finally, we restore the `_showEdit` function so that it is no longer spied upon.

The test for the second fragment looks very similar, but we need to trigger the function that will add it to the panel (see Listing 11.14).

```
QUnit.test("should display the display fragment for a supplier", functi
on(assert) {
  this.spy(this.oMasterController, "_showDisplay");
  this.oMasterController.onInit();
  this.oMasterController.onSave();
  assert.ok(this.oMasterController._
showDisplay.calledOnce, "showDisplay was called once");
    assert.strictEqual(this.oMasterController.byId("SupplierPanel").getC
ontent()[0].getMetadata().getName(), "sap.m.HBox");

  this.oMasterController._showDisplay.restore();
});
```
Listing 11.14 Testing if DisplaySupplier Fragment Is Shown

The second fragment is displayed in the original app when a user clicks on the SAVE button and the controller invokes the `onSave` method. We need to force this behavior now.

We're creating a spy first again, this time for the `_showDisplay` function called by `onSave`. Then, we initialize the master controller again. Next, we trigger the `onSave` method. Because we stubbed the model, no data really needs to be stored anywhere.

Afterwards, we check if the spy confirmed that `_showDisplay` was called once, and then we check if the content of `SupplierPanel` now contains a control of type `sap.m.HBox` instead of `SimpleForm`.

Finally, we restore the `_showDisplay` function again.

When you rerun the unit test page in your browser now, you should see all tests running through successfully.

With these two tests, we have not reached a code coverage of 100%, of course, but rather somewhere between 40% and 50%. However, these tests should give you insight how to create your own tests and how you might enhance your tests to achieve better code coverage.

Next, we'll turn to integration testing, and you'll see how to create tests with yet another framework, which will allow us to easily simulate user interaction as it would happen in a real application.

11.3 One-Page Acceptance Tests

OPA5 is an integration-testing framework for web applications built using SAPUI5 and is written in JavaScript. It ships with the SAPUI5 runtime in the sap.ui.core.test namespace. OPA provides an adaptor for QUnit to use its test queueing capabilities and the QUnit test results user interface. OPA can be used to test complex user interactions across the entire application and therefore can be seen as an alternative to other, similar frameworks like Selenium. Built and optimized for usage with SAPUI5, OPA is the first choice for testing SAPUI5 applications. It provides direct access to controls, properties, views, and many more SAPUI5-specific functionalities.

In this section, we'll try to give you an understanding of the general structure of OPA and explain more about its overall capabilities. First, we'll provide a high-level introduction into the architecture of OPA and the concepts and technologies we're working with. Then, we'll take a more detailed look into one of the main building blocks and central functionalities we'll use over and over when writing tests with OPA: the `waitFor` function. Then, we'll explain how to write tests using OPA and QUnit together. Finally, you'll learn how to structure tests more efficiently by working with page objects that also help to reuse `waitFor` functions across individual journeys.

11.3.1 Architecture

From an architecture perspective, OPA5 has a highly module structure. At its heart, OPA offers basic polling functionality that can be found in the sap.ui.core.test.OPA class. The sap.ui.core.test.OPA class is designed to check that a set of conditions remains true for a certain period of time. This class is frontend framework agnostic and can be used with other frameworks in the same way if a specific adapter is provided. SAPUI5 uses the `sap.ui.core.test.OPA5` adapter.

This adapter offers functions to start up applications via HTML files in an iFrame or the direct startup of SAPUI5 `UIComponents`. The `sap.ui.core.test.OPA5` adapter also provides a `waitFor` function, the central method to implement actions, specific checks, and error handlers that are needed to test applications. The `waitFor` function inspects a configuration object and tests this configuration against the application and against individual properties of controls. Here, the specific conditions to be checked are defined and handed over to OPA5 for validation (see Figure 11.13).

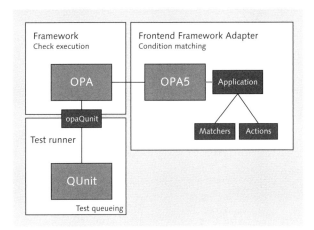

Figure 11.13 OPA5 Architecture

11.3.2 OPA Test Structure

Before we dive into the technical details of OPA testing, let's first talk about the general structure of tests written with OPA from a product or feature perspective. Because tests written with OPA start and run a complete application, the startup and teardown of the application itself is an important element to consider when planning your tests. This is especially important because OPA tests normally are not executed against a real backend but make use of a mocked data source, such as via `sap.ui.core.util.MockServer`.

Think of a scenario in which you want to test that deleting a certain product executes as expected. It's obvious that this will change the state of your application under tests from a data perspective. In order to decouple individual test scenarios from each other, you can use QUnit modules in which each module has its own startup and teardown. Within each module, you can now test several conditions and run modules individually from others during development to speed up your routines by only executing relevant tests.

Within your application, you'll have several modules that somehow relate to each other. Staying with the example of deleting a product, there might be also a module for changing the price of one product or other related modifications. With OPA, you can put several modules in one file, called a *journey*, which will be the second bucket used to structure your tests properly.

Finally, all your journeys will be included in one file. This file would be registered in your test suite and could be run in your CI environment.

11.3.3 Writing waitFor Functions

Let's get some hands-on experience and write our first simple OPA test using `sap.ui.core.test.OPA5` and its `waitFor` function. We want to find out if a particular control is displayed on the screen. We'll bootstrap SAPUI5, and, in the onInit callback of `sap.ui.core.Core`, we will instantiate the control and place a simple button. We can use OPA5 to find this button.

For this first test (see Listing 11.15), we'll keep it simple and use the `controlType` option. We specify `sap.m.Button` here, and in the `success` callback we retrieve the matching results as an argument. We can also perform refinement or assertions on the result, but for now we'll only log the control we retrieve as result to the console.

As soon as we call the `waitFor` function, OPA will internally queue this call. To execute it, we call the `emptyQueue` function.

> **Note**
>
> Classes in the `sap.ui.test` namespace are not loaded with the performance-optimized library preload of the `sap.ui.core` library. If you want to use assets in this namespace standalone, you have to request them manually.

```
<!DOCTYPE HTML>
<html>
<head>
  <meta http-equiv="X-UA-Compatible" content="IE=edge" />
  <meta charset="UTF-8">
  <title>First Simple OPA Test</title>
  <script id="sap-ui-bootstrap"
    src="https://openui5.hana.ondemand.com/resources/sap-ui-core.js"
    data-sap-ui-libs="sap.m"
    data-sap-ui-preload="async"
```

```
      data-sap-ui-theme="sap_bluecrystal"
      data-sap-ui-compatVersion="edge"
      data-sap-ui-onInit="init()">
  </script>
  <script>
  var init = function() {
    var oButton = new sap.m.Button("button", {
      text : "Click Me"}
    ).placeAt("content");
    sap.ui.require(["sap/ui/test/Opa5"], function(Opa5) {
      var opa = new Opa5();
      opa.waitFor({
        controlType : "sap.m.Button",
        success : function(oControl){
          console.log(oControl);
        }
      });
      opa.emptyQueue();
    })
  }
  </script>
</head>

<body class="sapUiBody" role="application">
  <div id="content"></div>
</body>

</html>
```

Listing 11.15 First Simple OPA waitFor

This is a simple example; the overall test structure will look different. The test execution will later be handled by a QUnit adapter. However, this is still helpful in that it shows what writing OPA tests is all about; the waitFor function is the central function you'll be using. Using this example, we'll continue to look at configurations for the waitFor function in more detail.

Besides querying all controls of one specific control type that will return an array of matching controls, you can also look for one specific control by searching for a control ID directly via the id-setting in the configuration. This will return one control directly (see Listing 11.16).

```
opa.waitFor({
  id: "button",
  success: function(oControl) {
    console.log(oControl);
```

```
  }
);
```
Listing 11.16 waitFor with Specific ID

Matchers

You could check for specific properties on the control found by OPA in the success handler of your `waitFor` functions. However, OPA also provides a specific predefined matcher that can be used to check if one of the control properties is set to a specific value, for example. To use the matchers, we can use the `matchers` property in the configuration object and instantiate the new matcher of your choice there (see Listing 11.17).

```
opa.waitFor({
  controlType : "sap.m.Button",
  matchers: new sap.ui.test.matchers.PropertyStrictEquals({
    name: "text",
    value: "Click Me"
  }),
  success : function(oControl){
    console.log(oControl);
  }
});
```
Listing 11.17 Usage of PropertyStrictEquals Matcher

You can also combine matchers by handing them over in an array. In this case, you can check for more than one condition on all matching controls. Another option is to pass one or many custom function(s). Finally, if you identify a missing matcher to reuse across your project, you can even create your own matcher by extending `sap.ui.test.machters.Matcher`. To make this work, you'll have to create a new module and implement an `isMatching` function in it that has to return a Boolean value based on the condition you want to check (see Listing 11.18).

```
sap.ui.define(
  ['sap/ui/test/matchers/Matcher'],
  function(Matcher){

    return Matcher.extend(my.Matcher, {
        metadata: {
          properties: {
            myPropertyForConstructor : {
              // config if needed
            }
          }
```

```
    },

    isMatching: function(oControl) {
      // your specific matcher logic goes in here
      return true||false
    }
  });
});
```

Listing 11.18 Custom Matcher Skeleton

The following OPA5 matchers are provided by SAPUI5:

▶ `AggregationFilled`
Returns `true` once the aggregation passed in as an argument is filled.

▶ `AggregationLengthEquals`
Returns `true` once the aggregation passed in as an argument holds as many items as passed in as an argument.

▶ `AggregationContainsPropertyEqual`
Returns `true` once the aggregation passed in as an argument contains an item that has a property passed in as an argument that matches the value passed in as an argument.

▶ `Ancestor`
Returns `true` if the control passed in as an argument is the ancestor of the given control.

▶ `Interactable`
Returns `true` if the given control is active (e.g., not busy, visible).

▶ `BindingPath`
Returns `true` if the `BindingPath` passed in as an argument matches the `BindingPath` of the given control property.

▶ `PropertyStrictEqual`
Returns `true` if the property of the control that has been passed in as an argument matches the value that has been passed in as an argument.

▶ `Visible`
Returns `true` if the property's visibility on the given control matches the value passed in as an argument (`true`/`false`).

Actions

Another handy property you can use when configuring the `waitFor` function is the actions setting. *Actions* are used in OPA5 to trigger user actions on the UI. This is another task you could implement on the `success` callback function. However, SAPUI5 provides some predefined actions for the most common control interactions. The usage is pretty similar to what you've seen for matchers. Simply pass the constructor for the action to the `actions` property. For this simple example with `sap.m.Button`, we'll showcase the usage of the `press` action:

```
opa.waitFor({
id: "button",
actions: new sap.ui.test.actions.Press()
});
```

For actions, the same plugin-like concept as for matchers is in place. This means you can implement your own custom actions. Create a new module that extends the `sap.ui.test.actions.Action` class and implement the `executeOn` function there (see Listing 11.19). For actions, you can omit the metadata implementation.

```
sap.ui.define(
  ['sap/ui/test/actions/Action'],
  function(Action){

    return Actions.extend(my.Action, {

        executeOn: function(oControl) {
          // your custom control interaction logic goes here
        }
    });
});
```

Listing 11.19 Custom Action skeletonActions Provided with SAPUI5

The following actions are provided by SAPUI5:

▶ `EnterText`
   Enters the text passed into the given control.

▶ `Press`
   Triggers the `tab` event on the given control.

waitFor Configuration Options

We've only covered a subset of the configuration options offered by the `waitFor` function. Much more is possible. For example, you can look for hidden controls or controls displayed within dialogs. For more information, look up the excellent JSDoc for this API that can be found in the SAPUI5 Demo Kit.

11.3.4 Writing an OPA Test

So far, we've discussed the basics of OPA5. Now, let's put the pieces together, but with limited scope. In this section, we'll use the QUnit adapter that comes with OPA5 and will create a first one-page test scenario. This way, we can keep more complex factors like multiple views and startup using a specific HTML file out of the way.

As a simple example application to test, we'll create a file called *Component.js* (see Listing 11.20). In it, we'll extend `sap.ui.core.UIComponent`, and in its `createContent` function we'll return some controls. We'll create a `sap.m.Button` instance that, once clicked on, will open a `sap.m.Dialog` instance, and the title of the dialog will be set to the button's text. This is a simple scenario that we can later test with OPA5. You might come across similar scenarios in real applications; for example, think of some approval workflows or data-loss protections.

> **Note**
>
> Please be aware that the following approach should not be used in productive applications unless you really know what you're doing and does not represent current best practices for SAPUI5 development.

```
sap.ui.define(
  [
    "sap/ui/core/UIComponent",
    "sap/m/Page",
    "sap/m/Button",
    "sap/m/Dialog",
    "sap/m/Text"
  ], function(UIComponent, Page, Button, Dialog, Text) {

  return UIComponent.extend("my.simple.component.Component", {

    createContent : function() {
      var oDialog = new Dialog({
      });
```

```
        var oButton = new Button('buttonToOpenDialog',
          {
            text : "hello",
            press : function(oEvt) {
              oDialog.setTitle(oEvt.getSource().getText());
              oDialog.open();
            }
        });
        var oPage = new Page({
            content : oButton
        });
        return oPage;
      }
   });
});
```
Listing 11.20 Simple Component-Based Application to Showcase OPA5

For all our test logic, we'll create a new file and call it *journey.js* (see Listing 11.21). In it, we'll first load all dependencies for our tests, perform the required configuration for QUnit and OPA5, and finally write the test itself.

```
jQuery.sap.require("sap.ui.qunit.qunit-css");
jQuery.sap.require("sap.ui.thirdparty.qunit");

QUnit.config.autostart = false;

sap.ui.require([
  'sap/ui/test/opaQunit',
  'sap/ui/test/Opa5'
], function(opaTest, Opa5) {

  // first we will extend OPA5 configuration
  sap.ui.test.Opa5.extendConfig({ … });

  // second we will write opaTests
  opaTest( … );
  QUnit.start();
});
```
Listing 11.21 Skeleton for a Single OPA5 Journey

As previously noted, OPA5 has an integration for use with QUnit to make use of QUnit's queueing and visual output capabilities. This is provided as an `opaTest` function that can be used once `sap.ui.test.opaQunit` has been required as dependency. Form minimal usage, the `opaTest` function expects the test name as a first argument and a callback function that holds the actual testing specification as a second argument. Listing 11.22 shows the general structure of an OPA5 test.

```
opaTest("test name", function (Given, When, Then) {

  // Arrangements : use this for application startup
  Given.iStartmyApp

  // Actions: use this for simulating user interaction
  When.iTriggerSomeAction

  // Assertions: use this to check for a certain condition
  Then.iSeeTheExpectedResult;
});
```

Listing 11.22 opaTest Structure

From this snippet, you can see that OPA5 supports writing readable tests that ease the understanding of what your tests actually do. If we translate this into our current scenario to be tested, the structure might look like in Listing 11.23. For now, let's take the application startup and teardown for granted. We'll look into the different options later. At this stage, it's important to understand that we'll run the `UIComponent` created before directly using the `componentLauncher`, triggered by calling `iStartMyComponent` with the component namespace as a configuration option, provided by OPA5.

```
opaTest("Should open the dialog", function(Given, When, Then) {

  Given.iStartMyUIComponent({
    componentConfig: {
      name: "my.simple.component"
    }
  });

  When.iPressAButtonById("buttonToOpenDialog");

  Then.iSeeTheDialogWithTheRightTitle().and
  .iTeardownMyUIComponent();

});
```

Listing 11.23 Sample Test Structure

Each of these function calls is executed by individual or even nested `waitFor` functions, which you worked with in the previous section. The difference now is that we'll write the functions as OPA5 properties and run them with QUnit, which offers some additional convenience.

One new option that we can use as soon as we write our functions in the context of OPA5 itself is the exchange of objects across the `waitFor` functions. For this functionality, OPA5 provides a context object. We can retrieve this object in any `waitFor` functions by calling `getContext()` on the global OPA5 instance. Into this instance, we can store, for example, our button and later retrieve it in another `waitFor` function. We'll do this in the implementation of `iPressAButtonById` in Listing 11.24. In this case, we'll use this functionality to check that the dialog title matches the button text.

Assume that we have a first `waitFor` function created that will serve as a click action to trigger a click on the button. We'll identify the button by using the ID we gave at initialization and hand it over as an argument. In general, you can use arguments for your functions, which makes test reuse across your application tests easy to achieve. For the assertion, we'll add a function that checks if `sap.m.Dialog` exists and if it has the right title.

Finally, we'll add an `errorMessage` property to the `waitFor` configuration now, because we can now visualize test results using QUnit.

Let's go over how to execute these functions as part of `Given`, `When`, or `Then`. From the comments in Listing 11.22, we can make a first guess and match the callback arguments to `arrangements`, `actions`, and `assertions`. These are part of the global OPA5 configuration, and each is a plain OPA5 object at initialization.

We'll call `extendConfiguration` on `sap.ui.test.OPA5` and make our test functions available across all tests. This will internally merge new and existing configurations. In order to add this function to the scope of the OPA test, we'll add it as a named property to the actions object of the OPA5 configuration. Adding the second function to the assertion follows the same principle.

```
sap.ui.test.Opa5.extendConfig({
  actions: new Opa5({
    iPressAButtonById: function(sId) {
      return this.waitFor({
        id: sId,
        actions: new Press(),
        success : function(oButton) {
          Opa5.getContext().oButton = oButton;
        },
```

```
          errorMessage : "Button with id " + sId + " not found"
      })
    }
  }),
  assertions: new Opa5({
    iSeeTheDialogWithTheRightTitle: function() {
      return this.waitFor({
        controlType: "sap.m.Dialog",
        matchers: function(oDialog) {
          return new PropertyStrictEquals({
            name: 'title',
            value: Opa5.getContext().oButton.getText()
          }).isMatching(oDialog);
        },
        success: function() {
          ok(true, "Open Dialog has the right title");
        },
        errorMessage: "no Dialog with the matching title found"
      })
    }
  })
});
```

Listing 11.24 Extend OPA5 Configuration

As a final step, we have to add a runnable HTML file in which we initially bootstrap SAPUI5 and prepare to display the test results. Let's call this file *test.qunit.html*, following QUnit conventions. The important part here is that we prepare the DOM content that QUnit expects to render the test result. We don't need to set any specifics for the bootstrap itself, but also should not forget to require the journey itself (see Listing 11.25).

```
<body>
  <div id="qunit-wrapper">
    <div id="qunit"/>
    <div id="qunit-fixture"/>
  </div>
</body>
```

Listing 11.25 DOM Structure for QUnit Test Result Display

If we run this test in a browser, we'll see QUnit and the application itself side by side, as shown in Figure 11.14.

Figure 11.14 First OPA Test in Browser

11.3.5 Application Lifecycle Handling

One last thing we want to look into is starting your application and tearing it down. As you've seen, OPA always needs running applications. This means that you as a test developer have to take care of application startup and teardown and restart whenever you want to run your journeys separately from each other.

OPA5 offers two ways to handle this lifecycle; both have advantages and shortcomings. For the current example, we used a UI component in combination with the so-called `ComponentLauncher`. This will load the component directly and share the same SAPUI5 runtime across individual startups. The other, more prominently documented way to start applications to be tested is within an iFrame embedded in the test page itself. When comparing both approaches, you'll realize that the application is displayed more nicely within the iFrame, but the startup generally takes longer, debugging is less accessible, and you might even run into cross-browser issues, especially in Internet Explorer. Still, both methods have advantages. For example, think about running your application in a container like SAP Fiori Launchpad and testing integration scenarios. This simply would not be possible with the `ComponentLauncher`.

Because the startup within an iFrame is well documented in the standard SAPUI5 Demo Kit, we won't go into details about it here. Instead, we'll take a closer look at the handling of the `ComponentLauncher` that we've used earlier in the chapter.

11.3.6 Structuring Tests with Page Objects

So far, you've learned all the basics of OPA and even created a first setup that will allow you to test simple, one-page applications. However, what about applications that are more complex, with more than one view, a large number of journeys, and even more individual `waitFor` functions? You could create different OPA5 objects and set up the OPA configuration for every journey individually or embrace complexity even more and add all your assertions, actions, and arrangements once for reuse centrally across all journeys—but neither of these options eases the handling of all this functionality.

That's why OPA offers *page objects*. The idea behind page objects is that every action or assertion always belongs to one dedicated screen or view. For example, think of a simple navigation scenario. Assume you have a list in one view—let's call this view *A*—and each click on a list item will trigger a navigation and a display of related details in a second view, called *B*. If we translate this example into pseudo OPA test syntax, we'd describe it like this:

```
When.onA.iPressItemX
Then.onB.iSeeTheDetailsForItemX
```

From this simple example, you can derive several facts. First, the example describes in more depth what the flow expected from the application itself should be and therefore helps explain the tested scenario, even for those who didn't write the test themselves. Second, it enforces a clear separation of concerns and ensures better design overall. The good news is that this example is pretty easy to achieve. Let's look at the details.

`sap.ui.test.OPA5` offers a function called `createPageObjects` that can be called to create this new `pageObject`. We can later use the `pageObject` under the name we pass in as a key for the object that holds all our actions and assertions. Listing 11.26 shows the general structure.

```
sap.ui.define([
  "sap/ui/test/Opa5"
], function(Opa5) {
  "use strict";
  Opa5.createPageObjects({
    onMyPage : {
      actions : {},
      assertions : {}
    }
```

```
      } );
  } );
```
Listing 11.26 Skeleton Coding for OPA5 Page Objects

11.3.7 Full Application Test Setup

Now, let's bring all the pieces together and create the general setup for OPA testing for your applications. Most of the coding we'll use in this section should be familiar by now, so we'll concentrate on the fine details and uncover some tricks and tweaks.

The starting point is the folder structure, which we created in Section 11.2.1. All files relevant to OPA will go into the *integration* folder, but we'll generally use the testsuite.qunit.html file as the endpoint to which all test pages should be registered.

Figure 11.15 shows the folders and files we'll create in this section. All the page objects will go in the *pages* folder, and we'll also create a file called Common.js in the *pages* folder. This file can be used to share functionality across page objects. In addition, with SelectionJourney.js, we'll create one journey and a simple OPA5 test page (opatest.qunit.html). For the application, we'll use the Master-Detail app created in Chapter 8. We'll test one simple scenario first as an example, testing that clicking a random item will display the related details on the details page.

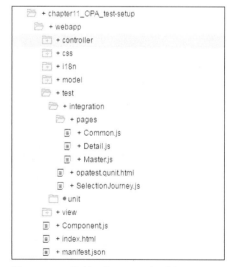

Figure 11.15 Folder Structure for OPA Tests

Let's start by creating the opa.qunit.html file (see Listing 11.27). The general structure of a test page should be familiar by now, so we'll concentrate on some basic configuration needed for the view namespace when working with views and `pageObjects`, and then we'll start the unit test by calling `QUnit.start()`. Note that we have to load the dependencies in two nested `sap.ui.require` functions; we have to set the global OPA5 configuration before we can load the journeys, because they will be queued instantly.

```
<script>
  var init = function(){
    jQuery.sap.require("sap.ui.qunit.qunit-css");
    jQuery.sap.require("sap.ui.thirdparty.qunit");
    jQuery.sap.require("sap.ui.qunit.qunit-junit");
    QUnit.config.autostart = false;
      sap.ui.require([
        "sap/ui/test/opaQunit",
        "sap/ui/test/Opa5",
        "my/app/test/integration/pages/Master",
        "my/app/test/integration/pages/Detail"
      ], function(opaTest, Opa5) {
        Opa5.extendConfig({
          viewNamespace: "my.app.view."
        })
        sap.ui.require([
          "my/app/test/integration/SelectionJourney"
        ]);
        QUnit.start();
      })
    }
</script>
```

Listing 11.27 Loading Page Objects and Journeys

Let's start with the content of the journey (see Listing 11.28). This is nothing more than a simple OPA test, but note the possibility to chain functions using the `and` keyword as used in the `When` block.

```
QUnit.module("MasterList Selections");

  opaTest("clicking an item on the master list should display the right
  details", function(Given,When,Then) {

    Given.iStartMyUIComponent({
      componentConfig: {
        name: "my.app"
      }
    });
```

```
When.onTheMasterPage.iWaitUntilAnAggregationIsFilled("items")
  .and.iClickOnARandomItem();

Then.onTheDetailPage.iSeeTheRightDetails()
  .and.iTeardownMyUIComponent();
});
```

Listing 11.28 Module and OPA5 Test in Journey

Now, we want to create the first page object for the master view. We want to simulate a random item being clicked on. In order to test this, the detail view needs
to show the matching details, so we'll save the binding path of the selected items
to later retrieve it on the `pageObject` for the detail view. To achieve this, we can
use the context OPA5 provides. This context is a JavaScript object that can be
used to share all kinds of values across `waitfor` functions. We'll also use plain
JavaScript to define the item to be clicked on using the `press` action. In the `wait-
For` statement in Listing 11.29, you can see clearly how you can refine the result
throughout the configuration; for example, we first retrieve the entire list using
the `id` setting and then shrink the result to one list item using a custom matcher
function.

```
sap.ui.define([
  "sap/ui/test/Opa5",
  "my/app/test/integration/pages/Common",
  "sap/ui/test/matchers/AggregationFilled",
  "sap/ui/test/actions/Press"
], function(Opa5, Common, AggregationFilled, Press) {
    "use strict";

    Opa5.createPageObjects({
      onTheMasterPage : {
        baseClass: Common,
        actions : {
          iClickOnARandomItem : function(){
            return this.waitFor({
              viewName : "Master",
              id : "list",
              matchers : function(oList) {
                var iItemIndex =
 Math.round(Math.random() * (oList.getItems().length - 1));
                return oList.getItems()[iItemIndex];
              },
              actions : new Press(),
              success : function(oListItem) {
```

```
                  var oPath = oListItem.getBindingContextPath();
                  Opa5.getContext().oBindingPath = oPath;
                  ok(true, "Item " + oPath + " was clicked");
                }
              });
            }
          },
          assertions : {}
        }
      });
    });
```

Listing 11.29 Page Object for Master View

We'll then read the binding path out of the OPA5 context and use the `sap.ui.test.matchers.BindingPath` matcher to compare it to the binding path set on the detail page in the assertion, as in Listing 11.30. We still have to perform some trickery here. Because the context will only be set once the click has been performed, we'll need extra scope to read it at the right time. This looks a little odd, because we'll then use the matcher within a custom matcher function, but it does the job.

```
iSeeTheRightDetails : function() {
  return this.waitFor({
    viewName : "Detail",
    id : "page",
    matcher : function() {
      return new BindingPath({
        path: Opa5.getContext().oBindingPath
      });
    },
    success : function() {
      var oPath = Opa5.getContext().oBindingPath;
      ok(true, "Details for " + oPath + "were displayed");
    }
  });
}
```

Listing 11.30 waitFor Used as Assertion for Detail Page

The last thing we still need to do is to ensure that the aggregation is filled, meaning that the list binding is already resolved and the list has items, before we can trigger the click on an item. We can use the `sap.ui.test.matchers.Aggregation-Filled` matcher for this. However, this might be a `waitFor` that we could reuse across different page objects, which is why we'll put it into a shared file called

Common.js. Remember that a line in Listing 11.29 defined Common.js as `base-Class` for this page object, which means that we can use all functions in the class with this alias. The full coding can be found in Listing 11.31.

```
sap.ui.define([
  "sap/ui/test/Opa5",
  "sap/ui/test/matchers/AggregationFilled"
], function(Opa5, AggregationFilled) {
  "use strict";
    return Opa5.extend("my.app.test.integration.pages.Common", {

      iWaitUntilAnAggregationIsFilled : function(aggregationName) {
        return this.waitFor({
          matchers : new AggregationFilled({
          name : aggregationName
        })
      });
    }
  });
});
```

Listing 11.31 Shared Page Object

You've now seen a small part of what OPA offers to application developers to ensure quality. At the beginning, everything seems to be very complex and a lot of coding is needed to cover all the functionality of your application. However, over time, you'll gain experience and start reusing your code across different projects. One last thing to note here is the use of a mock server to decouple tests from the actual backend. We'll take a closer look into what SAPUI5 offers in this respect in the next section.

11.4   Mocking Data: Using the Mock Server

`sap.ui.core.util.MockServer` is a class in SAPUI5 that can be used to simulate any backend on the client. It's a subclass of `sap.ui.base.ManagedObject`, and all of the parent class' capabilities can be used, including autogenerated getters and setters for its properties. Internally, it uses Sinon.js and wraps its fake server API to provide server capabilities. It's optimized for use with OData services and creates request handlers for all entities based on the OData service metadata document. However, it can be configured and used to mimic any data service or data source. You can also run more than one mock server at a time, listening outbound to different paths. This also means you can use several instances that are configured for individual OData services or even mix OData services with other REST services of your choice.

In this section, we'll first build up a general understanding of how the `MockServer` can be configured and started in order to mimic a specific OData service. In the second subsection, we'll then use more advances configuration concepts for mocking data and learn how individual responses can be customized.

11.4.1 Basic Instantiation and Configuration

For usage with OData, the minimal configuration of the `MockServer` requires a reference to the service metadata and the URI that should be answered with fake responses. For this example, we'll build on top of the application we built in Chapter 7. We'll add a *localService* folder into the *webapp* folder and put the service metadata there. You can easily extract the service metadata from any OData service straight out of the browser. We'll copy the metadata from the Northwind 3.0 service and create a metadata.xml file from its content.

Then, we will instantiate the `MockServer` as in Listing 11.32. In the constructor of the mock server, we'll give the root URI as a configuration option. Every request relative to that root path will not be sent out but will be responded to directly from the mock server. This setting is important especially if you have several data services you use within your app. Here, we'll use the same URI we used in Chapter 7 when defining the data source in manifest.json.

When calling the `simulate` function on the `MockServer` object that takes the path for the metadata.xml file, the mock server will internally create request stubs for all entities in the metadata. When calling the `start` function, all these stubs will be instantiated as request handlers and added to the requests to be handled by the mock server. Finally, we start the mock server by calling the `start` function. From then on, all request relative to the defined service URL will be responded to by the mock server.

```
<script>
  sap.ui.getCore().attachInit(function() {
    var oMockServer = new sap.ui.core.util.MockServer({
      rootUri : "/destinations/northwind/V2/
(S(xgoz33phgwr2uph42rkjj5b5))/OData/OData.svc/"
    });
    var sMetaDataPath =
  jQuery.sap.getModulePath("sapui5.demo.odata.readingdata.bestpractice"
```

```
+ "localService/metadata.xml");
    oMockServer.simulate(sMetaDataPath);
    oMockServer.start();

    new sap.m.Shell({
      app: new sap.ui.core.ComponentContainer({
        height : "100%",
        name : "sapui5.demo.odata.readingdata.bestpractice"
      })
    }).placeAt("content");
});
</script>
```
Listing 11.32 Basic Instantiation of MockServer: index.html

11.4.2 Advanced Concepts and Configuration

The simple setup we created in Listing 11.32 will be sufficient for basic use, such as in prototyping scenarios. With this example, we'll get only technical dummy data generated by the mock server on the fly based on the service metadata. We also have no way to control if the mock server should be active all the time. We might want to be able to stop it, or maybe even manipulate it at runtime. Also, if we want to run integration tests with the mock server and OPA5, we might want to keep an eye on performance and limit the request handles created to the ones that will be consumed by the application.

For more complex implementation, we'll create a new file called mockserver.js and put it into the *webapp/localService* folder right next to the metadata file. Let's start with a simple skeleton for the mock server. We'll create a new module using the sap.ui.define syntax and load `sap.ui.core.util.MockServer` as the only dependency.

We'll return an object in which we declare our functions and add an `init` function that we'll later call to instantiate and configure the mock server. We'll then copy the instantiation and configuration coding from last time. We'll also add the `MockServer` instance as a static variable and add a getter to retrieve later it at runtime (see Listing 11.33).

```
sap.ui.define(
  ["sap/ui/core/util/MockServer"],
  function(MockServer) {
    var oMockServer;
    return {
      init : function () {
        oMockServer = new MockServer({
```

```
        rootUri : "/destinations/northwind/V2/
(S(xgoz33phgwr2uph42rkjj5b5))/OData/OData.svc/"
      });
      var sMetaPath =
 jQuery.sap.getModulePath("sapui5.demo.odata.readingdata.bestpractice"
+ "localService/metadata.xml");
        oMockServer.simulate(sMetaPath);
        oMockServer.start();
      },
      getMockServer : function () {
        return oMockServer;
      }
    }
  });
```

Listing 11.33 Mock Server Skeleton

Now, let's load and initialize the newly created `MockServer` implementation in index.html. To do so, we'll modify how we load the dependency slightly by adding a `sap.ui.require` function to it. We'll load mockserver.js and, while we're at it, add `sap.m.Shell` to the dependencies here. Within the callback of the `init` event of the `sapui5` core, we'll call the `init` function of the mock server (see Listing 11.34).

```
<script>
  sap.ui.require([
    "sapui5/demo/odata/readingdata/bestpractice/localService/
mockserver",
    "sap.m.Shell"
  ], function(MockServer, Shell) {
    sap.ui.getCore().attachInit(function() {
      MockServer.init();
      new Shell({
        app: new sap.ui.core.ComponentContainer({
          height : "100%",
          name : "sapui5.demo.odata.readingdata.bestpractice"
        })
      }).placeAt("content");
    });
  });
</script>
```

Listing 11.34 Initialization of Mock Server in index.html

Options to Control Mock Server Usage

There are several ways to instantiate and control whether the mock server should be active from outside your application coding. The decision you make is dependent upon your scenario, distribution channel, and customer expectations. Options to control

> mock server usage include the `url` parameter, an independent HTML file, or even instantiation of `MockServer` in your component.

Now let's complete the `MockServer` configuration. All configuration related to the response data will be added as an object to the `simulate` function (see Listing 11.35). The API allows you to configure where the `MockServer` will take data for responses from, or whether missing data should be generated on the fly. It's expected that you use JSON files for the data you wish to use with `MockServer`, and that data for one specific entity set is found in your metadata.xml. In order to improve the performance in testing scenarios, we can specify the entity sets used in our application. Based on this setting, the handles to be created can be limited.

```
init : function () {
  oMockServer = new MockServer({
    rootUri : "/destinations/northwind/V2/
(S(xgoz33phgwr2uph42rkjj5b5))/OData/OData.svc/"
  });
  var sMetaPath =
 jQuery.sap.getModulePath("sapui5.demo.odata.readingdata.bestpractice"
+ "localService/metadata.xml"),
  sMockdataPath =
 jQuery.sap.getModulePath("sapui5.demo.odata.readingdata.bestpractice"
+ "localService/MockData");

  oMockServer.simulate(sMetaPath, {
    aEntitySetsNames: "Suppliers",
    sMockdataBaseUrl: sMockdataPath,
    bGenerateMissingMockData: true
  });
  oMockServer.start();
},
```

Listing 11.35 Extended Mock Server Configuration

So far, you've learned how to use a mock server with the OData service. Based on the service metadata, the setup is pretty simple, and you've seen that the server is productive in no time. However, you can also add custom request handles or even manipulate existing ones, both with a mock server configured for use with an OData service and for standalone mock servers that are instantiated to mimic individual paths. In the latter case, we could simply add the request we want to mock to the constructor on instantiation.

One use case in which you might manipulate existing paths for an OData-based mock server is when testing technical error handling within your app. In this situation, we can make use of the fact that the request created by the mock server in the `simulate` function call is modeled as a property on the `MockServer` class. All requests are stored in an array, which can be retrieved by calling `getRequests`. Each request object consists of three properties:

- The request HTTP method as an uppercase string
- The request path as a string or RegEx
- The response as a function

To simulate a failing metadata request, for example, we can identify the metadata request within the request array and manipulate it to return an XHR response with an HTTP code that indicates an error to the requesting OData model, the response headers, and a custom error message.

```
oMockServer.getRequests().forEach(function(oRequest) {
  if(oRequest.path.toString().indexOf("$metadata")){
    oRequest.response = function(oXhr) {
      oXhr.respond(500, {"Content-Type": "text/plain;charset=utf-
8"}, "metadata error");
    }
  }
});
```
Listing 11.36 Faking Individual Responses

> **Note**
>
> Manipulations to individual paths during `MockServer` instantiation have to be made prior to calling `start`.
>
> If you manipulate paths on the fly on already running mock servers, you'll have to stop and restart the running mock server instance to ensure that the newly created requests will be added as request handlers to the existing instance.

11.5 Linting Code

In this final section of this chapter, we now want to have a look into quality from a different angle. Quality is not only about functional correctness, but also has implications when it comes to the quality of code on a line by line basis. This is especially relevant when it comes to interpreted languages like JavaScript and even more important as we want to ensure that our code runs in different JavaScript engines. Here, syntactical issues are more likely to get overseen. Additionally, linting tools are often used to ensure code conventions and style guidelines. This fosters the readability of code by enforcing a common code formatting what will pay off once your applications are handed over from the development to maintenance and support teams.

When it comes to JavaScript, ESLint (*http://eslint.org/*) is the first choice linting tool for most developers. It`s broad usage and community footprint eases the adoption while a file based customization ensures the flexibility you will need to implement you custom checks and rules.

Fortunately we do not have to set up our own infrastructure for linting code but can make use of the functionality the SAP Web IDE provides. And at this point you will most likely already have seen it in action while working with this book and the examples in the SAP Web IDE. In Figure 11.16 you can see one example.

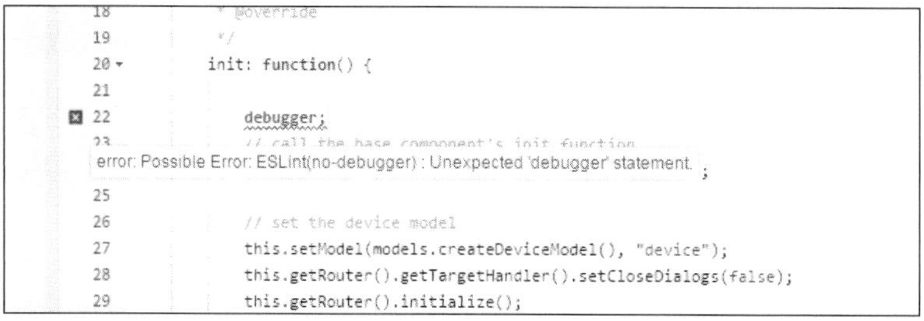

Figure 11.16 SAP Web IDE Linting Example

The rules enabled in the SAP Web IDE already reflect best practices and recommendations by the community. Still there is a possibility to customize existing rules or even create new ones. You can do this for every project individually. Right-click on your project in the workspace and selecting PROJECT SETTINGS from the context menu a new screen will open offering several configuration options. In here you can expand the CODE CHECKING section and select JAVASCRIPT to reach the customizing UI. In the example in Figure 11.17, you will find the rule corresponding to the response in Figure 11.16 and in here you can now customize or even disable the rule.

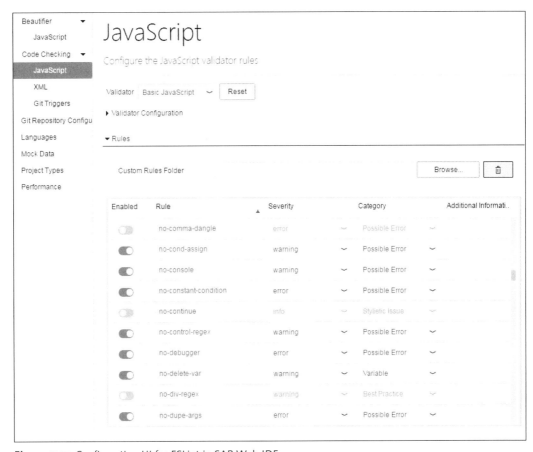

Figure 11.17 Configuration UI for ESLint in SAP Web IDE

Additionally, you could also upload your own rules or change between predefined rulesets. As we cannot cover this more broadly in this book, we highly recommend reading the documentation for ESLint and testing it out if you feel that the rules already available do not match your style of coding. To close this section testing we want to give one example on how to suppress ESLint to evaluate parts of your codes. For this you can simply use comments in your code. You can see in Figure 11.18 that you can use `eslint-disable` and `eslint-enable` to disable certain rules in parts of your files or even for the entire file.

549

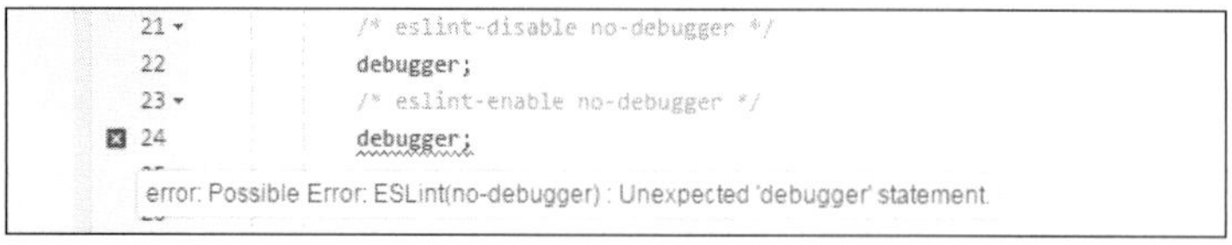

```
21 ▾          /* eslint-disable no-debugger */
22            debugger;
23 ▾          /* eslint-enable no-debugger */
⊠ 24          debugger;
    error: Possible Error: ESLint(no-debugger) : Unexpected 'debugger' statement.
```

Figure 11.18 Enable and Disable ESLint in Individual Files

11.6   Summary

In this chapter, you learned about debugging your application and creating unit tests and integration tests, which will ensure the stability of your application. You became familiar with QUnit and OPA as test frameworks and now know how to use them and what use cases they're for. You also learned how to guarantee certain code quality by adding ESLint to your applications during design time. You're now in perfect shape to start creating your productive, enterprise-grade apps.

To make it even easier for you to avoid any pitfalls, we'll look at the *worst* practices for SAPUI5 applications in the next chapter. If you've read this book thoroughly, you may already find some of these worst practices familiar. However, we found people stepping into these pitfalls so often that we felt an overview would be useful.

It's just as important to know what not to do as it is to know what to do. This chapter details common errors and missteps to make your applications as terrible as possible.

12   Don'ts

In previous chapters, you learned how to build applications with SAPUI5, write your own controls if required, make your applications enterprise-grade, and secure the quality of your code through proper test coverage.

However, we found that not absolutely every "do" can be explained, even in a book as comprehensive as this one, and hence it can be easier (and equally as important) to explain what *not* to do when implementing apps with SAPUI5. In this chapter, you'll see some of the worst practices, and you'll work through a how-to guide that will help you break your apps in case of any SAPUI5 updates. This guide will tell you what to do if you want your apps to be as hard to maintain, non-theme-able, and easy to break as possible. We'll also provide hints for how to check if you've been successful in your mission to apply our worst practices.

12.1   Worst Practices

There are certain sure-fire ways to make a mess of your apps. In this section, we'll look at three of the most common mistakes that can be made: wonky application styling, not following general development principles, and not taking performance into consideration.

12.1.1   Getting Application Styling All Wrong

In general, to get the worst out of your app, it's a good idea to change styling according to your personal preferences whenever and for whatever elements you want. That means putting your styling in a separate CSS file that you'll always load last, adding arbitrary style attributes to controls during runtime via jQuery or native JavaScript functions, and/or using the UI5 `addStyleClass` method frequently.

In this section, we'll look at common application styling mistakes.

Colors

If you want your customers to be unable to re-theme your apps to adopt their own style or if you want to have colors that won't adapt to any style-related accessibility settings, the first measure to take is to hard-code colors in your CSS files. Don't attempt to use any of the theming parameters delivered with SAPUI5, because they're too easy to change depending on users' needs. A good test here is to switch your application to high-contrast black mode.

If you can still see the same colors you manually set for your application, this is a good sign you were successful, and the beautiful dark-grey fonts you wanted will still be present against a dark-grey or black background. This will make the contrast as low as possible—but hey, you're the designer, and these were the colors you wanted; other themes should adapt to your choices, right?

Visibility

That said, if you want to bypass any information the framework includes about visibility or invisibility of controls at a certain point in time during runtime, it's a good idea to avoid using the respective control's own `setVisible` function; instead, set a CSS style to make the control invisible.

This will prevent SAPUI5 from realizing reliably if a control is currently rendered and if it needs re-rendering, and—most importantly—the control will still assume it's in its previous state, so it will try to apply any methods for moving or placing, resizing, or controlling the visibility according to the control's inherent logic.

If you see frequent messages in the console like UNDEFINED IS NOT A FUNCTION, referring to some DOM node that should be accessed, you can be sure you have been successful in truly messing things up.

Control-Internal Class Styling

When you find that the inner DOM of a control is not as you'd like to see it, assume that such elements along with their corresponding style classes will remain stable until the end of all time and across all frameworks. Overstyle any parts of the DOM rendered by one control, overriding the styles specified for these classes, and also add !important to your restyling in order to ensure that it will always be applied. Even better, write JavaScript code based on the assumption that a certain inner DOM element will always be there, don't bother checking for its existence, and wildly apply any modifications you can think of (also see Section 12.2 for more details).

Changes to the inner DOM of a control after updating SAPUI5 or error messages arising because SAPUI5 expects a certain styling to be present at the corresponding control are signs that you've been successful. The next step *always* is to complain to the developers about this bug and ask them to make their controls compatible with any changes you may come up with. Congratulations, you're the worst.

Styling DOM Elements Directly

If you need any DOM elements in your application like paragraphs or spans to adopt a different styling at some point, don't bother using any specific selectors that will restrict the new CSS styles to be applied to these particular elements only. Instead, define your CSS as generally as possible so that it's applied to as many elements as possible with just a few sleek lines of CSS. Rely on SAPUI5 controls never using anything as trivial as typical DOM elements, and assume that your own styles will only be applied to the elements you created in your own app code.

You've been successful if you can see your styling evenly distributed across the application, for any kinds of elements, be they inside or outside of any kinds of controls—and even in some most surprising places.

Misusing Theme Parameters

If you accidentally follow best practices guidelines instead, you may decide to use theme parameters instead of hard-coded colors—but what if the official list of theme parameters doesn't contain the color you're looking for with the semantic meaning you want to use it for? Naturally, you pick a different parameter that was designed for a completely different use case (like using background color theme parameters for font color), or you pick one of the internal ones, which are BY NO MEANS meant to be used by applications AT ALL! EVER! WE MEAN IT!

If you've picked a background color for your font and switch to HCB, and you see white text on a white background, then you were as successful as you can be! Bwahahahahaha!

Using (Generated) IDs in Selectors

When you need to reference an SAPUI5 view or control with a generated ID (like "`__xmlview1`") that's somewhere deep down in your application, check out its generated ID in the developer tools and use that generated ID in your CSS selector. You can apply whatever style you want to it, of course; after all, you used its ID, so the style can't possibly be applied to other elements, right?

When you see the same style you wanted to apply to one control or view popping up arbitrarily for other specimens of views or controls within your app, possibly depending on how you accessed the app (deep link vs. navigation), then you've done everything right.

Should SAPUI5 decide to change its ID-generating mechanism, your styling will end up in CSS nirvana, so another good measure of success is not seeing your styles anymore at all after an upgrade.

Never Namespace

Don't bother to namespace your style in any way. If you've added some really beautiful styling to your application, why not let the other, uglier apps around you benefit from your taste? You can nicely overstyle these other applications through a combination of DOM element selectors, maybe with simple class names (our favorites are `.red`, `.green`, and `.button`), along with no namespacing to prevent other apps from applying their own styles without interference from your CSS. Keep your CSS as general as possible, and all apps successively loaded in the same container as your app will be much prettier thanks to their new layout!

If you see your particular styles popping up in every other app loaded into, say, SAP Fiori Launchpad after your app, then you know you were successful, and they will all love you for it!

12.1.2 Ignoring General Rules in SAPUI5 Application Development

For those of you thinking "rules are meant to be broken," take a nice long look at this section.

Hard-Code or Concatenate Strings That Need to Be Translatable

If you need to use strings for things like titles and labels in your app, don't waste your time using a resource model for these texts. You can rely on the fact that most people who are interested in your app either speak [YOUR FAVORITE LANGUAGE HERE] or otherwise aren't in your target group. If they were, they would learn [YOUR FAVORITE LANGUAGE], right?

What's more, when you need to combine text with a value from a different model, don't bother using a text with a placeholder from the i18n properties file. Instead, concatenate several texts and put any dynamic texts from some business model somewhere, together with the necessary punctuation. If someone really wants to translate your app, he can choose the texts in such a way that they'll fit into this structure, regardless of their reading/writing direction!

When you switch to a different language and still see your language of choice, or when you see translated texts and the order of concatenated texts doesn't make any sense in the other language, or when you switch to a language using a right-to-left direction and your text insists on being structured in the same order it required in English, you know you've been successful!

Ignoring Text Directions

You can even go one step further in ignoring text directions: Ignore them for all styles and any order of elements! For instance, you could make sure that CSS for margins or paddings from a label to an input is only, and we mean only, applied to the right-hand border of the label.

When you have labels and inputs in your apps that are reversed when switched from right-to-left, the label will have a nice, clean margin on the right (your page border, let's assume), and your input will be neatly glued to the left border of your label (see Figure 12.1).

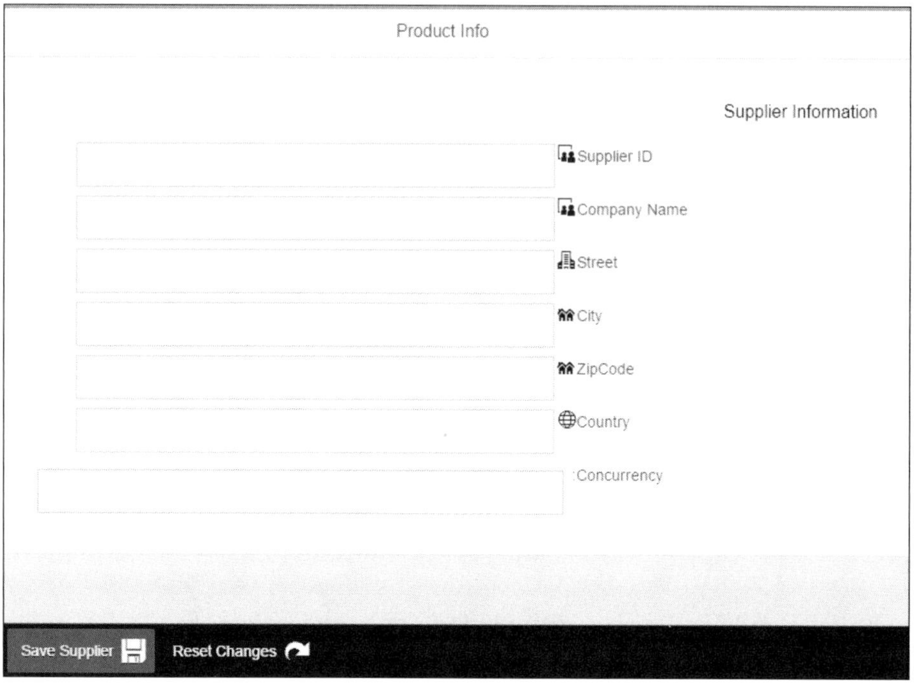

Figure 12.1 Right to Left Gone Awry

12.1.3 Performance Breakers

If you're looking to totally mess with your app's performance, you've come to the right place! The following subsections look at what you can do to slow and dumb down the performance of your apps.

Instantiate Everything, and Then Hide Half of It

This phrase is most probably one of the few ones in this book that's self-explanatory. Poor-performance-wise, it's a great idea to produce twice as many controls as there will ever be on screen concurrently—and then hide half of them away because they're not needed currently. This may break the performance of your app, but it'll speed up the developer—and after all, that's performance too, right?

It's easy to tell if you succeeded: Your app takes 10 seconds to load and you see the busy indicator (see Figure 12.2) forever; at least, it feels like forever.

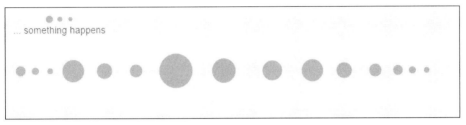

Figure 12.2 Busy Indicator Sample from Explored App

Loading Resources

Prevent asynchronous loading of libraries when your app starts. You need to prevent this loading by all means and only load the single files once they're needed. Someone talked about lazy loading in this book, so why not apply it here: Your performance will be all the "lazier" for it, because loading controls from libraries not declared as dependencies of your component causes each respective file to load in a synchronous request. So don't bother to write these dependencies into manifest.json; the libraries will load them when they need them.

Like instantiating everything and hiding half, when done correctly, this practice will make your app take forever to load. Oh, don't forget to check the console in the developer tools to watch all the nice, synchronous requests piling up in the NETWORKS tab.

12.2 How to Break your Apps during Updates

This section shows how to best make your apps break when someone runs them against the next SAPUI5 version. The hints given here will be helpful if you strongly dislike your teammates and you're leaving the team soon anyway.

There are no hints for how to know if you were successful for each practice, because it would be the same for all: If you were successful, your app will be broken after an update and will in the worst (or, for the purposes of our example, best) case resemble Figure 12.3.

Figure 12.3 Error Page in Google Chrome

12.2.1 Using Private and Protected Methods or Properties in SAPUI5

When you write your application code and you see that SAPUI5 has a method that you find useful, don't worry if it's labeled as private—or that its name starts with that underscore thingy. This just means the developers of the framework are jealous guys and want to keep these useful methods for themselves. It has nothing to do with the implementation that may change with every upgrade or patch of SAPUI5 because the names and existence of such methods are not part of the contract between SAPUI5 and its users. You can safely rely on these methods always being around and never changing their names or even the code inside them—after all, SAPUI5 claims to be backwards-compatible.

The same goes for properties at objects in the SAPUI5 libraries that start with one or two underscores in their name.

12.2.2 Using Deprecated or Experimental APIs

Using deprecated or experimental APIs is like using internal methods. If you've used a deprecated part of SAPUI5 and it's discontinued, you only need to complain to the SAPUI5 developers to support them again until you decide they should be dropped. Using an experimental API is also a nice idea; you can create precedents by doing so. After all, when enough people use an API, it can't be all that experimental anymore!

12.2.3   Extend SAPUI5 Controls

There are four steps to destroy your own controls during an SAPUI5 update:

1. First, extend a control from an SAPUI5 library.

2. Next, override the control methods—the public methods as well as the private ones. With your own control extension, you can do what you like.

3. Third, manipulate the inner DOM structure of the control however you'd like. Strip away elements you don't need personally, and add a few that look nice.

4. Fourth, with your own controls, you can completely forget about the control lifecycle, because it's only there for the "standard" SAPUI5 controls; you don't have to stick to it. Never destroy anything you've created, and make sure that you recreate most of the content of your control with each re-rendering.

12.3   Summary

This list of *don'ts* and *worst practices* is by no means meant to be exhaustive. If you're creative, you can come up with several new don'ts after you've read this book. We picked the ones that were either the most common or the most dangerous issues app developers introduced in their code. If you feel like we missed something important here, feel free to check out our repository, add your own don'ts to the list, and share them with other readers! We're looking forward to reading your stories! The URL for the list in the repository can be found in Appendix E.

This brings us to end of the last regular chapter in this book. Thank you very much for bearing with us until the bitter end; we hope you've enjoyed this journey. The three authors had a lot of fun writing it and hope we shared some of this fun and our own passion with you! All the best to you and to all the SAPUI5 apps you'll hopefully develop! Good luck!

Appendices

A   IDE Setup

For developing SAPUI5 applications, the SAP Web IDE currently has the best support and is the official IDE provided by SAP for SAPUI5 development. You can try out SAP Web IDE free of charge with a trial. All you need is a modern web browser to access this IDE. The Eclipse plugin for SAPUI5 development will not receive any further updates and their templates are quite outdated, so we highly recommend using the SAP Web IDE.

Feel free to use any other IDE of your choice—for example, WebStorm from Jet-Brains. WebStorm is a great IDE for JavaScript development that also has nice features like refactoring. We'll give you some tips and tricks about using WebStorm in Section A.2.

You could also use your favorite text editor, like Sublime or Atom. Code completion in JavaScript is a difficult topic, but there are parsers that can help—like Tern.js, which exists as a plugin for Sublime and Atom. However, the SAP-specific `sap.ui.define/require` syntax breaks those tools. One highlight to mention here from the user community is the tern-openui5 plugin by Timo Staudinger, which overcomes those issues. You can find tern-openui5 at *https://www.npmjs.com/package/tern-openui5*.

A.1   SAP Web IDE

The SAP Web IDE is a cloud-based development environment for SAPUI5 applications. You don't need to set up anything locally; all you need is a modern web browser to access the SAP Web IDE. The SAP Web IDE is part of the SAP HANA Cloud Platform (HCP), which is SAP's Platform as a Service (PaaS) offering. There is a trial version of SAP Web IDE available, which we use in this book. For productive usage, you need a productive account.

There is also a local trial version of the SAP Web IDE available, but we won't cover it in this book. As of the time of writing, there's no productive support for the local version. Stay up-to-date about the local trial version here: *http://scn.sap.com/docs/DOC-58926*.

> **Note**
>
> Learn more about the SAP Web IDE at *http://scn.sap.com/docs/DOC-55465* and in the free course "Build Your Own SAP Fiori App in the Cloud—2016 Edition" (see *https://open.sap.com/courses/fiux2*).

In this section, we'll walk through the steps to set up the SAP Web IDE for SAPUI5 applications.

A.1.1 Creating an Account on SAP HANA Cloud Platform

To begin our walkthrough, you'll need an account on the SAP HCP trial landscape. Proceed with the following steps:

1. Navigate to *https://account.hanatrial.ondemand.com/*. Click on REGISTER if you don't have an account, or click on LOGIN if you already have an account (Figure A.1), such as from the SAP Community Network (SCN).

Figure A.1 SAP HCP Trial Landing Page

2. If you select REGISTER, then you have to provide your name and email and choose your password, as shown in Figure A.2.

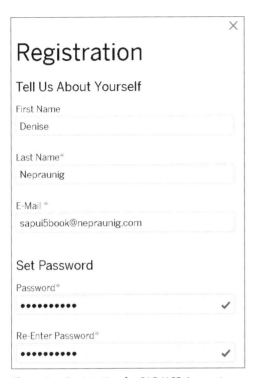

Figure A.2 Registration for SAP HCP Account

3. You should now see the success screen (Figure A.3); check your email (Figure A.4). Select CLICK HERE TO ACTIVATE YOUR ACCOUNT to successfully activate your account. Click on CONTINUE (Figure A.5).

Figure A.3 Successful Registration for SAP HCP

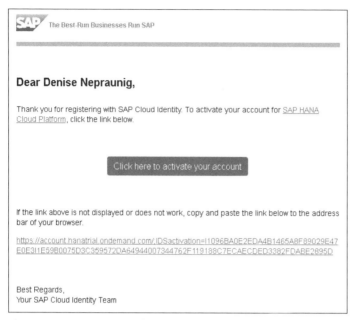

Figure A.4 Activation Email for SAP HCP

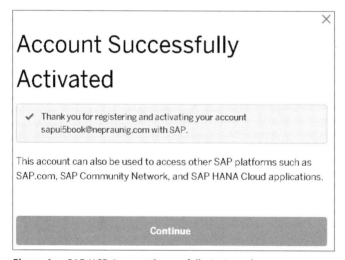

Figure A.5 SAP HCP Account Successfully Activated

In the SAP HCP cockpit, you'll see an overview of the different PaaS offerings from SAP, along with an overview of your JAVA or HTML5 applications (Figure A.6).

Within SAP HCP, it's possible to host HTML5 applications. Therefore, it's also possible to host SAPUI5 applications. Appendix C will explain how to deploy your SAPUI5 applications to SAP HCP.

Note

Learn more about SAP HCP in a free course on SAP HANA Cloud Platform Essentials (*https://open.sap.com/courses/hcp1*), the SAP Community Network page (*http://scn.sap.com/community/developer-center/cloud-platform*), or at *https://developers.sap.com*.

In the following subsections, we'll look at how to access SAP Web IDE in SAP HCP and how to use the different SAP Web IDE templates.

A.1.2   Accessing SAP Web IDE

Now that you've created or logged in to your SAP HCP account, you should find yourself in the SAP HCP cockpit (see Figure A.6).

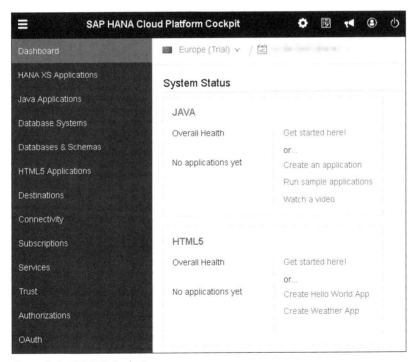

Figure A.6 SAP HCP Cockpit

We'll now access the SAP Web IDE via with the following steps:

1. On the left side of the SAP HCP cockpit, click on SERVICES. On the right side, click SAP WEB IDE (Figure A.7).

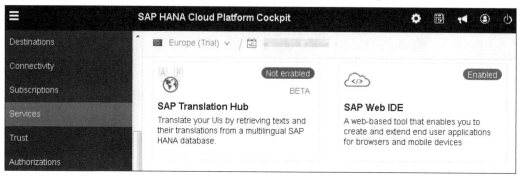

Figure A.7 Services in SAP HCP Cockpit

2. This opens up the dedicated service page of the SAP Web IDE (see Figure A.8). Here, click on the OPEN SAP WEB IDE link, which launches the SAP Web IDE in a browser tab (Figure A.9).

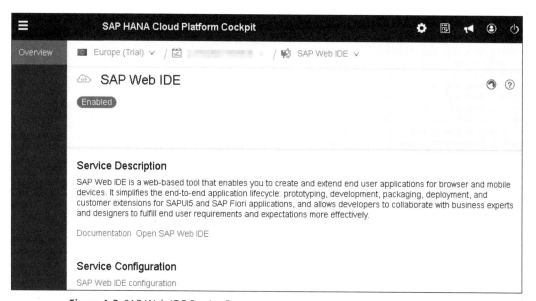

Figure A.8 SAP Web IDE Service Page

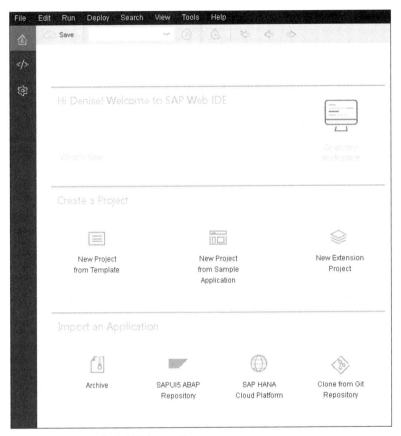

Figure A.9 SAP Web IDE Welcome Screen

You've officially accessed the SAP Web IDE welcome screen! Now, you can start working with the templates provided here.

A.1.3 SAP Web IDE Templates

One of the best features of the SAP Web IDE is the SAPUI5 application templates. In a click-through guide, you can choose your application style, such as master-detail or worklist (which you saw in Chapter 8); choose your backend connection; and wire certain UI fields to certain fields in your backend. With a few clicks, you have a fully functional and working SAPUI5 application which you can adapt further. There are also templates for smart templates available and a simple SAPUI5 Getting Started template with just one view.

First, we'll show you a simple Hello, World type of application and highlight the files that the template creates. Then, we'll show you how you can create a Worklist template with the Northwind service.

Simple SAPUI5 Application with Template

Let's create a simple SAPUI5 Hello, World application. Follow these steps:

1. From the welcome screen of the SAP Web IDE, choose NEW PROJECT FROM TEMPLATE, or select FILE • NEW • PROJECT FROM TEMPLATE from the menu.

2. On the next screen, select the SAPUI5 APPLICATION template tile and click on NEXT (Figure A.10).

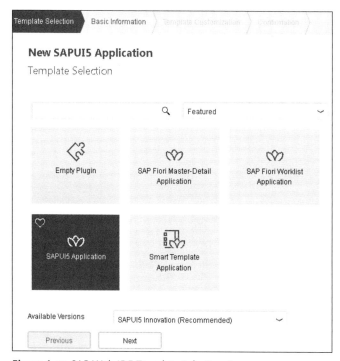

Figure A.10 SAP Web IDE Template Selection Screen

3. On the BASIC INFORMATION screen, choose the PROJECT NAME and NAMESPACE (Figure A.11) of the project and click on NEXT. PROJECT NAME will be the name of the project folder in the workspace and also the name of the application when deployed. NAMESPACE will be the SAPUI5 namespace of the application.

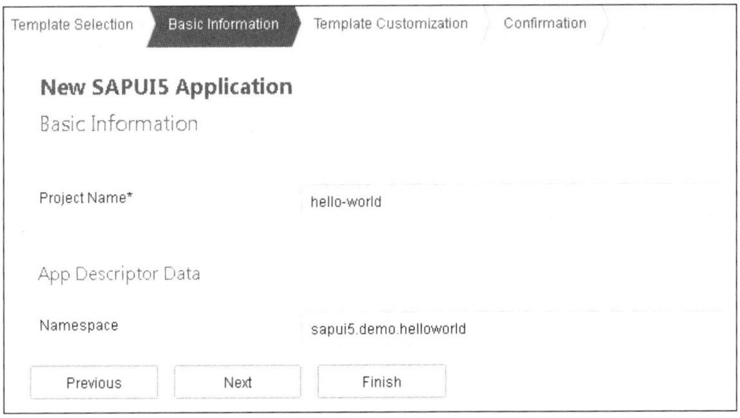

Figure A.11 Template: Basic Information

4. On the TEMPLATE CUSTOMIZATION screen, choose a name for the initial view (VIEW NAME) and the type (VIEW TYPE) and click on FINISH. Here, we've entered "XML" as the VIEW TYPE and "App" as the VIEW NAME (Figure A.12).

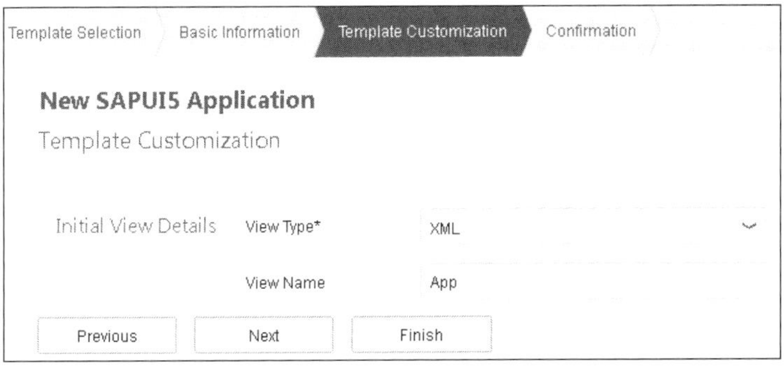

Figure A.12 Template Initial View Details

After the template creation finishes, you'll be in the SAP Web IDE workspace. There, you'll see the new HELLO-WORLD project (Figure A.13).

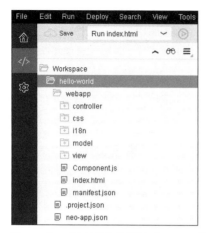

Figure A.13 SAP Web IDE Workspace with hello-world Project

The structure of the project should be familiar, expect for the *.project.json* and *neo-app.json* files, which are new. The project.json file is specific for SAP Web IDE and contains information such as which template was used. The neo-app.json file is specific for SAP HCP and is called the Application Descriptor, which contains, for example, a resource mapping to the SAPUI5 resources (Listing A.1). Therefore, index.html references to `src="../../resources/sap-ui-core.js"` instead of to a full URL to SAPUI5, like *https://sapui5.hana.ondemand.com/resources/sap-ui-core.js*.

> **Note**
>
> To learn more about neo-app.json (the Application Descriptor), navigate to *https://help.hana.ondemand.com/* and choose SAP HANA CLOUD PLATFORM • DEVELOP APPLICATIONS • HTML5: DEVELOPMENT • APPLICATION DESCRIPTOR FILE.

```
{   "routes": [{
      "path": "/resources",
      "target": {
        "type": "service",
        "name": "sapui5",
        "entryPath": "/resources"
    }, ...
```

Listing A.1 neo-app.json Resource Mapping

Let's quickly edit the *i18n.properties* file under *webapp/i18n* and change the value of `title` to `title=Hello World`. If you run the application (click on the green PLAY button shown in Figure A.13, or select RUN • RUN INDEX.HTML from the menu), you'll see the running application in a new browser tab (Figure A.14). The app doesn't look spectacular or fancy, but it's a good starting point for further development.

In the workspace (refer back to Figure A.13), you can perform all the actions you perform in any IDE, like editing files and copying and pasting files. The SAP Web IDE also has code completion capabilities for JavaScript and XML files built in. The XML code completion is available for properties (Figure A.15) and controls. For controls, there are also some neat snippets available (Figure A.16 and Figure A.17). There's also XML validation, which is handy if you forget to import a namespace or have syntax errors in your XML view.

Figure A.14 Running Hello World Application

Figure A.15 XML Property Code Completion

Figure A.16 XML Control Code Completion with Snippet Option

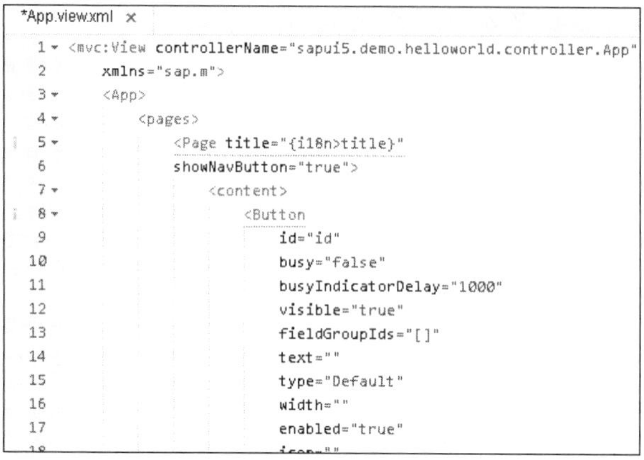

```
*App.view.xml  ×
  1 ▼  <mvc:View controllerName="sapui5.demo.helloworld.controller.App"
  2        xmlns="sap.m">
  3 ▼    <App>
  4 ▼      <pages>
  5 ▼        <Page title="{i18n>title}"
  6              showNavButton="true">
  7 ▼          <content>
  8 ▼            <Button
  9                  id="id"
 10                  busy="false"
 11                  busyIndicatorDelay="1000"
 12                  visible="true"
 13                  fieldGroupIds="[]"
 14                  text=""
 15                  type="Default"
 16                  width=""
 17                  enabled="true"
 18                  icon=""
```

Figure A.17 Snippet Added for Button

We've covered just a few highlights of the SAP Web IDE. Feel free to explore further the possibilities of the SAP Web IDE further on your own; we've only scratched the surface here to get you up and running.

Creating a Worklist SAPUI5 Application with a Template

Now, let's create a more sophisticated SAPUI5 application with a couple more views and fields. We'll choose the SAP Worklist application template with a back-end connection to the Northwind backend.

> **Setting Up the Backend Connection**
>
> We won't walk through the steps to set up the Northwind backend connection in this appendix; please refer to Appendix B for instructions.

Proceed with the following steps to start creating the worklist app:

1. In the TEMPLATE SELECTION screen of SAP Web IDE, select SAP FIORI WORKLIST APPLICATION and click on NEXT (Figure A.18).

2. Next, in the BASIC INFORMATION screen, give your project a name in the PROJECT NAME field. We've entered "worklist-demo" here (Figure A.19). Click on NEXT.

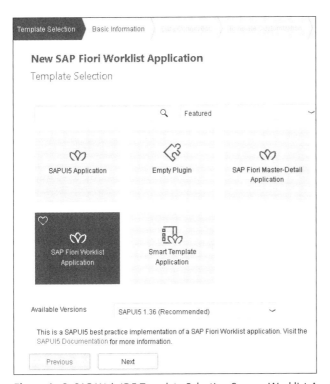

Figure A.18 SAP Web IDE Template Selection Screen: Worklist Application

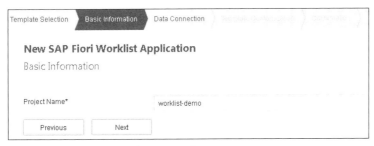

Figure A.19 Worklist Template Basic Information

3. On the DATA CONNECTION screen, under the SOURCES section, select SERVICE URL for the backend connection. In the SERVICE INFORMATION fields, enter the name of the service, "northwind," and the URL, *http://services.odata.org/V3/Northwind/Northwind.svc/*, and then click on the PLAY button so that you can see the entities of the service (Figure A.20).

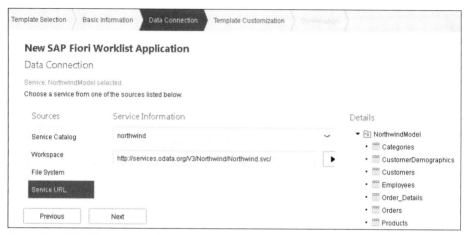

Figure A.20 Worklist Template Data Connection

4. Finally, configure the template and the fields you want to display (see Figure A.21).

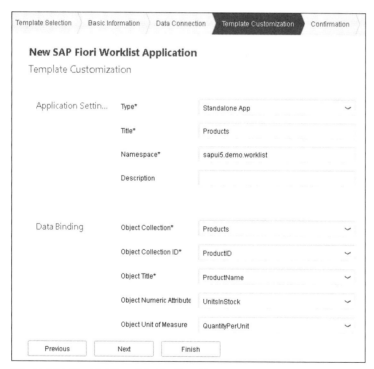

Figure A.21 Worklist Template Configuration

5. Then, click on the FINISH button and run the application.

Figure A.22 shows the first screen of the Worklist application; you can even navigate to the detail screen (Figure A.23). With just a few clicks, you have an app up and running that displays data from a backend. The application also contains unit tests and OPA tests.

Figure A.22 Running Worklist Template: Overview Screen

Figure A.23 Running Worklist Template: Detail Screen

Running the Worklist Template with Mock Data

Another great feature of the SAP Web IDE is the ability to run your application with mock data. If you don't have a backend connection, you also could choose a metadata.xml file from your workspace or another project, as in Figure A.20, via the WORKSPACE or FILE SYSTEM options. The SAP Web IDE template then provides the ability to run your application with the SAPUI5 mock server. You can see this option in the dropdown menu of the run configurations (Figure A.24). Chapter 11 covers the SAPUI5 mock server in greater depth.

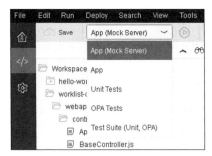

Figure A.24 Worklist Template Run with Mock Server

As of the time of writing, the template generates a *mockServer.html* file, which starts up the SAPUI5 mock server. Listing A.2 shows the startup code. When you run the application with the SAPUI5 mock server, you'll see some autogenerated data based on the data types of the fields of the service (see Figure A.25).

```
sap.ui.require([
        "sapui5/demo/worklist/localService/mockserver",
        "sap/m/Shell",
        "sap/ui/core/ComponentContainer"
], function(server, Shell, ComponentContainer) {
        // set up test service for local testing
        server.init(); ...
```

Listing A.2 Mock Server Startup in Worklist Template

←	Products	
Products (100)	Search	🔍
ProductName		UnitsInStock
ProductName 1	**6146.00** QuantityPerUnit 1	>
ProductName 10	**792.00** QuantityPerUnit 10	>
ProductName 100	**3655.00** QuantityPerUnit 100	>
ProductName 11	**1284.00** QuantityPerUnit 11	>

Figure A.25 Worklist Template Running with Mock Server

You can also provide your own mock data: Right-click on METADATA.XML and select EDIT MOCK DATA. This opens a handy editor to edit the mock data (Figure A.26). When you save the mock data, the data for the specific entity will be saved as *Entityname.json* (here, PRODUCTS.JSON) under a MOCKDATA folder (Figure A.27).

This is the same mechanism you'd see in place if you'd created a mock data file manually. When you run the application again with mock data, you'll see your own created mock data (Figure A.28).

Figure A.26 Edit Mock Data Dialog

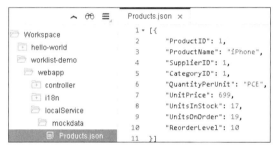

Figure A.27 Mock Data File for Products

Figure A.28 Worklist Template Running with Created Mock Data

A.2   WebStorm

According to JetBrains, WebStorm is the smartest JavaScript IDE and is perfectly equipped for client- and server-side development. Some of the primary benefits of WebStorm include the following:

▶ It includes all the latest frameworks, like Angular, React, and Meteor.

▶ It has a good code completion and offers refactoring features.

▶ It has built-in support for Grunt, Glup, or npm tasks. WebStorm does not support SAPUI5 out of the box, but we can configure it on a per-project basis to provide code completion for JavaScript files and for XML views.

You can download a 30-day trial version of WebStorm at *https://www.jetbrains.com/webstorm/*. For businesses and organizations, the yearly license is about $129, for individual customers it's $59, and there are also discounted licenses for startups available, as well as free licenses for students and teachers.

To make WebStorm work with SAPUI5, we need the OpenUI5 SDK. Keep in mind that OpenUI5 currently doesn't include any charts or smart controls. However, it's open source and we can use it for free. Proceed with the following steps:

1. Navigate to *http://openui5.org/download.html* and click on the DOWNLOAD OPENUI5 SDK button (Figure A.29). Extract the downloaded ZIP file to your machine.

Figure A.29 Download OpenUI5 SDK

2. Now, open WebStorm. We used WebStorm 2016.1.2 for this example. On the start screen, choose NEW PROJECT (Figure A.30), and then select EMPTY PROJECT (Figure A.31). Give the project a name, and then click on CREATE. We entered "sapui5-test". Now, you should see an empty project in your workspace (Figure A.32).

Figure A.30 Create New Project

Figure A.31 New Empty Project

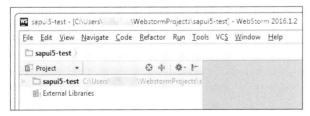

Figure A.32 Empty Workspace

3. Go to FILE • SETTINGSin the menu. In the SETTINGS dialog, chose LANGUAGES & FRAMEWORKS • JAVASCRIPT • LIBRARIES, then click on the ADD... button (Figure

A.33). In the NEW LIBRARY dialog, click on the green PLUS button (Figure A.34) and add the following two files (Figure A.35):

► Your OpenUI5SDK location/resources/sap-ui-core-all-dbg.js

► Your OpenUI5SDK location/resources/sap/m/library-all-dbg.js

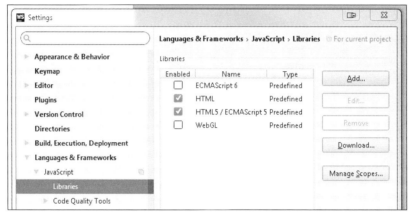

Figure A.33 Settings: JavaScript Libraries

Figure A.34 Add New Library

Figure A.35 Added Libraries

4. Here, we've chosen the VISIBILITY to be per PROJECT and entered "openui5" as the NAME. Click on OK in the NEW LIBRARY dialog and OK in the SETTINGS dialog to close the dialogs. The two files are now added as external libraries (Figure A.36).

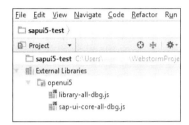

Figure A.36 External Libraries Added

5. Create a new file via the menu path FILE • NEW • FILE and give it the name "index.html". You'll find the source code of this file in the source code folder for this appendix at *www.sap-press.com/3980*. While you're typing in the source code (Listing A.3), you should see the code completion pop up (Figure A.37, Figure A.38, and Figure A.39). Press Ctrl+Space to manually trigger the code completion. The code in this section is only for demonstration purposes and does not represent a full application.

```
<script id="sap-ui-bootstrap"
  src="https://openui5.hana.ondemand.com/resources/sap-ui-
core.js" ... </script>
<script >
  sap.ui.getCore().attachInit(function() {
    var oApp = new sap.m.App();
    var oPage = new sap.m.Page();
    oPage.setTitle("Hello WebStorm");
    oApp.addPage(oPage);
    oApp.placeAt("content");
    var oModel = new sap.ui.model.json.JSONModel();
    oModel.setData({ test: true });
  });
</script>
```

Listing A.3 Demo Page for Code Completion

```
sap.ui.getCore().attachInit(function() {

    var oApp = new sap.m.App|
                    W    App (sap.m)
                    S    SplitApp (sap.m)
                    S    SplitAppMode (sap.m)
    });        Ctrl+Down and Ctrl+Up will move caret down and up in the editor >>

</script>
</head>
```

Figure A.37 Code Completion for Control

```
sap.ui.getCore().attachInit(function() {

    var oApp = new sap.m.App();
    var oPage = new sap.m.Page();
    oPage.setTi|
        m    setTitle(sTitle) (sap.m.Page)
        m    setTime([number] time) (Date)
```

Figure A.38 Code Completion for Method

```
oApp.addPage(oPage);
oApp.placeAt("content");

var oModel = new sap.ui.model.json.JSONModel();
oModel.setData
    m    setData([Object] oData, [boolean] bMerge = false) (sap.ui...
});      setLayoutData()
```

Figure A.39 Code Completion for JSON Model

If you want to use the code completion inside a Component.js file for the JSON model in which you've used the `sap.ui.define` syntax, then the code completion hints differ a bit (see Figure A.40 vs. Figure A.39). The data type could not be resolved correctly because of the SAP-specific `define` syntax, and therefore the (SEVERAL DEFINITIONS) hint pops up.

6. Now, set up the code completion for an XML file. First, you need to download two files:

▶ *https://openui5.hana.ondemand.com/downloads/schemas/sap.ui.core.xsd*

▶ *https://openui5.hana.ondemand.com/downloads/schemas/sap.m.xsd*

Keep in mind that this file location may change in the future and that it isn't officially documented at present. These XML schema files should exist for every library. You can also find these files in your OpenUI5 SDK by navigating to DOWNLOADS • SCHEMAS.

7. Next, create an XML view and set up the XML schema. You can use any view and create a new file inside your project. First, you'll see errors for the `sap.ui.core.mvc` and `sap.m` namespaces (Figure A.41).

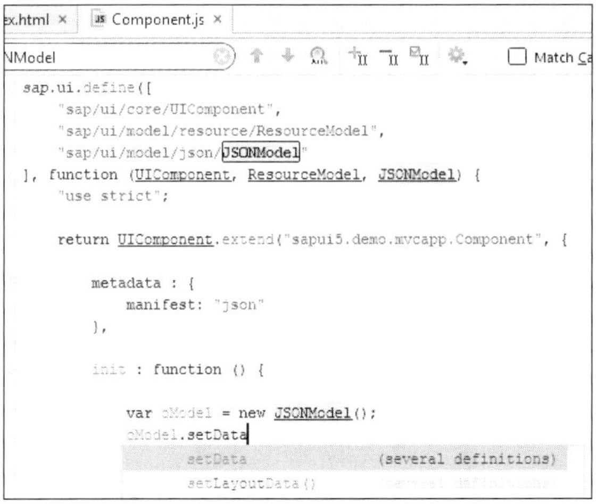

Figure A.40 Code Completion with sap.ui.define Syntax for JSON Model

Figure A.41 XML Namespace Error

8. Click inside the namespace (e.g., on SAP.M) and wait until the red light bulb appears (see Figure A.41). Hover over the light bulb and choose MANUALLY SETUP EXTERNAL RESOURCE from the dropdown menu (Figure A.42).

9. Select the sap.m.xsd.xml file that you have downloaded previously in the MAP EXTERNAL RESOURCE dialog and click on OK. Perform the previous step and this step again for the `sap.ui.core.mvc` namespace, mapping it to the sap.ui.core.xsd.xml file (see Figure A.43).

10. Place your cursor inside the PAGE tag and press ⎡Ctrl⎤+⎡Space⎤ to trigger the code completion. You should now see entries specific to `sap.m.Page`. Note that there are also some errors shown, like that the `controllerName` attribute isn't allowed here, or the same error for the `id` of the page or any other control (see these errors in Figure A.44).

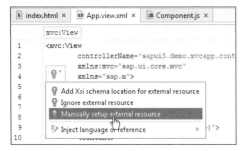

Figure A.42 Set Up External Resource for XML Schema

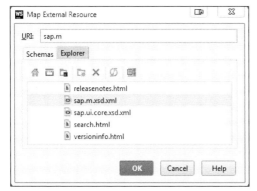

Figure A.43 Map External XML Schema

Figure A.44 XML Code Completion and Error

The code completion isn't perfect, but it's better than having no completion at all. Please keep in mind that the SAP community drives these code completion efforts for WebStorm and not by SAP itself; there is no official support for using WebStorm for SAPUI5 development.

Setting Up WebStorm

The following URL links to a great blog post by Robin van het Hof on how to set up WebStorm 9 for SAPUI5: *http://scn.sap.com/community/developer-center/front-end/blog/2014/09/22/configuring-jetbrains-webstorm-for-ui5-development*.

An additional blog post on performing further tweaks to WebStorm for SAPUI5 by Sergey Korolev can be found at: *http://scn.sap.com/community.developer-center/front-end/blog/2016/03/07/further-tweaking-of-jetbrains-webstorm-for-ui5-development*.

B   Accessing and Connecting to the Backend

When accessing the backend from your SAPUI5 application, you should be aware of the *same-origin policy*, an important web security concept. In this appendix, we'll look at the same-origin policy before diving into Google Chrome web security and SAP HANA Cloud Platform (HCP) destinations.

B.1   Same-Origin Policy

The same-origin policy prevents one web page from accessing data from another web page if the pages don't share the same origin. An *origin* is a combination of the URI scheme, hostname, and port number. Let's look at the same-origin policy example from Wikipedia (see *https://en.wikipedia.org/wiki/Same-origin_policy*).

As shown in Figure B.1, the first page has the URL *http://www.example.com/dir/page.html* and wants to access data from another URL. Microsoft Internet Explorer does not include the port when calculating the origin and is using its security zones instead.

Compared URL	Outcome	Reason
http://www.example.com/dir/page2.html	Success	Same protocol, host and port
http://www.example.com/dir2/other.html	Success	Same protocol, host and port
http://username:password@**www.example.com**/dir2/other.html	Success	Same protocol, host and port
http://www.example.com:**81**/dir/other.html	Failure	Same protocol and host but different port
https://www.example.com/dir/other.html	Failure	Different protocol
http://**en.example.com**/dir/other.html	Failure	Different host
http://**example.com**/dir/other.html	Failure	Different host (exact match required)
http://**v2.www.example.com**/dir/other.html	Failure	Different host (exact match required)
http://www.example.com:**80**/dir/other.html	Depends	Port explicit. Depends on implementation in browser.

Figure B.1 Same-Origin Policy Example[1]

---

1   Image Source: *https://en.wikipedia.org/wiki/Same-origin_policy*

When you're developing an SAPUI5 application with the SAP Web IDE, which is hosted in SAP HCP, and want to access data from the backend, you'll find that the backend doesn't have the same origin as the SAP Web IDE. Here are two URL examples for the SAP Web IDE and an SAP backend where you see that they don't have the same origin:

▸ SAP Web IDE URL:
  https://webide-usernametrial.dispatcher.hanatrial.ondemand.com/

▸ Backend URL:
  https://sapes4.sapdevcenter.com/sap/opu/odata/IWBEP/GWSAMPLE_BASIC/

In this example, you wouldn't be allowed to access the backend from within SAP Web IDE. If you develop an SAPUI5 application on a local computer and run it via a web server with a URL, like *http://localhost:port*, you'll run into the same problem. In addition, the same problem occurs if you host your SAPUI5 application as an HTML5 app on SAP HCP. Only an SAPUI5 app hosted on the backend system can access the data.

We'll illustrate this problem first as it would occur on a local machine. For this example, we prepared a simple backend written in PHP that can be hosted on any web hosting provider. The source code files for all examples are in the source code folder for this appendix at *https://www.sap-press.com/3980*. The backend for this example is in the no-cors.php file and has the following source code:

```
<?php
// returns {"products":10,"suppliers":3}
echo json_encode(array("products" => 10, "suppliers" => 3));
?>
```

We've hosted the backend on *http://nepraunig.com/sapui5book/backend/no-cors.php*, and the file returns a simple JSON structure, as shown in Figure B.2.

Figure B.2 Simple Backend

Let's look at the network trace for this URL and the response headers. Figure B.3 shows the network trace from Google Chrome. There is nothing special in this response header, butt keep it in mind, because we'll compare it later with another header when we talk about cross-origin resource sharing (CORS).

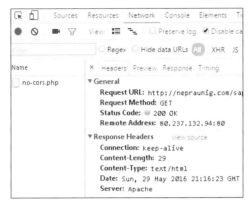

Figure B.3 Response Header for Simple Backend

If you wanted to access the data now from the server, you could make a GET request and use jQuery, which is included in SAPUI5. Listing B.1 shows such a request, which is from the no-cors.html file.

```
var sUrl = "http://nepraunig.com/sapui5book/backend/no-cors.php";
$.get(sUrl)
    .done(function(results) {
        alert("success");
        console.log("success", results);
    })
    .fail(function(err) {
        alert("error");
        console.log("error", err);
    });
```

Listing B.1 Accessing Data from Another Origin

When you run this example on your local machine, you'll see an error alert, because you're trying to access data from another origin. In this example, we're running on a local webserver. If we inspect the page in Google Chrome and look inside the console, we'll see an error message indicating that No Access-Control-Allow-Origin header is present on the requested resource; therefore, the local host is not allowed to access the data (see Figure B.4).

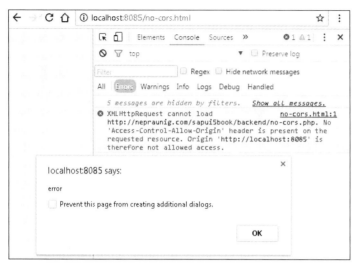

Figure B.4 Failing Request

One way to solve this problem is to use a CORS-enabled backend. This means that backend s explicitly allowed to access the data from such a backend from another origin. We've prepared such a backend for this book in PHP; Listing B.2 shows the source code from cors.php.

```php
<?php
header("Access-Control-Allow-Origin: *");
header("Access-Control-Allow-Credentials: true ");
header("Access-Control-Allow-Methods: OPTIONS, GET");
header("Access-Control-Allow-Headers: Content-Type, Depth, User-
Agent, X-File-Size,
    X-Requested-With, If-Modified-Since, X-File-Name, Cache-Control");
// returns {"products":10,"suppliers":3}
echo json_encode(array("products" => 10, "suppliers" => 3));
?>
```

Listing B.2 CORS-Enabled Backend

CORS

You can learn more about CORS at *https://developer.mozilla.org/en-US/docs/Web/HTTP/Access_control_CORS*.

The response from this CORS-enabled backend looks the same as in Figure B.2, but the response headers are different when you inspect the NETWORK trace in

Google Chrome, as shown in Figure B.5 (compare this with Figure B.3). The headers that we declared in Listing B.2 are returned as response headers.

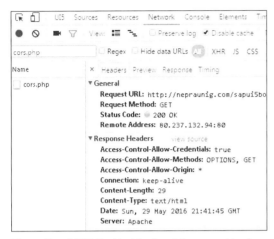

Figure B.5 CORS-Enabled Backend Response Headers

In the cors.html, the only change from Listing B.1 is that we use another URL:

```
var sUrl = "http://nepraunig.com/sapui5book/backend/cors.php";
```

With this CORS-enabled backend, we can now access the data and see it successfully logged to the console in Google Chrome (see Figure B.6).

Figure B.6 Successful Request to CORS-Enabled Backend

Normally, we can't change whether or not the backend is CORS-enabled. We used the previous examples to illustrate that some backends support CORS and others don't.

In the following sections we will see how we can overcome this problems with the same origin. First we will temporary disable the same-origin policy it inside

Google Chrome and next we will solve it permanently with the SAP HCP destination service.

B.2   Disable Web Security in Google Chrome

We can overcome same-origin-policy issues which prevents us from accessing data from a foreign origins with Google Chrome when we disable the web security via a command-line flag that looks like this:

```
--disable-web-security
```

As of Google Chrome version 49, the command-line flag has to look like this instead include the `--user-data-dir` parameter:

```
--disable-web-security --user-data-dir
```

For Microsoft Windows, you can change the target location for the shortcut to start Google Chrome via the following line of code (see Figure B.7):

```
"C:\Program Files (x86)\Google\Chrome\Application\chrome.exe" --
disable-web-security --user-data-dir
```

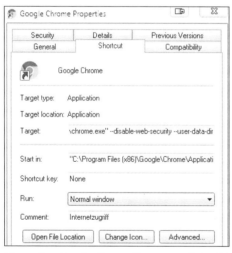

Figure B.7 Google Chrome Shortcut with Disabled Web Security

You must close all instances of Google Chrome and restart via the shortcut shown in Figure B.7 so that the parameters are taken into consideration. When you restart Google Chrome, you'll see a security warning, as shown in Figure B.8. If you try to access our simple backend again, which was not CORS-enabled, you can access it without any problems now, as shown in Figure B.8.

Figure B.8 Google Chrome with Disabled Web Security

When you don't want to fiddle around with the command-line flags for starting and restarting Google Chrome, we recommend a handy Google Chrome plugin called ALLOW-CONTROL-ALLOW-ORIGIN: *; you can find the plugin in the Google Chrome Web Store (see Figure B.9). You can then turn CORS on and off via the CORS symbol right to the URL bar (see Figure B.10).

Figure B.9 Allow-Control-Allow-Origin: * Plugin in Chrome Web Store

Figure B.10 Chrome Plugin to Toggle CORS

B.3   SAP HANA Cloud Platform Destinations

The plugin discussed in the previous section is a workaround during development, but when we want to access data in our running SAPUI5 application, we need another solution. Luckily, SAP HCP has such a solution in place: With the destination service, you can access data from foreign origins. SAP HCP then proxies your request, and the request is fired to the same origin from which your app is running.

However, if you run the previous example, no-cors.html, inside the SAP Web IDE on the cloud, then you'd face another issue: The backend URL is not served via HTTPS, but the SAP Web IDE URL is. The request is blocked because it mixes HTTP and HTTPS, as shown in Figure B.11.

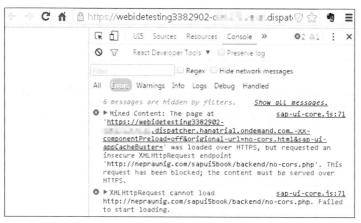

Figure B.11 Request Failing Due to Mixing HTTP and HTTPS

We can again overcome this issue with the destination from SAP HCP, and we'll create such a destination in this section. Begin by logging into the SAP HCP cockpit at *https://account.hanatrial.ondemand.com/cockpit*.

If you don't have access to SAP HCP, refer to Appendix A for instructions on how to set up an account. In the following subsections, we'll look at maintaining a connection to the backend via a simple backend destination, a Northwind destination, and an ES4 demo gateway destination.

B.3.1 Simple Backend Destination

For a simple backend destination, from the cockpit, choose DESTINATIONS on the left side, and click on NEW DESTINATION on the right. Click on the NEW PROPERTY button, then enter WEBIDEENABLED for the the ADDITIONAL PROPERTIES drop-down. You could also import the destination: It's called *simple-backend* and can be found in the source code for this appendix.

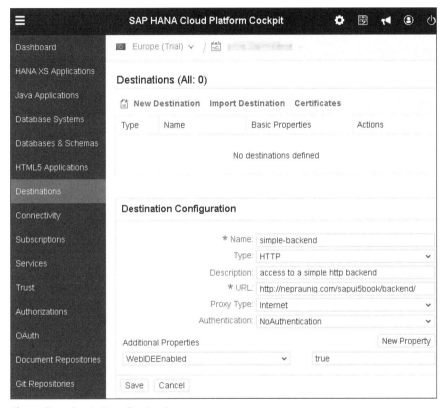

Figure B.12 Create New Destination

Open the SAP Web IDE—or restart it if it was already open, because the destinations are not automatically updated. In the workspace, right-click on the WORK-SPACE folder, choose NEW • FOLDER and enter "no-cors" for the FOLDER NAME. Right-click the new folder and create a new neo-app.json file with the content shown in Listing B.3.

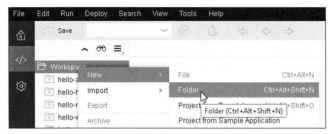

Figure B.13 New Folder in Workspace

Figure B.14 no-cors Folder Name

```json
{
  "welcomeFile": "/index.html",
  "routes": [{
    "path": "/resources",
    "target": {
      "type": "service",
      "name": "sapui5",
      "entryPath": "/resources"
    },
    "description": "SAPUI5 Resources"
  }, {
    "path": "/destinations/simple-backend",
    "target": {
      "type": "destination",
      "name": "simple-backend"
    },
    "description": "no cors backend"
  }],
  "sendWelcomeFileRedirect": true
}
```

Listing B.3 neo-app.json with Destination

Create an index.html file with the content shown in Listing B.4. This example is also in the source code for this appendix. Your project workspace should look like Figure B.15.

```html
<!DOCTYPE HTML>
<html>
<head>
  <meta http-equiv="X-UA-Compatible" content="IE=edge" />
  <meta charset="UTF-8">
  <title>Request to non CORS backend</title>
  <script id="sap-ui-bootstrap" src="/resources/sap-ui-core.js" data-sap-ui-theme="sap_bluecrystal">
  </script>
  <script>
    var sUrl = "/destinations/simple-backend/no-cors.php";
    $.get(sUrl)
      .done(function(results) {
        alert("success");
        console.log("success", results);
      })
      .fail(function(err) {
        alert("error");
        console.log("error", err);
      });
  </script>
</head>
<body class="sapUiBody" id="content">
</body>
</html>
```

Listing B.4 index.html File with Destination

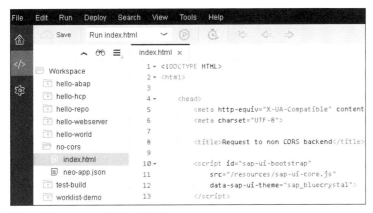

Figure B.15 no-cors Project Folder

In Listing B.3 and Listing B.4, notice that we included the `simple-backend` destination in manifest.json with the `/destinations/simple-backend` path, and in index.html, we're sending the request to `/destinations/simple-backend/no-cors.php`.

When you run the application now and inspect the network trace, you can see that the request to the backend has been sent via `/destinations/simple-backend` and that you were able to access the non-CORS and HTTP-only backend data inside SAP Web IDE (see Figure B.16).

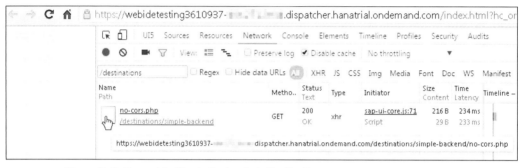

Figure B.16 Request to Simple Backend via Destination

B.3.2 Northwind Destination

In the same manner as we have maintained a simple backend connection as a destination in the SAP HCP cockpit, we can also maintain the connection to the Northwind service, which we discussed back in Chapter 7. Table B.1 lists the relevant parameters for the destination; you could also import the destination. We have named it `northwind`, and you'll find it in the downloaded content for this appendix. Figure B.17 shows the two maintained destinations.

Destination Settings for On-Premise Backend	
NAME	simple-backend
TYPE	HTTP
DESCRIPTION	Northwind OData Service
URL	http://services.odata.org

Table B.1 Destination Settings for Connecting to Northwind Backend

PROXY TYPE	INTERNET
AUTHENTICATION	NOAUTHENTICATION
Additional Destination Settings	
WebIDEEnabled	True
WebIDESystem	Northwind

Table B.1 Destination Settings for Connecting to Northwind Backend (Cont.)

Figure B.17 Two Destinations: simple-backend and northwind

Note

For a blog post about the Northwind connection for SAP Web IDE, visit *http://scn.sap.com/community/developer-center/front-end/blog/2014/07/07/how-to-use-northwind-odata-service-with-sap-river-rde*.

For a blog post about connecting to a remote system in SAP Web IDE, visit *http://scn.sap.com/community/developer-center/front-end/blog/2015/02/11/set-up-your-sap-web-ide-on-hana-cloud-part-3*.

In Appendix C, you'll learn how to maintain a destination for an on-premise backend connected via the SAP HANA Cloud Connector. You'll also learn how to deploy an application to SAP HCP. We want to show here that when your no-cors application is deployed, the required destination for the application is also listed as a required destination in the applications page (see Figure B.18). Feel free to deploy the application after you've read through Appendix C.

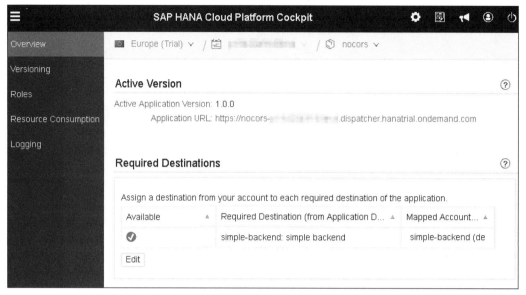

Figure B.18 Required Destination for Application

B.3.3 ES4 Demo Gateway Destination

There is also a demo SAP Gateway system available on the Internet, which you can access via the destination service. Table B.2 shows the necessary settings, and we've also included the *es4* destination file in the source code for this appendix for you to import.

Destination Settings for On-Premise Backend	
NAME	es4
TYPE	HTTP
DESCRIPTION	ES4 Demo Gateway
URL	*https://sapes4.sapdevcenter.com:443*
PROXY TYPE	INTERNET
AUTHENTICATION	BASICAUTHENTICATION
USER	Your username
PASSWORD	Your password

Table B.2 Destination Settings for Connecting to ES4 Demo Gateway

Additional Destination Settings	
WEBIDEENABLED	True
WEBIDEUSAGE	odata_abap
WEBIDESYSTEM	es4

Table B.2 Destination Settings for Connecting to ES4 Demo Gateway (Cont.)

Additional Information
For more information on the ES4 gateway connection for the SAP Web IDE, check out the blog post at *http://scn.sap.com/community/developer-center/front-end/blog/2014/06/22/how-to-configure-an-external-gw-system-with-sap-river-rde*.

C   App Deployment

After you've finished your application, you'll want to deploy it so that your users can begin using it. You have various options when deploying SAPUI5 applications, which we'll walk through in this appendix.

C.1   SAP HANA Cloud Platform

The easiest option is to deploy your application to the SAP HANA Cloud Platform (HCP), SAP's Platform as a Service (PaaS) offering. In SAP HCP, your application is hosted as an HTML5 application. SAP HCP acts like a web server in this case. The version management of the application is technically realized via a Git repository from which you can easily switch between the different versions of your application. You can directly deploy your application to SAP HCP from within the SAP Web IDE.

Let's start the SAP Web IDE and create a simple Hello, World like application. To review the basic steps of creating the app, refer back to Appendix A, then proceed with the following steps:

1. Call the app *hello-hcp*, and change the app `title` to *Hello HCP* in the i18n.properties file. Select your app folder, and then in the menu choose Deploy • Deploy to SAP HANA Cloud Platform (see Figure C.1).

Figure C.1 Deploy Application to SAP HCP

2. In the Deploy Application to SAP HANA Cloud Platform popup (see Figure C.2), you can specify an Application Name, a Version number (which is technically a Git tag), and whether or not the version should be active (with the Activate checkbox). We'll come back to versions later when to deploy an updated version of the application. Now, click on Deploy to deploy your application.

C | App Deployment

Figure C.2 Deploy Application to SAP HCP Settings

3. If the deployment was successful, you should see a popup (see Figure C.3) from which you can access the active version of the application and the application's page on the SAP HCP cockpit.

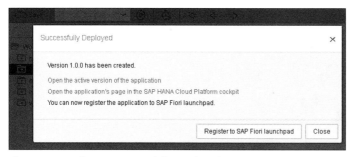

Figure C.3 Application Successfully Deployed to SAP HCP

4. Click on the OPEN THE ACTIVE VERSION OF THE APPLICATION link. A new browser tab will open, and there you'll see the running application (see Figure C.4). In the URL of the application, you'll notice that after *https://* comes your application

name, a hyphen, and your username, followed by DISPATCHER.HANATRIAL.ONDE-MAND.COM, which indicates that your app is running on the trial landscape of SAP HCP. An example URL looks like this: *https://appname-username.dispatcher.hanatrial.ondemand.com/index.html*.

Figure C.4 Application Running on SAP HCP

5. Returning to Figure C.3, click on OPEN THE APPLICATION'S PAGE IN THE SAP HANA CLOUD PLATFORM COCKPIT link. A new tab will open in which you can see the dedicated application page (see Figure C.5) inside the SAP HCP cockpit. On this application page, you can see the APPLICATION NAME, the APPLICATION URL, the ACTIVE APPLICATION VERSION, and if the application has STARTED.

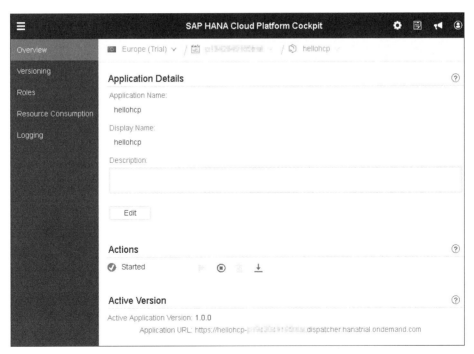

Figure C.5 Application Page in SAP HCP Cockpit

6. In the LOGGING menu entry on the left, you can check error logs for your application (Figure C.6); in RESOURCE CONSUMPTION, you can see some Git and network statistics (Figure C.7). We don't cover the ROLES option here, because roles are specific to SAP HCP.

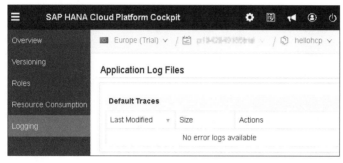

Figure C.6 Application Log in SAP HCP Cockpit

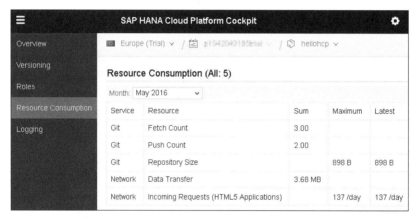

Figure C.7 Application Resource Consumption in SAP HCP Cockpit

7. Click on your user name for an OVERVIEW of all your HTML applications (see Figure C.8). You'll see a list with all the running apps (Figure C.9) and their active version by clicking VERSIONING. If you click on DASHBOARD in Figure C.10 you'll end up in the SAP HCP cockpit, where you'll also see the number of running HTML5 applications under the SYSTEM STATUS heading.

Figure C.8 Click on User Name for HTML Application Overview

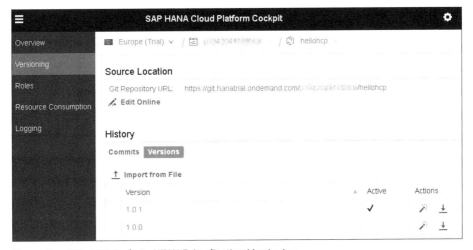

Figure C.9 SAP HCP Cockpit: HTML5 Application Versioning

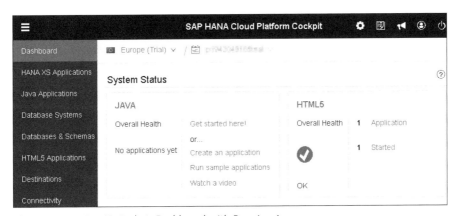

Figure C.10 SAP HCP Cockpit Dashboard with Running Apps

8. Now, switch back to the SAP Web IDE and change the application title to *Hello HCP Update*. Select the application folder, and then choose DEPLOY • DEPLOY TO SAP HANA CLOUD PLATFORM in the menu. In the DEPLOY APPLICATION TO SAP HANA CLOUD PLATFORM popup (see Figure C.11), you'll see that the UPDATE AN EXISTING APPLICATION radio button is selected, and the new version is prefilled as 1.0.1. Click on DEPLOY.

Figure C.11 Deploy Updated Application to SAP HCP

9. When the application is successfully deployed, you'll see the same SUCCESS-FULLY DEPLOYED popup as before (refer back to Figure C.3), and you can check the updated application via the OPEN ACTIVE VERSION OF THE APPLICATION link. If the application has not updated, clear your browser cache and refresh.

10. Now, check the application page again in the SAP HCP cockpit. Click on OPEN THE APPLICATION'S PAGE IN THE SAP HANA CLOUD PLATFORM COCKPIT in the SUCCESSFULLY DEPLOYED popup.

11. Click on the VERSIONING entry on the left (Figure C.12). From there, you can see the Git URL of your application; remember that versions are handled via Git. When you click on VERSIONS under the HISTORY heading (see Figure C.12), you'll see the two different versions of the application. The active version is indicated with a checkmark in the ACTIVE column. You can activate another version by clicking on the magic wand in the ACTIONS column (Figure C.13). You might do this if you think you may have introduced a bug in your current version and want to switch back to an old version quickly. We did not change the active version in our example.

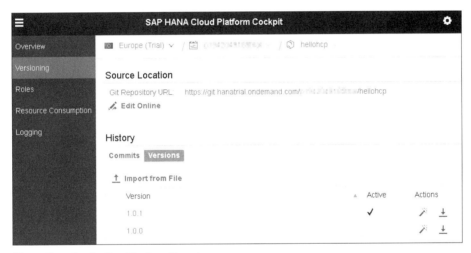

Figure C.12 Application Versions Overview

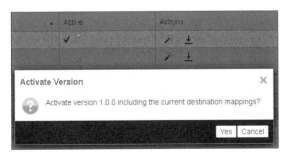

Figure C.13 Activate Particular Application Version

12. Click on the version number to open the corresponding version of the application. The URL will contain an `hc_commitid` URL parameter with the Git commit ID. Such a URL would look like this:

```
https://appame-username.dispatcher.hanatrial.ondemand.com/
index.html?hc_commitid=94f44412d2801f5009cba71981236f07f3ea8eb5
```

13. If you see the wrong version, then clear your browser cache or open the developer tools and make sure that the DISABLE CACHE (WHILE DEVTOOLS IS OPEN) checkbox is selected in Google Chrome.

14. In the application page in the SAP HCP cockpit, click on the OVERVIEW entry on the left (refer back to Figure C.5), and then click on the APPLICATION URL listed under the ACTIVE VERSION heading. Open the Google Chrome developer tools, refresh the page, and inspect the NETWORK trace. There, you can see that the minified version of your application is loaded, because Component-preload.js was loaded instead of all the separate view and controller files (see Figure C.14). The translation files (i18n.properties), the style file (style.css), and the manifest.json file were loaded separately.

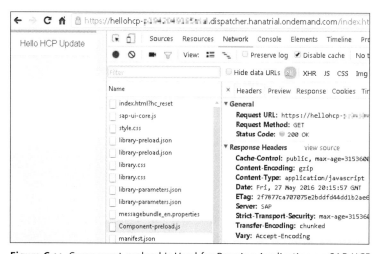

Figure C.14 Component-preload.js Used for Running Application on SAP HCP

15. If you switch back to the SAP Web IDE, you'll also notice the *dist* folder, which was created automatically when we deployed the app the first time (Figure C.15). The *dist* folder still contains all the files as a fallback option. If you open

the Component-preload.js file in the *dist* folder, you'll see which files have been packaged. We've included an excerpt in Listing C.1 and highlighted those files.

```
jQuery.sap.registerPreloadedModules({
"version": "2.0",
"name": "sapui5/demo/hellowebserver/Component-preload",
"modules": {
"sapui5/demo/hellowebserver/Component.js": ...
"sapui5/demo/hellowebserver/model/models.js": ...
"sapui5/demo/hellowebserver/view/App.view.xml": ...
"sapui5/demo/hellowebserver/controller/App.controller.js": ... } });
```

Listing C.1 Minified Component-preload.json from SAP Web IDE

Figure C.15 Application dist Folder in SAP Web IDE

16. The automatic build only works for apps created with the latest SAPUI5 application templates from SAP. However, you could also enable those build settings for previously created applications in the application settings. Right-click on your project folder and choose PROJECT SETTINGS (see Figure C.16).

Figure C.16 Project Settings for SAPUI5 Application

17. Here, under the PROJECT TYPES options (see Figure C.17), select the SAPUI5
CLIENT BUILD and SAP FIORI checkboxes. After making this selection, you'll see
the BUILD CONFIGURATION option (Figure C.18) where you can configure the
build settings.

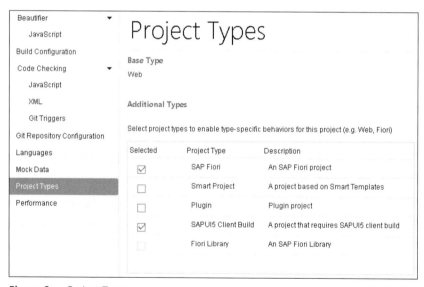

Figure C.17 Project Types

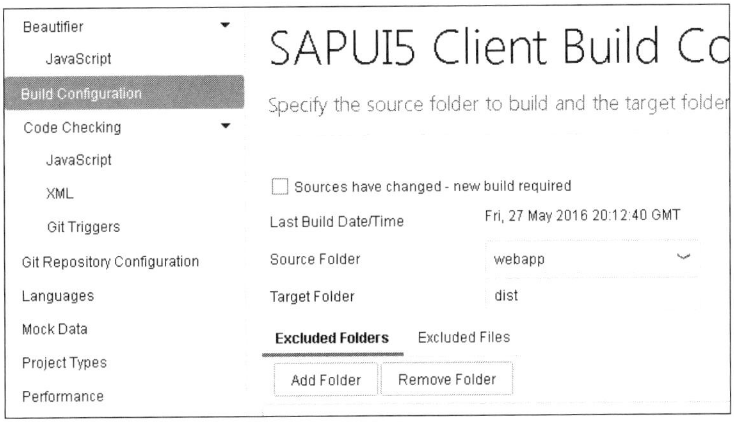

Figure C.18 Build Configuration

C.2   SAP Web IDE and SAP HANA Cloud Connector

Because the SAP Web IDE is hosted in the cloud and your data is, in general, in an on-premise system in a corporate network, you need to establish a secure connection between the SAP Web IDE and your on-premise system to access the data. You need a secure connection not only for accessing data, but also for directly deploying your application from the cloud to your on-premise ABAP system. SAP provides a tool for that: SAP HANA Cloud Connector.

SAP HANA Cloud Connector is a lightweight, on-premise agent, and runs on commodity hardware (e.g., PC, Linux, OS X), so no special hardware is needed. It establishes a secure SSL/TSL tunnel from an on-premise system to SAP HCP. You don't need a VPN solution to establish this connection, only Internet access. You also don't have to touch any firewall settings, because the firewall is handled inside the SAP HANA Cloud Connector. The SAP HANA Cloud Connector supports the HTTP and RFC protocols. In addition, database access via Java Database Connectivity (JDBC) is possible.

Figure C.19 shows an architectural overview of the SAP HANA Cloud Connector.

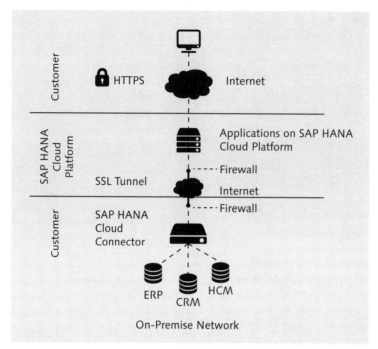

Figure C.19 SAP HANA Cloud Connector[1]

C.2.1 SAP HANA Cloud Connector Settings

We won't cover the detailed step-by-step installation and configuration of the SAP HANA Cloud Connector in this book. Instead, we'll guide you to the necessary resources so that you—or an admininstrator—can perform the necessary steps. What we will cover is how to maintain the destination for the on-premise system in the SAP HCP cockpit and how to consume the destination in the SAP Web IDE. Before exposing any on-premise system resources, you should always consult with your network and security colleagues.

To maintain the destination, proceed with the following steps:

1. Download the SAP HANA Cloud Connector from *https://tools.hana.onde-mand.com/#cloud*.

---

1 Source "Build Your Own SAP Fiori App in the Cloud, 2016 Edition" Open SAP Course, Week 1, All Slides, Page 33

2. There, you'll also find a link to the detailed installation guide with all the pre-requisites listed. There are two versions of the SAP HANA Cloud Connector: a *productive version* and a *developer version*. The developer versions do not include an installer; you just extract a ZIP file and run the file. The productive version starts the necessary services on your computer and is also upgradeable.

3. After you've downloaded and installed the SAP HANA Cloud Connector, you can access it via the information in Table C.1, as noted in the documentation.

Parameter	Value
URL	*https://localhost:8443/*
Username	Administrator
Password	Manage

Table C.1 Accessing SAP HANA Cloud Connector Locally

4. Choose MASTER as the installation type, because you're only running one SAP HANA Cloud Connector instance. When you first log in, you'll be asked to change your password (see Figure C.20).

Choose Installation Type
- Master (Primary Installation)
- Shadow (Backup Installation)

Apply

Figure C.20 Installation type of SAP HANA Cloud Connector

5. Next, connect your SAP HANA Cloud Connector to your trial account. Provide the mandatory settings in the initial configuration as shown in Table C.2.

Parameter	Value
LANDSCAPE HOST	*hanatrial.ondemand.com*
ACCOUNT NAME	Usernametrial
ACCOUNT USER	User
PASSWORD	your password

Table C.2 Initial Configuration Settings

6. When you're on a corporate network, you may need to provide additional proxy settings. After entering the necessary settings, click on the APPLY button (see Figure C.21).

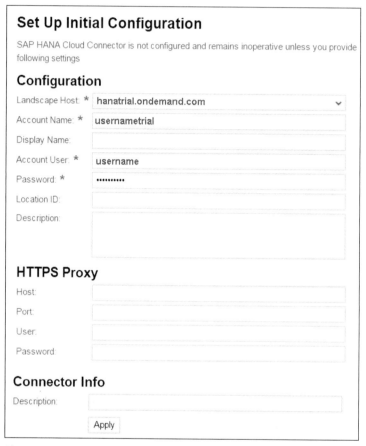

Set Up Initial Configuration

SAP HANA Cloud Connector is not configured and remains inoperative unless you provide following settings

Configuration

Landscape Host: *	hanatrial.ondemand.com
Account Name: *	usernametrial
Display Name:	
Account User: *	username
Password: *	••••••••••
Location ID:	
Description:	

HTTPS Proxy

Host:	
Port:	
User:	
Password:	

Connector Info

Description:	
	Apply

Figure C.21 SAP HANA Cloud Connector Initial Settings

7. You should see a successful connection to the SAP HCP trial instance now, as in Figure C.22. Click on ACCESS CONTROL on the left side of the screen. Next, click on the ADD button to add a new virtual mapping for an internal system.

Provide the information shown in Table C.3, depending on your backend system. We're using our internal SAP ABAP System GM6 as an example.

Figure C.22 Successful Connection from SAP HANA Cloud Connector to SAP HCP

Parameter	Value
VIRTUAL HOST	gm6.virtual
VIRTUAL PORT	44333
INTERNAL HOST	ldcigm6.wdf.sap.corp
INTERNAL PORT	44333
PROTOCOL	HTTPS
BACKEND TYPE	ABAP
PRINCIPAL TYPE	X.509 Certificate

Table C.3 System Mapping in SAP HANA Cloud Connector

8. After you provide a virtual host name and port for your real internal backend, you can decouple the real backend name from the virtual one. You can then use the virtual name in the SAP Web IDE, while the connection and ports to the real system could change. You wouldn't need to touch any code so long as you've referenced the virtual name. Now that you've created a virtual system, you can add a resource that will be accessible via SAP HANA Cloud Connector. Select the

virtual system and click on the ADD button in the RESOURCES ACCESSIBLE section. The ADD RESOURCE popup will appear (Figure C.23). When you add such a resource, it's explicitly whitelisted.

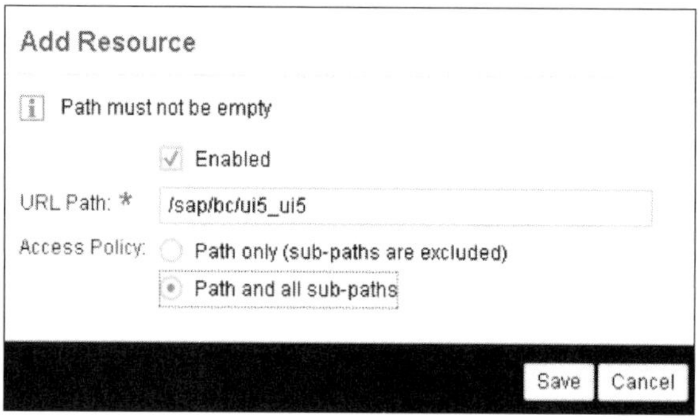

Figure C.23 Adding Resource to Virtual Host

Add the following URL paths, and select PATH AND ALL SUB-PATHS:

- /sap/bc/ui5_ui5
- /sap/opu/odata
- /sap/bc/bsp
- /sap/bc/adt

> **Note**
>
> Learn more about the SAP HANA Cloud Connector in the free SAP HANA Cloud Platform Essentials course, in week 3. See *https://open.sap.com/courses/hcp1/*.
>
> The following two URLs will point you to great blog posts by the SAP Technology Rapid Innovation Group (RIG) on how to set up the SAP HANA Cloud Connector and how to connect it to the SAP Web IDE:
>
> - *http://scn.sap.com/community/developer-center/front-end/blog/2015/02/11/set-up-your-sap-web-ide-on-hana-cloud-part-2*
> - *http://scn.sap.com/community/developer-center/front-end/blog/2015/02/11/set-up-your-sap-web-ide-on-hana-cloud-part-3*
>
> You can also find additional information about this topic in the SAP Web IDE Help at *https://help.hana.ondemand.com/webide/frameset.htm*; choose GET STARTED • OPTIONAL – CONNECTING REMOTE SYSTEMS.

C.2.2 Creating a New Destination in SAP HCP Cockpit

We're finished with the SAP HANA Cloud Connector settings; now, let's create a destination for your system in the SAP HCP cockpit. Proceed with the following steps:

1. Open the SAP HCP cockpit at *https://account.hanatrial.ondemand.com/cockpit* and select DESTINATIONS on the left side. Click on NEW DESTINATION (Figure C.24), and provide the settings from Table C.4. Notice that we're now using our virtual host name, *https://gm6.virtual:44333*, instead of the URL of the real backend, which is behind the corporate firewall. This is possible because of the SAP HANA Cloud Connector.

Figure C.24 Create New Destination in SAP HCP Cockpit

Parameter	Value
NAME	GM6
TYPE	HTTP
DESCRIPTION	GM6
URL	*https://gm6.virtual:44333*
PROXY TYPE	ONPREMISE
AUTHENTICATION	NOAUTHENTICATION

Table C.4 Destination Settings for Connecting to Backend

2. Click on the NEW PROPERTY button (Figure C.25) and provide the settings shown in Table C.5.

Figure C.25 Destination Configuration

Parameter	Value
WebIDEEnabled	true
WebIDEUsage	odata_abap,dev_abap,ui5_execute_abap,bsp_execute_abap
WebIDESystem	GM6

Table C.5 Additional Destination Settings

3. Click on the SAVE button to see the new destination, as shown in Figure C.26. The destination is now ready to be used to deploy an SAPUI5 application to the ABAP backend.

Figure C.26 New Destination Added

C.2.3 Creating an Application from a Template

You can also use this destination to access a gateway service from the backend. Let's open the SAP Web IDE and create a new application from a template, as we did in Appendix A when we created a worklist application with the Northwind backend. Proceed with the following steps:

1. Enter "onpremise-backend" as the PROJECT NAME, then click NEXT (Figure C.27).

Figure C.27 On-Premise Backend Application: Basic Information

2. On the DATE CONNECTION screen, select the GM6 backend and the RMTSAM-PLEFLIGHT service, then click NEXT (Figure C.28).

Figure C.28 On-Premise Backend Application: Data Connection

3. In TEMPLATE CUSTOMIZATION, provide the settings listed in Table C.6 (see also Figure C.29 and Figure C.30).

Parameter	Value
TYPE	STANDALONE APPLICATION
TITLE	Carrier
NAMESPACE	sapui5.demo.onpremise.backend
OBJECT COLLECTION	CARRIERCOLLECTION
OBJECT COLLECTION ID	CARRID
OBJECT TITLE	CARRNAME

Table C.6 Template Customization for On-Premise Backend Application

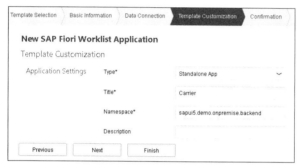

Figure C.29 On-Premise Backend Application: Application Settings

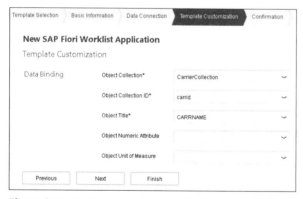

Figure C.30 On-Premise Backend Application: Data Binding

4. When you run the application now, you'll see that the data from the backend is displayed (Figure C.31). The backend connection is also listed in the neo-pp.json file, as shown in Listing C.2.

Figure C.31 Running On-Premise Backend Application

```
{  "path": "/sap/opu/odata",
   "target": {
     "type": "destination",
     "name": "GM6 ",
     "entryPath": "/sap/opu/odata"
   },
   "description": "GM6 "}
```

Listing C.2 Backend Connection in neo-app.json

It's also referenced in manifest.json as the data source, as shown in Listing C.3.

```
"dataSources": {
  "mainService": {
    "uri": "/sap/opu/odata/iwfnd/RMTSAMPLEFLIGHT/",
    "type": "OData",
    "settings": {
      "odataVersion": "2.0",
      "localUri": "localService/metadata.xml"
    } } }, …
```

Listing C.3 Backend Connection in manifest.json

C.3   ABAP Server

Now that we've set up the SAP HANA Cloud Connector, we can directly deploy the application to an ABAP system. If you didn't set the connector up, there's an alternative; you can also download the application from the SAP Web IDE as a ZIP file and import it into the ABAP system via the report /UI5/UI5_REPOSITORY_ LOAD.

In this section, we'll provide instructions for both scenarios: deployment via the SAP HANA Cloud Connector and via report /UI5/UI5_REPOSITORY_LOAD.

C.3.1 Deployment via SAP HANA Cloud Connector

In this section, we'll explain how to deploy an app via the SAP HANA Cloud Connector. Proceed with the following steps:

1. Quickly create a Hello, World like application like we did for SAP HCP in Appendix C, Section C.1 for deployment into the ABAP system. This app does nothing more than display HELLO ABAP, as shown in Figure C.32.

Figure C.32 Running Hello ABAP Application in SAP Web IDE

2. Select the application in the workspace and choose DEPLOY • DEPLOY TO SAPUI5 ABAP REPOSITORY (Figure C.33). In the popup that opens (Figure C.34), choose your backend system, make sure that DEPLOY A NEW APPLICATION is selected, and click on NEXT.

Figure C.33 Deploy to SAPUI5 ABAP Repository

Figure C.34 Deploy New Application to ABAP

3. Provide a NAME, DESCRIPTION, and PACKAGE (Figure C.35). Note that we've chosen a name that does not start with Z or Y (customer namespace), because we're deploying to an SAP internal system. We have selected the $TMP package, because we don't want to transport the application to another system. Click on NEXT, and on the confirmation screen (Figure C.36), click on FINISH.

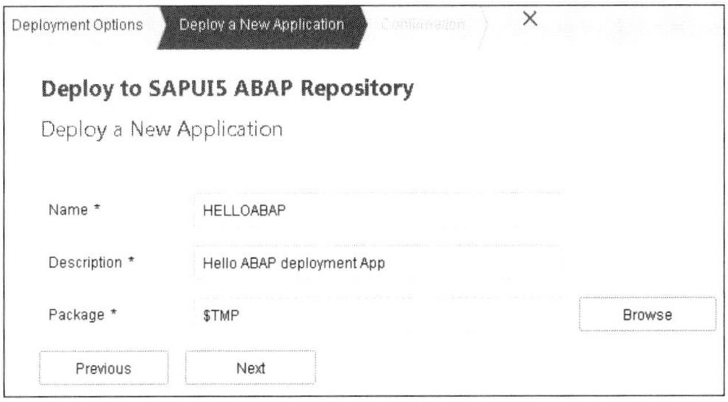

| Deployment Options | Deploy a New Application | Confirmation | ✕ |

Deploy to SAPUI5 ABAP Repository

Deploy a New Application

Name *	HELLOABAP	
Description *	Hello ABAP deployment App	
Package *	$TMP	Browse
Previous	Next	

Figure C.35 Choosing Name, Description, and Package for ABAP Deployment

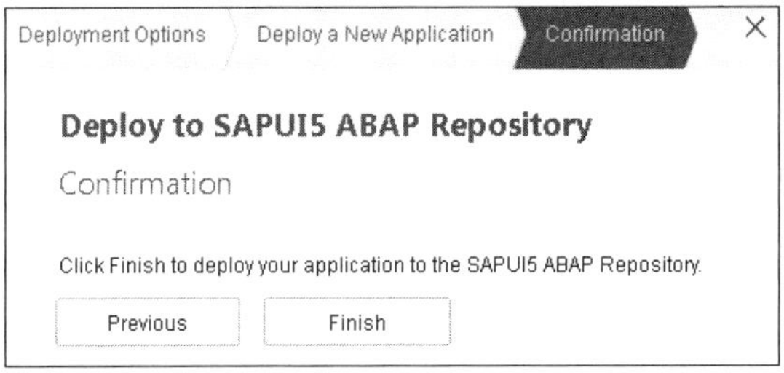

| Deployment Options | Deploy a New Application | Confirmation | ✕ |

Deploy to SAPUI5 ABAP Repository

Confirmation

Click Finish to deploy your application to the SAPUI5 ABAP Repository.

| Previous | Finish |

Figure C.36 Confirmation of Deployment to ABAP

Now, you'll see progress information in the top-right corner of the SAP Web IDE (Figure C.37). You can also check the deployment progress in the SAP Web IDE console.

Figure C.37 Deployment in Process

4. Choose VIEW • CONSOLE (Figure C.38) in the menu to see your deployed artifacts, as in Figure C.39.

File
Edit
Run
Deploy
Search
View
Tools
Help
Save
Workspace
hello-abap
hello-world
Unlink Workspace from Editor
Maximize Active Editor Ctrl+M
Problems Ctrl+Alt+P
Show Hidden Files
Console Ctrl+Shift+M
Clear Console

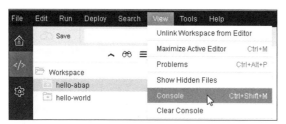

Figure C.38 SAP Web IDE View Console

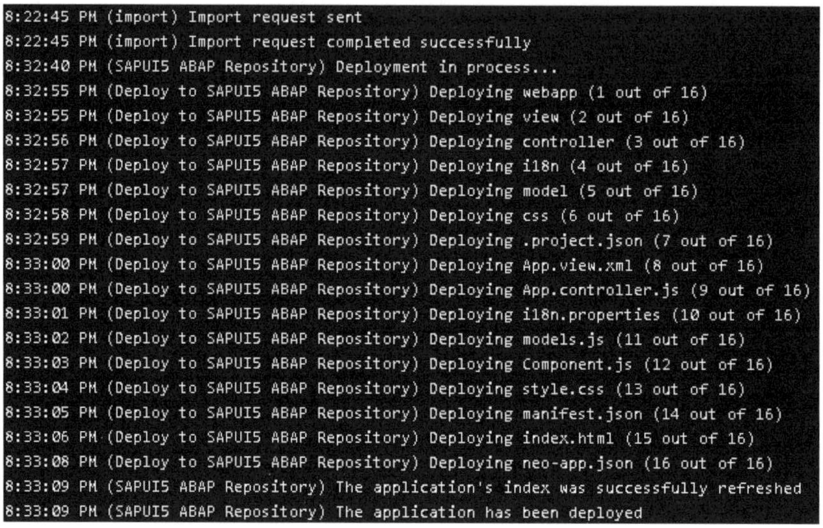

8:22:45 PM (import) Import request sent
8:22:45 PM (import) Import request completed successfully
8:32:40 PM (SAPUI5 ABAP Repository) Deployment in process...
8:32:55 PM (Deploy to SAPUI5 ABAP Repository) Deploying webapp (1 out of 16)
8:32:55 PM (Deploy to SAPUI5 ABAP Repository) Deploying view (2 out of 16)
8:32:56 PM (Deploy to SAPUI5 ABAP Repository) Deploying controller (3 out of 16)
8:32:57 PM (Deploy to SAPUI5 ABAP Repository) Deploying i18n (4 out of 16)
8:32:57 PM (Deploy to SAPUI5 ABAP Repository) Deploying model (5 out of 16)
8:32:58 PM (Deploy to SAPUI5 ABAP Repository) Deploying css (6 out of 16)
8:32:59 PM (Deploy to SAPUI5 ABAP Repository) Deploying .project.json (7 out of 16)
8:33:00 PM (Deploy to SAPUI5 ABAP Repository) Deploying App.view.xml (8 out of 16)
8:33:00 PM (Deploy to SAPUI5 ABAP Repository) Deploying App.controller.js (9 out of 16)
8:33:01 PM (Deploy to SAPUI5 ABAP Repository) Deploying i18n.properties (10 out of 16)
8:33:02 PM (Deploy to SAPUI5 ABAP Repository) Deploying models.js (11 out of 16)
8:33:03 PM (Deploy to SAPUI5 ABAP Repository) Deploying Component.js (12 out of 16)
8:33:04 PM (Deploy to SAPUI5 ABAP Repository) Deploying style.css (13 out of 16)
8:33:05 PM (Deploy to SAPUI5 ABAP Repository) Deploying manifest.json (14 out of 16)
8:33:06 PM (Deploy to SAPUI5 ABAP Repository) Deploying index.html (15 out of 16)
8:33:08 PM (Deploy to SAPUI5 ABAP Repository) Deploying neo-app.json (16 out of 16)
8:33:09 PM (SAPUI5 ABAP Repository) The application's index was successfully refreshed
8:33:09 PM (SAPUI5 ABAP Repository) The application has been deployed

Figure C.39 Console Output in SAP Web IDE

5. After the application has been deployed successfully, you can log in to your ABAP system and check the application. Go to Transaction SE80 or navigate manually to access the ABAP Workbench. In the ABAP Workbench, select Repository Browser and Local Objects, because we've deployed to the $TMP package (see Figure C.40). If you expand the HELLOABAP node, you'll see the URL of the application (bottom of Figure C.41), and you can copy and paste it to open it in your browser.

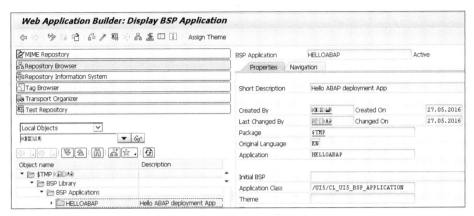

Figure C.40 Deployed SAPUI5 Application in ABAP Workbench: Transaction SE80

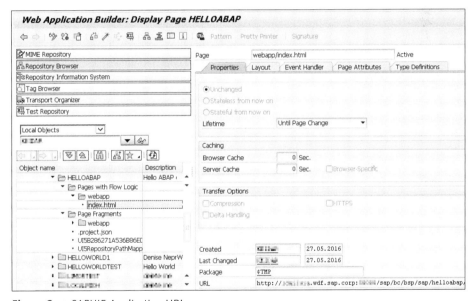

Figure C.41 SAPUI5 Application URL

SAPUI5 CDN

If you don't see a running application inside your browser after copying/pasting the application URL, then check the reference to `sap-ui-core.js` in the *index.html* file.

> **Note**
>
> Check the location of your sap-ui-core.js file in the ABAP system via the following URL:
>
> *http:///<HOSTNAME>:<PORT>/sap/public/bc/ui5_ui5* (Figure C.42)
>
> ---
>
> **SAP UI development toolkit for HTML5 from ABAP server**
>
> This Application provides a ready-to-consume version of SAPUI5.
> The SAPUI5 sap-ui-core.js bootstrap file is available at: /sap/public/bc/ui5_ui5/1/resources/sap-ui-core.js
>
> The following libraries are available:
>
> | Library | Version: none | Version: 1-next (1.38.4.201605280450) | Version: 1.30 (1.30.9) |
> |---|---|---|---|
> | META-INF | | | |
> | com.sap.apf.apf-lib | | 1.38.3.201605280246 | 1.30.9 |
> | com.sap.ca.scfld.md | | 1.38.1.201605280145 | 1.30.5 |
> | com.sap.ca.ui | | 1.38.1.201605280145 | 1.30.5 |

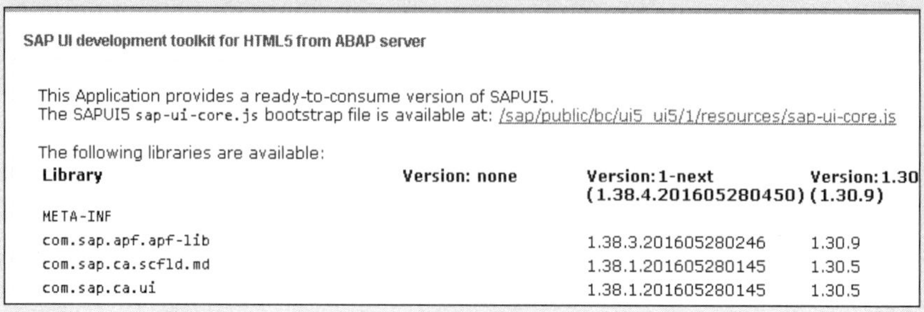

Figure C.42 SAPUI5 Version Overview in ABAP System

During the writing of this book, we encountered a problem: The paths in our deployed SAPUI5 application were not correct. To fix the problem, we changed the URL of the sap-ui-core.js file to *https://sapui5.hana.ondemand.com/resources/sap-ui-core.js*, which is the public version of SAPUI5 delivered via a CDN, as shown in Figure C.43.

Page	webapp/index.html		Active
Properties	Layout	Event Handler	Page Attributes	Type Definitions

```
 1   <!DOCTYPE HTML>
 2   <html>
 3
 4     <head>
 5       <meta http-equiv="X-UA-Compatible" content="IE=edge" />
 6       <meta charset="UTF-8">
 7
 8       <title>hello-abap</title>
 9
10       <script id="sap-ui-bootstrap"
11         src="https://sapui5.hana.ondemand.com/resources/sap-ui-core.js"
12         data-sap-ui-libs="sap.m"
13         data-sap-ui-theme="sap_bluecrystal"
14         data-sap-ui-compatVersion="edge"
15         data-sap-ui-resourceroots='{"sap.ui.demo.helloabap": ""}'>
16       </script>
```

Figure C.43 Modifed URL for sap-ui-core.js via CDN

Learn more about multiversion and CDN availability of SAPUI5 at *http://scn.sap.com/ community/developer-center/front-end/blog/2015/07/30/multi-version-availability-of-sapui5*.

When the app is deployed and you want to consume it via the SAP Fiori Launchpad, you don't need the HTML file and don't need to worry about the correct URL of the sap-ui-core.js file in the HTML file.

C.3.2 Deployment via Report /UI5/UI5_REPOSITORY_LOAD

As previously mentioned, it's also possible to manually upload an SAPUI5 application into the ABAP application server. Create a simple hello-repo application, as in the previous sections. Next, export the application from the SAP Web IDE. Proceed with the following steps:

1. Right-click the application folder in the workspace and choose EXPORT (Figure C.44).

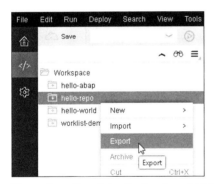

Figure C.44 Export Application from SAP Web IDE

2. The popup asks you if you want to save the ZIP file (Figure C.45). Download the ZIP file and extract it somewhere on your hard drive.

Figure C.45 Saving ZIP File from SAP Web IDE

3. Now, you can log into the ABAP system and go to Transaction SE38, or manually navigate to the ABAP Editor, where we'll run report /UI5/UI5_REPOSITORY_LOAD (Figure C.46). With this report, we can upload and download SAPUI5 applications, as well as delete them.

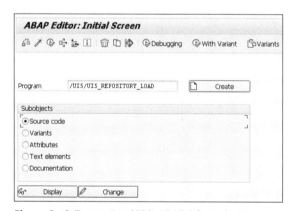

Figure C.46 Transaction SE38: ABAP Editor, /UI5/UI5_REPOSITORY_LOAD

4. When running report /UI5/UI5_REPOSITORY_LOAD via the clock and checkmark icon or by pressing F8 (in Microsoft Windows), you'll see the screen shown in Figure C.47, from which you can specify the name of the application

and whether you want to upload, download, or delete the SAPUI5 application you've named.

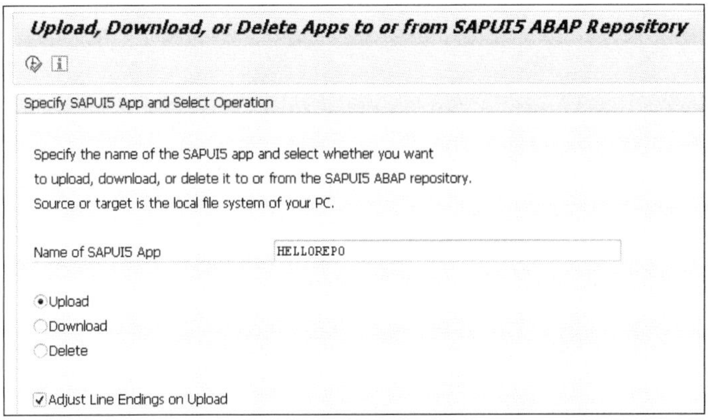

Upload, Download, or Delete Apps to or from SAPUI5 ABAP Repository

Specify SAPUI5 App and Select Operation

Specify the name of the SAPUI5 app and select whether you want
to upload, download, or delete it to or from the SAPUI5 ABAP repository.
Source or target is the local file system of your PC.

Name of SAPUI5 App   HELLOREPO

◉ Upload
◯ Download
◯ Delete

☑ Adjust Line Endings on Upload

Figure C.47 /UI5/UI5_REPOSITORY_LOAD Report Options

5. We've chosen the name "HELLOREPO" (Figure C.47), because we're on an SAP internal system; you should choose a name in the customer namespace starting with Y or Z. After executing the report, provide the folder location of your application. We chose the location where we previously extracted the ZIP file downloaded from the SAP Web IDE (Figure C.48). After clicking on OK, all the files are listed (Figure C.49), and you can click on CLICK HERE TO UPLOAD.

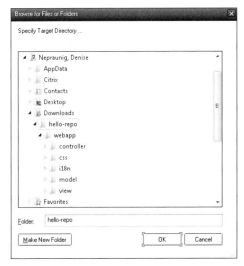

Figure C.48 Specify Folder for Uploading SAPUI5 Application

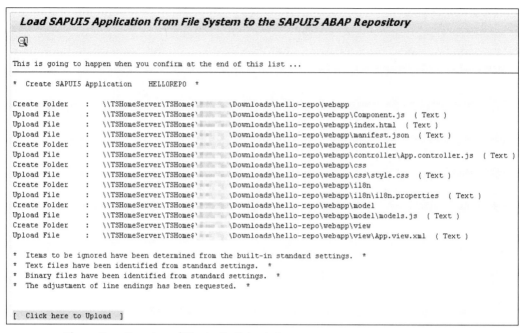

Figure C.49 Overview of Files to Be Uploaded

6. Next, provide information such as the application's DESCRIPTION and PACKAGE (Figure C.50). When you click the green checkmark to proceed (Figure C.50), several security warnings will pop up (Figure C.51), which is totally fine.

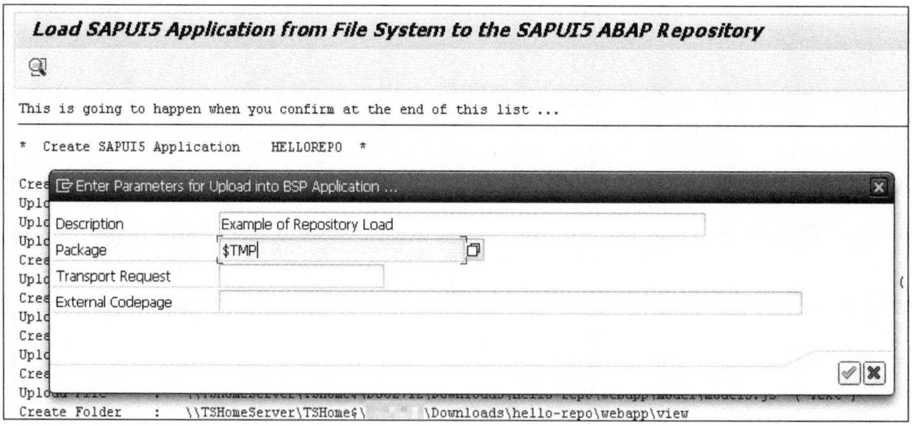

Figure C.50 Enter Parameters for SAPUI5 Application

Figure C.51 Security Warning When Uploading Files

7. At the end, you'll see confirmation that your app has been successfully uploaded (Figure C.52). You could also check in the ABAP Workbench (Transaction SE80) that your application was successfully uploaded (Figure C.53), as we did in the previous section.

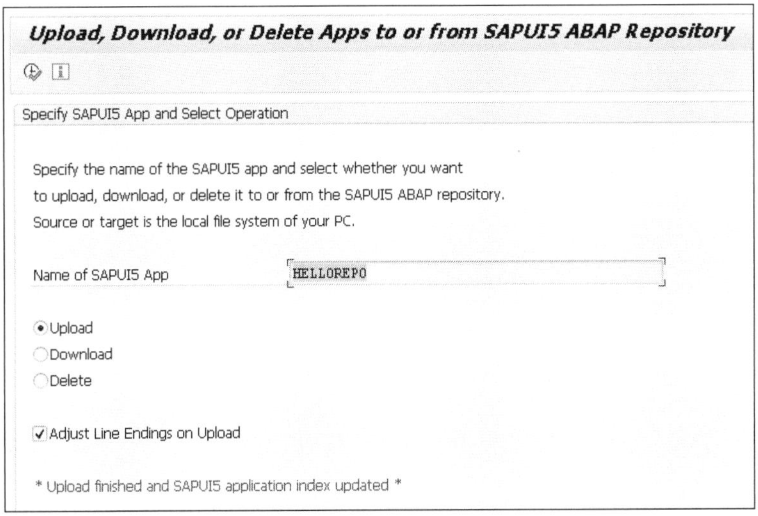

Upload, Download, or Delete Apps to or from SAPUI5 ABAP Repository

Specify SAPUI5 App and Select Operation

Specify the name of the SAPUI5 app and select whether you want
to upload, download, or delete it to or from the SAPUI5 ABAP repository.
Source or target is the local file system of your PC.

Name of SAPUI5 App   `HELLOREPO`

◉ Upload
○ Download
○ Delete

☑ Adjust Line Endings on Upload

* Upload finished and SAPUI5 application index updated *

Figure C.52 Finished Uploading Application

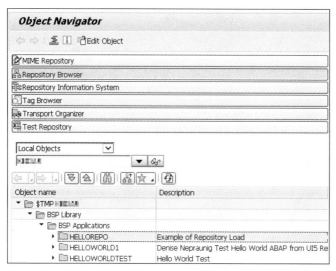

Figure C.53 Uploaded Application in ABAP Development Workbench: Transaction SE80

C.4   Other Web Servers

It's also possible to host an SAPUI5 application on an arbitrary web server. Hosting the application's UI is no problem, but when you want to access a certain backend and aren't using SAP HCP or are directly running your application inside the ABAP system with the backend data. Then, you have to figure out how to connect from the UI to the backend (on a remote server), as you will probably run into the same-origin-policy problem.

In SAP Web IDE, we created a simple Hello, World application as in the previous section and called it *hello-webserver*. When hosting an SAPUI5 application, we want to host the minified version of the application. The fastest way to achieve this is to deploy the application to SAP HCP, which automatically minifies the application. Keep in mind that this minification only works if you've created your app with the latest SAPUI5 application templates.

After you've deployed the application to SAP HCP, the application now includes a *dist* folder. You can download the whole application from the SAP Web IDE as we did in Section C.3.2.

To deploy the application, you'll need the files listed in Listing C.4.

```
|     Component-preload.js
|     index.html
|     manifest.json
|
+---css
|        style.css
|
\---i18n
         i18n.properties
```
Listing C.4 Files Needed for Deployment

Change the location of the sap-ui-core.js file in the index.html file as shown in Listing C.5. You can choose the publicly available CDN version of OpenUI5 for this example, because OpenUI5 is open source. We discussed using the CDN in Section C.3.1.

```
<script id="sap-ui-bootstrap"
  src="https://openui5.hana.ondemand.com/resources/sap-ui-core.js"
  data-sap-ui-libs="sap.m"
  data-sap-ui-theme="sap_bluecrystal"
  data-sap-ui-compatVersion="edge"
  data-sap-ui-resourceroots='{"sapui5.demo.hellowebserver": ""}'>
</script>
```
Listing C.5 CDN Version of OpenUI5

There is also a beta version of OpenUI5 available at *https://openui5beta.hana.ondemand.com/resources/sap-ui-core.js*, and there is even a nightly version available (for more information, see *http://openui5.tumblr.com/post/145001743062/new-nightly-builds-of-openui5-available-online*) available at *https://openui5nightly.hana.ondemand.com/resources/sap-ui-core.js*.

Keep in mind that OpenUI5 currently does not include any smart controls or charts. After you've adapted the index.html file, you can upload your files (as listed in Listing C.4) to the web server. We uploaded this example to *http://nepraunig.com/sapui5book/hello-webserver/*, and you can see the running app in Figure C.54.

Figure C.54 Running Application on Web Server

D   Cheat Sheets

In this appendix, we'll provide a handy cheat sheet for the most used and most useful functions, commands, and configurations in SAPUI5.

D.1   Starting the App

In this section, we'll look at important code for starting your SAPUI5 app.

D.1.1   SAPUI5 Bootstrap

Adapt the `src` property so that it points to your SAPUI5 resource (ABAP, HCP, SAPUI5 CDN, etc.; see Listing D.1).

```
<script id="sap-ui-bootstrap"
    src="https://sapui5.hana.ondemand.com/resources/sap-ui-core.js"
    data-sap-ui-libs="sap.m"
    data-sap-ui-theme="sap_bluecrystal"
    data-sap-ui-compatVersion="edge"
    data-sap-ui-preload='async'
    data-sap-ui-resourceroots='{"app.namespace": "./webapp/"}'>
</script>
```
Listing D.1 SAPUI5 Bootstrap

D.1.2   SAPUI5 Body

Within the body of the HTML document, you can add the SAPUI5 application:

```
<body class="sapUiBody" id="content">

</body>
```

D.1.3   SAPUI5 attachInit Event

With the `attachInit` event, the SAPUI5 core has been loaded, and now you can create the `app` component and place it in the DOM (see Listing D.2).

```
sap.ui.getCore().attachInit(function() {
  new sap.m.Shell({
    app: new sap.ui.core.ComponentContainer({
      height: "100%",
```

```
      name: "app.namespace"
    })
  }).placeAt("content");
});
```

Listing D.2 attachInit Function without require

Inside the `attachInit` function, you can require additional controls that are needed to create your application, like `sap.m.Shell` and `sap.ui.core.Component-Container`. See Listing D.3 for an example.

```
sap.ui.getCore().attachInit(function() {
  sap.ui.require([
    "sap/m/Shell",
    "sap/ui/core/ComponentContainer"
  ], function(Shell, ComponentContainer) {
    new Shell({
      app: new ComponentContainer({
        name: "app.namespace",
        height: "100%"
      })
    }).placeAt("content");
  });
});
```

Listing D.3 attachInit Function with require

D.2   Referencing Elements

There are a number of ways you can reference elements in SAPUI5. Check out the following subsections for examples.

D.2.1   Getting an Element by ID

You can access an element globally by its fully qualified ID, which is mainly used for debugging purposes, or you can access it within the controller of the corresponding view via its ID (which is specified in the view).

Getting an Element Globally

When you debug an application, you can access the specific control in your JavaScript console with the following line:

```
sap.ui.getCore().byId("full-qualified-id-of-the-control");
```

You can save the reference to the control in a variable and manipulate its properties and can see the ID of the control in the DOM of the rendered HTML page. In the Google Chrome browser, you'll see this information in the ELEMENTS tab. Figure D.1 shows the ID of the control in the DOM and the access and manipulation of a control. Note that the ID of the control is prefixed with ID of the view so that it's unique.

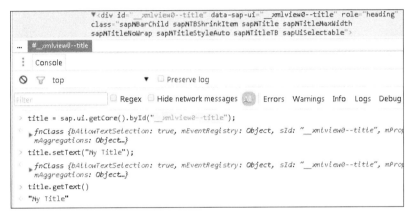

Figure D.1 sap.ui.getCore().byId("full-qualified-id-of-the-control")

Getting an Element inside a Controller

When developing apps, you may want to access certain controls from within the controller of the view to manipulate some of their properties or update data binding.

Inside the view, you give the control an ID as follows:

```
<Button
id="myButton"
text="My Button"
press="onPress"/>
```

Inside the controller, you can access the control via the following line:

```
this.byId("controlID");
```

The following is an example of how to access the button from the previous lines in the `onInit` function of the controller:

```
onInit: function() {
var oBtn = this.byId("myButton");
console.log(oBtn);
}, ...
```

Note that you only need the myButton ID of the button because it was defined inside the XML view; you don't need the fully qualified name as in earlier examples.

Getting a Control in a Fragment by Its ID

To retrieve a control instance in a fragment by its ID, you can use the following static function at the sap.ui.core.Fragment:

sap.ui.core.Fragment.byId(sFragmentId, sId)

This function takes the ID of the fragment and the ID of the control as parameters and returns the corresponding control instance, if it exists.

D.2.2 Finding the DOM Reference of a Control

If you want to retrieve the complete DOM reference to a control, you can use the following line:

```
oControl.getDomRef(sSuffix);
```

sSuffix is a placeholder for the ID that was assigned to the control without any prefixes for surrounding views or for components generated through preprocessors.

D.3 JSON Model

Here, you'll find the basics on everything from creating a JSON model to listening to events to implementing setter and getter functions.

D.3.1 Creating a JSON Model

To create a new JSON model, use the normal constructor like so:

```
var oJSONModel = new sap.ui.model.json.JSONModel();
```

You can also pass a URL directly to the service or file containing the data to the constructor:

```
var oJSONModel = new sap.ui.model.json.JSONModel(sUrl);
```

Or you can call the convenience method `loadData` after the instantiation and pass the URL to this method, like so:

```
oJSONModel.loadData(sUrl);
```

When you want to set data for the model you've already retrieved, you can also use the `setData` method at the model, passing a JSON formatted object in like so:

```
oJSONModel.setData(oSomeJSONObject);
```

D.3.2 Listening to Events

If you need to execute a certain code passage only after `JSONModel` has successfully loaded its data, you can attach to the `requestCompleted` event at `JSONModel` like so:

```
oJSONModel.attachRequestCompleted(oData, fnFunction, oListener);
```

You need to at least pass the function that should be executed when the event is fired, which also can be an anonymous function. If you want to retain the context present when you attached to the event, make sure to pass `this` as `oListener` to the method.

The same method can be applied to check whether the request for the model data failed. In that case, use `attachRequestFailed` instead.

D.3.3 Setting and Getting Properties

To retrieve or to set a particular property at a JSON model, you need to use the `getProperty(sPropertyName)` and `setProperty(sPropertyName, vPropertyValue);` methods. Property values can be simple data types or objects.

D.4 OData Model

This section provides the basics on everything from creating an OData model to listening to events.

D.4.1 Creating an OData Model

To instantiate an OData model manually (instead of having it instantiated automatically by the component when it's specified in manifest.json), you can call the constructor like so:

```
var oModel = sap.ui.model.odata.v2.ODataModel(sServiceUrl, mParameters);
```

Please see the API REFERENCE tab in the SAPUI5 Demo Kit for supported parameters.

Reading Data

When you want to trigger a `GET` request for an OData model, use the `read` method on the model, like so:

```
oModel.read(sPath, mParameters);
```

Data read in this way will be stored in the model.

If you want to access a particular value on the model, you can call the `getProperty` method at the model, passing the path to the value:

```
var myVal = oModel.getProperty(sPathToMyVal);
```

Writing Data

If you want to write data to your local OData model, use the `setProperty` method on the model, passing the path and the value you want to set:

```
oModel.setProperty(sPathToProperty, vValue);
```

The other parameters for this method are optional; please see the API documentation for further details.

When you're using two-way-binding (which is the default for OData models), changes to bound values are automatically collected through the `setProperty` method at the model.

To send data to the service, you can use the `submitChanges` method if you want to send changes that were collected because properties on the model changed. All parameters this method takes are optional.

If you're using batch groups, you can pass the `batchGroupId` parameter if you want to submit changes for a particular group only. Also, you can pass `success` and `error` callback functions to the `submitChanges` method, like so:

```
oModel.submitChanges({
batchGroupId: yourGroupIdHere,
success: fnSuccess,
error: fnError
}
```

Another method you can use to update data on the service is the `update` method at the model. Use this method if you want to send certain data that may not have been stored programmatically in the model previously as an update to the service:

```
oModel.update(sPath, oData);
```

Other parameters are optional; see the API documentation.

When you need to create a new, empty entry at the model, use the `createEntry` method, like so:

```
oModel.createEntry(sEntityName, mParameters);
```

`mParameters` is optional and contains options such as a batch group ID, additional headers, or success and error handlers.

D.4.2 Listening to Events

The OData model provides the same events as the ones listed in Section D.3.2 for the JSON model, plus some others. Because the OData model needs to retrieve a metadata document from the service on instantiation, there are metadata-related events you can attach to (and please also detach from, when no longer required):

```
metadataLoaded
metadataFailed
```

There are similar events for annotations, if you're using them for your model:

```
annotationsLoaded
annotationsFailed
```

The OData model also provides events related to the loading of the actual service data:

```
requestSent
requestCompleted
requestFailed
```

D.5   Bindings

Here, we'll cover how to create data bindings manually and retrieve information on existing bindings.

D.5.1   Creating a Binding Manually

If you need to create a binding outside of your declarative view, you can use the methods detailed in the following subsections.

bindElement

`bindElement(vPath, mParameters)` is used to bind a view, for instance, to a particular context (an object in your model). Note that when you're using a named model, you need to specify the model name as a parameter in the `mParameters` map. Take care to also include the path in this map; otherwise, it won't be taken into account for the specified model. The code then looks like the following:

```
oModel.bindElement({path: sPath, model: sModelName});
```

bindAggregation

If you need to create the binding for an aggregation manually, you can use the `bindAggregation` method at the parent control as follows:

```
oParentControl.bindAggregation(sAggregationName, { path: sPath,
template: oTemplateControl, model: sModelName});
```

This is a simplified example again. Note that you can also pass sorters or filters into this method and that you can also pass a factory function to create the aggregation manually. Again, when you're binding to an object in a particular named model, you need to specify the model name in the parameters object.

bindProperty

The `bindProperty` method allows you to programmatically create a binding for a particular control property, like so:

```
oControl.bindProperty(sPropertyName, {path: sPathToPropertyInModel,
model: sModelName});
```

You can again define formatters, sorters, and more options in the object passed as second parameter to the `bindProperty` method.

D.5.2 Getting Details of a Binding

When you want to retrieve information on an existing binding programmatically, you can use the `getBindingContext` method to find the context for which a binding was set—for example, the object a particular item in an aggregation is bound to:

```
oListItem.getBindingContext();
```

If the binding context was set using a particular named model, you need to specify the model name as a parameter for the method, like so:

```
oListItem.getBindingContext(sModelName);
```

You can do the same for an element binding, like you would set it on a view, by calling the following:

```
oView.getElementBinding(sOptionalModelName);
```

You only have to specify the model name if you're using a named model. Otherwise, the method will look for a binding on the default model.

D.6 Coding Conventions

When naming variables, we strongly recommend that you use the Hungarian notation in which the prefix indicates the type for the variables and attributes of classes. There are strong opinions about whether or not to use Hungarian notation, but from our experience it helps a lot during development if you don't have to think about whether a variable was an object or an array. When using the Hungarian notation, use the prefixes highlighted in Table D.1 and continue with an uppercase letter.

Example	Type
sUrl	String
oButton	Object
$DomRef	jQuery object
iCount	Integer
mParameters	Map / associative array
aEntries	Array
dInvoiceDate	Date
fNetAmount	Float
bVisible	Boolean
rPhonePattern	RegEx
fnSave	Function
vInput	variable Type

Table D.1 Hungarian Notation Examples

When creating classes and methods, use CamelCase notation, starting the class name with an uppercase letter. When creating private methods and attributes, start them with an underscore, like _isHoverable.

JavaScript Coding Guidelines

For more information on JavaScript coding guidelines for SAPUI5 development, navigate to *https://sapui5.hana.ondemand.com/* and select DEVELOPER GUIDE • DEVELOPING CONTENT • DEVELOPMENT CONVENTIONS AND GUIDELINES • JAVASCRIPT CODING GUIDELINES.

D.7   JSDoc

The source code of SAPUI5 is documented with JSDoc3, which mimics the behavior of a Javadoc. You can also use JSDoc to document your SAPUI5 application source code. In this section, we'll provide some basic examples. For all possible options, please refer to the JSDoc website at *http://usejsdoc.org/*.

JSDoc documentation starts with /** and ends with */. The different tags, like public or returns, start with an @ sign—so the tags are @public or @returns

(Listing D.4). The data type is defined inside the curly braces, so {dataType} (Listing D.5).

```
/**
 * Getter for the resource bundle.
 * @public
 * @returns {sap.ui.model.resource.ResourceModel} the resourceModel
 *          of the component
 */
getResourceBundle: function() {
  return this.getOwnerComponent().getModel("i18n").getResourceBundle();
}
```
Listing D.4 JSDoc for Method without Parameters and Return Value

```
/**
 * Convenience method for setting the view model.
 * @public
 * @param {sap.ui.model.Model} oModel the model instance
 * @param {string} sName the model name
 * @returns {sap.ui.mvc.View} the view instance
 */
setModel: function(oModel, sName) {
  return this.getView().setModel(oModel, sName);
}
```
Listing D.5 JSDoc for Method with Parameters and Return Value

Optional parameters are written inside square brackets, so [optionalData] (Listing D.6). You can also document @private methods (Listing D.7), which should start with an underscore.

```
/**
 * Convenience method for getting the view model by name.
 * @public
 * @param {string} [sName] the model name
 * @returns {sap.ui.model.Model} the model instance
 */
getModel: function(sName) {
  return this.getView().getModel(sName);
}
```
Listing D.6 JSDoc for Method with Optional Parameter and Return Value

```
/**
 * Shows the selected item on the object page
 * On phones an additional history entry is created
 * @param {sap.m.ObjectListItem} oItem selected Item
 * @private
```

```
*/
_showObject: function(oItem) {
  this.getRouter().navTo("object", {
    objectId: oItem.getBindingContext().getProperty("Id")
  });
}
```

Listing D.7 JSDoc for Private Method

D.8 Controls Cheat Sheet

To see all the different controls available in SAPUI5, visit the Explored app at *https://sapui5.hana.ondemand.com/sdk/explored.html*, or see the SAP Fiori design guidelines at *https://experience.sap.com/fiori-design/*. Another option is to use the control cheat sheet created by Abhishek Modi, which you can find at *http://scn.sap.com/community/developer-center/front-end/blog/2015/03/27/sapui5-controls-cheat-sheet*. The control cheat sheet shows the most important controls and their corresponding names (Figure D.2).

Figure D.2 SAPUI5 Control Cheat Sheet

E   Additional Resources

In this appendix, we've assembled various resources, from openSAP's massive online open courses (MooCs) to documentations, websites, books/E-Bites, communities, and tools that may help you during your SAPUI5 development journey.

E.1   openSAP Courses

- **Developing Web Apps with SAPUI5**—*https://open.sap.com/courses/ui51*
  Learn the basics and advanced topics of SAPUI5 from the SAPUI5 core team members.

- **Build Your Own SAP Fiori App in the Cloud (2016 Edition)**—*https://open.sap.com/courses/fiux2*
  Learn all about developing SAPUI5 applications in the cloud with SAP Web IDE, along with an introduction to other topics, including smart controls and smart templates.

- **SAP HANA Cloud Platform Essentials**—*https://openui5beta.hana.ondemand.com/*
  Learn how you can develop and host your applications (SAPUI5, Java, SAP HANA XS) on SAP HANA Cloud Platform, SAP's platform as a service (PaaS) offering.

E.2   Documentation

- **SAPUI5 Demo Kit**—*https://sapui5.hana.ondemand.com/*
  The official documentation contains a developer guide, great tutorials, API documentation, demo applications, and a controls overview.

- **OpenUI5 Beta Preview**—*https://openui5beta.hana.ondemand.com/*
  Check out the beta version of OpenUI5, with the latest features and the latest documentation and tutorials.

- **SAPUI5 Explored App**—*https://sapui5.hana.ondemand.com/explored.html*
  The dedicated controls website where you can explore most of the SAPUI5 controls with code examples.

- **Nabisoft SAPUI5 tutorials**—*https://nabisoft.com/tutorials/sapui5/*
  Nabi Zamani often helped write SAPUI5 documentation as an external contributor and has also written some of his own tutorials.

- **SAP Developers**—*http://go.sap.com/developer.html*
  All the development resources, tutorials, and events from the SAP Developer team, including those from SAPUI5, SAP Web IDE, SAP HANA, SAP HCP, and much more.

- **OData.org**—*http://www.odata.org/* and *http://services.odata.org/*
  Lots of examples and documentation about the OData protocol, including test services.

- **Web Accessibility Initiative (WAI)**—*https://www.w3.org/WAI/*
  General documentation and information on accessibility topics in web applications.

E.3 Websites

- **This book's web page**—*www.sap-press.com/3980*
  You'll find downloadable content for this book on the book's web page. After clicking the link, scroll down to the PRODUCT SUPPLEMENTS section.

- **OpenUI5 homepage**—*http://openui5.org/*
  The official homepage from OpenUI5, with simple getting started guides, SDK downloads, and a blog.

- **30 Days of SAPUI5**—*http://pipetree.com/qmacro/blog/2015/07/30-days-of-ui5/*
  To celebrate the release of SAPUI5 1.30, SAP mentor and SAPUI5 guru DJ Adams initiated a blog series in which he explains the latest and greatest features of SAPUI5.

- **SAP Fiori reference apps**—*http://scn.sap.com/docs/DOC-59963*
  These reference applications are also part of the SAP Web IDE shipment and contain best practices and coding examples for different application types.

- **SAP Fiori apps library**—*https://fioriappslibrary.hana.ondemand.com/sap/fix/externalViewer/*

- **SAP Fiori, Demo Cloud Edition**—*https://www.sapfioritrial.com/*
  Demo Cloud Edition with this trial.

▸ **SAP Fiori Design Guidelines**—*https://experience.sap.com/guidelines/*
Get an overview of the SAP Fiori Design Guidelines, the philosophy behind
SAP Fiori, application patterns, and how to use the different UI elements.

E.4   Books/E-Bites

▸ **SAP Gateway and OData (SAP PRESS) by Bönnen et al.**—*https://www.sap-press.com/3904*
Learn everything there is to know about OData and SAP Gateway—from the
steps of creating an OData service to how-tos for developing mobile, social, and
enterprise apps.

▸ **SAP Fiori Implementation and Development (SAP PRESS) by Anil Bavaraju**—*https://www.sap-press.com/3883*
Learn how to implement transactional, analytical, and fact sheet apps on an AS
ABAP or SAP HANA database, and further customize your options by creating,
developing, and extending your apps with SAP Web IDE.

▸ **JavaScript for ABAP Developers (SAP PRESS) by Miroslav Antolovic**—
https://www.sap-press.com/3933
Learn the basic principles behind JavaScript, including its variables, operators,
and control structures.

E.5   Communities

▸ **SAP Community Network (SCN)**

  ▹ SAPUI5: *http://scn.sap.com/community/developer-center/front-end*

  ▹ SAP Web IDE: *http://scn.sap.com/docs/DOC-55465*

  ▹ SAP Fiori: *http://scn.sap.com/community/fiori*

▸ **OpenUI5 Slack channel**—*http://slackui5invite.herokuapp.com/* (invite) and *https://openui5.slack.com/* (Slack channel)
Slack is a cloud-based team collaboration tool. In the OpenUI5 Slack channel,
you can chat with the creators of SAPUI5 and with engaged community members.

▶ **UI5Con 2016**—*https://wiki.scn.sap.com/wiki/display/events/UI5con+2016+-+Frank-furt*
In March 2016, the first ever SAPUI5/OpenUI5 conference (UI5Con) took place and brought together eager SAPUI5 team members and the SAPUI5 community. Slides and recordings from this event reside on the Wiki page.

E.6   GitHub Repositories

▶ **OpenUI5 on GitHub**—*https://github.com/SAP/openui5/*
Explore the source code of OpenUI5 and fork it.

▶ **DJ Adams' GitHub repository**—*https://github.com/qmacro*
DJ Adams has a lot of different SAPUI5 examples and snippets for various editors in his repository.

▶ **Denise Nepraunig's GitHub repository**—*https://github.com/denisenepraunig*
Denise likes to play around with SAP HCP and SAP HANA XS, and she shares examples on her GitHub repository.

▶ **openui5-googlemaps**—*https://github.com/jasper07/openui5-googlemaps*
John Patterson created an OpenUI5 Google Maps library.

▶ **openui5-sample-app**—*https://github.com/SAP/openui5-sample-app*
Check out a simple, OpenUI5 to-do app that stores changes in local storage.

▶ **grunt-openui5**—*https://github.com/SAP/grunt-openui5*
Discover Grunt tasks for OpenUI5, like minification and running a web server.

E.7   JavaScript Playgrounds

▶ **SCN JavaScript playgrounds**—*http://scn.sap.com/community/developer-center/front-end/blog/2014/12/20/openui5-jsbin-play-well-together-but-is-there-even-more*
Get information on the different JavaScript playgrounds via this blogpost on SCN.

▶ **JSFiddle and JSBin**—*http://jsfiddle.net/* and *http://jsbin.com/*
Share your SAPUI5 code snippets on these interactive playgrounds. In these two playgrounds, you can modify one HTML, JavaScript, or CSS file and share it with other people. These playgrounds are well-suited for smaller examples.

▶ **Plunker**
With Plunker, you can create many files and folders, like you would do in a real SAPUI5 application, so this playground is well-suited for bigger examples. Learn how you can tinker around with Plunker quickly via the following links:

  ▷ *http://scn.sap.com/community/developer-center/front-end/blog/2015/01/04/quickly-tinker-around-online-with-sapui5-explored-examples*

  ▷ *https://plnkr.co/*

E.8   Tools

▶ **XML and JSON tools**—*http://codebeautify.org/*
Check out a XML/JSON validator, viewer, and editor, which come in handy when your XML views or manifest.json file contains errors.

▶ **XOData**—*http://pragmatiqa.com/xodata/*
Visualize and explore OData services.

E.9   Google Chrome Plugins

▶ **UI5 Inspector**—*https://github.com/SAP/ui5-inspector*
Inspect SAPUI5 applications, get information about data binding, and modify control properties.

▶ **JSONView**—*https://github.com/gildas-lormeau/JSONView-for-Chrome*
Nicely formats JSON in your browser, which is handy when you deal with JSON responses from OData servers or from REST servers.

▶ **Access-Control-Allow-Origin***—*https://github.com/vitvad/Access-Control-Allow-Origin*
Handy plugin to turn on the web security in Chrome, as illustrated in Appendix B.

▶ **Postman**—*http://www.getpostman.com/*
Postman is a REST client that we used for OData CRUD operations in Chapter 7.

▶ **Advanced REST client**—*https://advancedrestclient.com/*
This is an alternative REST client that's easy to use. If you run into problems with Postman, we can recommend this REST client.

- **Octotree**—*https://github.com/buunguyen/octotree*
  Browse GitHub repositories in a tree view, which is handy when navigating the OpenUI5 GitHub repository.

- **Sight**—*https://github.com/tsenart/sight*
  Sight is a syntax highlighter that makes reading source code much more enjoyable inside the browser.

- **OneTab**—*https://www.one-tab.com/*
  If you have too many browser tabs open and tend to lose track of them, we recommend this tool. It closes all your tabs and displays them on one page. Remember that too many open browser tabs eat up a lot of memory.

F   The Authors

Christiane Goebels has been in web development ever since starting her career at SAP in 2000. Over the years, she has worked on SAP-related and non-SAP-related projects big and small for customers for all over the world. She led her own internet agency from 2005 to 2010, and re-joined SAP in 2012 as part of the central SAPUI5 development team.

She is an experienced speaker and has been giving numerous trainings and talks on JavaScript and SAPUI5 at SAP and at international conferences.

Denise Nepraunig is a software developer at SAP in Walldorf, where she creates SAPUI5 applications and was involved in the development of the SAP Web IDE. Before she joined SAP, she worked at an SAP partner company, where she worked with SAPUI5 and OData development with ABAP, gaining hands-on experience with SAP Fiori and the SAP Mobile Platform.

Prior to that, she worked at an SAP customer as an ABAP developer and was part of international SAP ERP and SAP CRM rollouts. Denise is an experienced speaker, SAPUI5 coach, and SAP Mentor. She loves to explore new technologies, and in her free time tinkers around with SAP HCP and SAP HANA.

Thilo Seidel built his first web page back in 2002 and instantly fell in love with the browser. He has taken on various roles since then, including sales, designer thinker, traveler, student, and project manager. Before joining SAPUI5, his technological journey involved freelancing with jQuery, Bootstrap, and Ruby on Rails. Currently, Thilo is the product owner of SAP Fiori Launchpad on the weekdays and an occasional hacker on weekends.

Index

X

Interested in reading more?

Please visit our website for all new
book and e-book releases from SAP PRESS.

www.sap-press.com